EUROPEAN SECURITY SINCE THE FALL OF THE BERLIN WALL

There have been dramatic changes to the landscape of European security in the years since the fall of the Berlin Wall. The essays in *European Security since the Fall of the Berlin Wall* collectively take stock of how approaches to security in Europe have changed, both in practice and in theory, since the end of the Cold War.

Organized into three sections, the collection begins with an exploration of the broad changes in Europe's security environment relating to issues such as terrorism and the rising importance of energy security. The second section describes the adaptations of Europe's institutional framework, including the transformation of NATO and the evolution of European armed forces, while the closing essays examine regional security issues with the Middle East, the Balkans, and Russia. Covering a broad spectrum of theoretical approaches and written in a clear, engaging style, *European Security since the Fall of the Berlin Wall* will illuminate European security debates for years to come.

(European Union Studies)

FRÉDÉRIC MÉRAND is an associate professor in the Department of Political Science at l'Université de Montréal.

MARTIAL FOUCAULT is an assistant professor in the Department of Political Science at l'Université de Montréal.

BASTIEN IRONDELLE is a research fellow at CERI–Sciences Po Paris and Deakin Fellow (2009–10) at St Antony's College, University of Oxford.

European Union Studies

European Union Studies features the latest research on topics in European integration in the widest sense, including Europe's role as a regional and international actor. This interdisciplinary series publishes the research of Canadian and international scholars and aims at attracting scholars working in various disciplines such as economics, history, law, political science, and sociology. The series is made possible in part by a generous grant from the European Commission.

The first series of its kind in Canada, and one of only a few in North America, *European Union Studies* is unique in looking at the EU 'from the outside,' making sense not only of European integration but also of the role of the European Union as an international actor.

GENERAL EDITORS:

Jeffrey Kopstein
Professor of Political Science
Director, Centre for European, Russian, and Eurasian Studies
University of Toronto

Amy Verdun
Professor of Political Science
Director, Jean Monnet Centre of Excellence
University of Victoria

EDITED BY FRÉDÉRIC MÉRAND, MARTIAL
FOUCAULT, AND BASTIEN IRONDELLE

European Security since the Fall of the Berlin Wall

UNIVERSITY OF TORONTO PRESS
Toronto Buffalo London

©University of Toronto Press Incorporated 2011
Toronto Buffalo London
www.utppublishing.com
Printed in Canada

ISBN 978-1-4426-4240-9 (cloth)
ISBN 978-1-4426-1130-6 (paper)

Printed on acid-free, 100% post-consumer recycled paper with vegetable-based inks.

Library and Archives Canada Cataloguing in Publication

European security since the fall of the Berlin Wall / edited by Frédéric Mérand, Martial Foucault, and Bastien Irondelle.

(European Union studies series)
Includes bibliographical references and index.
ISBN 978-1-4426-4240-9 (bound). – ISBN 978-1-4426-1130-6 (pbk.)

1. National security – Europe.   2. Europe – Military policy.   3. Europe – Defenses.   4. Europe – Foreign relations – 1989–.   I. Mérand, Frédéric, 1976–   II. Foucault, Martial, 1972–   III. Irondelle, Bastien   IV. Series: European Union studies.

UA646.E87 2011   355'.03304   C2010-906219-1

University of Toronto Press acknowledges the financial assistance to its publishing program of the Canada Council for the Arts and the Ontario Arts Council.

 Canada Council   Conseil des Arts
for the Arts   du Canada

 ONTARIO ARTS COUNCIL
CONSEIL DES ARTS DE L'ONTARIO

University of Toronto Press acknowledges the financial support of the Government of Canada through the Canada Book Fund for its publishing activities.

To REGIS, 1995–2009

Contents

Acknowledgments

This volume is the product of a conference that was held on a freezing day in February 2007 at the University of Montreal, in its beautiful Art Deco main building. The conference was funded by the Institute of European Studies and supported by the Research Group on International Security (REGIS). We would like to thank the directors of these research centres, Gérard Boismenu and Michel Fortmann. We would also like to thank the students and colleagues who helped us organize the conference: Stéfanie von Hlatky, Véronique Dumais, Gaëlle Rivard-Piché, and Stéphane Léman-Langlois. Finally, this book would not have been possible without the support of the European studies series editors, Amy Verdun and Jeffrey Kopstein, two anonymous reviewers, and Daniel Quinlan, our indefatigable editor at University of Toronto Press.

The book is dedicated to REGIS, its founding director, Michel Fortmann, and its staff. A rare example of collaboration between two Canadian universities, one English-speaking (McGill) and the other French-speaking (Montréal), REGIS passed away in October 2009. But like a phoenix it is now reborn under a new name: the Centre for International Peace and Security Studies (CIPSS). REGIS is dead, long live CIPSS!

EUROPEAN SECURITY SINCE THE FALL
OF THE BERLIN WALL

1 Theorizing Change in the European Security Environment

FRÉDÉRIC MÉRAND, BASTIEN IRONDELLE, AND MARTIAL FOUCAULT

This book begins with a banal assertion: European security is no longer what it used to be. A little over twenty years ago, the iron curtain divided East from West. Although *détente* was in the air, the arms race was not over: the Soviet Bloc and the Atlantic Alliance still pointed their missiles at each other. Today the European Union claims to be the main regional actor of a reunited continent. Russia is a 'strategic' if difficult partner, and the United States, long a dominant player in the region, seems busy elsewhere. But Islamic terrorism and climate change are high on the agenda of European leaders, and conflicts in the Middle East and in Africa are anything but solved. While a lot of ink has been spilled on the end of the Cold War, we believe it is worth reflecting again upon how different the world looks twenty years after the fall of the Berlin Wall.

Our focus is on *European* security. By that we do not primarily mean the security of European states, or the continent's security architecture, but security as it is experienced by *Europeans* – be they political leaders or ordinary citizens. Security means different things to different people. Our perspective, so to speak, is a phenomenological one. In line with contemporary developments in security studies, we believe that the definition of security cannot be limited to 'objective' criteria like state survival or even the preservation of state values. By these traditional yardsticks, security should not even be an issue for today's Europeans. As we will argue below, objectively speaking, there is no specific threat to the European continent, to the territorial integrity of European states, or even to their core political values. And yet there remains a sense of insecurity among people and leaders, there remain international security risks that affect Europe, and there is a growing range of actors and institutions that purport to deal with European security. So clearly, however we define it, security matters.

Although – or rather because – we adopt a phenomenological perspective on European security, our theoretical stance is pluralist. The scholars gathered in this volume come from different theoretical schools: institutionalism, foreign policy analysis, structural and classical realism, neofunctionalism, and constructivism of various stripes. All of these approaches, we believe, can meet around the notion that security is bound to be a contested, shifting concept. This does not mean that the concept is elusive, however, and we hope that, by focusing on European issues, we can get a better purchase on it. Mindful of our commitment to theoretical pluralism, we have asked our contributors not to betray their preferred theoretical approaches, but to engage in a fruitful dialogue on the evolution of the European security environment since 1989.

Before we outline the main arguments pursued in the book, this introductory chapter discusses two starting points. *First*, we observe a European security environment that is much more complex but also more benign than it was during the Cold War. While the point about complexity has often been made, we dig deeper into its various facets: terrorism, non-proliferation, regional crises, energy security, and so forth. But more importantly, we believe that the security environment's benign character is unduly underestimated. *Second*, in large part because Europe's security situation is so favourable, practitioners and scholars who work on this continent have gone the furthest away from the pre-1989 orthodoxy in security studies, exploring referents other than the state, enlarging their conception of security to include more diffuse risks, and developing new 'legitimate' fields of inquiry. In other words, Europe's unique security politics has led to a broader and deeper conception of security studies. Borrowing from Thomas Kuhn's (1962) sociology of science, we argue in this Introduction that, so far as European security is concerned, the paradigmatic consensus dominated by realism and liberalism until 1989 has been broken, and we evaluate the extent to which it is being replaced by another paradigm. Our conclusion is that the field of European security studies today is characterized by pluralism and will remain in flux for the foreseeable future.

The Evolution of the European Security Environment since 1989

Beyond the clichés about 9/11, how can we best describe the European security environment today? In the first chapter of the book, Alexandra Gheciu describes changes in definitions of threat and conceptualizations of the enemy, particularly in response to the 9/11 attacks and, more broadly, to what is widely perceived as the growing threat of Islamist terrorism. Current developments however are also rooted in the reaction of Western states to the end of the Cold War. In line with Ulrich Beck's theory of the 'risk society,' the promotion of democracy that dominated the 1990s was gradually replaced by more complex practices of risk management. Gheciu examines the ways in which new conceptualizations of threat/enemy have inspired a particular ethos of risk management in the Euro-Atlantic sphere. That ethos, she suggests, has translated into a specific combination of practices of inclusion and exclusion, whereby global partnerships are forged beyond Europe but so-called illiberal regimes and movements are increasingly disciplined.

Compared with the pre-1989 era, it is clear that Europe has been displaced as the main front line in any putative war. Where does Europe fit in the new strategic equation? Can it play a key role in Asia, the Middle East, and Africa? Is Russia still a partner in an oil- and gas-shocked relationship? To answer some of these questions, it is useful to briefly discuss two cases that have monopolized the Europeans' attention over the past two decades. In their respective chapters, Costanza Musu describes the frustrating engagement of the European Union in the Middle East peace process, while Vincent Pouliot tells the story of Europe's uneasy relationship with Russia. Both in their own ways come to the conclusion that not much has changed over the past twenty years. And both, interestingly, argue that an important part of the responsibility for this paralysis lies with the Europeans, who have not been able to create the united, credible voice that could exert an influence in Washington. In the Middle East, the EU arguably acts as one: the peace process is in fact one of its oldest common foreign policies, the Europeans having agreed among themselves since the early 1980s on a two-state solution. But their cheque-book diplomacy suffers from a lack of strategic clout, especially vis-à-vis Israel, which will only accept a US-led policy. As Musu argues, borrowing from the foreign policy analysis literature, being an *actor* is not the same as having a *presence*. And towards Moscow, the Europeans are divided as ever. On all the files that matter (Iran, Georgia, Moldova, Ukraine, Chechnya, etc.) they have been able to influence neither Russia nor US/NATO policy vis-à-vis Russia. The resurgence of Russia, which Pouliot argues from a theoretical perspective inspired by constructivism should have been expected given the diplomatic mistakes which in the 1990s led to a NATO enlargement that Moscow never accepted, promises to haunt European security for a long time.

The larger strategic context in which these two relationships unfold is addressed by Sten Rynning, who in his chapter uses the angle of NATO's transformation to analyse the place of Europe in today's geopolitics. Working from a realist perspective informed by geopolitics, Rynning shows the relative marginalization of Europe in world politics. As we argued at the outset, Europe is no longer the dominant security player, like France, Germany, and the UK were until the First World War; nor is Europe the most likely theatre of operation that it remained until 1989. But that does not mean that the old continent has fallen into strategic irrelevance, as the infamous characterization by Robert Kagan (2003) would suggest. Rynning argues on the contrary that European leaders realize that they have an objective interest, together with North America, in stabilizing Eastern Europe and gaining influence in the border regions, such as Central Asia, the Middle East, and North Africa. Because military capabilities are key to geopolitics and the Europeans are dependent upon the Americans, Rynning expects the Atlantic Alliance to remain the cornerstone in European security affairs.

While this big strategic equation may be at the back of the mind of many European leaders, they do not talk much about it. If we look at public statements, the three biggest security issues on the agenda of European leaders today seem to be terrorism, non-proliferation, and climate change, which our contributors address sequentially. In their thought-provoking chapter, Bastian Giegerich and Raffaelo Pantucci look at new forms of terrorism. Successful terrorist attacks in Madrid and London, the murder of Dutch filmmaker Theo van Gogh, as well as other failed or foiled terrorist activities in numerous EU member states have made clear that radicalized members of Europe's Muslim communities pose a threat in the form of jihadist terrorism. Taking a micro-sociological approach that emphasizes group dynamics, social networks, and ideology formation, Giegerich and Pantucci address the process of radicalization before looking at the issues of leadership and the international links of homegrown terror as well as the role of the internet in contemporary terrorist activities. Despite all the hype surrounding al Qaeda, one should not forget that Europeans were dealing with terrorist groups long before 9/11, ranging from nihilists in the late nineteenth century to radical organizations in the 1970s and 1980s. Giegerich and Pantucci help us understand why today's political responses differ from the ones that prevailed then.

So terrorism in older clothes has been present for a long time in Europe. The same is true of the nuclear question, which makes cyclical appearances in the European public discourse. There are still hundreds of US nuclear weapons stockpiled in Belgium, Italy, Germany, the Netherlands, and the UK, in addition to the French *force de frappe*, Britain's own nuclear deterrent, and Russia's aging, diminishing, but still atomic strength. From 1990 to the early twenty-first century, as Stefanie von Hlatky and Michel Fortmann document, it seemed as though the debate had shifted from arms control and disarmament on the European continent to non-proliferation outside of Europe, notably in North Korea, Iran, Syria, but also India, Pakistan, and Israel. Continental issues are now coming back with a vengeance, as the US decision to deploy its missile defence system in Europe, with NATO approval, threatens for many to trigger a new arms race with Russia. Will the deep unpopularity of this initiative among European public opinion lead to political movements reminiscent of the early 1980s? Will Moscow succeed in convincing the Obama administration to drop his predecessor's plan?

Shifting the debate somewhat, von Hlatky and Fortmann's chapter focuses on the nuclear future of Europe by inquiring into the possibility of a European nuclear doctrine. This speculative theme allows them to explore changing European attitudes toward nuclear weapons, the development of the European Security and Defense Policy (ESDP), the respective postures of the two European nuclear powers, France and the UK, as well as the transatlantic relationship. They show that the European stance on non-proliferation has the potential to highlight core contradictions in its nuclear policy, as commitments taken under the non-proliferation treaty (NPT) stand in opposition to Europe's stagnant nuclear legacy. Their analysis provides crucial insight into the ongoing debate on ballistic missile defence, a Bush-era project which several European countries continue to support, cautiously in the West, more enthusiastically in the East, in the face of Russia's resurgence.

One issue that barely existed in the public conscience in 1989 was climate change. Increasingly, however, climate change is construed as a major security challenge, which in the long run threatens the survival of mankind. In the short run, the security dimension of climate change seems more salient outside of Europe, especially in Africa and Asia. There is perhaps one important exception: energy security. The explosion of energy demand around the world, which fuels a steep rise in CO_2 emissions, is a growing concern for Europeans, who fear becoming dependent on unreliable producers such as Russia. The European Union has made a direct connection between the need to ensure

Europe's energy security, combating climate change, and economic competitiveness. However, as Maya Jegen argues, it is not clear that the Europeans have learned much from the 1970s, when energy security was also high on the agenda, albeit without the environmental concerns that prevail today. Harnessing Thomas Kuhn's (1962) epistemological notion of paradigm shift to the securitization literature (Krause and Williams 1996), which shows how public discourse transforms 'normal' social phenomena into 'threats,' Jegen shows that, thanks to the environmental challenge, the energy security paradigm is in the process of being enlarged and politicized.

To these three global security issues we should add regional conflicts that, although localized, will continue to attract a great deal of European leaders' attention. Suffice it to mention the long-frozen conflicts of Transdniestra, Abkhazia, and South Ossetia, which, as Vincent Pouliot tells us, warmed significantly in the summer of 2008. While we cannot do justice to all these conflicts, it is impossible not to mention the Western Balkans. Are they really out of trouble? Eva Gross's chapter offers a rather sanguine assessment. While the EU's 'baptism by fire' in successive conflicts – between Serbia and Slovenia, between Serbia and Croatia, between Bosnian Serbs, Croatians and Bosniaks, and between Serbia and its Kosovar minority – has often been considered as a major failure, Gross argues that Europe's fifteen-year crisis management effort in the region has not been in vain. Through NATO, and in close cooperation with the US, the Europeans have put boots on the ground and helped stop the war in Bosnia; prevented another one in Macedonia; and possibly averted the worst form of ethnic cleansing in Kosovo. Through the EU, they have provided considerable economic help and, perhaps more importantly, a promise of membership which has done much to stabilize the region. All in all, the EU's rise to strategic actorness was painful, but several lessons were learned that should prove useful in dealing with future regional conflicts, in Europe and at the periphery. Gross however identifies strong securitization tendencies in the EU's treatment of the Balkans, notably with an increasing obsession of organized crime and immigration, which threaten to confine this region to the role of the eternal 'Other.'

Indeed, major developments in Europe's security institutions since 1989 are linked to the Balkans war. Two in particular deserve mention: the evolution of NATO and the development of ESDP. In less than twenty years, the Atlantic Alliance has gone from being a defence pact of sixteen nations, pledged to each other against the Soviet Union and held together by Washington's firm hand, to an unwieldy security organization whose membership, now at twenty-eight, includes many of the states that were once the enemy's satellites. Long posted along the front line in a layer cake pattern, Allied forces are now constantly on the move: they were deployed to the Balkans in the 1990s and, since 2002, more or less occupy Afghanistan. This transformation from a static defence structure to a flexible organization geared to force projection, Sten Rynning argues, demonstrates not only the Alliance's resilience but also its usefulness.

Not everybody agrees on NATO's usefulness, however. For a variety of reasons, many of which have to do with the suspicion that NATO will not always be there or serve their aims, EU countries have been working since 1998 on a common security and defence policy, ESDP. Its purpose is to allow the EU to deploy troops in addition to other crisis management capabilities when NATO does not wish to be politically engaged, such as in Bosnia, the Congo, or Chad, countries where EU military operations have been launched since 2003. European defence was – and remains – a contentious issue. The UK and its Atlanticist partners harbour suspicions that Paris is trying to decouple Europe from the US. We should expect this suspicion to be attenuated as the French rejoin NATO's military command, which they left in 1966. But the most interesting aspect of both ESDP and NATO, as Hanna Ojanen shows in her chapter, may be the level of acceptance of international military cooperation by military leaders and public opinion. By historical standards, the fact that European armed forces deploy together most if not all the time – whether in an ESDP format as in Chad or with NATO in Afghanistan – deserves mention. This unprecedented level of political-military integration makes Europe quite unique among the world's regions (Katzenstein 2005). But it also brings up one potential paradigm shift in the functions of the state. Security and defence, traditionally associated with sovereignty and statehood, seem today more loose and more easily transferable than before. In part, they are being conferred to the EU. Such transfer of functions, Ojanen argues, changes the ways in which European states legitimize themselves vis-à-vis both their citizenry and the international community.

Most Eastern European countries joined the EU between 2004 and 2007. Between 1999 and 2004, they had joined the Atlantic Alliance. To a large extent, they now see their security situation through Western, some would say pre-1989 Western, eyes. It is thus tempting to analyse the evolution of the European security environment only from a Western perspective. Vincent Pouliot's chapter invites us to resist this temptation. In an important shift of perspective, he forces us to observe European security through Russian eyes. The decision to enlarge NATO geographically and functionally, argues Pouliot, radicalized Russia as early as 1994. Moscow's inflexible positions – e.g., regarding ballistic missile defence, the Conventional Forces in Europe treaty, or NATO's presence in Russia's traditional sphere of influence – are generally attributed to President Putin's rule since 1999. In fact, they flow directly from this critical juncture of 1994, when the West formally extended its hand to the Visegrad countries. For Moscow, the 1990s remain a decade of darkness, the result of their leadership's weak response to Western pressure. In this constructivist perspective inspired by the sociology of Pierre Bourdieu, Russia's resurgent power constitutes an inevitable return of the balance to the pre-1989 situation.

While the fall of the Berlin Wall certainly had a profound impact in the East, the transformation of European armed forces is, perhaps, the only consequence that can be directly attributed to it in the West. While the European military is often criticized for being stuck in Cold War structures and ways of doing, notably with its over-reliance on territorial defence (with its scattered bases, outdated tanks, etc.) and the attachment of many countries to conscription (which weighs heavily on personnel costs and deployability), Anthony Forster tracks the progress made since the early 1990s. In fifteen years, Forster shows in his institutional analysis, ten European countries have relinquished conscription and several have created or strengthened their rapid reaction forces. Forster distinguishes four models: expeditionary warfare (France, UK), territorial defence (Finland, Czech Republic), late modern (Netherlands, Belgium), and post-neutral (Ireland, Switzerland). While army formats remain diverse, a distinctly European model of *civil-military relations* has emerged in which peace operations sanctioned by an international organization such as the EU, NATO, or the UN play a predominant role.

Germany is a case in point. Constitutionally barred from going abroad until 1994, the *Bundeswehr* has since deployed large numbers of troops to Kosovo, Afghanistan, and Congo in combat-moderate missions. Crisis forces have been created and conscription reduced to what is minimally acceptable at the political level. For Pascal Vennesson and his co-authors, who in their chapter look specifically at *army doctrine* in France, Germany, Italy, and the UK, European security institutions such as NATO have contributed to a 'major shift in the use of force in the

Table 1.1
Perceived threats for the next ten years

	Europe	USA	Fr	GER	UK	IT	NL	PL	SP
International terrorism	66	74	70	70	48	71	48	59	81
Large numbers of immigrants and refugees coming into (Europe/USA)	63	71	53	74	68	80	55	51	78
Iran acquiring nuclear weapons	59	72	63	63	58	62	37	51	67
Global spread of a disease	57	57	49	52	57	43	55	69	62
Energy dependence	**78**	**88**	**69**	**88**	**76**	**87**	**72**	**75**	**87**
Major economic downturn	65	80	57	55	64	71	53	63	77
Global warming	**85**	**70**	**89**	**82**	**80**	**87**	**77**	**83**	**93**
Islamic fundamentalism	53	59	61	57	50	65	48	28	71

Note: Each cell corresponds to the percentage of people telling how likely or somewhat likely they are personally affected by each threat.
Source: *Transatlantic Trends, 2007,* German Marshall Fund.

region.' So, while European armed forces surely remain diverse in strength, role conceptions, and projection capabilities, there has been a convergence towards reduced, more mobile, professionalized forces. These forces are used mostly for peace support operations in which international legitimacy is cherished by public opinion. Slowly, Europe's 'way of war' is freeing itself from the Cold War.

In sum, relations among European states have gone the furthest away from the balance of power. The language of threats has been replaced by that of risks. Regional and domestic security institutions are being retrofitted to address the needs of a security community that lives in relative peace with its neighbours and can afford to choose its role abroad. Table 1.1 suggests that Europeans are generally less fearful than Americans, and what they fear is predominantly linked to non-traditional referents, especially global warming or energy dependence. By and large, compared with twenty years ago, Europe's security environment appears quite benign. It is thus not surprising, as we will argue in the next section, that a new generation of security scholars have found in Europe an ideal terrain for their analyses.

A Paradigm Shift in European Security Studies?

The strongest blow to orthodox security studies was dealt on the European ring, almost single-handedly by the end of the Cold War. In international relations (IR) theory more generally, the fall of the Berlin Wall generated competing explanations but also gave life to new theoretical approaches that contest the dominance of neorealism and neoliberalism. Often subsumed under the 'constructivist' heading, these approaches share a principled rejection of the 'national interest' and the 'balance of power' as overarching causal models. Whether we agree with it or not, there is no denying that constructivism has forced a rethink of the discipline's main assumptions and fault lines. Some of the authors gathered in this book have made important contributions to this constructivist literature. Others have worked towards the reconstruction of classic paradigms like realism, institutionalism, and foreign-policy analysis. The richness of the theoretical landscape is reflected in the contributions to this volume.

Indeed, our objective in this book is to showcase different theories and how they illuminate complex security phenomena. Some of our contributors apply refreshing approaches that are rarely used in security studies, such as functionalism in Ojanen's chapter on ESDP, sociology in Giegerich and Pantucci's treatment of terrorism, or policy sciences in Biscop's analysis of CFSP. The other perspectives we present in this book are more common in European security studies. Vennesson et al.'s and Forster's respective chapters rely on the institutionalist literature to show how civil-military relations and military doctrines carry the weight of Europe's past despite the end of the Cold War. Gross and Jegen borrow from the constructivist notion of securitization to tackle the rising security themes of organized crime, migration, and energy. Also firmly aligned with the constructivist camp, Gheciu and Pouliot go back to the social theory of Ulrich Beck and Pierre Bourdieu to introduce the notions of risk and social relations in the analysis of European security. Finally, and at the opposite end of the theoretical spectrum, Rynning and von Hlatky and Fortmann argue forcefully for the continued relevance of realist approaches, which, however, they adapt to twenty-first-century developments.

Can the theoretical effervescence that these chapters represent be described as a *paradigm shift* in the words of Thomas Kuhn? Although our authors suggest nuanced answers, we argue that there is at least the beginning of a shift, precisely because no one sees European security in

the same way as before. The assumption that environmental degrada-
tions or humanitarian crises do not constitute 'real' security problems is
only sustained by the most extreme neorealist fringes. Starting with
Barry Buzan's *People, States, and Fear* (1991), the idea that our definition
of security should include environmental, societal, economic, and political dimensions in addition to state security (in a strict military sense)
has gained broad acceptance, even by neoclassical realists who include
these considerations into their conception of state purpose. In the political field, the human security agenda promoted first by NGOs, then by
a large segment of the 'international community,' illustrates the enlargement of security definitions.

This does not mean that the enlargement of security is uncontested.
Many realists in particular (including some of our contributors) would
argue that security suffers from conceptual overstretch. Again, our
point is not to say who is right and who is wrong (to paraphrase
Alexander Wendt, security 'is what people make of it'), but rather to
emphasize that the boundaries and cleavages of the security debate
have changed, among both scholars and practitioners. In an important
way, IR scholars have always liked to refer to their discipline in the sin-
gular, as in IR *theory*. This reflected the intellectual consensus driving
the discipline well into the 1980s, when neorealists and neoliberals disagreed on a very narrow set of theoretical hypotheses but shared the
same ontological and epistemological assumptions (unitary state, international system, positivism, etc.). The 'neo-neo' synthesis, as it was
then called, carried the promise of a single paradigm for security studies (Waever 1996).

It is useful at this stage to remind ourselves of what are, for Kuhn, the
conditions and causes of a paradigm shift. A paradigm is a set of practices and assumptions that define a scientific discipline such as physics,
chemistry, but also, arguably, international relations and security studies. In *The Structure of Scientific Revolutions*, Kuhn argues that a paradigm usually helps scholars answer the following questions: (1) What
is to be observed (ontology)? (2) What kinds of question can be asked
(epistemology)? (3) What counts as evidence (methodology)? A paradigm is not a theory that seeks to explain something but a world view
or, to use Michel Foucault's terms, an *episteme* shared by all scholars.
This world view determines what can be said to be true or false; it is the
core of assumptions upon which theories are developed.

Normally a paradigm is not to be questioned; this is what Kuhn calls
'normal science.' It may happen, however, that a series of anomalies

occurs which leads to a crisis in the discipline. By anomaly, we mean an occurrence which flies in the face of the paradigm's most cherished assumptions, be they ontological, epistemological, or methodological. One such anomaly may not throw scholars in doubt; they may choose to believe that it is an isolated event or that they can produce a new explanation using the same assumptions. But a *severe* anomaly or the multiplication of anomalies forces scientists to admit that certain research questions or possible answers have been neglected. Deeply held assumptions do not seem to fit these new questions and objects. New ideas are then tried out and an intellectual battle ensues. Whether we observe a shift in the paradigm depends on the outcome of these institutional and political struggles around what is to be observed, what kinds of question can be asked, and what counts as evidence.

We believe that, with respect to these three questions, European security scholars now bring answers that are significantly more diverse than those provided before the end of the Cold War.[1] To be sure, the security environment has changed; but so have fundamental assumptions about security studies. According to Charles Kegley (1993: 141), the end of the Cold War has changed 'all the answers and all the questions' for two reasons. First, the blatant failure of orthodox IR theory to account for the post-1989 world gave strength to alternative approaches in the struggle that ensued. Second, this struggle led to the emergence of new paradigmatic claims which, although they built to some extent on an already existing critical tradition, refused the post-positivist label, engaged squarely with the orthodoxy, in the event making concessions on the epistemological and methodological fronts, and fashioned themselves self-consciously as the new dominant perspective.

Despite resistance from some realists who maintain that military force remains the alpha and omega of security studies, the field has undergone both a 'broadening' and 'deepening' (Paris 2001). This book's contributors illustrate these two developments, which have contributed to 'open' ontological and epistemological issues, thus breaking the former paradigm of European security studies.

By *broadening* the scope of security studies, European security scholars have come to take into account non-military threats, such as resource scarcity, climate change, overpopulation, poverty, pandemics, and terrorism. The definition of security has moved beyond its political and military dimension to encompass the environment (in Jegen's study of European energy security) or human security (in Biscop's and Gross's 'comprehensive' approach to crisis management). All kinds of 'soft' issues that were considered beyond the realm of security studies have now become key epistemological questions. In parallel, there has been a move from security *threats*, with their strong connection to the study of war, to a greater focus on diffuse *risks* that can affect mankind in different ways. Gheciu's, Ojanen's, and Vennesson et al.'s chapters are all predicated on a transition from clearly formed threats that need to be *defended against* to the much more complex equation of risks that need to be *predicted* and *managed*. The language of crisis management and conflict prevention, which dominates European discourses, testifies to this broadening of the paradigm.

By *deepening* the concept of security, our contributors in turn consider the security of referents other than the state. New ontological referents emerge, such as religious movements (as in Giegerich and Pantucci's chapter), energy actors (as in Jegen's chapter), and even the more abstract referent of security 'functions,' which in Ojanen's chapter allows for a rethinking of the state and its eventual replacement by the European Union. Internal and external boundaries are blurred in a European- and global-level system of security governance (Kirchner and Sperling 2007). In our book, the interpenetration of internal and external security, which used to delineate the state as a key unit of analysis, forms the basis for Gheciu's study of the Euro-Atlantic risk society, Giegerich and Pantucci's analysis of terrorism, and Gross's story of the securitization of organized crime and migration in the Balkans.

This opening of the security studies paradigm, as the reader will have recognized, corresponds more or less to the rise of constructivism and the development of new methodologies, such as discourse analysis, the ethnography of social practices, and the study of culture to complement systemic approaches. It is interesting to note that social constructivists have developed their hypotheses primarily, although not exclusively, in relation to European security. The work of Thomas Risse, Lena Hansen, Peter Katzenstein, Jeffrey Checkel, or Barry Buzan, all of whom use the European continent as their primary source of evidence, provides a good illustration. With the end of the Cold War and the double enlargement of the EU and NATO, Europe has emerged as a pacified security community, bound together by norms and rules, in an extremely dense institutional and symbolic environment where common understandings and practices are produced and reproduced. This 'object' did not seem to exist before. Enthused with the peaceful pacification of a continent, and supported by a political rhetoric that stressed the importance of common values in a post-Westphalian order, scholars began to look for instances where international relations did not seem to be ruled by the security dilemmas of major states. In Europe they found several.

Why would European governments and NGOs devote so much attention and resources to a regional conflict like that in the Balkans, where no existential threat to their state could be discerned? Why would they use soft instruments such as judicial reform and conditionality? None of this seemed to make sense unless one factored the dense institutional and social fabric of Europe, which tends to suppress external anarchy. Military capabilities and the use of force not being so useful anymore, ideational and social resources become paramount (Williams 2006). In the post-1989 European imaginary, one's internal problem becomes the other's external threat, and vice versa. This, of course, does not mean the end of all conflicts: while interstate war seems unlikely, security practitioners and scholars have focused increasingly on the fleeting sense of insecurity felt by Europeans, a sense of insecurity which encompasses both external (e.g., international crime) and internal (e.g., street violence) elements.

Two words of caution, however. First, we are not arguing that rivals to orthodox security studies appeared only after 1989. On the contrary, an alternative reading of security was already available in the form of various post-positivist approaches such as feminism, constructivism, Marxism, and so on. In 1983 already, Richard Ullman criticized the 'excessively narrow' and 'excessively military' conception of security that prevailed. The opening of the security paradigm was anticipated by critical perspectives which, in the 1980s, began to deconstruct state practices of securitization and called for a normative project of emancipation. These critical approaches, which remain quite marginal in the US, are now almost dominant in Europe, under the labels of the 'Aberyswyth,' 'Copenhagen,' and 'Paris' schools (CASE Collective 2006). Europe, a space without internal borders, with porous external borders, and with its complex intermingling of internal and external security concerns, remains the main field of inquiry for these scholars.

Nor has there been what Michel Foucault would have called a clean epistemological break. Clearly, no new orthodoxy has emerged to replace the neo-neo synthesis of the 1970s–1980s. We do not argue that the fall of the Berlin Wall has become the graveyard of orthodox security studies. Indeed, as some authors show in this book, realism and liberalism still provide a great deal of insight into some security issues, even in Europe. Rynning's sceptical tone, for instance, is a useful reminder that the state remains a key geopolitical player and that state boundaries have all but vanished. In contrast to the other contributors in this volume, he finds that 'change is important but it happens on the familiar chessboard of Eurasian geopolitics.' It is also quite possible that European security constitutes an exception in terms of disciplinary paradigm, and that the former paradigm continues to hold outside of European studies. Pouliot, for instance, suggests instances of a paradigm shift in European security policy are looked at with great suspicion in Moscow, which considers them as cheap talk or window dressing for traditional state interests.

So if there is a paradigm shift, it may be limited to Europe, and it is not complete yet. But we believe that, at the very least, the former paradigm has been *shattered*: the questions pursued and the answers provided by European security scholars are more diverse today than they were prior to 1989. Put differently, the neo-neo synthesis has been replaced by fragmentation and diversity. What we suggest, in effect, is that European security studies are currently in flux, which is confirmed by the variety of approaches developed in this book. The battle between orthodox thinkers and their constructivist contenders is far from over. This book is a demonstration of this continuing struggle.

Structure of the Book

To explore the interplay of, on the one hand, evolving perceptions of the European security environment and, on the other, theoretical developments in security studies, the book is structured around three main headings. Within these headings, each important issue is addressed though a specific theoretical approach of the author's own choosing, ranging from structural realism to critical constructivism via institutionalism. This, we hope, will provide a broad picture of the discipline's diversity of approaches and a key to assess their explanatory power. In the first section, 'The New European Security Environment,' we focus on shifting representations of security in Europe. If security is defined in its traditional sense as the integrity of the state and the absence of major political or military threats, the vast majority of Europeans live in a benign security environment. Thus our conception of security needs to be broadened and deepened.

As Gheciu argues in the first chapter of this section, despite the language of war and the attempt to frame terrorism as an assault on state sovereignty – that is, as a *threat* – conceptualizing terrorism as a *risk* posed by illiberal entities means that it can be 'managed' and 'disciplined' with the development of a new ethos and practices of inclusion/exclusion, many of which entail domestic instruments such as the police or the judiciary in addition to international security organizations. Giegerich and Pantucci, by contrast, take the 'new' terrorist threat more head on. Eschewing the language of risk, they show how certain Muslim communities have become radicalized in Europe. The domestic purveyors of insecurity are sometimes immersed in transnational networks, and their home bases in Africa or Asia. But still they suggest that what Europeans fear is better understood as matters of public safety, or internal security, than external security. Thus, like Gheciu, they emphasize the blurring of internal and external boundaries and the displacement of the state as the main referent of security studies. Globalization notwithstanding, security issues seem to have been largely domesticated: in Europe, there is no more anarchy *between* states than there is *inside* them. Although Europeans may have developed a greater interest in stopping transnational flows, as migration and crime are increasingly associated in the public conscience, Europe's borders have never been so secure.

While under the radar, nuclear issues are trickier. There is no fear comparable to the existential annihilation caused by nuclear war or even the human ravages of total war. Europe has moved from being a source of nuclear threat to being a base of stability, although one that can be expected to feel the side effects of world developments. Today, as von Hlatky and Fortmann show, the EU is the main proponent of non-proliferation and disarmament efforts, which are pursued through treaty ratifications, conditionality, and diplomacy (such as in Iran). In this context, the porosity of borders may be a problem, but it is probably minor compared with the inability of Europeans to solve the tension between deterrence and non-proliferation. The fact that nuclear risks are more diffuse – or the origin of the threat harder to locate – may give a false sense of security to Europeans.

A political and symbolic travail of securitization is necessary so that the threat is construed as one. Among diffuse risks none seems greater than the environmental challenge. With climate change, the loss of biodiversity, or the dangers associated with nuclear energy, the survival of mankind is at stake. It is not quite clear how traditional security institutions can tackle these risks, although they will certainly have to deal with their side effects. One important dimension that organizations such as NATO and the EU have begun to address, however, is energy security, covered in Jegen's chapter. This is a popular objective, for which the right combination of economic, diplomatic, and military tools is sought, so far without much success.

In the second section of the book, 'The Transformation of European Security Institutions,' our contributors describe how Europe's institutional framework has adapted to and in turn shaped perceptions of the security environment. As Biscop shows in his chapter, the notion that the nexus between failed states, civil wars (abroad), and crime (at home) can be broken by armed intervention has enjoyed significant currency in Europe since 2001. This has certainly informed institutional developments around the CFSP and ESDP. Robert Cooper, perhaps the EU's most influential diplomat after Javier Solana, wrote a book on 'the breaking of nations' (2004) which makes a similar argument. While diluted due to the reluctance of some governments, the 2003 *European Security Strategy* develops the same philosophy. The idea is that Europe can only be secure if it addresses the five following 'threats': terrorism, proliferation of weapons of mass destruction, regional conflicts, failed states, and organized crime, all of which are assumed to be interconnected in some ways. What is interesting about these perceived threats is that, again, they are all diffuse and all carry risks pertaining to both external and internal security.

Part of the explanation may come from the very density of Europe's institutional fabric, which raises the profile of security issues at the same time as it erases borders. The last two decades have been characterized by constant institutional innovation in the field of security. At the regional level, the EU has launched and developed its common defence policy, which, Ojanen argues, is justified by a transformation of the security functions traditionally bestowed upon the state. In parallel, as Rynning shows, NATO has undergone a complete overhaul, gearing itself for force projection after forty years of territorial defence, but with a continuing concern for the stability of Eurasian power relations. At the domestic level, European countries have worked hard to restructure their armed forces to fit new security challenges and, perhaps more importantly, the demand of regional security organizations. Forster focuses on civil-military relations and Vennesson and his colleagues focus on army doctrines. Both come to the conclusion that, despite attempts at rebooting the culture and format of European defence organizations, the weight of institutional legacies from the past means that adaptation will take a long time. As a result, these authors find more heterogeneity than homogeneity in the way practitioners approach security questions.

Finally, in 'Regional Challenges: Continuity and Change,' we look more specifically at three regional issues at Europe's border: Russia, the Balkans, and the Middle East. The Middle East, covered by Musu, serves as a good illustration of Europe's challenges in broadcasting its influence beyond the continent. We could have selected other areas where Europe is currently engaged, such as Afghanistan, but we wanted to analyse in greater detail three regions that have been intimately linked to the security of Europeans for a long time, at least since the last years of the Cold War.

Despite Mearsheimer's sombre predictions at the beginning of the 1990s, none of our contributors would feel uncomfortable with the characterization of Europe as a security community (Cottey 2007). Eurasia has become a spaghetti bowl of security institutions that serve to increase social interaction, resolve disputes, and build confidence. Long the main problem, as Europe implicated the rest of the world in its 'world' wars, Europe has now become an island of peace. While still volatile, the situation in the Balkans is unlikely to contaminate the neighbourhood. As Gross argues, the EU has largely succeeded in its crisis management efforts. Having stabilized its Eastern flank with NATO and EU enlargement, Europe now seeks to project stability in the Mediterranean (Union for the Mediterranean) and the Caucasus (European Neighborhood Policy and Eastern Partnership). Even the delicate status of Kosovo, which unilaterally declared its independence in 2008, and the Georgian war have not so far seriously undermined Russia-EU relations, which, in political and economic terms, remain characterized by interdependence. But, as Pouliot shows, this pacification has come without collective identification, which explains the difficulties that Europe faces in its dealings with Russia. Deep misunderstandings as to how European security should be organized resurface periodically and can be expected to continue to do so.

Conclusion

Theories are supposed to describe a reality. But they are social constructs and, as such, cannot be separated from social representations of the security environment. Too often, books on European security pretend to offer an 'objective' description of the main security threats to Europe and the strategic challenges that lie ahead. The assumptions and the political commitments that support such descriptions are rarely made explicit. This leads to, at best, theological discussions about whether Europe is (should be) a 'normative power' and, at worst, pop-psychological oppositions between Europeans who come from Venus and Americans who come from Mars. In between these two extremes is a rich intellectual production that simply repeats whatever happens to be fashionable in the foreign ministries of London or Paris. With a view to minimizing such temptations and generating a more reflexive account of European security, we have asked our contributors to make constant to and fro's between empirical description and theoretical development. As we have argued in this introductory chapter, theory and reality are interdependent; in Europe since the fall of the Berlin Wall, theoretical representations have shaped the security environment as much as empirical developments have informed security studies.

In the seminal 1993 book, *After the Cold War*, Robert Keohane, Joseph Nye, and Stanley Hoffmann identified the dismantling of the Berlin Wall as a 'perfect real-time laboratory' in which to test IR theories. Writing as history unfolded, they reported how states transformed international institutions as a result of the withdrawal of Soviet troops from Eastern Europe and the reunification of Germany. Looking from the vantage point of some twenty-odd years past, we can begin to ponder how this set of events circa 1989 profoundly transformed the lives of Europeans, the fate of security institutions, but also security studies themselves. In the conclusion, we will return to some of these themes. Building on the book's findings, we will outline a theory of the dynamics of European security that holds, we believe, the promise of bringing together different theoretical perspectives.

NOTES

1 In doing so, we adopt a soft definition of paradigm shift. We are cognizant of the fact that Kuhn did not intend his model to be applied to social science, where theoretical models are more diverse and contested than in the hard sciences.

REFERENCES

Buzan, Barry. 1991. *People, States, and Fear: An Agenda for International Security Studies in the Post-Cold War Era*. Boulder, CO: Lynne Rienner.
CASE Collective. 2006. 'Critical Approaches to Security in Europe: A Networked Manifesto.' *Security Dialogue* 37, no. 4: 443–87.

Cooper, Robert. 2004. The *Breaking of Nations: Order and Chaos in the 21st Century*. New York: Atlantic Monthly Press.

Cottey, Andrew. 2007. *Security in the New Europe*. Houndmills: Palgrave.

Giegerich, Bastian. 2006. *European Security and Strategic Culture: National Responses to the EU's Security and Defence Policy*. Baden-Baden: Nomos.

Kagan, Robert. 2003. *Paradise and Power: America and Europe in the New World Order*. New York: Knopf.

Katzenstein, Peter. 2005. *A World of Regions*. Ithaca, NY: Cornell University Press.

Kegley, Charles. 1993. 'The Neoidealist Moment in International Studies? Realist Myths and the New International Reality.' *International Studies Quarterly* 37: 131–46.

Keohane, Robert, Joseph Nye, and Stanley Hoffmann. 1993. *After the Cold War: International Institutions and State Strategies in Europe, 1989–1991*. Cambridge: Cambridge University Press.

Kirchner, Emil, and James Sperling. 2007. *EU Security Governance*. Manchester: Manchester University Press.

Krause, Keith, and Michael Williams. 1996. 'Broadening the Agenda of Security Studies: Politics and Methods.' *Mershon International Studies Review* 40, no. 2: 229–54.

Kuhn, Thomas. 1962. *The Structure of Scientific Revolutions*. Chicago: University of Chicago Press.

Meyer, Christoph. 2006. *The Quest for a European Strategic Culture: Changing Norms on Security and Defence in the European Union*. Houndmills: Palgrave.

Paris, Roland. 2001. 'Human Security: Paradigm Shift or Hot Air.' *International Security* 26, no. 2: 87–102.

Risse-Kappen, Thomas, and Richard Lebow, eds. 1995. *International Relations Theory and the End of the Cold War*. New York: Columbia University Press.

Ullman, Richard. 1983. 'Redefining Security.' *International Security* 8, no. 1: 129–53.

Waever, Ole. 1996. 'The Rise and Fall of the Inter-Paradigm Debate.' In *International Theory: Positivism and Beyond*, ed. Steve Smith, Ken Booth, and Marysia Zalewski, 149–85. Cambridge: Cambridge University Press.

Williams, Michael. 2006. *Culture and Security: The Reconstruction of Security in the Post-Cold War*. London: Routledge.

PART ONE

The New Security Environment

2 Towards Security? The Politics of Managing Risks in Twenty-First-Century Europe

ALEXANDRA GHECIU

In this chapter, I start by providing a brief overview of changes in definitions of threat and conceptualizations of the enemy in Euro-Atlantic security discourses, particularly in response to the 9/11 attacks and, more broadly, to what is widely perceived as a significant threat of international, Islamist terrorism. I then focus more specifically on NATO, examining the ways in which new conceptualizations of threat/enemy have inspired a particular ethos of risk management in the Alliance. That ethos, I suggest, has translated into a specific combination of practices of inclusion and exclusion. The chapter analyses the dynamics of those practices and reflects on some of the normative problems and challenges generated by them.

Redefining the Field of Security Following the Collapse of Communism

The end of the Cold War marked the start of a significant transformation in European security practices. Following the collapse of the Eastern bloc, a heavy emphasis came to be placed not just by individual states but also by international institutions – including by NATO, the Organization for Security and Cooperation in Europe (OSCE), and the EU – on international practices of promoting liberal democracy, especially in former communist states. In the period of flux that followed the demise of communist regimes, such practices were identified as a key dimension of efforts to enhance European and international stability. The new practices carried out by the institutions of the Western security community occurred in the context of the reconfiguration of the field of security, which led decision makers in the Euro-Atlantic area to understand the diffusion of knowledge and dispositions of self-restraint as the key to long-term regional and international stability. The concept of field is used here in a Bourdieusian sense, as analogous to a game in that it is a socially constructed, historically specific domain of activity that is governed by a specific set of rules.[1] The field of international security is the domain where authoritative definitions of the culture of security – that is, a common system of intersubjective, socially constructed meanings about 'what frightens' in international politics, or the 'face of the enemy' – are shared by a given community of agents.[2]

In the immediate aftermath of the end of the Cold War, the field of security was reconfigured in ways which involved a partial de-valorization of military factors and a new emphasis on culture as a source of security. In brief, in the field of security the collapse of communism and the end of the Cold War led to the rise to prominence of a Kantian-inspired democratic peace set of ideas, practices, and institutional arrangements, and the privileging of non-military forms of capital seen as necessary for the enactment of those practices. Those developments were informed by a prevailing view in Western policymaking circles that the demise of the Eastern bloc had created conditions for the start of a process of constructing, in President Bush Sr's words, a 'new world order' of democratic peace.[3] The rise to prominence of Kantian-inspired ideas and practices represented a significant transformation in the field of security. Note, for instance, that they involved a move away from Cold War intersubjective understandings of the 'face of the enemy' (a clearly constituted geopolitical entity) and the rise to prominence of a collective idea that, with proper self-discipline and international support, even former enemies (ex-communist states) could become partners worthy of inclusion into some if not all of the institutional structures of the liberal-democratic security community. In that sense, the European security environment was seen by Western policymakers – and many academics – as far more benign than had been the case prior to 1989.[4]

In the 1990s, conventional military threats seemed to be declining in importance, while, simultaneously, more fluid and multifaceted security challenges were assuming centre stage. Thus, key security documents and statements issued by Western actors after 1989 depict a new ontology of European security, significantly different from the picture of power-balancing in an anarchic environment that was so often depicted in mainstream (primarily structural realist) IR analyses. In the European context, after 1989 the spotlight came to be placed not on geostrategic rivalries but, rather, on domestic problems allegedly generated by the lack of good, liberal-democratic norms and institutions, and associated particularly with the former communist countries. It was argued that domestic instability generated by problems of transition towards post-communist institutions threatened to be one of the key – if not the key – sources of instability in Europe.[5] In that context, in Western political circles the prevailing view was that the promotion of 'good,' liberal democratic norms and institutions within those states would be a vital ingredient in the pursuit of security in the new era. This collective view regarding changes in the field of security translated into a development identified by Frédéric Mérand, Bastien Irondelle, and Martial Foucault as the blurring of the boundary between internal and external security.[6] One of the most significant manifestations of the new view of blurred boundaries was the idea that, by helping to stabilize and reconstruct fragile post-communist states, Western actors were also playing a significant role in promoting regional and international security.

That shared understanding concerning the importance of pursuing international security through the construction of a particular type of institution within potentially problematic states of Central/Eastern Europe was inscribed in the key documents, conventions, and charters of European reconstruction signed in the early 1990s. These included both declarations issued by individual Western leaders and, more importantly, collective statements embedded in the basic documents of all the important European institutional forums, from the Council of Europe, to the European Community/Union, the Conference/Organization for Security and Cooperation in Europe (OSCE), as well as NATO (Adler 1998; Flynn and Farrell 1999; Gheciu 2005; Williams 2007). With the series of treaties, conventions, and other agreements signed in the early 1990s, the establishment or maintenance of a political system that did not respect these principles was de-legitimized as incompatible with the normative foundation of the new Europe.

Against the background of that redefinition of the field of security, several international actors, including the EU, NATO, and the OSCE – as recognized expert institutions in the Euro-Atlantic area, institutions that embodied the norms of liberal-democracy and possessed the accumulated material, cultural, and symbolic capital of the security community – initiated a series of practices of socialization aimed at expanding the Western security community into the former Eastern bloc (Gheciu 2005). In other words, in the 1990s, the EU, NATO, and the OSCE assumed important roles in promoting the norms of liberal democracy – and cultivating dispositions of self-restraint underpinning liberalism

– in what were seen as potentially vulnerable ex-communist polities. While the EU and the OSCE had always had the promotion of democracy, the rule of law, and human rights at the heart of their mandates, for NATO the adoption of Kantian-inspired democracy-promotion practices constituted a more significant transformation. True, as reflected in the Preamble and Article 2, the language of the Washington Treaty depicted the Atlantic Alliance as an institution that would represent and promote the liberal-democratic values and principles of the founders. In practice, however, in the context of the Cold War, the principles and aspirations inscribed in Article 2 were subordinated to the perceived strategic demands of the East-West power balancing. It was only following the collapse of the Soviet bloc, and against the background of the recognition in NATO decision-making circles that the Euro-Atlantic security environment was changing, that efforts aimed at constructing 'good' liberal-democratic polities came to the fore in NATO's repertoire of security practices. In that sense, NATO's practices both reflected and contributed to the post–Cold War transformation in the field of security.

Before we go any further, it is worth noting that all these developments in the field of security were far from generating uniform interpretations within the IR academic community. As Mérand, Irondelle, and Foucault note in the Introduction to this volume, after 1989 the paradigm that had dominated security studies during the Cold War came under sustained attack from critics emboldened by the mainstream scholars' apparent inability to account for changes in European security. Thus, many critical voices (Barry Buzan, Ole Waever, Jef Huysmans, Keith Krause, Michael Williams – to name but a few) intensified their critique of the ontological and epistemological assumptions associated with the neorealist-neoliberal synthesis. They, and other critical IR scholars, insisted on the need to acknowledge the importance of new (non-state) security referents, and to systematically inquire into the social construction of particular security environments – including the use of symbolic, institutional and cultural power in those exercises of social construction. Meanwhile, prominent mainstream IR scholars – John Mearsheimer and Ken Waltz, most notably – insisted that no fundamental change had occurred, and that the structural patterns highlighted in neo-realist writings were bound to persist, leading to a return of European security 'back to the future.'[7]

This dissonance in IR interpretations of post–Cold War European security is also reflected in academic analyses of NATO. Thus, while critical scholars such as Iver Neumann, Michael Williams, Emanuel Adler, and Rachel Epstein have focused their attention on NATO's adaptation to the post–Cold War environment, and have implicitly or explicitly linked the Alliance's success (or failure) to its ability to use symbolic and cultural power to expand the liberal-democratic security community and address non-conventional threats, influential voices within the mainstream tradition (particularly structural realists, such as Ken Waltz and John Mearsheimer) have continued to conceptualize NATO as a conventional geo-strategic arrangement. Consequently, in discussing the Alliance's future, scholars who belong in the latter camp have continued to focus on NATO's material capabilities and its (in) ability to perform traditional 'hard' security functions.

The Rise of the Logic of Risk Management

While the emphasis on promoting regional and international security through Kantian-inspired democracy-promotion practices is still alive, the enactment of those practices was complicated, after 9/11, by a growing concern about a new set of enemies to international peace. Following the terrorist attacks in the US, and later in Madrid and London, the prevailing discourses on security in the Euro-Atlantic area came to depict a new kind of existential threat: international Islamist terrorism. Extremist Islamists, it is argued, endanger not only the people and territory of particular Western polities, but, more fundamentally, threaten the key values of modern civilization.

The events of 9/11 and their aftermath can thus be seen as a second key point (after the collapse of communism) in the transformation of the field of security. In some ways, 9/11 only served to reinforce transformations that had occurred in response to the end of the Cold War. Thus, the focus on promoting international security via adopting an 'inside' approach (transforming polities, rather than constraining their behaviour via conventional geo-strategic arrangements) continues to occupy a privileged position in Euro-Atlantic security practices. In a similar vein, the focus on non-conventional threats and multiple security referents has become even more intense. Linked to that, perceptions of the blurred boundary between inside/outside were rendered more acute in a situation in which a key argument in Euro-Atlantic political circles has been that internal 'problems' could quickly become international threats, particularly when terrorists are involved. Yet, one can also point to some discontinuities between pre-9/11 and post-9/11 shared understandings of the security environment. In particular, I would suggest, the new concern with international terrorism prompted a partial reconceptualization of the space of security, in a situation in which those identified as the new enemies operate both within and outside the Western (liberal) world. Gone are the early post–Cold War days when the transatlantic security community was seen as a haven of democratic peace, stability, and prosperity, and all security challenges were associated with the *outside* realm. In the fluid security environment of the post-9/11 world, there is a new sense that enemies of civilization both target the Western world and use it as a base for some of their activities, taking advantage of extensive liberal freedoms to finance and plan their operations.

The new concern with internationally organized terrorism is reflected in a multitude of documents and statements issued over the past few years by many states in the Euro-Atlantic area, and also by institutions like NATO, the EU, and the OSCE. While debates and even tensions persist in many international forums as regards the best way to prevent and combat terrorism, those debates occur against the background of a shared understanding that international terrorist groups/networks that support those groups are particularly dangerous (and at the same time highly elusive) enemies of civilization (Gheciu 2008).

For our purposes, it is particularly revealing that, in recent years, NATO has repeatedly identified international terrorism as a key threat to the allied security. In light of recent changes – and prevailing perceptions of those changes – this move is hardly surprising. Given the dominant intersubjective understandings in policymaking circles in NATO member states concerning the prominence of non-conventional enemies and diffuse security risks, in order to demonstrate its continued relevance in the context of Euro-Atlantic relations, and thus secure persisting support by its members, the Alliance had to demonstrate that it would be able to address this multitude of risks, including by combating terrorism. For instance, the North Atlantic Council (NATO's key decision-making body) stated at its June 2003 meeting in Madrid its commitment to the fight against international terrorism. Thus,

Terrorism continues to pose a grave threat to Alliance populations, forces and territory, as well as to international peace and security. It also poses a threat to the development and functioning of democratic institutions, the territorial integrity of states, and to peaceful relations between them … To fight terrorism effectively, our response must be multi-faceted and comprehensive. (North Atlantic Council 2003)

As an expression of the broader emphasis on counter-terrorism in European decision-making circles, it is interesting to note that a very similar reading of the danger posed by non-conventional enemies, especially international terrorist groups – represented as the new 'dangerous others' for the entire civilized world – can be found in the 2003 *European Security Strategy* and the OSCE documents, including the 2001 Action Plan to Combat Terrorism. As stated in that Action Plan, 'The 55 participating states of the OSCE stand united against terrorism, a scourge of our times. The barbaric acts of terrorism that were committed against the US on 11 September 2001 represented an attack on the whole of the international community ... These heinous deeds, as well as other terrorist acts in all forms and manifestations, committed no matter when, where or by whom, are a threat to international and regional peace, security and stability. There must be no safe haven for those perpetrating, financing, harbouring or otherwise supporting those responsible for such criminal acts' (OSCE 2001).

Based on this intersubjective understanding of the changing nature of new enemies, what we see in Euro-Atlantic circles is a growing tendency to conceptualize security as a process of risk management. That is, in the face of a highly elusive and mobile enemy that combines 'modern technology and radicalism,' an enemy that, instead of being confined to a spatially distant realm is 'also part of our [liberal-democratic] society, with the alleged potential to generate chaos, there has been a tendency to move away from a dream of security as a stable positive outcome (the 'new world order' enunciated by President Bush Senior) and towards a more pessimistic view of security as a constant process of management of a plurality of risks (Rassmussen 2002; Coker 2002).

The concept of risk management occupies a prominent position in the analyses put forward by scholars concerned with a general sense of insecurity that, they argue, prevails in our – 'late modern' – era.[8] In their view, the current international concern with risk is largely a product of globalization, and a related sense of vulnerability in being part of a world system in which old protections (usually provided by nation-states) are increasingly becoming obsolete. According to sociologists like Ulrich Beck and Anthony Giddens, an unprecedented anxiety about risks is common to what they call 'second modernity' or 'late modernity,' that is, a period when humanity is more sober about progress and about the future. Thus, while many accept that things may still progress, they also recognize that there is a price to be paid – for instance, in terms of global, often unanticipated consequences of our actions.

Particular attention is paid to global risks, which cannot be delimited spatially (think, for instance, of the threat of a nuclear attack, or even an attack by terrorist groups using WMDs), just as they cannot be delimited in time, for actions taken today can have unforeseen consequences affecting future generations (Coker 2002). Ulrich Beck famously argued in 1996 that risk society 'is not an option which could be chosen or rejected in the course of political debate' (28). Instead, it represents an inescapable structural condition of advanced industrialization where the produced hazards of that system 'undermine and/or cancel the established safety systems of the provident state's existing risk calculation' (31). Risk theorists argue that terrorism represents yet another manifestation of the 'world risk society' (Beck 2002: 39–55). For Beck, 11 September demonstrated that we now live in a world risk society, a society in which we have to face unpredictable dangers that defy the traditional approach to the management of risk: insurance. Terrorism, it is argued, is a risk that goes 'beyond the realm of rational calculation into the realm of unpredictable turbulence' (43).

More broadly, the notion involved in arguments about risk is that in globalized, late-modern societies some risks are so grave as to justify extraordinary measures, measures which suspend or place serious limits on key constitutive norms of those societies in the name of reducing risk (as in the case of terrorism). The irony, however, is that making decisions in the present to take a particular course of action in the name of managing a risk creates new risks; in the process of pre-empting the unfolding of a virtual scenario, decision makers in a risk society can create what Beck called the 'boomerang effect': the effects of the decision taken at present in the name of acting on a future risk may come back to haunt their authors, as the attempt to recapture certainty – that fundamental goal of modernity – gives rise to a spiral of uncertainty. Thus, 'the more we attempt to "colonize" the future, with the aid of the category of risk, the more it slips out of our control' (Beck 1999: 139).

In the field of international security, consistent with the ethos of risk management and in contrast to the promise of a peaceful new world order that was so popular in the early years of the post–Cold War period, recent developments have inspired more cautious statements about the future. Today, few would boast about definitive solutions to security challenges and a stable, peaceful new world order. Instead, in a multitude of contexts we see a plurality of actors, including security institutions, articulating and seeking to implement discourses that conceptualize security as a process of risk management. This move has occurred in a situation in which, as Jef Huysmans has argued, 'uncertainty is the primary threat' in today's world (Huysmans 1998). The main approach to security issues is now preventive defence against a multitude of dangers, most of which are ill-defined and often poorly understood.

In particular, these new security discourses cast international Islamist terrorism as an extreme form of risk, due to a combination of two elements – exceptional danger, particularly should terrorists acquire WMDs, and absolute uncertainty regarding the identity, location, and plans of terrorist groups like al Qaeda. This particular portrayal of terrorism as a form of extreme risk has been used in different institutional settings to justify extraordinary measures of prevention in a multitude of areas, ranging from exceptional policing measures to economic measures designed to disrupt terrorist financing and even military action to destroy terrorist groups and/or prevent a country from becoming a breeding ground for terrorism. As I have argued elsewhere, these measures entail significant redefinitions and blurring of established categories such as private/public sphere, military action/policing, high/low politics, and give rise to a number of serious normative problems and dilemmas for liberal-democratic polities (Gheciu 2008).

For NATO, the past few years have been a time marked by the rise to prominence of a very ambitious agenda of risk management. Thus, practices of risk management carried out by the Alliance in the name of combating international terrorism have taken the concept of preventing harm far beyond its conventional understanding of acting to minimize the risk of particular accidents/incidents. Indeed, risk management has come to represent an extremely complex project, involving a continued effort to mould as many individuals and communities as possible into the kinds of responsible (liberal, self-disciplined) actors that are unlikely to be a source of threat to international security – in particular, unlikely to engage in or support international terrorism. In the first years of the twenty-first century there has been a reassertion – sometimes a muscular reassertion – of the (Kantian) project of building self-disciplined selves and polities that was so powerful in Euro-Atlantic political circles in the first decade following the end of the Cold War. In the new context, practices of building responsible subjectivity that were so influential in the 1990s (in particular practices of expansion of the Western security community through the socialization of former communist subjects into the norms of liberalism) have been further developed but also combined with newer methods and technologies. Particularly interesting has been the development of programs and technologies that seek to 'deepen' the security community by enhancing the commitment to the norms and values of liberal democracy of those vulnerable individuals and groups which reside within the community of liberal democracy.

This approach has been accompanied by a more exclusionary set of practices, aimed at identifying, containing, and, ideally, displacing beyond the space of normal politics of liberal democratic polities those who are deemed 'beyond salvation,' that is, those who have allegedly refused to evolve into such rational, self-disciplined subjectivities. All those practices cross established boundaries between the public/private sphere, military/policing, high/low politics and create an assemblage of methods and technologies for the monitoring and guidance of a multitude of subjects – all in the name of reducing (though not eliminating) the risks posed by actors identified as a new type of enemies of civilization.

Managing Risks in an Uncertain World: The NATO Case

In response to 11 September, NATO acted quickly to invoke, for the first time in its history, the mutual defence clause (Article 5). The allies then proceeded to redefine NATO's role in the new world of elusive threats to international security. Senior allied officials pointed out that NATO would have to adapt to a new environment – an environment in which many threats come from non-conventional sources (Robertson 2002; Donnelly 2003).

In the new security environment, combating terrorism has been identified as 'a core mission for NATO' (Robertson 2003). Indeed, the North Atlantic Council (NATO's key decision-making body) stated at its June 2003 meeting in Madrid its commitment to the fight against terrorism. In their words:

> Terrorism continues to pose a grave threat to Alliance populations, forces and territory, as well as to international peace and security. It also poses a threat to the development and functioning of democratic institutions, the territorial integrity of states, and to peaceful relations between them ... To fight terrorism effectively, our response must be multi-faceted and comprehensive. (North Atlantic Council 2003, Paragraph 25)

In the course of a meeting held in 2002, the defence ministers of Member States argued that NATO needed to adapt to a security environment in which many of its enemies were hard to identify (NATO 2002a). The notion involved here is that, in the new context, NATO must be prepared to deal with an enemy that is 'like cancer,' operating anywhere and, potentially, everywhere, simultaneously attacking the West in different ways and on multiple fronts. The 'enemy,' in other words, consists of 'those groups that threaten our social order, blurring the boundaries between war and non-war' (Donnelly 2003).

Under these circumstances, consistent with the principles of risk management, NATO officials and representatives of allied governments have argued that the Alliance must be increasingly able and willing to adopt a preventive approach to security, 'preventing instability from growing into crises and managing crises before they get too out of hand ... if we wish to prevent the organized crime generated by these conflicts from darkening our doorsteps' (Robertson 2002a). Importantly, for NATO:

> What has changed – and what has changed dramatically – is the way in which [our] common values are threatened, and the manner in which we have to defend them. In the face of threats from terrorism, the proliferation of weapons of mass destruction and failing states, a reactive approach is simply no longer good enough. These new and complex threats call for much more active engagement, including well away from our own borders – and that is what the NATO Alliance is very much geared towards these days. (Jaap de Hoop Scheffer 2006a)

In the twenty-first-century NATO discourse, there is little talk about definitive solutions to security challenges and a stable, peaceful new world order. Instead, the emphasis is on the challenges of responding, via a plurality of means, to a multitude of fluid problems and threats. The sense of uncertainty as a characteristic of the new security environment was evident at the Alliance's Riga Summit, in November 2006. Thus, the *Comprehensive Political Guidance* – the key strategic document produced by the allies at the summit – states that NATO must be prepared to face 'unpredictable challenges' that 'arise at very short notice.' Under these circumstances, the priority for the Alliance is to develop procedures and capabilities that enable it to 'respond quickly to unforeseen circumstances,' for instance by launching and sustaining 'concurrent major joint operations and smaller operations for collective defense and crisis response on and beyond Alliance territory, on its periphery and at strategic distance' (NATO 2006).

NATO's current focus on risk management has translated into a dual approach to the pursuit of security. This involves an attempt to broaden and deepen the Western security community by inclusive practices aimed at cultivating or enhancing support for liberal norms outside the allied territory, especially by diffusing liberal norms and seeking to construct polities worthy of inclusion into that community. On the other hand, there has been a renewed emphasis on exclusionary practices aimed at identifying, excluding from allied space – or at least from the normal political and socio-economic life of allied states – and defeating that new category of dangerous others. Particularly dangerous, according to the NATO discourse, are those actors accused of involvement in or support for Islamist terrorism, who allegedly pose a threat not only to the allied publics but more broadly to the values of civilization.

Towards an Expanded Euro-Atlantic Security Community?

Building on practices carried out in the 1990s, NATO has sought to intensify its effort to shape transitional, potentially unstable polities in an attempt to turn them into 'like-minded' liberal-democratic countries. The aim behind those practices is to expand the liberal-democratic zone of peace, to help construct polities that deserve the respect of/integration into the Western security community. The focus, in other words, is on guiding a process of *becoming* – and rewarding those states that accept the responsibility to undertake such a process along the lines prescribed by NATO. The logic behind this approach to security is the same Kantian-inspired logic of building international security via an 'inside' approach, which became prevalent in the 1990s. Now, however, there is an additional rationale for engaging in building 'good,' self-disciplined liberal-democracies: these polities are seen as more reliable partners in efforts to address the risks posed by international terrorist groups and other non-conventional enemies. Importantly, such liberal democracies tend to be identified as societies where extremist groups and organized criminals are less likely to be able to organize and gain supporters.[9] Moreover, the argument is that such polities can support allied efforts to carry out 'policing at a distance' (for instance in the Balkans, where many Central/East Europeans are involved in reconstruction efforts). In a similar vein, they can help stabilize post-conflict societies (recall, for instance, the contributions of countries like Poland and Romania in Afghanistan).

   In the name of helping build self-disciplined, democratic societies, NATO has continued to carry out a plethora of socialization practices. Those practices, initiated in the 1990s and dramatically expanded over

the past few years, are aimed at cultivating NATO-prescribed conceptual and practical dispositions (or *habitus*) to partner states. NATO's efforts at international norm promotion have involved, in particular, a
series of initiatives designed to strengthen and expand the Partnership
for Peace (PfP) Programme and to continue the process of NATO enlargement (François 2000). Its explicit aim of spreading the Alliance's
ways of thinking and acting, and its emphasis on the usefulness of
programs that teach people from partially or non-democratic states
Western-defined norms and rules are powerful indicators of the importance attached by the Alliance to the construction of self-disciplined liberal subjects who can presumably act as 'like-minded' partners and
potential future members of the Euro-Atlantic security community.

The summit held by NATO in Istanbul in June 2004 was especially
important for partnerships, not least because the Alliance decided to establish some partnership programs built on the PfP model in the
Mediterranean region and even in the so-called 'Broader Middle East'
(including the Caucasus and Central Asia). The Istanbul Cooperation
Initiative (ICI) was extended to interested countries of the broader
Middle East region, especially the members of the Gulf Cooperation
Council,[10] in order 'to foster mutually beneficial bilateral relationships
and thus enhance security and stability. The initiative focuses on practical cooperation where NATO can add value, notably in the Defense
and security field' (NATO 2004a). At Istanbul, NATO also decided to
'elevate the MD [the Mediterranean Dialogue] to a genuine partnership.' This is to be accomplished through 'greater emphasis on practical
cooperation' on the model of PfP tools (ibid. §8). In addition to allowing
participation, on a case-by-case basis, in appropriate PfP exercises, the
Alliance also suggested the establishment of a liaison between the ministries of defence of partner countries and NATO at NATO Headquarters
and the Partnership Coordination Cell at Mons. The ICI and an enhanced MD supplement NATO's activities in Afghanistan and are
thus part of NATO's post-9/11 strategy to use partnership and region-
building practices to stabilize and – according to the allies – spread
democratic norms to and thus help reform the Broader Middle East.

NATO has also reaffirmed its commitment to the 'open door' policy
and has sought to (re)shape the countries that are currently queuing to
join NATO in the next wave of enlargement. If candidates accept the responsibility to evolve into stable liberal-democracies, they can expect to
receive NATO's guidance in the process of preparation for accession,
and eventually to be rewarded with inclusion into the Western security

community. Albania and Croatia are the latest examples of states that have been integrated into NATO following long accession dialogues and reforms monitored – and partly guided – within the framework of NATO's *Membership Action Plan* (the program designed to provide guidance and monitor the performance of countries that wish to join the Alliance). Meanwhile, the widely anticipated invitation to a third country – the Former Yugoslav Republic of Macedonia – has been delayed by a bitter dispute with Greece over the name 'Macedonia.' At the 2008 Bucharest Summit, two other countries, Ukraine and Georgia, were promised membership in the Alliance at a future point in time, though at present there is no clear timeline for the accession of those states. In the course of consultations and accession dialogues with all those states, NATO officials have insisted that enlargement decisions will be heavily influenced by the democratic credentials of candidates.[11]

Within the framework of the Membership Action Plan (MAP), candidate states have been subjected to repeated assessments of their reform processes and have been receiving systematic advice on the reforms they still have to carry out in order to become eligible for admission into the NATO club. Vis-à-vis third-wave candidates, the Alliance has sought to enhance its ability to carry out continuous surveillance and guidance of candidate states by initiating a series of institutional innovations, such as the establishment of NATO Headquarters in those countries. Reform programs formulated within the framework of MAP involve comprehensive plans for democratic transformation in a host of areas, ranging from fighting corruption and organized crime, strengthening the rule of law, enhancing the independence and efficiency of the judiciary, to implementing defence reforms (primarily aimed at promoting transparency, efficiency, and strengthening of democratic control of the military).[12]

In essence, in various ways and through diverse forums, NATO has been involved in spreading Western-prescribed liberal concepts, norms, and corresponding practical dispositions of self-restraint beyond its borders, thereby seeking to contribute to the construction of liberal polities. This effort is based on the assumption that the establishment of stable liberal democracies is an important dimension of the quest for international security – and a key ingredient in the fight against international terrorism. But those practices of democratic norm promotion – and the rewards officially associated with the completion of democratic reforms – have been complicated by a series of developments, particularly by dynamics associated with the fight against international terrorism. For example, prevailing NATO definitions of what constitute acceptable liberal norms – and what are the acceptable exceptions to those norms – have suffered a significant transformation over the past couple of years. While the Alliance has continued to stress the importance of norms of transparency, democratic accountability, and judicial independence, evidence regarding post-9/11 NATO enlargement suggests that, in the context of the perceived threat of international terrorism, there was a certain willingness to allow a series of compromises and exceptions to liberal norms in the name of protecting the Euro-Atlantic world from the threat of international terrorism (Gheciu 2008).

Excluding Enemies from the Security Community

If NATO has sought to expand the security community that it claims to embody, it has also focused on efforts to exclude from the territory of that community a new type of dangerous *others*. Those are identified as actors who, due to their ('barbaric') actions, have placed themselves beyond the realm of humanity. They are in particular terrorist groups who 'pose a threat to civilization itself' due to their (alleged) refusal to transcend their irrational behaviour (as reflected in the 'mindless slaughter of so many innocent civilians'), and their 'willingness to commit acts of violence without precedent in the modern era' (North Atlantic Council 2001). Vis-à-vis such actors (e.g., al Qaeda and their supporters, both non-state and state actors), NATO's self-defined role is not that of a guide in the process of transition from an unlawful state of nature to – borrowing a Kantian term – a 'lawful state' (i.e., a state governed by liberal norms). Indeed, those actors' wilful acts of violence 'against civilization' have made such a course of action impossible: according to the NATO discourse, terrorists and their supporters not only insist on living in an 'unlawful state,' but they explicitly seek to destroy the 'lawful' world. Therefore, it is argued, it is necessary to find the right coercive measures to 'combat this scourge' and thus to prevent terrorists and their sponsors from harming the 'civilized nations' (North Atlantic Council 2001).

In the words of Lord Robertson, then NATO Secretary General, in the twenty-first century it is particularly important for the Alliance to find effective ways to protect its citizens 'from criminal terrorists and criminal states, especially when they are armed with weapons designed for massive and indiscriminate destruction' (Robertson 2002). In the new security environment, NATO's aim must be 'to maintain the will and the capabilities ... to root out and defeat [criminal terrorists and criminal states] ... NATO played the key role in defeating the threats of the Cold War and the instability that followed it. We must now transform our Alliance so it can play an equally pivotal part in the war against terrorism and the dangers of weapons of mass destruction' (Robertson 2002a).

One of the most important assumptions underpinning contemporary practices of exclusion is that the new, unconventional enemies are located within as well as outside the NATO territory. Gone are the optimistic days of the early post–Cold War era, when the Western allies did not see any existential threats on the horizon and the Euro-Atlantic world was regarded as a haven of security. The notion of existential threats and the perceived need to fight a war against them are back – though in a form that differs from the existential threats of the Cold War era. The new focus on enemies and boundaries is instantiated in practices of direct war (though, interestingly, not wars directed at the entire population of a state) and in the use of judicially sanctioned or extra-judicial incarceration, as well as the use of special measures aimed at excluding from the normal political and socio-economic life of the liberal-democratic security community those individuals/groups suspected of involvement in organized crime and terrorism.

It is noteworthy that NATO statements and documents that call for an intensified anti-terrorist struggle also state that this should be done with minimal disruption to the socio-economic activities and political life of the citizens of member states and their partners.[13] In a situation in which the new others are seen as unusually elusive, operating 'like cancer, everywhere' (Donnelly 2003b), one of the priorities for NATO has been to develop new technologies, going well beyond the mandate of a military alliance, and to acquire new powers of identification, surveillance, and exclusion of dangerous individuals and groups. One of the key aspects of this has been the blurring of the boundary between performing defence-related functions and carrying out law enforcement operations.

As early as November 2002, at the Prague Summit, NATO leaders endorsed a whole package of measures and initiatives, most of which can be considered as designed to combat terrorism. It is interesting to note that, in reforming NATO to address the new challenges of the twenty-first century, the allies have placed particular emphasis on the need to improve intelligence sharing both within and outside of the Euro-Atlantic area, with particular emphasis on intelligence concerning organized crime and potential terrorist activities within member and partner states. The allies made a commitment to review current intelligence structures at NATO and to strengthen the Terrorist Threat Intelligence Unit at NATO headquarters in Brussels. This Unit, which was created after 11 September, has now become permanent and will analyse general terrorist threats, as well as those more specifically aimed at NATO. However, so far, progress in the area of intelligence sharing has been limited, not least because the Alliance still lacks an integrated analytical staff, resulting in confusion and compartmentalization, and because in several instances there was reluctance even among close partners to share intelligence that might deter or even endanger the lives of sources. Nevertheless, more developments are expected in this area in the future, and many analysts have expressed high hopes regarding the prospects for cooperation within (and around) the new NATO Intelligence Fusion Centre, established at RAF Molesworth, in October 2006.[14]

Meanwhile, the *Partnership Action Plan against Terrorism* (endorsed by allies and partners in 2002) provides for the development of an EAPC/PfP Intelligence Liaison Unit designed to facilitate the surveillance of groups deemed to be dangerous. The Plan also provides for the enhancement of allied/partner cooperation in the area of border control, aimed primarily at providing assistance and training to partners in their struggle to prevent illicit movement of people and material across international borders.

In other areas, too, NATO has taken a series of steps designed to enable it to assume some of the functions traditionally attributed to domestic law enforcement agencies, thereby further blurring the boundary between the 'inside' and 'outside' realms. For example, at NATO's June 2004 Istanbul Summit, the Allies agreed on a Policy on Combating Trafficking in Human Beings. Describing human trafficking as a 'modern day slave trade' that fuels organized crime and potentially finances terrorism, the allies made a commitment to ratify and accept the UN Convention against Transnational Organized Crime, to review national legislation and report on national efforts to meet all obligations under the Convention and relevant Protocol, to exchange information and cooperate with the EU and other international institutions in order to ensure maximum effectiveness of the new policy, and to identify and punish all those responsible for organized crime.[15]

For its part, Operation Active Endeavour in the Mediterranean also illustrates the evolution of NATO into an organization that combines military and policing functions in the name of managing a multitude of non-conventional risks. Operation Active Endeavour evolved out of NATO's immediate response to the terrorist attacks of 9/11. NATO initially deployed its Standing Naval Forces to the Eastern Mediterranean in October 2001, in a demonstration of allied resolve and solidarity. Together with the dispatch of Airborne Warning and Control Systems (AWACS) aircraft to the US, it was the first time that NATO assets had been deployed in support of an Article 5 operation (the operation was launched just before the start of Operation Enduring Freedom in Afghanistan). The initial aim of the operation in the Mediterranean was to provide a deterrent presence and surveillance in strategic international waters at a key moment. In March 2003, Active Endeavour was expanded to include providing escorts through the Straits of Gibraltar to merchant ships from allied states that requested them. This extension of the mission was designed to help prevent terrorist attacks such as those on the USS *Cole* in 2000. In May 2004 the escorts were suspended as a result of a declining number of requests – but with the understanding that they may be reactivated at any time. In April 2003, NATO further expanded the mission and began boarding suspect ships (with the compliance of the ships' captains and flag states). In October 2004, NATO put in place a new operational pattern. Since then, the focus has been on gathering and processing information and intelligence so as to target specific vessels of interest. Also, as part of its expanded operation, which now covers the entire Mediterranean, NATO has been involved in civilian emergencies (e.g., helping to rescue civilians on stricken oil rigs and sinking ships), and has become involved in efforts to combat illegal migration in that region. Allied officials also claim that the experience that NATO has accrued in Active Endeavour has given the Alliance unparalleled expertise in the field. That expertise is relevant to wider international efforts to combat terrorism, particularly in the area of proliferation and smuggling of weapons of mass destruction, but also, perhaps more surprisingly for NATO, in controlling international criminality (e.g., illegal migration).

Finally, in recognition of the prevailing view among the allies that '9/11 transformed terrorism from a domestic security concern into a truly international security challenge,' NATO has sought to improve its 'out-of-area' policing functions, particularly in the context of failed states, where, it is argued, domestic organized crime might be associated with or at least help finance international acts of terrorism (Robertson 2003). Thus, for instance, in Kosovo the NATO-led international security force (KFOR) seeks to perform important law-enforcement functions, ranging from riot control and protection of ethnic minorities to the fight against organized crime, paramilitary groups, and terrorist activities.[16] In order to enhance its ability to perform these functions, KFOR has enhanced its surveillance and investigative capabilities, has already arrested several suspected terrorists with alleged links to the al Qaeda network, has taken steps to purge from the Kosovo Protection Corps[17] individuals suspected of involvement in organized crime or terrorism, and is continuing to investigate the activities of foreign nationals who came to the region as volunteer soldiers during the fighting and who appear to have remained in the province after the end of the conflict.[18]

As part of its effort to adapt to a changing field of security, NATO also took a series of steps aimed at enhancing its ability to apply effective military force (in defensive as well as offensive operations) against terrorists and those state or non-state actors suspected of harbouring them. For the NATO allies, the nature of contemporary (terrorist) threats is such that, in certain conditions, it may be necessary to apply military force in order to prevent terrorists from bringing violence 'to our doorstep.' At their meeting in May 2002, NATO foreign ministers agreed that: 'To carry out the full range of its missions, NATO must be able to field forces that can move quickly to wherever they are needed, sustain operations over distance and time, and achieve their objectives' (Bennett 2003). This inspired a new capabilities initiative, the Prague Capabilities Commitment (PCC), aimed at improving, among other things, the Alliance's terrorism-related capabilities and in general ensuring that allied militaries are equipped to move faster and further afield, to apply military force more effectively, and to sustain themselves in combat (Bennett 2003). It includes eight fields: intelligence, surveillance, and target acquisition; air-to-ground surveillance; chemical, biological, radiological, and nuclear defence; command, control, and communications; combat effectiveness; strategic air and sea lift; air-to-air refuelling; and deployable combat support and combat service support units. Another Prague initiative, the NATO Response Force, is designed to reflect the new realities in which the Western allies might have to respond to surprise attacks – or threats of attack – carried out by enemies anywhere in the world, and possibly using unconventional weapons. Thus, the idea behind the NATO Response Force is to give the Alliance a new capability to respond quickly to an emergency, wherever that emergency might occur.

To Create or Not to Create a System of Global Partnerships

A discussion of NATO's transformation in response to the perceived needs of risk management beyond its borders would be incomplete without a discussion of the issue of global partnerships. The complexity of that issue makes it impossible to fully analyse it within the space of this section, but I would like to at least highlight some of the dilemmas and challenges associated with global partnerships. The key proponents of this idea – particularly the US and Britain – insist that the formation of global partnerships is essential to efforts to transform NATO into an institution that can manage risks and, when necessary, respond to crises anywhere in the world. As then Secretary of State Condoleeza Rice noted at the Riga Summit: 'I think it is very clear that we are indeed in a global struggle and we don't have the luxury of sitting home and allowing the threat to come to us … We have to fight back on the offensive' (Rice 2006).

That view, however, is far from representing the consensual position of all NATO allies. Indeed, significant disagreements persist among the allies over the idea of a global system of partnership with a series of 'Contact Countries.' Several European allies, including Germany, Belgium, Luxembourg, Greece, and Spain, have serious concerns about creating a formal system of global partnership, fearing that such a development might involve additional commitments on their part and dilute the potency of Article V of the Washington Treaty. By contrast, Central and East European NATO members seem to have signalled their tentative – if not unambiguous – support for the idea of global partnerships. Even clearer support has been granted by the UK in a situation in which, as Clemens has pointed out, 'UK defense officials have grown accustomed to working closely with Pentagon colleagues on out-of-area contingencies. For many politicians as well, notions of the Alliance as a police force fit well with residual sentiment for the Anglo-American special relationships' (Clemens 1997: 185).

In spite of disagreements on this topic, at NATO's 2006 Summit the allies were able to move – at least partly – towards embracing the concept of global partnerships. Thus, at Riga, NATO resolved to: 'Fully develop the political and practical potential of NATO's relations with Contact Countries [and to] increase the operational relevance of relations with non-NATO countries, including interested Contact Countries' (NATO 2006b). The idea emphasized at Riga was that it was important for the allies to enhance NATO's ability to work with those existing and potential contributors to NATO operations and missions that share 'our interests and values' (NATO 2006b). That idea was reaffirmed at the 2008 Bucharest Summit, where the heads of government of NATO member states said:

> The Alliance places a high value on its expanding and varied relationships with other partners across the globe. Our objectives in these relationships include support for operations, security cooperation and enhanced common understanding to advance shared security interests and democratic values ... We particularly welcome the significant contribution by Australia, Japan, New Zealand and Singapore to NATO-led efforts in Afghanistan. (North Atlantic Council 2008)

The particular importance attached to the Contact Countries mentioned in the Bucharest Declaration is indicative of the US-led effort within NATO to strengthen cooperation with stable, relatively rich liberal-democracies that have the potential to act as 'security providers' (rather than security 'consumers') in the Alliance's current missions, for instance by providing not only troops but also material support for those missions. What is involved here is an initiative designed to partly redefine the concept of partnership: immediately following the collapse of the Cold War, as we have noted, NATO used the concept (and practice) of partnership to forge new relations with – and carry out extensive international socialization in – a series of former communist countries. The vast majority of those countries were far from being in a position to make significant contributions to NATO missions. Nevertheless, their inclusion into allied structures and programs was seen by NATO as an important step in the process of stabilizing that region and contributing to the construction of reliable, self-disciplined (liberal-democratic) countries in the former Eastern bloc.

That particular understanding of partnership has certainly not disappeared, as NATO – we noted above – continues to attach significant importance to the socialization of former communist countries. Simultaneously, however, and in part as a result of debates and disagreements regarding inter-allied burden sharing in missions such as the one in Afghanistan, some NATO allies seem increasingly keen to establish more formal partnerships with 'like-minded,' reliable countries such as Australia and New Zealand that can make significant contributions to allied out-of-area operations. This novel approach is different from the previous 'partnership' concept in at least one key area. Though a number of the previous partners were accepted despite their infinitely meagre military potential, the new global partnership aims at attracting militarily strong states to NATO. 'Partnership' arrangements with states such as New Zealand, Japan, or South Korea are not designed to export democracy to the partnership regions, but rather to strengthen cooperation with 'out-of-area' stable democracies in order to enhance the Alliance's ability to manage a plurality of risks and (when necessary) respond to crises anywhere in the world.

If these Contact Countries support NATO missions, commit significant financial resources, and put their soldiers' lives on the line, it seems reasonable to argue that it becomes essential to integrate them beyond simply planning the operations and to incorporate them in the consultation process within NATO itself. For this purpose, a new, permanent forum for 'global partners' should be created. Yet, any moves in this direction would be fraught with difficulties. In spite of the public expression of support for the idea of global partnership issued at the Bucharest Summit, some of the European allies remain uncomfortable with the vision of global partnerships, as they continue to fear that such a system might one day compel the allies to become militarily involved in distant regions in missions that are far removed from the original mandate of NATO.[19] Indeed, it continues to be the case that public NATO affirmations of support for the concept of global partnerships conceal inter-allied tensions on this topic and fail to address a number of significant dilemmas and challenges for the Alliance. Let me briefly highlight just some of those dilemmas and challenges.

To begin, the very concept of global partnerships remains ambiguous, and the implications that such partnerships might have for the role, modes of operation, and reach of the Alliance have yet to be fully understood. For all references to a prominent set of Contact Countries (the 'like-minded' democracies mentioned above), it is still unclear which countries would qualify for inclusion in that club and on the basis of what criteria. For example, are military contributions to NATO's existing operations essential in processes of deciding which states qualify for the status of Contact Countries? Is there – and should there be – a limit to the number of Contact Countries that NATO would be willing to cooperate with? What are and what should be the processes for selecting Contact Countries? Crucially, what are their specific obligations, and what are they entitled to in return for their (potential) support for and participation in NATO's missions?

At present, Contact Countries do not have legal obligations towards NATO and are not embedded in the Alliance's procedures and institutional structures. Hence, their status – and particularly the extent to which such countries could expect protection and support in the case of a crisis – is highly ambiguous. Contact Countries, it could be argued, can only complicate an already complex and unclear set of commitments made by NATO vis-à-vis its numerous partner states (in their various guises). On the one hand, some statements issued by senior NATO officials would seem to suggest that the Alliance is prepared to extend its protective shield to a wide set of partners. In a powerful statement, former NATO Secretary General Solana insisted in 1999 that 'the Alliance has repeatedly made clear that the security of all NATO member-states is inseparably linked to that of the partner countries … Your security is of direct and material concern to the Alliance' (Whitney 1999).

In principle, at least, such a broad commitment could raise the prospect that Contact Countries might conceivably seek to involve NATO in regional disputes or crises, should such crises be seen as a threat to their security. For instance, both Japan and Australia – not to mention South Korea – have repeatedly expressed concern about (what they perceive as) the hostile behaviour of nuclear North Korea (Abe 2007). The prospect of potential NATO involvement in crises in faraway regions is precisely the reason – or at least one of the main reasons – behind the reluctance of countries like Germany, Belgium, and France to support global partnership arrangements.[20] It is thus unlikely that, in the foreseeable future, the Alliance will be able to make significant progress in this area. Furthermore, the topic of global partnerships could further reinforce tensions within the Alliance, potentially making it even more difficult for the allies to agree on a common vision for the future of NATO.

At the same time, the inter-allied differences and disagreements that came to light in the context of the 2008 crisis in Georgia (when the US, UK, and several Central/East European allies were in favour of a strong response to Russian aggression, while countries like Germany and France were more reluctant to antagonize Moscow) demonstrate that even in the case of a clear act of aggression against a partner state the Alliance can find it difficult to speak with one voice. It is reasonable to assume that those actual or potential Contact Countries interested in securing NATO's protection would interpret the Alliance's hesitation over the Georgian crisis as a sign that, at least in the absence of a formal commitment by the Alliance, they cannot be confident of such protection. The next logical step for them would be to insist on the creation of a formal legal framework to govern their relationships with NATO. Indeed, in private communications, NATO officials have already indicated that, in their view, there will be a real effort by proponents of the global partnership concept within the Alliance to create such a framework in the next few years.[21]

Such a development, however, would be far from unproblematic, not least because it could complicate the Alliance's decision-making procedures, especially the rule that the more troops a country is willing to put on the ground, the greater its voice should be in NATO decision-making processes (Asmus 2006). For argument's sake, let us assume that a new legal framework for global partners is created, and that, in a given NATO-led mission, a partner country like Australia is prepared to deploy more troops than some of the allied states. Would that mean that Australia would de facto acquire a greater voice in NATO's decision-making processes than those allies with a more limited military involvement in that operation? If so, it is not difficult to anticipate significant tensions within the Alliance, which could potentially lead some of the European allies to rethink their involvement in NATO.

Linked to this, if a formal partnership structure does emerge, it might soon overshadow the existing partnership forums (e.g., the Euro-Atlantic Partnership Council, which has already been weakened following the accession to the Alliance of many of the Central/East European partners). Such a shift towards preferential treatment vis-à-vis Contact Countries would probably antagonize existing partners, many of which have been working through existing PfP channels since their creation. To mention just one example: according to NATO officials, Sweden – one of the key PfP states – has already expressed opposition to the idea of formalizing global partnerships. It is unclear that NATO could maintain strong PfP arrangements while at the same time pursuing global partnerships; and, should the former falter, the Alliance could weaken some of the instruments that have played important roles in enhancing cooperation and addressing crises in post–Cold War Europe. In light of persisting problems and crises on the 'old continent,' it is doubtful that such a development would be desirable.

These and many more questions related to the idea of global partnerships have yet to be adequately addressed. It is only fair to admit, at this point, that, particularly in a situation in which some of the allies are less than willing to contribute to NATO's programs and operations (e.g., as revealed in the national caveats in Afghanistan), the Alliance will have no option other than to pursue closer cooperation – and possibly more formalized arrangement – with a host of 'out-of-area' partners. At the same time, however, it remains the case that the allies need to reflect more carefully than they seem to have done so far on the potentially problematic implications of global partnerships and, to the extent that they do decide to move forward, to seek to avoid or at least minimize those problems.

Conclusion

I argued in this chapter that in the context of a security environment seen as highly fluid, and marked by the rise of non-conventional enemies, NATO has sought to demonstrate its persisting relevance in the context of Euro-Atlantic relations by evolving into a complex risk management institution that pursues security via a combination of inclusive and exclusionary practices, blurring conventional boundaries between international security and domestic law enforcement, between the public and the private spheres, and operating both within and outside the Euro-Atlantic area. Contrary to a series of pessimistic predictions, NATO has certainly survived the recent changes in the international system. Yet, its evolution has been far from unproblematic. Indeed, some of the recent developments within NATO, and particularly its contemporary 'out-of-area' activities have triggered inter-allied tensions and problems, raising questions about the Alliance's evolving mandate and, more broadly, its future.

In spite of its self-confident statements, and its efforts to adapt to the new security environment, it is not yet clear that NATO, even if it survives, will continue to be seen as a relevant Euro-Atlantic security institution. As noted above, given prevailing ideas – in allied decision-making circles – regarding the changed nature of the European security environment, in order to continue to be perceived as a relevant institution, NATO has to constantly demonstrate that it can , indeed, manage a multitude of risks – including risks posed by non-conventional enemies. On the plus side, one can argue that NATO has taken promising steps in this direction, for instance by developing new capabilities for fighting non-conventional enemies (e.g., the Prague Capabilities Commitment) and launching innovative operations that have a strong civilian component (such as the expansion of its efforts to expand the security community of 'good' governance) or that combine civil and military dimensions (such as policing at a distance and reconstructing polities emerging from conflict in order to keep them from re-becoming breeding grounds for terrorism – most notably in the case of Afghanistan).

From a less optimistic angle, we cannot forget that many of these initiatives and missions have yet to prove successful. The most problematic issue currently faced by NATO is, arguably, the inability of the allies to reach agreement on what – and by whom – should be done in Afghanistan (as reflected in the endless debates regarding the aims and means of the international mission, not to mention the disputes over who should provide more troops and material resources). More broadly, tensions persist among the allies over the question of how far the Alliance should go in pursuit of its risk management role. As noted above, while some allies seem prepared to turn NATO into a global risk management institution, others are much more reluctant to support such a broadening of the Alliance's mandate.

It is only fair to admit that many of those problems, far from being confined to NATO, reflect difficulties associated with some of the new security practices conducted by Euro-Atlantic actors, often in the name of combating international terrorism. Such practices challenge traditional boundaries between friend/enemy, inside/outside, war/peace, and, in many cases, seek to redefine norms governing the behaviour of liberal democratic actors vis-à-vis particular types of dangerous *others*. In the case of NATO, some of those questions have been raised, directly or indirectly, in a situation in which the allies have tried to redefine relations with partners and to acquire powers and competences going far beyond the Alliance's original mandate. Whether or not the allies will be able to address such complex – and as yet unanswered – questions in the foreseeable future remains to be seen.

NOTES

This chapter does not address developments that occurred in 2010, when the book was already in production.

1 Bourdieu (1990). For helpful analyses of Bourdieu's work see also Haugaard (1997) and Michael C. Williams (2007).
2 See, on this topic, Pouliot (2003: 25–51). However, Pouliot restricts the definition of threats to those arising from rivalries among states. In my view, the field of security now needs to be defined in a broader sense, to encompass a broad set of non-state threats and enemies. On the field of security see also Bigo (1996).
3 For a more detailed analysis, see Alexandra Gheciu (2005).

4 On the widespread perception that the European security environment was becoming more benign in the post-1989 world, see the Introduction to this volume.

5 For different visions of desirable security scenarios that were being articulated at that time, and their shared focus on the need to strengthen political and cooperative solutions, rather than military/confrontational ones, see, for example, David Mutimer (1995) and Ingo Peters (1996). For the US perspective, see also James Baker (1995: 232). On the pro-CSCE scenario, particularly as seen from the French perspective, see Mitterrand's biography by Alain Genestar (1992). For a view of a CSCE-centred security system articulated on the other side of the former divide, see Gorbachev (1996).

6 See the Introduction to this volume.

7 For a broader discussion on this point, see the Introduction to this volume. As Mérand, Irondelle, and Foucault note, while no paradigmatic consensus has emerged after 1989, it is clear that the positivist paradigm that enjoyed hegemonic status during the Cold War has been the target of unprecedented attacks, as the answers provided by scholars who focus on European security are far more diverse than they were prior to 1989.

8 For particularly interesting analyses see Beck (1999) and Douglas and Wildavsky (1982). See also Coker (2002) and Rasmussen (2002) and Michael J. Williams (2005, 2009). In criminology, particularly influential has been Ericson and Haggerty (1997).

9 In the words of a senior NATO official, 'Many of us believe that by integrating the Balkans and former Soviet republics into allied structures, we are helping to stabilize Europe and minimizing many security risks. Just imagine the kinds of problems that a country like Albania, with a majority Muslim population, and currently plagued with corruption and organized crime could generate in Europe if it were to become a pariah state. It's not hard to see that this could be an ideal safe haven for some extremist Islamist groups. We believe that, by encouraging liberal-democratic reforms and helping Albania to become a member of Western institutions, we can help avoid such a scenario.' Interview with senior NATO official, Brussels, May 2005.

10 More specifically Bahrain, Kuwait, Oman, Qatar, Saudi Arabia, and the United Arab Emirates.

11 See, for instance, the speech by NATO Secretary General Jaap de Hoop Scheffer (2006a). This view was reiterated in interviews by the author with NATO officials in Brussels and NATO, 2006–7.

12 Interviews with two NATO officials, London, 15 January 2007. For an analysis of the kinds of non-military as well as military reforms that NATO

expects of candidate states, as well as some of the steps the Alliance has taken to monitor and guide those reforms, see also the NATO Parliamentary Assembly Report (2004).

13 See, for instance, NATO Parliamentary Assembly's Resolution 319 on Terrorism Financing (2002) and Report on Financing Aspects of the Fight against Terrorism (2004).

14 Interviews with NATO officials, fall–winter 2006–7, Brussels, London, and Oxford.

15 See for example 'NATO Policy on Combating Trafficking in Human Beings' (2004b).

16 See International Crisis Group (2004) and (2006). See also Mustafa and Xharra (2003).

17 After the end of the NATO/Yugoslavia war in June 1999, the former Kosovo Liberation Army was transformed into the Kosovo Protection Corps (KPC), a civilian agency charged with providing emergency response and reconstruction services. The KPC's mission is to protect the Kosovo population against natural or man-made disasters and to assist in the rebuilding of the province.

18 See for example Bennett (2001).

19 Interview with NATO official, Brussels, 27 April 2008.

20 Interview with NATO official, Brussels, 20 April 2008.

21 Interview with NATO official, Brussels, 27 April 2008.

REFERENCES

Abe, Shinzo. 2007. 'Japan and NATO: Toward Further Collaboration.' Statement to the North Atlantic Council, Brussels, 12 January.

Adam, Barbara, Ulrich Beck, and Joost Van Loon, eds. 2000. *The Risk Society and Beyond: Critical Issues for Social Theory*. London: Sage.

Adler, Emanuel. 1997. 'Imagined (Security) Communities.' *Millennium: Journal of International Studies* 26, no. 2: 249–77.

– 1998. 'Seeds of Peaceful Change: The OSCE's Security Community-Building Model.' In *Security Communities*, ed. Emanuel Adler and Michael Barnett, 119–60. Cambridge: Cambridge University Press.

– 2005. 'Communities of Practice in International Relations.' In *Communitarian International Relations: The Epistemic Foundations of International Relations*, ed. Emanuel Adler, 3–28. London: Routledge.

Aradau, Claudia, and Rens Van Munster. 2007. 'Governing Terrorism through Risk: Taking Precautions, (Un)Knowing the Future.' *European Journal of International Relations* 13, no. 1: 89–115.

Asmus, Ronald. 2006. *NATO and the Global Partners: Views from the Outside*. Riga Papers, *The German Marshall Fund of the United States*, 27–9 November.

Baker, James. 1995. *The Politics of Diplomacy*. New York: Putnam's Sons.

Beck, Ulrich. 1992. *Risk Society: Towards a New Modernity*. London: Sage.

– 1996. 'World Risk Society as Cosmopolitan Society? Ecological Questions in a Framework of Manufactured Uncertainties.' *Theory, Culture and Society* 13, no. 4: 1–32.

– 1999. *World Risk Society*. Cambridge: Polity Press.

– 2002. 'The Terrorist Threat: World Risk Society Revisited.' *Theory, Culture and Society* 19, no. 4: 39–55.

– 2004. 'The Silence of Words: On Terror and War.' *Security Dialogue* 34: 255–67.

Bennett, Christopher. 2001. 'Aiding America.' *NATO Review* 4 (Winter). http://www.nato.int/docu/review/2001/0104-01.htm.

– 2003. 'Combating Terrorism.' *NATO Review* 1 (Spring). http://www.nato.int/docu/review/2003/issue1/english/art2pr.html.

Bigo, Didier. 1996. *Polices en réseaux: L'expérience européenne*. Paris: Presses de Sciences Po.

Bourdieu, Pierre. 1977. *Outline of a Theory of Practice*. Cambridge: Cambridge University Press.

– 1990. *The Logic of Practice*. Stanford, CA: Stanford University Press.

– 2002. 'Social Space and Symbolic Power.' In *Power: A Reader*, ed. Mark Haugaard, 225–44. Manchester: Manchester University Press.

Bourdieu, Pierre, and Loïc Wacquant. 1992. 'The Purpose of Reflexive Sociology (The Chicago Workshop).' In *An Invitation to Reflexive Sociology*, ed. Pierre Bourdieu and Loïc J.D. Wacquant, 61–216. Chicago: University of Chicago Press.

Buzan, Barry, Ole Waever, and Jaap de Wilde. 1998. *Security: A New Framework for Analysis*. London: Rienner.

Clemens, C., ed. 1997. *NATO and the Quest for Post-Cold War Security*. London: Macmillan.

Coker, Christopher. 2002. *Globalization and Insecurity in the Twenty-First Century: NATO and the Management of Risk*. Adelphi Paper no. 345. London: The International Institute for Strategic Studies, June.

Donnelly, Chris. 2003a. 'Special Interview with Chris Donnelly.' Brussels, 5 June. www.nato.int/docu/speech/2003/s030605b.htm.

– 2003b. 'Security in the 21st Century: New Challenges and New Responses.' Paper published in NATO's online library, June. http://www.nato.int/docu/speech/2003/s030605a.htm.

Douglas, Mary, and Aaron Wildavsky. 1982. *Risk and Culture: An Essay on the Selection of Technical and Environmental Dangers*. Berkeley: University of California Press.

Epstein, Rachel. 2008. *In Pursuit of Liberalism*. Baltimore, MD: Johns Hopkins University Press.

Ericson, Richard, and Kevin Haggerty. 1997. *Policing the Risk Society*. Toronto: University of Toronto Press.

Flynn, Gregory, and Henry Farrell. 1999. 'Piecing Together the Democratic Peace: The CSCE, Norms and the "Construction" of Security in Post-Cold War Europe.' *International Organizations* 53, no. 3: 505–35.

François, Isabelle. 2000. 'Partnership: One of NATO's Fundamental Security Tasks.' *NATO Review* 48, no. 1. http://www.nato.int/docu/review.htm.

Gartner, Heinz, and Ian Cuthbertson, eds. 2005. *European Security and Transatlantic Relations after 9/11 and the Iraq War*. London: Palgrave.

Genestar, Alain. 1992. *Les Péchés du Prince*. Paris: Bernard Grasset.

Gheciu, Alexandra. 2005. *NATO in the 'New Europe': The Politics of International Socialization after the Cold War*. Stanford, CA: Stanford University Press.

– 2008. *Securing Civilization?* Oxford: Oxford University Press.

Gorbachev, Mikhail. 1996. *Memoirs*. London and Toronto: Doubleday.

Haugaard, Mark. 1997. *The Constitution of Power*. Manchester: Manchester University Press.

Huysmans, Jef. 1998. 'Security! What Do You Mean? From Concept to Thick Signifier.' *European Journal of International Relations* 4, no. 2: 226–55.

– 2004. 'A Foucaultian View on Spill-Over: Freedom and Security in the EU.' *Journal of International Relations and Development* 7, no. 3: 294–318.

International Crisis Group. 2004. 'Collapse in Kosovo.' ICG Report, 22 April. http://www.crisisgroup.org/home/index.cfm.

– 2006. 'An Army for Kosovo?' Europe Report no. 174, 28 July. http://www.crisisgroup.org/home/index.cfm.

Johnston, Les. 2000. *The Rebirth of Private Policing*. London: Routledge.

Kant, Immanuel. 1970. 'Perpetual Peace.' In *Kant Political Writings*, ed. H. Reiss, 116–24. Cambridge: Cambridge University Press.

Lindley-French, Julian. 2007. *The North Atlantic Treaty Organization: The Enduring Alliance*. London and New York: Routledge.

Mutimer, David. 1995. 'Chaos and Constitution in the European Security Order: A Study in International Change.' PhD diss. York University, Toronto.

Mustafa, Artan, and Jeta Xharra. 2003. 'Kosovo Officers under Investigation.' *Balkan Crisis Report*. London: Institute for War and Peace Reporting, 11 December.

NATO Parliamentary Assembly. 2002. 'Resolution 319 on Terrorism Financing.' Brussels. http://www.nato-pa.int/default.asp?CAT2=0&CAT1=0&CAT0=576&SHORTCUT=282.

– 2004. 'NATO Parliamentary Assembly Report: Financing Aspects of the Fight against Terrorism.' EAPC/PFP Conference, Brussels, 14–15 October.

North Atlantic Council. 2001. 'Statement by the North Atlantic Council.' NATO Press Release PR/CP(2001)122, 11 September. http://www.nato.int/docu/pr/2001/p01-122e.htm.

– 2003. 'Final Communiqué, Ministerial Meeting of the North Atlantic Council Held in Madrid on 3 June 2003.' http://www.nato.int/docu/pr/2003/p03-059e.htm.

– 2008. 'Bucharest Summit Declaration,' issued by the Heads of State and Government participating in the meeting of the North Atlantic Council in Bucharest on 3 April 2008. PR/CP(2008)049. http://www.nato.int/cps/en/natolive/official_texts_8443.htm.

North Atlantic Treaty Organization [NATO]. 1991. 'The Alliance's Strategic Concept Agreed by the Heads of State and Government Participating in the Meeting of the North Atlantic Council.' Rome, 8 November. http://www.nato.int/cps/en/natolive/official_texts_27433.htm.

– 1995. 'The Study on NATO Enlargement.' Brussels: NATO Press Office.

– 2002a. 'Informal NATO Defence Ministers Meeting, Warsaw.' 24–5 September. http://www.nato.int/docu/comm/2002/0209-wrsw.htm.

– 2002b. 'Prague Summit Declaration.' Press Release 127, 21 November 2002. http://www.nato.int/docu/pr/2002/p02-127e.htm.

– 2002c. 'Partnership Action Plan Against Terrorism.' Prague, 22 November. http://www.nato.int/docu/basictxt/b021122e.htm.

– 2002d. 'NATO Military Concept for Defence against Terrorism.' Endorsed by the NATO Heads of State and Government at the Prague Summit, November 2002. http://www.nato.int/ims/docu/terrorism.htm.

– 2003a. 'NATO-EU Cooperation Taken to a New Level.' NATO Update. Brussels, 17 March. http://www.nato.int/docu/update/2003/03-march/eo317a.htm.

– 2003b. 'Final Communiqué, Ministerial Meeting of the North Atlantic Council Held in Madrid.' 3 June. http://www.nato.int/docu/pr/2003/p03-059e.htm.

– 2004a. 'Istanbul Summit Communiqué.' Press Release (2004)096, Istanbul, 28 June. www.nato.int/docu/pr/2004/p04-096e.htm.

– 2004b. 'NATO Policy on Combating Trafficking in Human Beings.' NATO Policy Document, 29 June. www.nato.int/docu/comm/2004/06-istanbul/docu-traffic.htm.

– 2006a. 'New Chapter for NATO in Afghanistan.' NATO Update. Brussels, 4 May. http://www.nato.int/docu/update/2006/05-may/e0504a.htm.

– 2006b. 'Comprehensive Political Guidance.' Endorsed by NATO Heads of State and Government on 29 November 2006. http://www.nato.int/issues/com_political_guidance/index.html.

– 2007. 'The Three Adriatic Aspirants: Capabilities and Preparations.' NATO
Parliamentary Assembly Report, prepared by the Sub-Committee on Future
Security and Defence Capabilities, Brussels. Report 165 DSCFC 07 E rev 1.
http://www.nato-pa.int/default.asp?SHORTCUT=1167.

Organization for Security and Cooperation in Europe. 2001. *Bucharest Plan of
Action for Combating Terrorism.* MC(9)DEC/1, Bucharest, 4 December, 2001.
http://www.osce.org/documents/cio/2001/12/670_en.pdf.

Peters, Ingo, ed. 1996. *New Security Challenges: The Adaptation of International
Institutions: Reforming the UN, NATO, EU and CSCE since 1989.* New York:
St Martin's Press.

Pouliot, Vincent. 2003. 'La Russie et la communauté atlantique: Vers une
culture commune de sécurité?' *Études Internationales* 34, no. 1: 25–51.

– 2006. 'The Alive and Well Transatlantic Security Community: A Theoretical
Reply to Michael Cox.' *European Journal of International Relations* 12, no. 1:
119–27.

Rasmussen, Mikkel Vedby. 2002. 'A Parallel Globalization of Terror: 9-11, Security and Globalization.' *Cooperation and Conflict* 37, no. 3: 323–49.

– 2004. 'It Sounds Like a Riddle: Security Studies, the War on Terror, and
Risk.' *Millennium* 33, no. 4: 381–95.

Rice, Condoleeza. 2006. 'Interview with Eberhard Piltz.' *ZDF,* Riga. http://
www.state.gov/secretary/rm/2006/77105htm.

Robertson, George. 2002a. 'Defence and Security in an Uncertain World.'
Keynote Speech at Forum Europe, Brussels, 17 May. http://www.nato.int/
docu/speech/2002/s020517a.htm.

– 2002b. 'Opening Statement by Lord Robertson at the NATO Defence Ministers Meeting, Warsaw, 24–5 September 2002.' http://www.nato.int/docu/
speech/2002/s020924a.htm.

– 2002c. 'Speech to the NATO Parliamentary Assembly: Towards the Prague
Summit.' 15 November. http://www.nato.int/docu/speech/2002.

– 2003. 'Transforming NATO.' *NATO Review* (Spring): 3.

Rupp, Richard. 2006. *NATO after 9/11: An Alliance in Continuing Decline.* London and New York: Palgrave.

Scheffer, Jaap de Hoop. 2006a. 'Speech by NATO Secretary General Jaap De
Hoop Scheffer at the Albanian Parliament, Tirana, 6 July.' http://www.
nato.int/docu/speech/2006/s060706a.htm.

– 2006b. 'Statement by Secretary General on Situation in Belarus.' NATO Update, 19 July. http://www.nato.int/docu/update/2006/07-july/index-e.htm.

– 2006c. 'Monthly Briefing by NATO Secretary General, July.' http://www
.nato.int/docu/speech/2006/s060624a.htm.

Smith, Jeffrey, and Glenn Kessler. 2005. 'US Opposed Calls at NATO for Probe
into Uzbek Killings.' *Washington Post,* 14 June.

Thompson, John. 1991. 'Editor's Introduction' to Pierre Bourdieu, *Language and Symbolic Power*. Cambridge, MA: Harvard University Press.

Valverde, Mariana, and Michael Mopas. 2004. 'Insecurity and the Dream of Targeted Governance.' In *Global Governmentality. Governing International Spaces*, eds. Wendy Larner and William Walters, 233–50. London: Routledge.

Waever, Ole. 'Insecurity, Security and Asecurity in the West European Non-War Community.' In *Security Communities*, eds. Emanuel Adler and Michael Barnett, 69–118. Cambridge: Cambridge University Press, 1998.

Walker, R.B.J. 1993. *Inside/Outside: International Relations as Political Theory*. Cambridge: Cambridge University Press.

– 2006. 'Lines of Insecurity: International, Imperial, Exceptional.' *Security Dialogue* 37, no. 1: 65–82.

Waltz, Kenneth. 1993. 'The Emerging Structure of International Politics.' *International Security*, 18, no. 2 (Fall): 75–6.

Weaver, Robert. 2000. 'Continuing to Build Security through Partnership.' *Nato Review* 52, no. 1. http://www.nato.int/docu/review.htm.

Whitney, C. 1999. 'Conflict in the Balkans: The Alliance.' *New York Times*, 25 March.

Williams, Michael C. 2001. 'The Discipline of the Democratic Peace: Kant, Liberalism and the Social Construction of Security Communities.' *European Journal of International Relations* 7, no. 4: 525-53.

– 2007. *Culture and Security*. London: Routledge.

Williams, Michael C., and Iver Neumann. 2000. 'From Alliance to Security Community: NATO, Russia and the Power of Identity.' *Millennium: Journal of International Studies* 29, no. 2: 357–87.

Williams, Michael J. 2004. *Risky Business: The European Union and International Security in the 21st Century*. Paper presented at the 2004 Standing Group on International Relations Conference, the Hague, September 2004.

– 2005. 'The Politics of Risk: The US, Europe and Proactive Security for the Twenty-First Century.' Paper presented at the Annual Meeting of the International Studies Association, Hilton Hawaiian Village, Honolulu, Hawaii. March.

– 2009. *NATO, Security and Risk-Management: From Kosovo to Kandahar*. London: Routledge.

Wörner, Manfred. 1990. 'Opening Statement to the NATO Summit Meeting.' London, 5 July. http://www.nato.int/docu/speech/1990/s900705a_e.htm.

Yost, David. 1998. *NATO Transformed: The Alliance's New Roles in International Security*. Washington: United States Institute for Peace Press.

3 Understanding the Islamist Terrorist Threat to Europe

BASTIAN GIEGERICH AND RAFFAELLO PANTUCCI

From the attacks on London and Madrid, to the arrest of terrorist cells, to groups of supporters pouring funds and fighters into foreign organizations, Europe appears to have become a central battlefield of global jihad. Nonetheless, the European public continues to display a puzzling sense of indifference or, rather, a fairly low perception of a threat that increasingly comes from within their societies and seems bent on destroying it. As has been argued in a volume on European counterterrorism policies, 'Europeans are divided as to whether they consider their own cities, civilians and assets targets for future attacks' (von Hippel 2005: 10).

Of course, the reason for this indifference might be the fact that European societies have had to grapple with the phenomenon of terrorism for decades.[1] Groups like the Rote Armee Fraktion or the Brigate Rosse have been a problem, as have groups seeking regional independence and deploying political violence in Europe, like ETA in Spain, terrorists in Northern Ireland or Corsica, or the PKK in Turkey, most of whom remain active to this day. The terrorist threat that Europe is accustomed to has not disappeared. However, while these groups still account for the majority of terrorist incidents across Europe, they are no longer the main threat, nor are they apparently the focus of counterterrorism security services across Europe (Europol 2007, 2008). While many definitions of terrorist groups exist, this article will follow Wilkinson's typology of factional terrorists (Wilkinson 2005: 11): extreme nationalists (for example ETA and the PKK); ideological terrorists (left- or right-wing groups); exile group terrorists; issue group terrorists (for example animal rights or abortion); and, finally, religious extremist groups.

This chapter focuses on the latter group and more specifically on the Islamist terrorist groups driven by a jihadi-Salafist ideology that currently make up the threat that is often-times broadly captured under the banner name of al Qaeda. This threat is different from the previous incarnations of terrorist threats Europe has faced. It does not come from individuals who pursue a defined political aim comprehensible to the population around them, but instead from a group who employ tactics like suicide bombings to achieve the highest possible damage to lives and property in the pursuit of a, some will say, perverted interpretation of religion. In Europe, these networks are home-grown in the sense that they are self-forming and are dominantly manned by individuals who have been living in Europe for a long time and often have citizenship or legal resident status in an EU member state.[2]

While the extent and importance of their international links to terrorist networks beyond Europe is open to debate, their aim is to cause mass casualties, and major economic damage. They claim to adhere to the belief of imposing a sharia-inspired caliphate upon European populations and punish them for their ongoing support of governments they perceive to be conducting crusades against their Muslim brethren. Their modus operandi is inspired (and sometimes directed) by al Qaeda (AQ) and includes the use of coordinated multiple attacks, including suicide attacks, aimed at soft and symbolic targets where many civilians are present. These groups do not constitute a random phenomenon, but rather are part of an ideology which seems to have enveloped portions of Europe's young Muslim communities like a 'social wave,' reminiscent of previous such social 'waves' except that this has encouraged some of them to take the drastic step of self-immolation while attempting to murder as many of their fellow European citizens as possible (Roy 2008: 1). And it is this element that lies at the heart of European government's fears – presenting as it does a paradigm shift in the threat faced. Previous terrorists may have been willing to die for their cause, but they did not appear to be as eager to actively embrace death while inflicting misery on others.

The terrorist threat to Europe is driven by new methods, new motivations, and new actors. While the risk posed by this type of terrorism does not currently amount to an existential threat to European societies and governments, it is nonetheless severe. The transformation, with regards to this particular issue, has to be understood as adding layers of complexity to the terrorist threat. Whereas individuals and symbols representing 'the state' were traditionally attacked, now societies as such are targets as well. While most terrorism was previously confined to certain national boundaries, now a transnational threat is the main concern. And whereas motivations were either ethno-separatist or ideological, they now seem to be much more individualized. Given that the traditional terrorist threat to Europe has not gone away, an element of continuity is present. However, the transnational Islamist terrorist threat that has emerged over the last decade is fundamentally different from what went on before and hence justifies the notion of a new paradigm. To capture this development it seems necessary to apply a sociological approach in order to analyse social, cultural, and religious factors that may help to understand what drives and sustains this new form of terrorism and how it might evolve.

Takfiri-Salafi Ideology

Before we proceed, it is useful to first define the underlying religious ideology that appears to drive the Islamist threat facing Europe.[3] Salafism is a revivalist interpretation of Islam which demands a more literal reading of the Quran in an attempt to try to marry modern life with medieval Islamist beliefs. Its retrospective-looking revivalism is similar to its Saudi-driven counterpart, Wahhabbism, though the Saudi version is more explicit in seeking a 'pure' society that adheres to the practices of seventh-century Arabia and was born in the dunes of the Nejd desert among the loyal fighters of ibn-Wahhab who were seeking to restore their rigid form of Islam to the Arabian peninsula.

Salafism, originally Egyptian in origin, is instead founded upon the belief that the purest form of Islam existed in the Prophet's time and seeks therefore to return it to this time. Under King Faisal of Saudi Arabia, this belief was blended with the dominant Wahhabbi strain in the kingdom as he went about dominating the territory now known as Saudi Arabia, creating the foundations of the ideology that exists today. In parallel to this, and pertinent to the threat faced in Europe, is the Deobandi school of Islam, formed initially as a counter to British rule in South Asia during the late 1800s. Similar to Wahhabism and Salafism (and sharing many similar ideological parents), this ideology proliferated throughout the Indian sub-continent and remains to this day influential among the global South Asian community. (It must also be noted that the Ahl-e-Hadith school, while less influential than Deobandism, has a substantial impact upon extremist South Asian Islam and equally espouses a purist form of Islam.)

The important details to note are that both the Wahhabi and Deobandi schools were initially born in conflict, while the Salafi school was seeking to merge modern life with a medievalist reading of Islam. The merger and cross-pollination of much of this thought has resulted in the ideological cornerstone of most European extremist Islamist groups: the desire to impose a world-wide caliphate under sharia law. As a report by the New York Police Department has pointed out, this version of Islam has spread widely in the West's Muslim diasporas and is in fact what many young Muslims are exposed to (NYPD 2007: 17). It is also important to pause for a moment to highlight that Deobandism and Salafism are practised by many Muslims in Europe, in many cases without resulting in any terrorism or extremist behaviour. For British Pakistani Muslims, for example, Deobandism is increasingly the prevailing school, a vestige of their cultural heritage, and many credit Salafi centres of worship as being behind key counter-radicalization initiatives. It is for this reason that we have to add the term 'takfiri' (the practice of invoking apostasy in others) before the term Salafi, as this more cleanly separates the sub-group of violent extremists from the benign majority.

Bassam Tibi (2007) has suggested that jihadists in fact form a social movement based on a transnational religion that is becoming increasingly politicized. This movement rejects the secular and democratic order of Europe and tries to raise cultural differences 'to the level of military conflict, but also [tries to revive] traditional worldviews in a way that widens the sense of a gap between civilisations' (Tibi 2007: 48). As another observer adds, Salafism 'has become a powerful magnet for generations of young Muslims,' offering a revivalist and globalist interpretation of religion that is better attuned to their needs than the more traditional versions espoused by their parents. Problematically, however, '[it] preaches an Islam that calls for cultural rupture with Europe' (Stemmann 2006: 10). For some, Salafist ideology has permutated into a call for revolt against the West (Tibi 2007) and at the same time has proved to be a powerful tool to strip cultural content from Islam in its search for a pure religion. However, the 'quest for authenticity' in original Salafism has been replaced by a 'de-culturation' of Islam and a resulting 'non-historical, abstract, and imagined model of Islam' (Roy 2005: 7).

For violent Takfiri-Salafists, the community of Muslims has lacked proper leadership since its earliest days. Hence they make historical Islam into the reference point for a current desirable societal order. Islamist militants link their use of violence to the Prophet's rebellion against oligarchic rulers of the time and by trying to cast themselves in the light of pious and virtuous figures of the past. They furthermore point to military exploits in the past, victories of Muslim armies for example, to suggest that Muslims will prevail even if the odds are against them. Finally, militant Islamists weave a narrative that describes their use of violence as a defensive measure necessary to counter an alleged oppression and persecution of Muslims.[4]

In their reading, Islam does not make a distinction between public and private lives or between political and religious institutions. Religion regulates all walks of life, and the separation of state and church is unknown. The interests of the community of Muslims, the *umma*, are more important than those of the individual. There is thus a conceptual conflict between God's rule and the democratic political system: sharia law does not permit the separation of these spheres. Orthodox Muslims who follow Salafist ideology believe that sharia is the only valid notion of order and can thus not be governed by democracy (where man makes laws). Islamism is thus more than a religion in that it, in particular in its proper form, merges Islam, the religion, with the reinvention of society based on fundamentalism and is, in extremists' minds, brought about by violence if necessary.

While this chapter recognizes the undeniable fact that the jihadi-Salafist (or takfiri-jihadist) interpretation of Islam is clearly at the core of the Islamist threat that Europe faces, the reality is that it is increasingly hard to point to any sort of rigorous religious awareness or doctrine among Islamist plotters. Some display a certain religious knowledge, and others a particular zeal for the beliefs they claim to be fighting for, but at the same time, one of the most striking facts is the relative religious illiteracy of most individuals (MI5 2008). Furthermore, unlike many other political prisoners, AQ or affiliate members do not use their court appearances to made grand political gestures or statements, but rather 'keep silent or deny any involvement during their trial' (Roy 2008: 13), which is surprising given the proselytism inherent in their ideology and the potential for the court-room to provide a forum for broadcasting their views to the world. Furthermore, the seeming rise of 'lone wolf' terrorism – in which autodidact individuals with no apparent connections to networks, but nonetheless apparently identifying with what they perceive to be the al Qaeda ideology and seeking to demonstrate their adherence through performing a terrorist act – casts further doubt over the religious motivation of such individuals.

What is clear, however, is that the jihadi-Salafist ideology plays some sort of a role in the radicalization of Muslim communities in Europe, if for no other reason than it seems to be the one constant among them all and is clearly the ideology that is best associated with the key radicalizing individuals. Hence, one of the main sections of the chapter will address the process of radicalization before we look at the issues of leadership and international links of European home-grown terrorists. Radicalization is not just a major part of the puzzle for anyone who tries to understand the terrorist threat to Europe; it is also a key counter-terrorism concern, as halting radicalization would presumably help to prevent terrorist attacks. As the NYPD argues, a focus on radicalization is vital: 'The tools for conducting serious terrorist attacks are becoming easier to acquire. Therefore intention becomes an increasingly important factor in the formation of terrorist cells' (NYPD 2007: 2). Understanding intentions implies understanding how and why individuals radicalize. To provide the necessary context, the next section will offer a brief threat assessment.

Jihadi-Salafist Terrorism in Europe: A Threat Assessment

While estimates vary and hard figures are difficult to come by, it is safe to assume that approximately 16 million Muslims live in EU member states, making up 3.3 per cent of the total population (Armitage 2007: 3). Within this broader community is a smaller group consisting of Jihadi terrorists, the networks that support them, and the groups that sympathize with them. What is crucial to recognize is that the broader European Muslim communities are an embedded and increasingly integral part of European society. They represent a highly diverse mix in terms of their origin, though they tend to be concentrated in the Western European states, with relatively small populations literally and proportionally present in Central and Eastern European states (the exception of course being Albania, Bosnia, and Macedonia, which are predominantly Muslim states but currently remain outside the European Union, though within the European space). Within the nations where they are based, there tends to be a further concentration. For example, Muslims in France or Spain are mostly of North African extraction, whereas in Germany they are mostly of Turkish origin. In the UK the majority is either Pakistani or Bangladeshi, while the community in the Netherlands is dominated by Moroccan and Turkish immigrants and the Italian community displays a remarkable diversity drawn from the Balkans and from across Africa.

The communities originated in a combination of previous colonial connections and post–Second World War worker populations who were brought to Europe to provide a workforce to replace the decimated European populations (with some further groups the result of specific migrations reflecting events in home countries – for example, the construction of the Mangala Dam in Pakistan in the 1960s, or Idi Amin's expulsion of South Asian tradesmen from Uganda in the 1970s, both of which led to substantial population movements to the UK). The exceptions to this trend are Spain and Italy, where, despite long-standing connections to Muslim Africa, the majority of the Muslim immigration is relatively recent. With the historical migrations, entire communities were constructed to house these workforces on the peripheries of major cities, or they were planted in areas of the nation where the workers were then needed.

Naturally, over time, the mostly male population sought to bring over wives, children, and other family members, leading to substantial and isolated communities emerging on the peripheries of states and cities without much effort to integrate them into the broader communities – both a reflection of their natural tendencies and a sense of inhospitality from the European nations. At the same time, these populations retained strong ties with their home communities, bringing wives or husbands for children born in Europe, as well as seeking religious leadership from communities back home and inviting their Imams, who had little understanding of the nations they were moving to. In the UK, for example, it was discovered that only 8 per cent of Imams preaching in the nation were born in the UK (BBC 2007).

In addition to this predominantly economically driven migration, a number of political refugees sought either overt or covert refuge in Europe, driven from the Muslim world either as a result of their membership of the Muslim Brotherhood (or other Islamist political organizations who clashed with their secular governments), or because of their unwelcome reception in their home states – the so-called Arab Afghan fighters who fought alongside Osama bin Laden and were drawn from across the Muslim world met with a frosty reception when they tried to return to their home states after jihad in Afghanistan. Many individuals from both of these groups chose to relocate to Europe, where liberal political attitudes, a long history of welcoming political dissidents from around the globe, and a growing Muslim population among which

Table 3.1
European Union member states by Muslim populations

Largest Muslim population (%)	Largest Muslim population (millions)
Cyprus (17.8)	France (5)
Bulgaria (12)	Germany (3.5)
France (8.3)	UK (1.6)
Netherlands (6.3)	Italy (1)
Denmark (5.1)	Netherlands (1)
	Spain (1)

Source: Armitage (2007: 3).

they could hide provided a highly attractive environment. Many of these individuals remained highly active in Islamist and extremist politics after their shifts, however, and provided the initial tangible connection between jihadist terrorism and Europe. Prominent examples include Omar Bakri Mohammed, Abu Hamza al-Masri, and Abu Qatada – all of whom relocated to the United Kingdom and formed the nub of what later became known as 'Londonistan.' Similar patterns can be found around less prominent individuals in other European countries. Table 3.1 shows the European states with significant Muslim populations.

While it is necessary to emphasize once again that not all Muslims in Europe are by any means attracted to extremism or terrorism, there is an inevitable link between immigration and jihadism that makes the latter a dangerous threat to Europe in terms of both actual terrorism and in the sense of inflaming social cohesion in one way or another (Sendagorta 2005: 66). Examples of this include the infamous spring 2001 riots in northern England, where tensions between impoverished South Asian and white communities led to some of the most violent rioting the UK had seen in years, further reflecting tensions that had been seen previously in the late 1980s with the Rushdie affair.[5] Similar problems can be seen in the autumn 2005 rioting in which young, disenfranchised North African-French communities living both literally and figuratively on the periphery of France's major cities went on a rampage across the country. Most recently, the rioting and violent protests across Europe in 2006 in the wake of the publication of the Danish cartoons of the Prophet showed a clear motivational link to Islam, as was the case in the Rushdie affair. The riots in France and the UK do not display such direct connections, except that they occurred in predominantly Muslim areas which have also proved recruiting grounds for jihadist causes. The purpose of highlighting them, however, is to point to the considerable societal tensions for Muslim communities in Europe, even though such tensions are not in themselves necessarily linked to terrorism.

What is new is that this anger can also produce a desire among some individuals to use violent jihad as their method of expression. In numerical terms, Bakker's study (2006: 17–29) counted 31 jihadi terrorist incidents in Europe between September 2001 and October 2006 (most of them foiled or failed) involving no less than 28 networks – a figure which is higher today. In the UK, some 200 groups have been identified and some 2,000 individuals are considered to be involved in some 30 identified plots (IISS 2007: 8), though according to the head of Britain's MI5, the actual number could be twice as high. The Dutch internal intelligence service estimated in 2003 that 200 extremists liable to commit violence plus another 1,200 supporters were in the country (AIVD 2003). In Germany, the security services have listed 28 Islamist organizations with 30,000 fee-paying members. Some 2,000 are assessed as tolerating violence with another 400–600 individuals judged to be ready to commit violence (ICG 2007: 14–16). Germany's domestic intelligence agency pointed to an increasing number of websites that were calling for an attack on German soil, some of them in German and others in Arabic with German subtitles. Another study in 2007, entitled 'Muslims in Germany' and conducted by researchers at the University of Hamburg but supported and published by the German Ministry of the Interior, suggested that 6 per cent of the approximately 3.5 million Muslims living in Germany showed acceptance of 'massive forms of political/religious motivated violence.' Earlier estimates had put this number at 1 per cent.

The actual threat posed by home-grown jihadi terrorism in Europe is more complex than the highly visible successful or foiled attacks. Kilcullen (2007: 649–50) has suggested a useful classification of five clearly discernible phenomena, or aspects, to the threat. First are terrorist cells, including those with external, international linkages to AQ or AQ-inspired groups. Both the Madrid and London attacks were carried out by individuals who were recruited, or self-recruited, in the country where they carried out the attacks and then sought (and in the case of the London group found) external connections to the global jihad. They were able to raise the relatively meagre funds required to finance their operations, as highlighted in Table 3.2, through petty crime. Thus, their method of operation is inherently different from the attacks of 11 September 2001, in which a group was selected from abroad and sent

Table 3.2
Comparison of costs of 3/11 (Madrid) and 7/7 (London) terrorist attacks

	Madrid	London
Total estimated cost of operation	Less than €10,000 (although police found €25,000 in apartment)	Less than £8,000, sometimes estimated to be as low as £1,000
Financing	drug trafficking	self-financed
Explosives per bomb	ca 10 kg	ca 10 kg
Number of bombs	14	4
Victims	191 killed	56 killed (including the four bombers)

Sources: IISS (2007: 25, 29); Jordan et al. (2008: 30); Nesser (2007: 328); Kirby (2007: 421).

to carry out operations in the United States with a clear funding support network sending money from the outside. The total costs have been estimated to have been less than $500,000. Evidence suggests that these new networks are far more complex and loosely organized, making them harder to detect and less predictable.

Second are so-called subversive networks, which foster extremist objectives but do not themselves resort to violence. Their methods are manifold and include intimidating community members, trying to take control of political parties and other social organizations, and generating civil unrest through strikes, boycotts, and demonstrations. These networks may or may not have direct links to terrorist cells; this will likely be reflected in the local government's reaction to their presence. These networks are prime generators of the takfiri-Salafist ideology, which uses the religious tolerance of European societies and the legal safeguards that their political systems provide against them. A clear example would be the recently reformed (and then banned) al Muhajiroun group in the UK, who actively espouse and possibly participated in jihad abroad while leading a vocal and aggressive campaign to promote their ideology in the UK, and whose trail can be found in many terrorist plots.[6]

The third group, extremist political movements, are closely related to but do not engage in subversive activities and resort primarily to political means. Hence, they offer non-violent avenues to address grievances and could thus actually be exploited in a positive sense against their subversive counterparts. While their activities, insofar as they accept the rule of law and the democratic political process, are legal, these movements provide a potential recruiting base and radicalizing environment which terrorist cells and subversive networks might use to gain members. Hizb ut-Tahrir and its mixed history could fall under this category (the former UK government has concluded that the group is harmless while the Conservative-Liberal Democrat coalition entering office in 2010 is reviewing this position and Germany has had the group banned); other examples might include the Milli Görüş organization which has Turkish roots and a large presence in Germany.

Fourth, networks of sympathizers are important because they are involved in channelling fighters into conflicts and potentially back into European societies. Although they are thought to lack any kind of formal structure, they still serve as a recruiting base to terrorist groups, as well as providing groups abroad with funding and media support. Sometimes these networks come together around specific individuals or mosques or other places of public congregation, which replace the aforementioned political groups as the recruiting ground. Again, it is very hard to distinguish between the networks that provide support and some of the earlier groupings – for example, Abu Hamza's Supporters of Shariah group operated with impunity out of the Finsbury Park Mosque in London, acting as both a subversive group and as a network of sympathizers.[7] Similar parallels can probably be drawn to the Multi-Kultur Haus in Ulm, Germany, which provided a locus and radical network with connections to extremists in Pakistan. This sort of loose affiliation can also be seen in the networks that funnel money, equipment, and occasionally individuals from Europe to groups waging jihad in different parts of the world.

Finally, there is a partial overlap between criminal and extremist networks. Narcotics trafficking, people smuggling, money laundering, document fraud, and cyber crime are all of concern because these activities can directly finance terrorism, as in the case of the Madrid attack and many recent UK plots. In the Spanish case, it was revealed that a broader criminal network masked the presence of a terrorist group; Spanish authorities realized only later that some of the plotters had already appeared on the periphery of narcotics investigations.

It is clear, therefore, that the jihadi terrorist threat has to be located in the larger framework of radical Islam in Europe. Ed Husain, himself a former radical, argued that 'home-grown British suicide bombers are a direct result of Hizb ut-Tahrir disseminating ideas of jihad, martyrdom, confrontation … and nurturing a sense of separation among Britain's

Muslims' (Husain 2007: 119). A more specific example of this is the evolution of al Muhajiroun from the group to which Husain belonged, and in particular his mentor Omar Bakri Mohammed, who was one of the many political dissidents who fled the Muslim world and hid among Europe's Muslim communities. Angry at Hizb ut Tahrir's refusal to take more aggressive action, Bakri Mohammed broke away to found a splinter group called al Muhajiroun (the emigrants), a number of whom have since turned up in terrorist plots or have been arrested for antisocial activity.

Takfiri-Salafists exploit the openness of European societies for their recruitment purposes. The AIVD, the Dutch domestic intelligence service, has argued that the radical ideology 'works like a magnet on some sections of the Muslim communities' (AIVD 2005: 5). Different organizations, from mosques to gyms and youth organizations, are penetrated by extremists, who seek to manipulate 'grievances for the purpose of recruitment to insurgent and terrorist activities' (Kilcullen 2007: 656).

The desire to inflict mass casualties by deploying suicide bombers has already been highlighted as a fundamental difference between the kind of terrorism that Europe has experienced in the past and this new form of domestic jihadism in Europe. Traditionally, terrorist attacks in Europe had been limited in their severity because terrorists used violence in order to force their issue up the political agenda in the face of popular indignation. However, they were interested in maintaining a level of popular support, which is why they did not target indiscriminately and tended to call in warnings to the security services ahead of time (though this was not always the case). The fact that terrorists wanted many people to watch but not to die has been summed up by the phrase 'terrorism is theatre' – a saying that has been transformed by the jihad-salafi approach, which seeks to massacre many with as big an audience as possible. There are signs, however, that even Islamist militants are aware of the fact that they need to communicate favourably with potential supporters and sympathizers – witness Dr Ayman al Zawahiri's letter to Abu Musab al-Zarqawi chiding his mass slaughter of Shia Muslims, or his online question-and-answer session in 2008 in which he sought to address the *umma*'s complaints about al Qaeda's actions. For some analysts the conclusion reached is that this need may act as a restraint if the level of violence associated with their attacks becomes so high as to mean that they are unable to communicate any messages to the target population (Ryan 2007: 26–30).

Domestic jihadi terrorists have successfully attacked several European countries. Furthermore, dozens of additional plots have been foiled or have failed, networks funnelling fighters and money to current conflicts in Afghanistan, Pakistan, Iraq, and Somalia have been uncovered across the continent, and charismatic extreme individuals (both Imams and others) have become beacons for plots internationally. It seems that 'Europe is a transit area for extremists, a source of intellectual capital, exploitable grievances, and legislative safe haven, and an actual battle ground' (Kilcullen 2007: 662) in the confrontation with Islamist terrorists. This is the backdrop of the new threat facing Europe, which represents a step-change in complexity and underlying causes from previous terrorist threats which European security forces have faced (though it must also be remembered that old threats remain, and in some ways, elements of the new threat are similar). The key to understanding the way Europe might attempt to counter this threat is through knowledge about the process of radicalization among Muslim communities.

Radicalization – The Process

Before we go into detail about understanding current trends in radicalization, it is worth emphasizing the increasing difficulty with which one can point to any single pathway to violent extremism. In fact, to talk of a pathway probably suggests something that is clearer than it really is. Highlighted specifically in a leaked report by Britain's Security Service (MI5 2008), but increasingly clear to observers, this trend is broadly observable in the extraordinary diversity of the individuals who become embroiled in terrorist activity in Europe and the variety of ways in which they get involved. It is possible to discern some general patterns, or at least clusters of issues, that seem to identify individuals who become susceptible to extremist ideologies. But using these vague clusters as templates to understand who else might become a terrorist is very likely to throw up many false positives. As the MI5 report (2008) puts it, it is important not to assume that those who share these experiences will therefore become terrorists.

In the academic debate, this variety of explanations is expressed in a number of different ways, and authors are divided regarding the underlying logic of radicalization. Some authors point to a loss of identity among second-generation immigrants that makes them vulnerable to an ideology that rebuilds identity around a community of fighters. Others identify resentment for an immoral Europe and the notion of

'Islam under threat' as the driving factor. A more recent explanation combines elements of both schools of thought and stresses individual experiences, group dynamics, and outside influence in a multi-step process (Sageman 2007; NYPD 2007; MI5 2008).

Sageman argues that traumatic events experienced personally or learned about indirectly can spark moral outrage. The events often are related to incidents of Muslim suffering in other parts of the world. Individuals interpret this outrage through a specific ideology, which is based on the notion that the West is at war with Islam. In chat rooms or other Internet-based venues, adherents share this moral outrage, which resonates with the personal experiences of others and often with experiences of people still living in the respective individual's 'home' state. For example, the conflict in Kashmir was an early rallying cry for South Asian Muslims in Europe, while the brutal Algerian civil war provided a direct connection for many North Africans. Both incidents remain salient today and have been supplemented by the situations in Afghanistan, Iraq and Somalia. In addition, the rallying call of Muslim oppression in Palestine or Bosnia seems to resonate with Muslims around the world (and particularly in Europe), highlighting the increasingly transnational appeal of the 'globalized umma' as defined by Olivier Roy. Global grievances thus become fused with local and personal experiences. Finally, from the broad online and real-world community the individual is brought into contact with a self-selecting group that identifies a real-world connection to the global jihad and the individual then becomes involved in a terrorist cell.

The NYPD report distinguishes four phases in the radicalization process: pre-radicalization, self-identification, indoctrination, and jihadization. The first stage involves the personal circumstances of individuals before radicalization begins. It is not always possible to profile individuals who set off on a path of radicalization. As Jordan et al. (2008: 19) write, 'a reliable uniform portrait cannot be established.' Neumann (2006: 73) asserts that 'very little in terms of quantifiable attitudes or socio-economic indicators connects these groups.' Finally, Kirby (2007: 418) states, regarding the London 7/7 bombers, that 'it is interesting to note the relative diversity of personal backgrounds and personality-profiles within the group' beyond a general common heritage. Nonetheless, the NYPD (2007: 23) points to several general commonalities among individuals at the pre-radicalization phase. Paraphrasing the NYPD report, by and large the perpetrators of jihadist attacks in the West are:

- male Muslims under the age of 35 (though one has to highlight the presence of women, as well as older and much younger individuals);
- local residents and citizens of Western liberal communities;
- often second- or third-generation immigrants although from different ethnic backgrounds (recent immigrants and converts to Islam seem vulnerable as well);
- middle class;
- educated;
- not radical or devout Muslims initially (this is particularly hard to ascertain, as much of the information regarding individuals' piousness at a young age is available only from close family members);
- unremarkable as far as their daily lives and jobs are concerned.

The second phase, self-identification, is triggered by some kind of perceived individual crisis, which can be economic, social, political, or personal and which validates the individual's sense of rejection from the community they inhabit. This crisis is believed to shake previously held beliefs and opens the mind to new thoughts. The MI5 (2008) points out that one similarity among the individuals involved in extremism is that they have faced some rejection or hostility from society. Frequently, individuals in this stage try to find other individuals also experiencing similar inner conflicts. This, then, leads to the formation of clusters organized around some kind of social activity.

Central to the indoctrination phase is the acceptance 'of a religious-political worldview that justifies, legitimizes, encourages, or supports violence against anything ... un-Islamic, including the West, its citizens, its allies, or other Muslims whose opinions are contrary to the extremist agenda' (NYPD 2007: 36). Subscribing to this world view leads these individuals to redefine their goals in non-personal terms and to aim for some greater good.

During the final phase of jihadization, the group that has formed initially out of a cluster of individuals in crisis situations has taken on much stronger structures. 'Individuals see themselves as part of a movement and group loyalty becomes paramount above all other relationships' (NYPD 2007: 43).

Ultimately, the NYPD report is too deterministic in its predictions; in reality, radicalization is less of a trajectory than a confluence of the first three aspects in no particular order in an individual who is actively involved in the global jihad (Innes et al. 2007). However, the NYPD structure is a useful and coherent attempt to grasp the phenomenon of radicalization in its conceptual entirety.

Three issues warrant further explanation, namely the role of the internet, the importance of small group dynamics, and the role of external causes. The internet is a crucial enabler of radicalization because it provides direct and fast access to ideology and an opportunity for cut-and-paste religious knowledge. Further down the radicalization process the Web is a virtual meeting place and provides information on potential targets and weapons including bomb-making manuals (NYPD 2007: 83). Kirby (2007: 425) observes that the internet has

> effectively removed many of the practical barriers that once limited entry into the formal jihad ... The tactical and operational tradecraft that can be gleaned from the thousands of existing sites is comparable to that once only available in physical training camps ... [The internet has] introduced a deformalized experience in which a once-Al Qaeda sympathizer now enjoys a radically enhanced opportunity to become a full-fledged jihadist.

However, whether the internet is really a space were individuals can 'learn' jihad is still unproven. It should be pointed out that skills transfer via the internet does not seem to be as complete as Kirby suggests. While it is possible to discern among some more recent plots the contours of a completely isolated terror cell that is able to move from radicalization to constructing a viable device using only the internet, it is unclear whether these sorts of cells (often made up of a single person) have anything to do with what one might term 'the global jihad,' or whether they are simply disaffected individuals who would seek to carry out some action with or without the pretext of the global jihad. Some authors (Ryan 2007) see the user-driven internet as a chance to instil debate, challenge jihadist ideology, and promote engagement and thus as a useful area for counter-terrorism efforts, while another recent report states that blocking the parts of the internet which may help the radical narrative may not in fact prove an effective strategy (Neumann and Stevens 2009).

In terms of small-group dynamics, the formation of a group of like-minded individuals often consolidates radical indoctrination. In other words, in many cases, such as the 7/7 bombers, social networks predate an accelerated radicalization process. Sageman (2004; 2007) uses the explanation of clique dynamics to come to terms with this phenomenon, while Quintan Wictorowicz (2005) has shown in some detail how individuals can become tied to groups that require an almost total rejection of the world around them. This implies a certain analytical shift away from the individual towards such groups. As bonds between group members become stronger, isolation from other groups and individuals grows. In other words, the group facilitates the growth of commitment among its members to the detriment of other ties. Through this process, moderating influences disappear over time. While similarities do exist with previous terrorist-like activity that has taken place in Europe (left- or right-wing groups can be seen as having similarly insular perspectives), the extreme detachment from societal norms coupled with an ability to fully function within society presents a new and dangerous shift in radicalization in Europe.

International events can play a role and are sometimes referred to as 'humiliation by proxy' (Kirby 2007: 422). Situations in such places as Afghanistan, Palestine, Kashmir, Chechnya, Bosnia, Somalia, or Iraq suggest to some Muslims that the Muslim community in general is suppressed and abused, create a feeling of solidarity, although the humiliation is not necessarily felt and experienced personally. Kirby explains that the video statements of the 7/7 ringleader Khan clearly express this dynamic, framing his actions as essentially defensive – coming to the aid of Muslim brothers and sisters around the world (Kirby 2007: 420). Explaining that the Bosnian crisis in the 1990s had radicalized many British Muslims, Ed Husain recalls his own experience inside radical organizations: 'We had been trained always to link local issues to the global concerns of Muslims' (Husain 2007: 125); in other words, to ensure that humiliation by proxy is intensified by linking it to whatever local grievance might possibly exist. Other writers have stressed the importance of the 2003 invasion of Iraq because it provided a rallying point for diverse ideological factions across the radicalized spectrum (Neumann 2006: 74). The connection of international and local levels is clearly important and has been confirmed in case studies. Vidino (2007: 585), for example, found that for members of the Hofstadt group in the Netherlands, international events 'may have contributed to the men's radicalization' even though their declared enemies where those whom they perceived as oppressing or even fighting Islam in a local context, in the Netherlands (also compare Nesser 2006: 337).

International Links and Leadership

The question of whether home-grown jihadist terrorism is an autonomous phenomenon has not yet been resolved conclusively. Several authors have pointed out that radicalized individuals self-recruit and are largely free of outside interference or influence (Leiken 2005; Bakker 2006:

53–4). Kirby's (2007) concept of the 'self-starter' is a strong and tempting one because it suggests that radicalization is driven by social dynamics aided by radical Islamist rhetoric and ideology. The ability to identify with the global *umma* furthermore makes particular geographic or historical roots less important, and countries of origin no longer form reference points for action (Haine 2007: 34). But in counter to this argument, it is increasingly notable that there are clear connections and contacts that appear to exist between autonomous cells in Europe and the global jihad in one way or another. As MI5 (2008) concluded about British extremists, 'What is different about those who ended up involved in terrorism is that they came into contact with existing extremists who recognised their vulnerabilities (and their usefulness to the extremist group),' suggesting that isolated radicalization to violence is a rare (but not unheard of) phenomenon. In fact, several plots in the UK, the Sauerland Group in Germany, and other groupings in Denmark and Spain provide ample evidence for a clearly discernible international dimension that goes beyond Europe.

Another concept introduced to the debate by Jordan et al. (2008) in their work on the Madrid network is that of a grassroots jihadi network (GJN) of individuals that operate in their country of residence and objectives of the broader global jihadi movement, including AQ, but are not actually in close contact with other groups. While Jordan et al. stress that the GJN has tactical and operational autonomy, they also emphasize that its members may have some contact with international members of the jihadi movement.

The Hofstad group, which carried out the murder of Theo van Gogh in 2004, is usually thought to be a prime example of autonomous radicalization (Vidino 2007). Its members were formed from the three likely groups of recruits, including a small number of converts to Islam, several recent and mostly illegal immigrants, and a larger number of second- and third-generation immigrants. The Hofstad group does not seem to have been brought together by a facilitator or recruiter, though they congregated around a Syrian preacher named Redouan al-Issar and established contacts with other European extremist networks. Initially, however, the members used their own research, driven primarily by the internet, to form their own versions of militant Islamist thinking. Given that recruitment and radicalization in this case seem to have been free of outside interference, the Dutch security services refer to the group as self-radicalized.

The apparent absence of facilitators and/or recruiters outside the group of aspiring jihadis has been noted in other studies as well. Jordan et al. (2008) show that none of the operational members of the Madrid network attended a foreign training camp, and only one of the group members had existing links to militants (in Algeria).[8] And research into the international plot focused around Bradford native Aabid Khan and online jihadist Younis Tsouli, aka Irhabi007 (terrorist007), and their global network of conspirators stretching from Georgia, USA, through to Canada, Bosnia, Denmark, and across the United Kingdom, shows that new networks may be emerging that only seek a connection after they have advanced quite far down the path of radicalization (Pantucci, 2008). Kirby (2007) in her work on the 7/7 group cautions that the absence of such recruiters or facilitators does not mean that no connection to broader international networks and more experienced actors exists – in fact, time has shown strong connections between the 7/7 group and a number of other plots and networks. Other writers insist that AQ logistics networks in Europe remain strong, in particular in France and Spain (a claim supported by government statements) and similarly claim that just because connections were not found in certain cases does not mean that they did not exist. As a result, the phenomenon of home-grown, autonomous terrorism and radicalization might be overrated (Steinberg 2007).

Even though the degree of autonomy and the extent of their connections to experienced jihadists are subject to debate, a few strengths and weaknesses of such home-grown networks stand out (see Jordan et al. 2008). First, decision-making autonomy on tactical and operational matters is a clear strength because it allows for flexibility and efficient running of daily tasks since the need for consultation is minimized. Furthermore, given that attacks are relatively cheap to carry out and can be financed through personal funds and common delinquencies, these groups also enjoy logistical autonomy. This makes counter-terrorism efforts aimed at international financial flows mostly ineffective. Finally, until a network acquires weapons and bomb-making materials, their activities may not be chargeable under European laws or if they can be charged with anything it is most likely going to be related to common crimes such as drug trafficking.

On the side of weaknesses, the lack of experience among the group members and an inability to practise their trade before they attempt an action is the most important one because it leads to mistakes. The attempted car bombings in London and Glasgow in the summer of 2007 failed as a result of an incorrect combustible mixture in the vehicles; similar parallels can be drawn with the attempt in Germany to bomb passenger trains in Koblenz and Dortmund in the summer of 2006 and a more recent attempt by a radicalized individual to carry out a suicide bombing in Exeter, England, in May 2008. However, in order to be able to practise, the members of the autonomous home-grown group will need exposure beyond their immediate network in order to improve their skills – which may bring them to the attention of security services.

Neumann goes even further and insists that there is a link between the sophistication of an attack and 'the degree to which its perpetrators were able to capitalise on the finance, weapons, training and skills provided through existing structures' (Neumann 2006: 77). Thus, the phenomenon of autonomous European jihad is not yet clearly established, which is good and bad news from a counter-terrorism point of view. Good since it means some training and therefore contact with extremists is essential, all of which increases possibilities for capture; bad, since the future direction seems clear: autonomy is increasing. One of the leading scholars on the issue, Marc Sageman, has changed his view about the link to the original AQ and no longer claims that such a link is necessarily vital.[9]

Conclusion

It is unclear how the current terrorist threat to Europe might further evolve. On the one hand, the lack of successful attacks suggests that a plateau may have been reached. On the other hand, threat assessments by most security services, as well as anecdotal evidence of individuals going to fight abroad, suggest that the threat remains. For Europe as a whole the threat perceptions remain uneven, with many EU member states not having experienced a successful attack in decades.

Although there are several commonalities among individuals who have been radicalized, recent studies show that these individuals by and large appear to be unremarkable and ordinary people. Socio-economic factors do not offer a direct explanation for radicalization and jihadist violence, and neither do Islamic beliefs. However, radical preachers exploit socio-economic factors to create a sense of victimhood and identification with a global Muslim community in order to justify violence.

The evidence presented in several recent studies mostly suggests a focus on sociological aspects. For example, group dynamics and pre-existing social networks have been identified as being entry points for jihadism and as instilling a dynamic that may lead to violence. Leading scholars in the field are in no doubt about the severity of the threat. Neumann argues that 'Europe has evolved into a nerve centre for the global jihad, and it is here that future attacks against Western interests are most likely to be planned and executed' (Neumann 2006: 71). As Kilcullen confirms, 'a substantial part of the threat both emanates from, and targets Europe (Kilcullen 2007: 648). Recognizing this reality, and the fact that arresting their way out of this threat is impossible, European security services have focused on pouring their resources into preventing radicalization in Muslim communities and hence manage this particular risk. Only once they have tackled how to prevent radicalization will they be able to effectively counter what former British Prime Minister Gordon Brown has defined as a 'generational struggle.'

NOTES

1 This paper uses Wilkinson's (2005: 9) definition of terrorism as 'the systematic use of murder, injury and destruction or threat of the same to create a climate of terror, to publicise a cause and to intimidate a wider target into conceding to the terrorists' aims.'
2 A study of 242 jihadists in Europe reveals that 40 per cent were born in Europe and a further 55 per cent were raised in or were long-term residents of Europe. See Bakker (2006).
3 This summary of different schools of Islam in the Muslim world is by no means comprehensive. Only a brief summation is possible within the confines of this chapter to capture the key salient ideological points.
4 Johnny Ryan (2007: 43–56) has coined the phrase 'The 4Ps' to describe the different aspect of this call to violence: precedent, perseverance, piety, persecution.
5 The publication in 1988 of Salman Rushdie's *The Satanic Verses* led to an uproar across the Muslim world, culminating in a fatwa issued by Ayatollah Khomeini of Iran condemning Rushdie to death. In the UK, much of the initial public disorder focused around Britain's Muslim communities in northern cities.
6 While connections appear to exist between this group and the 7 July 2005 plotters, the May 2009 report by the Intelligence and Security Committee (ISC 2009) of the British Parliament states quite bluntly that 'there is no evidence of any links between the London bombings and al Muhajiroun.' However, this is followed by a heavily redacted section that suggests more detail exists, and research carried out by the authors shows clearly that the

group is one of a few that provide a connective thread through a number of terror networks in the UK.

7 O'Neill and McGrory's *The Suicide Factory: Abu Hamza and the Finsbury Park Mosque* (2006) is an authoritative piece of investigative journalism that looks at Abu Hamza's activities.

8 Petter Nesser (2006) disagrees with this assertion, claiming strong connections were established.

9 See his debate with Bruce Hoffman in *Foreign Affairs* triggered by Hoffman's book review of Sageman's work (Hoffman 2008; Sageman and Hoffman 2008).

REFERENCES

AIVD (Algemene Inlichtingen en Veiligheidsdienst, Dutch General Intelligence and Security Service). 2005. 'Saudi Influences in the Netherlands. Links between the Salafist Mission, Radicalisation Process and Islamic Terrorism.' The Hague, http://www.aivd.nl.

Armitage, D. 2007. *The European Union: Measuring Counterterrorism Cooperation.* Strategic Forum 229. National Defence University (NDU), Institute for National Strategic Studies (INSS). Washington, DC: NDU Press.

Bakker, E. 2006. *Jihadi Terrorists in Europe: Their Characteristics and the Circumstances in Which They Joined the Jihad: An Exploratory Study.* Clingendael Report, The Hague. http://www.clingendael.nl/publications/2006/20061200_cscp_csp_bakker.pdf.

BBC. 2007. 'Ban Foreign Language Imams – Peer.' http://news.bbc.co.uk/1/hi/uk/6275574.stm.

Europol. 2007. *EU Terrorism Situation and Trend Report* (EU TE-SAT). Europol Annual Report, The Hague. http://www.europol.europa.eu/publications/EU_Terrorism_Situation_and_Trend_Report_TE-SAT/TESAT2007.pdf.

Europol. 2008. *EU Terrorism Situation and Trend Report* (EU TE-SAT). Europol Annual Report, The Hague. http://www.europol.europa.eu/publications/EU_Terrorism_Situation_and_Trend_Report_TE-SAT/TESAT2008.pdf.

Haine, J.-Y. 2007. 'The European Security Strategy Coping with Threats.' In *The EU and the European Security Strategy: Forging a Global Europe,* ed. S. Biscop and J.J. Andersson, 21–41. London: Abingdon.

Hippel, K. von. 2005. *Europe Confronts Terrorism.* London: Palgrave Macmillan.

Hoffman, B. 2008. 'The Myth of Grass-Roots Terrorism: Why Osama Bin Laden Still Matters.' *Foreign Affairs* (May/June). http://www.foreignaffairs.org/20080501fareviewessay87310/bruce-hoffman/the-myth-of-grass-roots-terrorism.html.

Husain, E. 2007. *The Islamist: Why I Joined Radical Islam in Britain, What I Saw Inside and Why I Left*. London: Penguin.

IISS. 2007. *Home-Grown Terrorism: What Does It Mean For Business?* IISS-Lloyd's Joint Report. London: IISS-Lloyd's. http://www.lloyds.com/NR/rdonlyres/CEB33D83-7917-4CE9-A1FD-43DF8498890C/0/360_HomeGrownTerrorism ReportFinalwebversion_031207.pdf

Innes, Martin, et al. 2007. *Hearts and Mind and Eyes and Ears: Reducing Radicalization Risks through Reassurance-Oriented Policing*. Cardiff University Police Science Institute.

Intelligence and Security Committee. 2009. *Could 7/7 Have Been Prevented? Review of the Intelligence on the London Terrorist Attacks on 7 July 2005*. London: The Stationary Office. http://www.cabinetoffice.gov.uk/media/210852/20090519_77review.pdf.

International Crisis Group (ICG). 2007. *Islam and Identity in Germany*. Europe Report no. 181.

Jordan, J., F. Manas, and N. Horsburgh. 2008. 'Strength and Weaknesses of Grassroot Jihadist Networks: The Madrid Bombings.' *Studies in Conflict and Terrorism* 31: 17–39.

Kilcullen, D. 2007. 'Subversion and Countersubversion in the Campaign against Terrorism in Europe.' *Studies in Conflict and Terrorism* 30: 647–66.

Kirby, A. 2007. 'The London Bombers as "Self-Starters": A Case Study in Indigenous Radicalization and the Emergence of Autonomous Cliques.' *Studies in Conflict and Terrorism* 30: 415–28.

Leiken, R. 2005. 'Europe's Angry Muslims.' *Foreign Affairs* (July/August). http://www.foreignaffairs.com/articles/60829/robert-s-leiken/europes-angry-muslims.

MI5. 2008. *Understanding Radicalization and Violent Extremism in the UK*. Excerpts published in Alan Travis, 'The Making of an Extremist,' *The Guardian*, 20 August.

Nesser, P. 2006. 'Jihadism in Western Europe after the Invasion of Iraq: Tracing Motivational Influences from the Iraq War on Jihadist Terrorism in Western Europe.' *Studies in Conflict and Terrorism* 29: 323–42.

Neumann, P. 2006. 'Europe's Jihadist Dilemma.' *Survival* 48, no. 2: 71–84.

Neumann, P., and T. Stevens. 2009. *Countering Online Radicalisation: A Strategy for Action*. London: International Center for the Study of Radicalisation (ICSR).

New York Police Department. 2007. *Radicalization in the West: The Homegrown Threat*. NYPD Intelligence Division.

O'Neill, S., and D. McGrory. 2006. *The Suicide Factory: Abu Hamza and the Finsbury Park Mosque*. London: Harper Perennial.

Pantucci, R. 2008. 'Operation Praline: The Realization of Al-Suri's *Nizam, la Tanzim?' Perspectives on Terrorism* 2, no. 12: 11–17.

Roy, O. 2005. 'A Clash of Cultures or a Debate on Europe's Values?' *ISIM Review* 15: 6–7.

– 2008. *Al Qaeda in the West as a Youth Movement: The Power of a Narrative*, MICROCON Policy Working Paper no. 2. http://www.microconflict.eu/publications/PWP2_OR.pdf.

Ryan, J. 2007. *Countering Militant Islamist Radicalisation on the Internet*. Dublin: IIEA Press

Sageman, M. 2004. Understanding Terror Networks, Philadelphia, PA: University of Pennsylvania Press.

– 2007. *Leaderless Jihad: Terror Networks in the Twenty-First Century*. Philadelphia: University of Pennsylvania Press.

Sageman, M., and B. Hoffman. 2008. 'Does Osama Still Call the Shots? Debating the Containment of al Qaeda's Leadership.' *Foreign Affairs* (July/August). http://www.foreignaffairs.org/20080701faresponse87415/marc-sageman-bruce-hoffman/does-osama-still-call-the-shots.html.

Sendagorta, F. 2005. 'Jihad in Europe.' *Survival* 47, no. 3: 63–72.

Steinberg, G. 2007. *Die Wiederkehr von al-Qaida: Aktuelle Entwicklungen im internationalen Terrorismus und ihre Folgen für Europa*. SWP-Aktuell no. 62.

Stemmann, J. 2006. 'Middle East Salafism's Influence and Radicalization of Muslim Communities in Europe.' *Middle East Review of International Affairs* 10, no. 3: 1–14.

Tibi, B. 2007. 'The Totalitarianism of Jihadist Islamism and Its Challenge to Europe and to Islam.' *Totalitarian Movements and Political Religions* 8, no. 1: 35–54.

Travis, A. 2008. 'The Making of an Extremist.' *The Guardian*, 20 August.

Vidino, L. 2007. 'The Hofstad Group: The New Face of Terrorist Networks in Europe.' *Studies in Conflict and Terrorism* 30: 579–92.

Wetzels, P., and K. Brettfeld. 2007. *Muslime in Deutschland: Integration und Integrationsbarrieren*. Bundesministerium des Inneren, Berlin.

Wictorowicz, Q. 2005. *Radical Islam Rising*. Oxford: Rowman and Littlefield.

Wilkinson, P. 2005. *International Terrorism: The Changing Threat and the EU's Response*. Chaillot Paper no. 84. EUISS.

4 Nuclear Weapons in Today's Europe: The Debate That Nobody Wants

STEFANIE VON HLATKY AND MICHEL FORTMANN

To a superficial observer, the nuclear issue, which was central to any discussion about European security during the Cold War, seems to have completely disappeared from public view since the early 1990s. For many commentators, this is as it should be. As a 'senior diplomat' noted in 1999, nuclear deterrence is an issue that should remain 'in a box in a corner' and stay there for the foreseeable future (Smith 2004). But like a rash that refuses to go away, the nuclear issue reappears time and again in the headlines, making it seem unlikely that a European debate over nuclear weapons and their status in Europe can be avoided forever. To paraphrase the editors of this volume, the boundaries of the nuclear debate have changed, but this has not produced a concurrent shift in NATO policy. Despite clear disagreements over the role of nuclear weapons in today's security environment, concerns over nuclear proliferation have resisted the trend toward the regionalization of security (Lake and Morgan 1997). After being avoided and postponed, is it not time to revisit the traditional concept of deterrence in a European context and to reopen finally the nuclear Pandora's box? Now that the divisions over the war in Iraq have been mended, is it time for France, Germany, the United Kingdom, and the United States to address the nuclear question? At the very least, the great European powers will increasingly feel pressed to tackle the nuclear dimension of their common defence policy. Continued reliance on the tenets of deterrence while simultaneously pursuing an increasingly active non-proliferation agenda appears unsustainable. Is a paradigm shift inevitable?

This chapter will focus on the nuclear future of Europe by inquiring into the possibility of a common European position on nuclear issues. Its point of departure is a realization that there is much European enthusiasm for non-proliferation initiatives but that certain Cold War legacies, like deterrence, may be hampering progress on the development of an ambitious and enforceable non-proliferation agenda. The realist view taken here suggests that dependence on the United States' security guarantees is part of the answer, even in the post–Cold War era. However, this broad theme is inevitably linked to other issues, four of which will be discussed here. First, we will look at how European attitudes toward nuclear weapons have changed, especially since the end of the Cold War. Second, we will discuss three plausible scenarios for the formulation of a European nuclear doctrine: classical deterrence, existential deterrence, and post-deterrence, an updated version of deterrence as envisioned in the nuclear posture review (NPR). We argue that existential deterrence is the most likely option, since the leading European powers have opted out of a renewed debate on a shared nuclear doctrine. Third, we assess how Germany, France, and the UK have responded to the post–Cold War security environment with regards to nuclear weapons. Throughout the nineties and today, there are growing divisions between the nuclear states, France and the UK, and other European powers. Finally, we will look at the transatlantic relationship, since NATO has continued to dominate the nuclear field. In this section, we will also discuss actions undertaken under the banner of European security and defence with regards to its non-proliferation policies. It is apparent that the European stance on non-proliferation has the potential to highlight core contradictions in its nuclear policy, as commitments taken under the non-proliferation treaty (NPT) stand in opposition to Europe's nuclear legacy. This chapter offers a realist reading of how nuclear issues have evolved since the end of the Cold War from a European and transatlantic perspective.

Nuclear Weapons and Strategic Culture

The fundamental question behind any policy debate on nuclear weapons has been set against two options: should the status quo persist, which is based on the American guarantee of nuclear protection; or should nuclear weapons in Europe be disposed of, as an anachronism from the Cold War? In other words, are nuclear weapons still useful for Europe in the current geostrategic context? In this section, we will focus on the relevance of deterrence in this new European security environment. We will also look at public and elite attitudes towards nuclear weapons and the policy of deterrence in particular.

The Cold War Status Quo Revised

Since the early 1990s, NATO allies have reiterated their Cold War poli-cy on nuclear weapons as weapons of last resort. This apparent consen-sus was reaffirmed in the 1999 NATO strategic concept which states that the alliance's nuclear weapons act as a guarantee for the protection of its members and that NATO will seek a balance of strategic and nu-clear forces based in Europe. This consensus is thus based on four main assumptions (Smith 2004): (1) nuclear weapons in Europe, including French and British nuclear forces, must act as an insurance policy, with a guarantee of minimal deterrence against the risk, even if remote, of a resurgent and aggressive Russia, or the risks of nuclear and WMD pro-liferation in Europe's periphery; (2) these nuclear weapons must ensure the coupling of American and European defence, in an effort to keep the US in the European theatre; (3) NATO nukes represent the solidari-ty of the alliance members in facing nuclear threats and continental de-fence. The NATO nuclear doctrine thus engaged nine members: the United States, Great Britain, Germany, the Netherlands, Belgium, Italy, Turkey and Greece; (4) finally, by offering assurances for the protection of Europe, the presence of nuclear weapons on European soil must also serve to discourage the nuclear ambitions of individual states, which would otherwise be isolated in the pursuit of their own security, in ac-cordance with the realist principle of *self-help*.

These postulates have survived the end of the Cold War but are in-creasingly being scrutinized. In February 2006, during the Munich con-ference on security policy, German Chancellor Angela Merkel suggested that NATO's strategic concept be revised, arguing that the world had fundamentally changed since 1999 (Smith 2006). This suggestion was taken up in 2009, at the Strasbourg/Kehl Summit. It appears that a de-bate on the nuclear question in Europe may jeopardize the most funda-mental aspects of deterrence, including the above-stated pillars of NATO's strategic concept.

Germany is not alone in expressing reluctance toward the NATO deter-rence posture. Broadly speaking, it can be argued that European solidar-ity has gradually been eroding since the end of the Cold War. For example, Greece abandoned its deterrence mission in 2001; and today, only seven NATO states (excluding France) are participants in the nuclear mission, which constitutes a mere 25 per cent of the Alliance, with twenty-six mem-bers. The idea of coupling the European and American nuclear doctrines has equally been weakened. According to Bruno Tertrais, the American strategic culture with regards to extended deterrence is undergoing a shift (Tertrais 1999). In this sense, it is not surprising that the arsenal of American nuclear weapons in Europe is smaller than the French and British national deterrent capabilities. American nuclear capabilities in Europe have been receding, given the removal of one hundred bombs in 2005 and 2008 (Kristensen 2005, 2007, 2008). Equally uncertain is the extent to which these American weapons have truly halted nuclear proliferation in Europe, in accordance with the fourth stated postulate as listed above. We can here point out that the removal of American nuclear weapons from Korea in 1992 did not provoke a chain reaction of nuclear proliferation in the region (Japan, South Korea, and Taiwan). Furthermore, the promise of EU membership serves as a major incentive against proliferation for applicant countries (Tertrais 2006b). Attitudes toward the nuclear component of NATO's strategic concept have been rather complacent. If not completely sidelined, deterrence is progressively being abandoned in favour of more popular initiatives, such as a new European brand of non-proliferation policies, as we will discuss further below.

Public Attitudes toward Nuclear Weapons

If we look at surveys done in recent years in Europe, there is strong public support for non-proliferation initiatives and general ambivalence with regards to deterrence as a policy. It should be mentioned that the French and British publics are generally more favourable to deterrence than the German public, for instance, but there is overwhelming and shared support for policies aimed at halting the proliferation of nuclear weapons and weapons of mass destruction (WMDs) more broadly. This shift in attitudes towards deterrence is not surprising in itself, given that the nuclear threat posed by Russia has considerably diminished. What *is* surprising is that people are generally unaware that American nuclear weapons remain on European soil. Surveys conducted in 2006 in six different countries (Belgium, Germany, Great Britain, Italy, the Netherlands, and Turkey) confirm this (Stratcom 2006). As for the question about whether these weapons should stay or be removed, there is a strong response in favour of a nuclear-free Europe, with the strongest showing in Turkey (88.1 per cent) and the lowest in Great Britain (55.7 per cent) (Stratcom 2006: 3–6). When we look at European attitudes toward nuclear weapons, Britain and France, the two states that actually possess nuclear weapons, are slightly more favourable to the concept of deterrence and of retaining a nuclear capability, while

Germany and Italy show clear support for nuclear disarmament (Stratcom 2006). In October 2007, there was even a public demonstration in Italy, where people marched for the withdrawal of stationed US nuclear weapons from Italian territory (Abolition 2000, 2007). What this tells us is that Europe is divided on the nuclear question. These findings, combined with a weakening elite consensus, indicate that support for traditional extended deterrence in Europe is eroding.

We have already mentioned the German chancellor's appeal to revise the NATO strategic concept with regards to the nuclear posture. Indeed, opposition to the nuclear status quo can also be found in conservative circles in the United States. Prominent groups are speaking out publicly and questioning the utility of nuclear weapons more generally. In a 2008 *Wall Street Journal* article, renowned conservative figures such as Henry A. Kissinger, George P. Shultz, William J. Perry, and Sam Nunn described nuclear weapons as anachronistic and endorsed the view of 'a world free of nuclear weapons' (Shultz et al. 2008). This message has been embraced by the Obama administration. Both elite and public attitudes serve as powerful indicators for this broad shift away from the Cold War posture, enshrined in successive NATO strategic concepts.

For now, the European nuclear question is mostly framed in terms of non-proliferation. Consequently, there has not been much public debate on deterrence or the use of nuclear weapons in Europe. This stance has endured in the absence of an imminent threat. This would seem to buy European audiences ample time to think about their nuclear future. However, with the development of the European security and defence policy, the nuclear debate may emerge sooner than later. Let us now turn to the plausible alternative in reformulating a European nuclear doctrine.

Scenarios for a European Nuclear Doctrine

Beyond the public debate on the desirability of nuclear weapons, the question of developing or renewing a general nuclear doctrine for Europe has not been thoroughly explored. This section will assess the different alternatives for a European nuclear doctrine, which describes the ways and means through which nuclear weapons may be employed. Essentially, the choice is threefold, each doctrine corresponding to doctrines associated with France, the Alliance, and the United States. The three models, which are by no means exhaustive, are as follows: classical deterrence, existential deterrence, and post-deterrence, inspired by the American Nuclear Posture Review (NPR) of 2002. We argue that existential deterrence has been the most pervasive and enduring of the three models.

The first model, which is based on classical deterrence, posits that nuclear weapons are weapons of last resort. Their purpose is to prevent an aggressor from threatening a state's vital interests by demonstrating the capability of imposing unbearable costs if the threat is executed. In this view, nuclear weapons are meant as a political tool, rather than an actual weapon of war, as envisioned by the doctrine of flexible response during the Cold War. Thus, a hypothetical nuclear strike would always have strategic significance, sending a clear signal to the aggressor that his very survival is at risk if the aggression is pursued.

In the current European context, there are several problems with this approach. First, it is meant to address threats posed by other states, with no application for threats such as terrorism or nuclear proliferation in the periphery (Bentégeat 2004). In other words, nuclear weapons have the potential of deterring other states that also possess nuclear weapons, but may be inappropriate or ineffective in other cases. Second, since this model of deterrence implies centralized control, it could not be easily adapted to a multilateral setting. As De Gaulle reminds us, deterrence may be difficult to share. As such, how can we reconcile the centralized control of nuclear weapons, which is implied by the classical deterrence stance, with the Europeanization of the doctrine? The alternative, which was proposed by France with the notion of *concerted deterrence*, implies sharing the nuclear risk (Tertrais 1999; Chirac 1996). However, since its introduction in 1992, no follow-up debate has occurred, as will be discussed in the next section. More fundamentally, the definition of vital interests cannot easily be enlarged without undermining the credibility of the threat. Would France choose to sacrifice its survival to defend an ally? Expanding the nuclear umbrella to the rest of Europe highlights the dilemma of extended deterrence for France.

The second model can be called existential deterrence or latent deterrence and fits well with NATO's current nuclear stance. According to this perspective, the mere presence of nuclear weapons within a region has a deterrent effect. These weapons do not have to be operational, since it is assumed that in the event of an emerging threat, there would be ample time to prepare a nuclear response. The advantage of existential deterrence is that it is the most discrete but still retains the option of nuclear use in extreme contingencies. The main problem is that these weapons, and their modes of delivery, will grow outdated. Contemplating the new security environment, some observers have expressed such concerns in terms of *obsolescence by neglect* (Buteux 2000–1: 49). In response, European leaders will find it increasingly difficult to justify the maintenance of defunct weapons on their soil. The alternative, the modernization of these weapons, would open the debate that this very option sought to prevent.

The last model of deterrence, *deterrence plus*, is the model thought up by the Bush administration, in the context of the Nuclear Posture Reviews of 2002. This option recognizes that classical deterrence is not equipped to meet today's unconventional threats. The assumption is that, contrary to the USSR during the Cold War, new enemies may be irrational and hence undeterrable. It also moves from a reactive stance to a pre-emptive one, in order to neutralize potential threats before they materialize. Finally, this approach views classical deterrence as immoral because the doctrine of mutually assured destruction threatens civilian populations.

To replace classical deterrence, proponents of this approach suggest an offensive doctrine, where threats are met with the full spectrum of military force, from conventional to nuclear, representing a seamless web of defence. In this context, the utility of nuclear weapons decreases in comparison to the technologies of the revolution in military affairs (RMA), as well as missile defence systems. These technologies hold an appealing promise by offering a low-cost and efficient method to counter the threat of weapons of mass destruction. The threat of military use of force to counter a threat is thus more credible and can serve to strengthen the deterrence posture of this doctrine (Fortmann and von Hlatky 2009).

The major problem with this approach is that this doctrine, the Bush Doctrine, has been quite unpopular among European audiences, even if it is the most thorough attempt at adapting deterrence to the post–Cold War context. The war in Iraq has considerably weakened the appeal of this option, and it will unlikely be considered seriously now that Bush is out of office.

Among these three nuclear doctrines, no single approach appears to hold broad enough support for the creation of a European nuclear strategy. Moreover, the context may not be ripe for such a project, as the prospects of reconciling the French and British approaches to nuclear weapons with the broader objectives of the Common Security and Defence Policy (CSDP) are pessimistic (Tertrais 2007). Even if none of these options appears well-suited to become a truly European nuclear doctrine, existential deterrence is the doctrine by default, a basic reassurance of the American security guarantee in Europe. In fact, one author talks of *existential deterrence plus,* commenting on the nuclear posture since the end of the Cold War: 'the maintenance of a numerically small and limited TNF stockpile was judged to be sufficient for deterrence purposes now that the Soviet threat no longer existed' and was complemented by 'the continued deployment of US nuclear warheads widely dispersed geographically amongst European NATO member states' (Smith 2004: 536). Moving away from existential deterrence appears likely only if European players take on the leadership role. Such attempts have been uneven at best. In the next section, we will look at the alternatives or European initiatives on the nuclear issue.

Taking the Nuclear Lead

The idea of a group of states leading a European nuclear initiative is appealing, but unlikely within the CSDP. In this sense, France has been the most active in attempting to initiate a nuclear dialogue with other European great powers. In this section, we focus on French and British attitudes toward European nuclear cooperation, through diplomatic initiatives undertaken by both countries since the end of the Cold War. We also discuss German reactions to French overtures. Finally, we consider European initiatives, especially those undertaken under the Western European Union. On all fronts, efforts by the French to reopen the nuclear dialogue have been thwarted by indifference or downright opposition. A European position on nuclear doctrine is thus unlikely to emerge in the near future, as states defer to the status quo, under American rather than French leadership.

The UK and France

In November 1993, British Defence Secretary Malcolm Rifkind announced the establishment of a French-British Joint Nuclear Commission which would look at the role of nuclear weapons in the post–Cold War era (United Kingdom 1995). Cited as the 'main forum for strategic cooperation,' its activities have since been shielded from the public eye, as the forum's deliberations are highly classified (French Embassy 2010). The 1994 Anglo-French Summit at Chartres featured discussions to coordinate both countries' approach to the NPT but went further when Major and Mitterrand suggested that deterrence should be the basis for European security (Butcher, Nassauer, and Young 1998).

A more public display of French and British cooperation on nuclear issues was seen at the annual Franco-British Summit, held on 29 October 1995. At the meeting, President Chirac and Prime Minister Major insisted on a high degree of convergence between the two countries on matters of nuclear policy. The summit, through the solidarity expressed by the two leaders, had a symbolic significance. Considering France's difficult position following the resumption of its nuclear tests, appealing for the Europeanization of the French deterrent was largely perceived as a cover-up. Though the meetings covered a broad range of security and defence issues linking the two governments, the nuclear relationship was set at the forefront, with attention-grabbing slogans enshrined in official documents. For instance, a commitment to a shared understanding of deterrence is expressed in the *Joint Statement on Nuclear Cooperation*:

> We do not see situations arising in which the vital interests of either France or the United Kingdom could be threatened without the vital interests of the other also being threatened. We have decided to pursue and deepen nuclear co-operation between our two countries. Our aim is mutually to strengthen deterrence, while retaining the independence of our nuclear forces. The deepening of co-operation between the two European members of the North Atlantic Alliance who are nuclear powers will therefore strengthen the European contribution to overall deterrence. (Anglo-French Summit 1995)

Such principles were reiterated on several occasions, such as the Franco-British Summit in Le Touquet in February 2003, but nuclear cooperation between the two states did not develop beyond that. Despite this, there was yet another attempt to relaunch a nuclear discussion, after Chirac's speech at L'Ile Longue in 2006, during which he made explicit the French doctrine of deterrence, again referring to the extension of France's vital interests (Favin-Lévêque 2006). Once again, French efforts fell flat. Britain's Secretary of State for Defence John Reid did not reciprocate, saying that there was no 'common or joint approach to nuclear deterrence outside the framework of NATO' (United Kingdom 2006). Even with France's return to the ranks of the NATO defence mechanism, there is little chance that nuclear cooperation between the two countries will go further.

France and Germany

As for Germany, the prospects of a nuclear dialogue with France are even slimmer. There are three main reasons for this: First, Germans are not keen on entering a partnership where they would be a junior member, while the political and strategic advantages of such a partnership are still uncertain; second, a special nuclear relationship with France might undermine both countries' positions within NATO, especially in regards to their nuclear responsibilities; and finally, the nuclear question is a particularly sensitive issue in Germany, as political parties have mobilized against the deployment of nuclear weapons (Schmidt and De Spiegeleire 1999; Schmidt 2004). This has not prevented France from attempting to lure Germany into an understanding, with sustained efforts since the 1990s. For example, the French initiated a controversial exchange when a secret document was published by *Le Monde*. The document hinted at an agreement made between Helmut Kohl and Jacques Chirac to 'open a dialogue on the role of nuclear deterrence in the context of a European defence policy' (Whitney 1997).

Calls for *concerted deterrence*, whereby the French nuclear deterrent is extended to the rest of Europe, were not taken up by the German government, which was not favourable to furthering a debate on nuclear weapons and doctrines within the European context. This anti-nuclear German attitude was apparent as NATO adopted its strategic concept in 1999. During the meetings, the German government, with the support of Canada, sought the removal of the first-use policy, with little success. German reactions to the American NPR of 2002 were equally critical (Staatsminister Ludger Volmer 2002). We should also note that the German domestic context had been set for an anti-nuclear stance: Schröder's red-green coalition (1998-2005) had positioned itself against the policy of first use and in favor of the complete abolition of nuclear weapons.

More recently, Germans have expressed concerns over France's deterrence posture, as articulated in 2006 and in 2008. This posture, which seeks an extension on the notion of vital interests, was perceived as lowering the nuclear threshold (Janning 2006). Sarkozy's latest overtures to Germany in the summer of 2007 did not elicit any enthusiasm from either Chancellor Angela Merkel or Foreign Affairs Minister Frank Walter Steinmeier.

From the above discussion, it is clear that Europe is not yet ripe for a big debate on the nuclear question. For the time being, the dialogue is restricted to the French-British-German triad. Moreover, it is hardly surprising that the nuclear dialogue sought by France has taken the form of conflicting monologues. No consultative mechanism has been put in place since the bilateral summit of Nuremberg in 1996, where the two countries had agreed to initiate a 'dialogue on the future role of nuclear deterrence in the context of a European Defense Policy' (Franco-German

Summit 1996). Finally, there is a sense that the nuclear question might overwhelm the European agenda and could impair the unification process (Schmidt 2004). Despite French efforts, it is clear that no credible attempt has been made to engage in European concerted deterrence. Beyond the symbolism of bilateral talks, between the French and the British and between the French and the Germans, no significant dialogue on the nuclear question has taken root since the early 1990s. Finally, European deliberations have not translated into concrete initiatives. Perhaps a truly multilateral framework is more appropriate for undertaking nuclear cooperation.

NATO, Europe, and the US

In the absence of an immediate threat, following the collapse of the Soviet Union, NATO has adapted and renewed its mandate. Although the implications of the new security environment were acknowledged in the 1991 and 1999 versions of the strategic concept, there was no fundamental shift with regards to NATO's nuclear doctrine. In practice, however, this lack of attention to nuclear weapons within the NATO framework is significant. The abandonment of deterrence, in the way it was actively pursued throughout the Cold War, means that nuclear extended deterrence has been downgraded in the rank of NATO priorities. In practice, this became even more apparent, as the Bush administration cancelled its nuclear modernization programs between 1989 and 1991, while American theatre nuclear weapons or forces (TNW/TNFs) were massively withdrawn from Europe.

In this section, we argue that NATO has lost much of its relevance as a credible forum of consultation on the Alliance's nuclear doctrine. Indeed, the Nuclear Planning Group (NPG), NATO's highest-level advisory body on nuclear forces, has progressively been sidelined since the end of the Cold War (Smith 2002). Under the Bush presidency, there was a growing rift between the official position espoused by NATO and the American nuclear posture. The United States then preferred to focus on bilateral relationships to develop the nuclear dimension with its allies. In this respect, France and the UK updated their nuclear doctrine outside the NATO framework, and in a way consistent with the Bush NPR. The NPR produced by the Obama administration in the spring of 2010 is more promising in terms of allied consultation. On the other hand, the United States has been less successful in the alignment of its non-proliferation initiatives, an area where European countries have developed a common framework. To the extent that these initiatives highlight a contradiction between commitments made under the NPT, and NATO's nuclear doctrine, the latter may be further undermined.

NATO under the Nuclear Radar

The 1991 NATO strategic concept stresses continuity in matters related to nuclear forces. Though short, the section on the Alliance's nuclear doctrine enshrines the concept of deterrence, under the guidance of American, French, and British nuclear capabilities. Extended deterrence is also reaffirmed, as nuclear weapons continue to be the symbolic embodiment of transatlantic solidarity. Indeed, the document states that 'nuclear forces based in Europe and committed to NATO provide an essential political and military link between the European and the North American members of the Alliance' (North Atlantic Treaty Organization 1991). By highlighting the remoteness of resorting to the use of nuclear weapons, NATO's 1991 strategic concept translates into minimal deterrent capabilities through the maintenance of American sub-strategic forces in Europe, albeit on a much reduced scale.

As previously mentioned, instead of updating its nuclear policy through NATO, the United States has privileged unilateral moves and bilateral channels with its allies. Will this change under the Obama administration? The Obama administration's NPR and NATO deliberations surrounding the 2010 Strategic Concept are promising in this respect. In contrast, during the Cold War, NATO had established a permanent and institutionalized framework for allied consultation on nuclear weapons policy through the NPG. After introducing its nuclear posture review in January 2002, followed by its unilateral withdrawal from the ABM Treaty later that year, the Bush administration set a new pattern. Quiet bilateral cooperation with the United Kingdom on nuclear weapons policy progressed outside the NATO framework. For example, the two allies tightened their cooperation in matters of stockpile stewardship and renewed their nuclear cooperation agreement, while the UK developed and modernized its nuclear weapons infrastructure (Millar and Ipe 2004). As for France, policymakers have inconsistently leveraged counter-proliferation and non-proliferation approaches to nuclear weapons policy. There is a split between a more robust deterrent, akin to the NPR-inspired *deterrence plus* doctrine, and the maintenance of traditional French deterrence: 'unless the nation's vital interests are endangered, France cannot explicitly threaten nuclear attack to deal with proliferation challenges, yet it cannot afford the conventional capabilities that would allow it to face such challenges on its own and forgo nuclear threats' (Yost 1996: 117).

The Bush National Security Strategy of 2002 further distanced the United States' approach from NATO and the EU. The reassertion of preemption to address threats of WMDs, and the realization of this doctrine in Iraq, contributed to tensions in transatlantic relations. These tensions are passing with the Obama administration's approach to NATO diplomacy. Moreover, and as Bruno Tertrais suggests, European involvement in non-proliferation efforts can contribute to enhancing deterrence and reinforcing the transatlantic link. He mentions specific initiatives to deter Iran's nuclear ambitions, such as closer military cooperation in the region with allied countries, the formulation of a joint UK-France doctrine to strengthen nuclear deterrence, and finally, facilitating diplomatic ties between the United States and the Gulf countries (Tertrais 2006c).

The European Non-Proliferation Agenda

Since non-proliferation efforts benefit from enormous support among both European and American populations, they might represent a model for broader cooperation on the nuclear question (Simons Foundation 2007). While the United States and Europe are aligned in their perception of the threat, namely proliferation concerns in North Korea and Iran over the last decade, they have devised different strategies to achieve this goal and have even been in opposition at times. Under the Bush administration, the United States has demonstrated a certain reluctance towards UN leadership on non-proliferation initiatives and confidence-building measures in the Biological Weapons Convention (BWC), while the EU faces political challenges with regards to the implementation and effective application of sanctions when faced with non-compliance (Allin et al. 2008). EU plans for making commercial agreements conditional upon compliance with non-proliferation agreements, holds promise, as laid out in its recent Strategy against the Proliferation of Weapons of Mass Destruction.

The transatlantic gap in non-proliferation initiatives has been manifest since 9/11, as the United States de-emphasized its commitments to the NPT and the multilateral framework. As suggested in the 2002 NPR, the US government instead opted for counter-proliferation as a way to meet the challenges of proliferation of WMDs. Smith makes a clear distinction between non-proliferation and counter-proliferation:

'Non-proliferation implies a diplomatic and soft power-based approach, based, in nuclear terms, on ensuring maximum respect for and compliance with the NPT and associated agreements. Counter-proliferation ... suggests a willingness to use coercive hard power should softer options be deemed inadequate' (Smith 2004, 538). Following the same logic, European experts agree that the EU should pursue initiatives under the NPT, even in the absence of the United States, perhaps leading to renewed efforts by the EU to draw up its own course of action on non-proliferation (European Union 2003). The new impetus given to non-proliferation efforts under the Obama administration is unlikely to provoke fundamental changes within the NPT.

The EU has been officially engaged in planning a common policy toward Iran. France, Germany, and Great Britain have been leading these negotiations, with a strong public backing going as high as 83 per cent in France (Ottolenghi 2006; Transatlantic Trends 2007). What is interesting about the case of EU non-proliferation efforts is that it represents a key area where the EU is both willing and recognized to be a key player. The EU is supporting the treaty-based approach and committed to strengthening the NPT (Howlett et al. 2005). This broad consensus on nuclear non-proliferation could foster the common ground needed for a debate on the nuclear future of Europe. Still, its NATO commitments could pose a challenge. As previously mentioned, NATO's nuclear legacy, which Europe inherited from the Cold War, stands in contradiction to its current non-proliferation policies. In principle, there are three functions for NATO nukes: (1) to contribute to a credible nuclear deterrence capability of NATO; (2) to provide an essential political and military link between the European and the North American allies and to symbolize nuclear risk sharing within NATO; and (3) to enable the European NATO partners to participate in nuclear consultations and nuclear planning processes with NATO's NPG (Kamp 1999: 300).

But it is the concept of nuclear sharing that poses a problem for commitments made under the NPT. It involves consultations on nuclear policy, along with the storage and maintenance of equipment required for the use and delivery of nuclear weapons. It means that 'the non-nuclear NATO-partners, in effect, become nuclear powers in times of war' (Johnson 1964). Nuclear sharing is against Article One of the NPT, where nuclear states commit 'not to transfer to any recipient whatsoever nuclear weapons or other nuclear explosive devices or control over such weapons or explosive devices directly or indirectly' (United Nations 1968). As a response, there has been particularly strong opposition in

Italy and Germany (Simons Foundation 2007), with calls for the removal of theatre nuclear weapons (TNW) from Europe altogether. However, the Americans might benefit from avoiding this confrontation since TNWs in Europe still act either as a backup insurance against a more aggressive Russia or as bargaining chips for disarmament negotiations (Beste and Szandar 2005). From the European standpoint, TNWs offer a basic level of nuclear reassurance from the United States (Smith 2002).

Another thorny issue concerns the expansion of NATO and whether or not the nuclear umbrella will apply to new member states (Tertrais 1999). A public commitment was made, stating that 'enlarging the Alliance will not require a change in NATO's current nuclear posture and therefore, NATO countries have no intention, no plan and no reason to deploy nuclear weapons on the territory of new members nor any need to change any aspect of NATO's nuclear posture or nuclear policy – and we do not foresee any future need to do so' (North Atlantic Council 1996). It was explicitly recognized that no nuclear weapon storage sites would be built on the territory of new members (Smith 2004). Meanwhile, American plans for a missile defence system in Eastern Europe remain the more controversial issue.

In sum, non-proliferation efforts undertaken by the Europeans are not necessarily aligned with the American position. Recent developments highlight contradictions between the NPT and the post–Cold War nuclear status quo, but specific actions undertaken during the last ten years directly challenge commitments made under the NPT. For example, the unilateral withdrawal of the ABM Treaty, followed by the 2002 NPR, have enhanced the American nuclear position, creating a gap when compared with its allies' commitments to the NPT (Makhijani and Smith 2003). These concerns linger, even if Obama's brand of alliance politics is likely to break that pattern.

Conclusion

The goal of this chapter was twofold: to make sense of European attitudes and policies toward nuclear weapons since the end of the Cold War and to address the theoretical apparatus of deterrence in light of those changes. These areas of inquiry are important mainly because they seem to have fallen below the public radar despite an outdated nuclear weapons policy on the European level and for the transatlantic relationship. From this reflection, we have reached a number of conclusions. First, European attitudes, for both the elite and public, illustrate deep tensions with regards to nuclear weapons, a departure from the elite-driven deterrence stance of the Cold War. Second, the doctrine of deterrence has been re-examined and adapted to the new security realities of the twenty-first century but has not fostered a common approach between nuclear European powers, non-nuclear European powers, and the United States. In the end, deterrence appears overstretched as a common strategy for the transatlantic relationship. Third, European initiatives to draw up a nuclear weapons policy, at the bilateral level or through the EU apparatus, have failed to produce substantial results. Finally, and perhaps of more immediate concern, NATO has been inefficient as the preferred forum for consolidating transatlantic aims. It may prove difficult to reconcile NATO's strategic concept with the non-proliferation ambitions of its members, as professed within the NPT framework.

In the final analysis, is a European position on nuclear issues possible? We have identified the main hurdles that need to be overcome. In the absence of a European consensus and with French efforts leading to a dead end, we are left with the option of a broader European framework. To foster a new nuclear consensus, the role of nuclear weapons may need to be minimized and France should demonstrate that its nuclear approach is complementary to the American guarantee upheld through NATO. It may also be desirable to pursue a harmonization of European policies within the framework of non-proliferation. This would address the presence of theatre nuclear weapons in Europe, which has become the more anachronistic feature of the current nuclear posture.

REFERENCES

Abolition 2000 Europe. 2007. 'Mayors of Aviano and Ghedi Launch Campaign for Italian NWFZ.' 5 October 2007. http://abolition2000europe.org/index.php?op=ViewArticle&articleId=243&blogId=1.
Allin, Dana H., Gilles Andréani, Philippe Errera, and Gary Samore. 2008. 'Chapter Two: Confronting Proliferation.' *Adelphi Papers* 47, no. 389: 35–58.
Anglo-French Summit. 1995. 'British-French Joint Statement on Nuclear Co-operation.' 29–30 October. Quoted in Butcher, Nassauer, and Young (1998).
Bentégeat, Henri. 2004. 'Dissuasion.' *Défense nationale et sécurité collective* 8–9 (août-septembre): 11–17.

Beste, Ralf, and Alexander Szandar. 2005. 'Europe's Atomic Anachronism.' *Spiegel Online International*, 23 May. http://www.spiegel.de/international/spiegel/0,1518,357281,00.html.

Boyer, Yves. 2006. 'L'avenir de la force de dissuasion britannique.' *Défense Nationale et Sécurité Collective* 7 (juillet): 35–45.

Butcher, Martin, Otfried Nassauer, and Stephen Young. 1998. 'Nuclear Futures: Western European Options for Nuclear Risk Reduction.' BASIC/BITS Research Report (December). http://www.basicint.org/pubs/Research/1998nuclearfutures1.htm.

Buteux, Paul. 2000–1. 'Symbol or Substance? The Role of Nuclear Weapons in NATO's Updated Strategic Concept.' *Canadian Military Journal* (Winter): 45–50.

Chirac, Jacques. 1996. 'Discours de M. Jacques Chirac, Président de la République, devant l'Institut des hautes études de défense nationale (IHEDN) sur la réforme de la défense française, la mise en place de l'architecture de défense européenne, la restructuration des industries d'armement et la limitation des armements nucléaires et conventionnels.' Paris, le samedi 8 juin 1996.

Croft, Stuart. 1996. 'European Integration, Nuclear Deterrence and Franco-British Nuclear Cooperation.' *International Affairs* 72, no. 4: 771–87.

Dumoulin, André. 2000. 'L'identité européenne de sécurité et de défense et la dissuasion nucléaire.' *Défense Nationale et Sécurité Collective* 8–9 (août-septembre): 20–37.

European Security and Defence Assembly. 2008. 'European Security Policy, Collective Defence and Nuclear Deterrence.' *Assembly Fact Sheet No. 2* (May). http://www.assembly-weu.org/en/documents/Fact%20sheets/2E_Fact_Sheet_nuclear_deterrence.pdf?PHPSESSID=f3137d60.

European Union, Political and Security Committee. 2003. 'Action Plan for the Implementation of the Basic Principles for an EU Strategy against the Proliferation of Weapons of Mass Destruction.' 13 June. http://www.sipri.org/contents/expcon/eu_wmd_ap.pdf.

Favin-Lévêque, Jacques. 2006. 'Discours de l'Ile Longue: Tournant pour la doctrine de dissuasion nucléaire de la France?' *Défense Nationale et Sécurité Collective* 5 (mai): 5–12.

Fortmann, Michel, and Stefanie von Hlatky. 2009. 'The RMA: Impact of Emerging Technologies on Deterrence.' In *Complex Deterrence: Theory and Practice in a Complex Era*, ed. T.V. Paul, Patrick M. Morgan, and James Wirtz, 304–19. Chicago: University of Chicago Press.

Franco-German Summit. 1996. 'Joint Franco-German Security and Defense Concept.' 9 December. Nuremberg.

French Embassy. 2010. 'Moving Together towards a European Defence Capability.' http://www.ambafrance-uk.org/Defence-cooperation.html.

Howlett, Darryl, John Simpson, Harald Miller, and Burno Tertrais. 2005. 'Effective Non-proliferation. The European Union and the 2005 NPT Review Conference.' *Chaillot Paper 77* (April).

Janning, Josef. 2006. 'L'Allemagne et le renouvellement de la stratégie nucléaire française.' *Défense Nationale et Sécurité Collective* 2 (février): 25–34.

Johnson, Charles E. 1964. 'U.S. Policies on Nuclear Weapons.' Washington, 12 December, Lyndon B. Johnson Library.

Kamp, Karl-Heinz. 1999. 'The Relevance of Nuclear Weapons in NATO.' *Defence and Security Analysis* 15, no. 3: 293–304.

Kristensen, Hans M. 2005. *U.S. Nuclear Weapons in Europe. A Review of Post-Cold War Policy, Force Levels, and War Planning.* Natural Resources Defense Council. February 2005.

– 2007. 'United States Removes Nuclear Weapons from German Base, Documents Indicate.' Federation of American Scientists Security Blog, 9 July. http://www.fas.org/blog/ssp/2007/07/united_states_removes_nuclear.php.

– 2008. 'U.S. Nuclear Weapons Withdrawn from the United Kingdom.' Federation of American Scientists Security Blog, 26 June. http://www.fas.org/blog/ssp/2008/06/us-nuclear-weapons-withdrawn-from-the-united-kingdom.php.

Lake, David A., and Patrick M. Morgan. 1997. 'The New Regionalism in Security Affairs.' In *Regional Orders: Building Security in a New World*, ed. David A. Lake and Patrick M. Morgan, 3–19. University Park, PA: Pennsylvania State University Press.

Makhijani, Arjun, and Brice Smith. 2003. 'Conflit nucléaire au sein de l'OTAN.' *Énergie et Sécurité* 27. http://www.ieer.org/ensec/no-27/no27frnc/nato.html.

Millar, Alistair, and Jason Ipe. 2004. 'Nato's Nuclear Posture: What's Next?' BASIC's NATO E-mail Series, 8 December. http://www.basicint.org/update/NATO041208-PF.htm.

North Atlantic Council. 'Final Communiqué Issued at the Ministerial Meeting of the North Atlantic Council.' Brussels: NATO, 1996. http://www.nato.int/docu/pr/1996/p96-165e.htm.

North Atlantic Treaty Organization. 1991. 'The Alliance's New Strategic Concept.' http://www.nato.int/docu/comm/49-95/c911107a.htm.

Ottolenghi, Emanuele. 2006. 'Not All Is Lost in Europe.' *National Review Online*, 13 February. http://www.nationalreview.com/comment/ottolenghi200602130806.asp.

Schmidt, Peter. 2004. 'La question nucléaire dans les relations franco-allemandes.' *Défense Nationale et Sécurité Collective* 8–9 (août-septembre): 72–83.

Schmidt, Peter, and Stephan De Spiegeleire. 1999. 'The Nuclear Question in a Post-Westphalian Europe.' In *Pondering NATO's Nuclear Options. Gambits for a Post-Westphalian World*, ed. David Haglund, 37–58. Kingston, ON: *Queen's Quarterly*.

Shultz, George, William Perry, Henry Kissinger, and Sam Nunn. 2008. 'Toward a Nuclear-Free World.' *Wall Street Journal*, 15 January, A13.

Simons Foundation. 2007. 'Global Public Opinion on Nuclear Weapons.' Vancouver. http://www.angusreidstrategies.com/uploads/pages/pdfs/Simons%20Report.pdf.

Smith, Julianne. 2006. 'Munich's Security Conference: Déjà Vu or Defining Moment?' *Democracy Arsenal*. http://www.democracyarsenal.org/2006/02/munichs_securit.html.

Smith, Martin A. 2002. 'In a Box in the Corner? NATO's Theatre Nuclear Weapons, 1989–99.' *Journal of Strategic Studies* 25, no. 1 (March): 1–20.

– 2004. 'To Neither Use Them Nor Lose Them: NATO and Nuclear Weapons since the Cold War.' *Contemporary Security Policy* 25, no. 3 (December): 524–44.

Staatsminister Ludger Volmer. 2002. Declaration quoted in Mark Bromley, David Grahame, and Christine Kucia, *Bunker Busters: Washington's Drive for New Nuclear Weapons*. BASIC Research Report (July). http://www.basicint.org/pubs/Research/2002BB.pdf.

Strategic Communications (Stratcom). 2006. 'Nuclear Weapons in Europe: Survey Results in Six European Countries.' 25 May.

Tertrais, Bruno. 1999. 'Nuclear Policies in Europe.' *Adelphi Papers* 327 (March): 1–96.

– 2006a. 'Memorandum from Bruno Tertrais.' Presented to the Select Committee on Defence, United Kingdom Parliament, SND 43, 17 February.

– 2006b. 'Nuclear Proliferation in Europe: Could It Still Happen?' *Nonproliferation Review* 13, no. 3: 569–79.

– 2006c. 'Deterring a Nuclear Iran: What Role for Europe?' *Policy Focus* 72: 16–19.

– 2007. 'The Last to Disarm? The Future of France's Nuclear Weapons.' *Nonproliferation review* 14, no. 2 (July): 264–7.

Transatlantic Trends. 2007. *Key Findings 2007*. http://www.transatlantictrends.org/trends/doc/Transatlantic%20Trends_all_0920.pdf.

United Kingdom. 1995. *Parliamentary Debates*, 16 November, vol. 267, col. 136.

– 2006. *Parliamentary Debates*, 23 January, vol. 441, col. 136.

United Nations. *Treaty on the Non-Proliferation of Nuclear Weapons (NPT)*. New York: 1968. http://disarmament.un.org/wmd/npt/npttext.html.

Western European Union. 1987. 'Platform on European Security Interests.' The Hague, 27 October . http://www.weu.int/documents/871027en.pdf.

– 2007. 'The Future of Nuclear Non-proliferation.' Document A/1982, 3 December. ·

Whitney, Craig R. 1997. 'France and Germany to Discuss Joint Nuclear Deterrent.' *New York Times*, 25 January.

Yost, David S. 1996. 'France's Nuclear Dilemma.' *Foreign Affairs* 75, no. 1 (January/February): 108–18.

5 Energy and Security in the European Union

MAYA JEGEN

The European Union's former Energy Commissioner Andris Piebalgs liked to joke that the best thing that happened to him in his job was Gazprom's restriction of gas deliveries to the Ukraine in early 2006. It led to fears of shortages across the European Union (EU)[1] and brought to mind the vulnerability of energy supply and infrastructures (Crooks 2007). The repetition of this incident in early 2009, which exposed hundreds of thousands of Europeans to fiercely cold weather, illustrates that increased awareness alone did not produce a more securing approach. It would also seem that the problem is not limited to animosity among former Warsaw Pact members: two years before the 2006 events, the International Energy Agency (IEA) had warned against increasing short-term risks to energy security. The Paris-based energy adviser argued that oil and gas supplies would come more and more from fewer countries and, in particular, from politically sensitive areas such as the Middle East members of OPEC (IEA 2004). The soaring oil and gas prices of the new millennium have made energy policy issues salient not only for experts but also for the average citizen. In other words: energy security is high on the political agenda of the twenty-first century.

Some authors even argue that a paradigm shift took place in energy policy around 2000. Rising prices, network failures, and increasing dependence on imports shifted the goals of energy policy away from competition and liberalization towards energy security and climate change (Helm 2005). Others argue that 'energy security had been displaced as a matter of international debate and policymaking by such issues as energy efficiency, deregulation, and climate change,' but that energy security is back on the agenda today (Barton et al. 2004: 4). Thus, energy security is an old 'new issue.' This chapter addresses energy security from a conceptual angle, analysing whether the move from a planned monopolized energy system to liberalized markets impact on energy security and whether environmental, national, and supranational issues reframe the concept. The question I ask is whether we can observe a genuine paradigm shift in the way energy security is conceptualized in Europe.

To answer this question, I will argue that three external developments have altered the meaning of energy security in Europe. The first development is the success of the EU's Single Market Program in the 1980s. European integration through market liberalization provided a template for the European Commission to justify its intervention into a domain, energy policy, where it has a rather weak treaty competence. This strategy was fairly successful for the liberalization of electricity markets, and the Commission has tried in recent years to apply it to energy security as well. The present challenge, however, is to move from what Scharpf (1999) calls 'negative integration' to 'positive integration,' namely the creation of new European rules regarding the functioning of these markets in order to allow for greater investment in infrastructure, providing sufficient reserves, and so forth. This is what I call the economic attribute of energy security.

The second development was the rise of environmental concerns – especially but not exclusively climate change – and their gradual 'securitization.' Climate change in particular is increasingly portrayed as an energy-related threat. The association of environmental issues with energy security entails a shift of focus from a concern with increasing *supply* (to meet the growing demand) to the challenge of managing *demand*. This is the environmental attribute of energy security.

The third and last development is related to the external relations of the EU with producer countries. Of special concern in this regard is the perception of Russia as an emergent energy superpower: its abundant gas reserves have replaced Middle East oil as the key 'threat' to the security of energy supplies for Europe. Deteriorating relations between Russia and its former USSR satellites – some of them now Member States of the EU – have resulted in a politicization of energy security (political attribute).

The chapter starts with an outline of the general evolution of energy policy in the EU to contextualize the notions of energy security and paradigm shift. After these conceptual clarifications, I will delineate the concept of energy security as it has been used by the Commission over the last forty years; this description is based on official documents of the Commission such as directives, communications, and Green and White Papers.

Energy Policy Shifts

The notion of paradigm has been used as an epistemological concept since the eighteenth century to describe scientific ways of thinking. With Thomas Kuhn's publication of *The Structure of Scientific Revolutions* in 1962 the concept entered language beyond epistemology. For Kuhn, science does not progress evenly, but passes through 'normal' and 'revolutionary' stages. Normal science is described as 'puzzle-solving' (Kuhn 1970: 35–42), where the paradigm guides scientific research by proposing theoretical and methodological propositions. Therefore, the scientific community works on familiar puzzles and their solutions and contributes to the cumulative knowledge within normal science; meanwhile it tends to neglect research that might challenge the dominant paradigm. By contrast, the scientific revolution brings qualitative and quantitative change by revising scientific belief or practice and reverting the existent paradigm (Kuhn 1970: 92). The notion of paradigm is closely associated with the existence of a given scientific community. However, the suggestive and equivocal use of the concept has provoked criticism and Kuhn added specifications in later writings and, eventually, talked about 'disciplinary matrix' or 'exemplars' (Kuhn 1992: 390 ff.).

Dieter Helm takes up the analogy to Kuhn's scientific revolution with regard to the field of energy policy. He argues that a paradigm shift occurred around the turn of the millennium when the energy policy debate shifted from issues of liberalization and deregulation to issues of energy security and climate change. Besides, and for historical reasons, 'energy industries are entering into a major investment phase, both to replace existing assets and to meet new demands. This investment is occurring at a time when there has been an exogenous shock to energy prices (encouraged by the endogenous consequences of low investment and asset-sweating in the last two decades)' (Helm 2005: 14). For Helm, paradigm shifts in the policy domain bring about new objectives and new policy instruments, implying a change of ideas.

From the Second World War to the late 1970s regional and national monopolies structured energy markets. Electric utilities considered fulfilling the demand as their main task and never questioned the growing demand, which was meant to epitomize economic upswing. Fulfilling the demand stood as well for guaranteeing the security of supply. Monopolies did not aim at maximizing profits, but at increasing their sales on new markets (Jegen 2001). This self-conception of electric utilities was widely shared by politicians and the public. Hirsh (1999) argues that there was an implicit 'utility consensus' – a kind of paradigm – between electric utilities, the state, and the public: electric utilities were recognized as natural monopolies that gave them the opportunity to sell electricity without competition. In return, they committed themselves to stable rates (ensured by monopoly profits) and public service, including security of supply. Following Hirsh, electric utilities gained considerable political and economic clout due to this utility consensus. They sought to restrain external influence and enlarge their control ('closure of the system'), pursuing a conservative technological renewal policy.

Political elites backed the utility consensus not only by adhering to technological choices, but also by sharing the belief in progress. Economic growth was equated with increasing electricity production: viewed from this growth-based ideology, increasing energy consumption was positively valued. As long as the public approved this equation of economic growth and increasing energy consumption, the discretionary power of electric utilities was not challenged: 'Just as the doctrine of the divine right of kings established a moral basis for governance by monarchies in the Middle Age, the ideology of growth provided the justification for utility managers to control an important infrastructural element of modern society' (Hirsh 1999: 50–1). The grow-and-build strategy of electric utilities was an integral part of this growth-based ideology, responding to the growth forecast with the extension of their production capacity. More efficient technologies led to lower costs of production, bringing about lower electricity rates, which in turn increased the demand and entailed a downswing of costs and rates (Hirsh 1999: 46). There was no incentive in this system for energy efficiency.

In the 1980s and 1990s, states began to back out of this utility consensus and moved toward more competitive energy markets. Taking off with the liberalization and deregulation[2] of publicly owned electric utilities in England and Wales under the Thatcher government, network industries have since been reformed worldwide. Several factors drove this restructuring process: changes in generation technology and fuel prices made it profitable to generate with smaller units, and the integration of separate utility systems into larger regional networks increased the size of the market. Some authors concluded from these changes that government regulation was no more required for electricity markets than for other commodities (Borenstein and Bushnell 2000: 48). Whereas electric utilities fixed quantities and rates within the traditional utility consensus, markets established these entities within the market approach: 'planners concentrated on quantity first, ensuring security of supply (which was the primary objective of energy policy). The resulting cost determined the prices, moderated from time to time by explicit and implicit state subsidies ... The market approach assumed that competition between generators and suppliers would ensure sufficient supply, but at whatever price emerged from the competitive process' (Helm 2005: 7). It was assumed that prices would be lower because the private sector would be more efficient than the electric utility consensus model. According to Helm, the historical context endorsed this reasoning: quantity was not a problem because of excess capacities in electricity and oil markets and the attention focused on reducing operation costs. Excess capacity helped as well to envisage cheap energy as the objective of market liberalization without putting at risk the security of supply.

Around the millennium the historical context of excess capacities and relatively low fossil fuel prices changed and put pressure on the liberalized or partly liberalized markets, in particular on electricity markets. As Borenstein and Bushnell (2000: 49) explain: 'The combination of very inelastic short-run demand and supply (at peak times) with the real-time nature of the market (costly storage and grid reliability requirements) makes electricity markets especially vulnerable to the exercise of market power.' It became obvious that the deregulation of electricity markets carried some risk. If deregulation neglects the issue of market power, it can undermine the objectives of industry restructuring and produce a regulatory backlash. Thus, Borenstein and Bushnell (2000: 52) conclude that 'any restructuring initiative must recognize that the lack of economic storage and of price-responsive demand can produce serious market disruptions. Furthermore, levels of transmission capacity that may have been adequate under regulation may not be able to support effective competition. In restructured electricity markets, some level of market power seems likely to persist.' As a consequence, most countries responded with some kind of regulatory measures to avoid market power, but also to ensure energy supply.

In sum, there have been important market-related shifts in energy policy during the last forty years: a move from a planned production model that was controlled by regional and national monopolies toward transnational liberalized markets, often leading to private oligopolies, and finally to some kind of reregulation in order to keep up with market failures and obligations of energy security. These shifts brought along new policy ideas or priorities as well as new actors. Energy security is a long-standing issue of energy policy, but the question is if and to what extent its meaning has changed in the course of these energy policy shifts. The next section will examine the evolution of the concept over the last forty years, focusing primarily on the discourse of the European Commission. Thus, I put the emphasis on the narrative of an institutional actor whereas the narrative is understood as a way of ordering and constructing shared meaning and organizational reality. A narrative can 'create a collective centering that informs policy actors' choices about what to do and, by providing a "plot," can help define operational solutions' (Hajer and Laws 2008: 260). To introduce this section, I will begin with some general definitions of energy security.

Defining Energy Security

There is no shortage of definitions of energy security in the literature, but most references contain the basic elements mentioned by Barton and his co-authors (2004: 5): 'We define energy security as a condition in which a nation and all, or most, of its citizens and businesses have access to sufficient energy resources at reasonable prices for the foreseeable future free from serious risk of major disruption of service.' A first element is the *sufficiency* of the resources, whereas the plural of resource may imply a *diversification* of sources. A second element refers to the *price* that should be 'reasonable.' Energy *in*security can therefore be understood as the loss of welfare that may occur as a result of a change in available energy or its price (Bohi and Toman 1996). A third element alludes to the notion of *public service* ('most of its citizens and businesses have access'). Finally, there is often a reference to *time*, that is, a distinction between short-term and long-term security of supply.

Some authors seek to specify the *nature of risk*, often in association with geopolitical considerations:

> Energy security has three faces. The first involves limiting vulnerability to disruption given rising dependence on imported oil from an unstable Middle East. The second, broader face is, over time, the provision of adequate supply for rising demand at reasonable prices – in effect, the reasonably smooth functioning over time of the international energy system. The third face of energy security is the energy related environmental challenge. The international energy system needs to operate within the constraints of 'sustainable development' – constraints which, however uncertain and long-term, have gained considerable salience in the energy policy debates in our countries. (Martin, Imai, and Steeg 1998: 4)

In their definition, Martin, Imai, and Steeg explicitly address *sustainable development* – a term that entered the discourses of national and international politics from the late 1980s on and attempts to reconcile economic progress with an environmentally and socially sound development.[3]

In sum, the origins of energy insecurity are diverse, and, as a consequence, policy responses tend to be diverse, too. The perception of major causes changes over time and within a specific policy context. The focus of policy responses may be recapitulated as follows (IEA 2007: 33–4):

- policies may address disruptions of energy supply due to extreme climate conditions or accidents (e.g. the impact of Hurricane Katrina on the energy system) by, for example, releasing oil stocks;
- policies may address the short-term balancing of demand and supply in electricity markets by, for example, creating independent Transmission System Operators (TSOs);
- policies may address regulatory failures;
- policies may address the problem of the concentration of fossil fuel resources by, for example, reducing the exposure to a resource concentration risk.

As the perception of energy security changes over time and according to the context, energy security issues are mostly politicized, that is, they are 'part of public policy, requiring government decision and resource allocation or, more rarely, some other form of communal governance.' Once in a while, however, energy security issues may be securitized, requiring emergency action beyond the state's standard political procedures. Securitization is thus a more extreme form of politicization (Buzan et al. 1998: 23).

Starting from these elements of definition, I will turn now to the use of the energy security concept in the European Union.

Energy Security in the European Union

1970s–1980s: About Oil and Cooperation

Although the energy security objective was at the core of the Paris (1951) and Rome (1957) treaties, the relative neutralization of the European Coal and Steel Community and the European Atomic Energy Community meant that, from the late 1960s on, the EU became mainly concerned with the security of *oil* supply. Hence, the Council of Ministers adopted a Directive (68/414/EEC) in 1968 asking its Member States to maintain minimum stocks of crude oil and/or petroleum products equating to 65 days of consumption. The justification of the directive was the protection of economic activity from supply reduction and interruption. With the amendment of the directive in 1972, the quantity of the strategic reserve was raised from 65 to 90 days (Directive 72/425/EEC). This modification reflected a concern about growing imports by and dependency of the Member States. Another amendment followed the oil crisis of 1973 obliging Member States to maintain minimum stocks of fossil fuel at thermal power stations; that is, electricity producers were to be able to assure the continuation of electricity supplies for a period of at least 30 days (Directive 75/339/EEC). Besides minimum quantities to maintain, the EU decided as well on measures, including drawing on oil stock (Directive 73/238/EEC).

The oil price shock led to increased intergovernmental cooperation – both among consumers and among consumers and producers – to ensure energy security. One of the consequences of this cooperation was the creation of the International Energy Agency (IEA) after the 1974 Washington Conference. During the negotiations, concerned with overall energy security and with oil supply security in particular, the European Community sought 'the best form of dialogue to avoid any confrontation between oil-consuming and energy-producing countries' (European Communities 1986: 19). The final Agreement included specific chapters on an emergency sharing system, but it also asked Member States for an overall reduction in 'dependence on imported oil by undertaking long-term cooperative efforts on conservation of energy, on accelerated development in the energy field and uranium enrichment' (Scott 1994: 48). In other words: the oil price shock may be understood as a moment of securitization of the energy issue that gave way to several institutional measures. The lesson learned from the oil crises was that energy security depended on all available energy sources, the availability of alternative sources such as coal and nuclear, environmental considerations, and investments in energy R&D (Scott 1994: 38). This lesson has since been politicized and is part of energy policy discourses.

In the 1980s, Europe managed to decrease temporarily its dependence on OPEC oil and energy security was increasingly framed in the context of finding new energy sources and their geographical diversification (European Communities 1988). At the end of the decade, the report of the Groupe des Sages indicated that imports were expected to increase and that 'the availability of these supplies at secure and moderate prices remains an important consideration for the Community'; they concluded that 'Energy security will remain a major concern. The issues mentioned reflect the interaction between global developments and changes in the Community with the implementation of the internal market and environmental policies' (European Communities 1990). Thus, during the 1970s and 1980s, energy security meant mainly reducing the level of oil imports and managing risks with regard to unstable producing countries. In other words: energy was politicized rather than securitized. It is interesting to note that the Groupe des Sages does refer to environmental issues, but not as an integrated part of energy security.

1990s–2000s: Restructuring Energy Markets in a New Geopolitical Context

As already announced by the Groupe des Sages, the 1990s brought about an energy policy shift that was reflected in the concept of energy security: the focus turned away from monopoly-controlled supply to the opening of electricity markets; moreover, oil supply was not the primary concern any more. It mirrored another historical change: the fall of the Berlin Wall altered the relationship of the EU with the members of the former USSR and put the Energy Charter firmly on the political agenda.

A political declaration of principles for international energy cooperation, 'based on a shared interest in secure energy supply and sustainable economic development,' was signed in 1991. The intent of the Energy Charter was to integrate the energy sector of the former USSR into European and world markets. A legally binding treaty followed the political declaration in 1994 and became effective in 1998. The treaty sought to establish common rules to encourage investment and trade, to ensure reliable cross-boarder energy transit, and to promote energy efficiency (Energy Charter Secretariat 2004). The concept of energy security was seen in the context of market integration and restructuring where stable conditions for investments were crucial.

This context was exemplified by the Treaty on European Union, which set a number of objectives for the general policy framework of the EU, including energy policy, and which affected the elaboration of the *Green Paper for a European Union Energy Policy* published in 1995 and the *White Paper on an Energy Policy for the European Union* published in

1996. Thus, the Green Paper insisted on the importance of promoting economic and social progress via an internal competitive market, where 'the availability of energy at the best price and under the best conditions governs this economic progress and strengthens the overall competitiveness of the Community.' Moreover, it emphasized the incorporation of the environmental dimension into other policies as well as the 'growing stature of the Community on the international scene, in particular through the implementation of a common foreign and security policy' (European Commission 1995: 17).

The Green Paper defines security of supply as 'ensuring that future essential energy needs are satisfied by means of a sharing of internal energy resources and strategic reserves under acceptable economic conditions and by making use of diversified and stable, externally accessible sources.' The concept covers physical security and economic security as well as the continuity of supply. In addition, the Green Paper takes up the distinction between short-term and long-term supply. The former refers to the capacity to avoid supply interruptions to users caused by exceptional circumstances, primarily with regard to oil and gas resources. The latter affects the energy industry's capacity to guarantee a reliable and economic supply of sufficient energy in the long term. Interestingly, the Green Paper highlights that 'the definition of security of supply differs depending on the circumstances' (European Commission 1995: 24).[4]

This means that available quantities and risks vary with each resource. For example, coal is a negligible security issue in the sense that there are large reserves and diverse and reliable suppliers, most of them members of the OECD. In contrast, import dependence on oil is high and there is a perceived strategic necessity for long-term contracts between consumption, production, and transit countries as a means of limiting negative impacts. In this context, energy security refers also to the conditions of investment to secure exploration, production, and transportation outside the European borders. Considering gas supplies, security of supply is supposed to be ensured by an open competitive market (European Commission 1995: 25–7).

The freer movement of energy goods necessitates, according to the authors of the Green Paper, a Community approach with regard to energy security that is based on the instruments of the treaty. Such an approach should benefit both companies and Member States of the EU: the companies' interest is in the market dimension necessary for investments; the members' interests may be in complementarity with domestic resources and policies (European Commission 1995: 24). In short, the Green Paper considers the integration of the Community's energy market as an instrument of energy security in itself: once the rules have been established (contracts, conditions for investment), the market contributes to energy security.

The *White Paper on an Energy Policy for the European Union* is a revision of the Green Paper, incorporating a number of critics: the EU Council focusing on a rapidly integrating common market looks for diversification, supply flexibility, and energy efficiency to enhance energy security. Furthermore, it asks for an integrated view of environmental and energy policies. The European Parliament, for its part, speaks up for liberalization, too, but emphasizes public service and the protection of the environment. Thus, the White Paper stipulates three main energy policy objectives: global competitiveness, security of supply, and protection of the environment (European Commission 1996: 9–10). As the former head of the General Energy Policy Division Christian Waterloos states, these objectives have to be pursued by a market economy approach where the EU has four priorities (1995: 56–7):

- facilitating the proper functioning of the internal energy market;
- intensifying dialogue and cooperation with EU's partners (Eastern Europe, the Mediterranean, the Gulf; OECD/IEA; WTO);
- promoting activities with regard to a better environmental protection;
- strengthening solidarity within the Community and creating the means to face disruption of supplies.

A ranking of these priorities is, however, implicit: 'environmental goals should be achieved through measures that do not impact on industrial competitiveness and integrated energy and environmental technologies should be preferred to add-on ones' (European Commission 1996: 19). In other words, the competitive market approach dominates the discourse, but the Commission seeks to subsume the environmental dimension as well as to add the notions of solidarity and external relations.

The salience of the market issue in the Green and White Papers should come as no surprise: the proposals came forward within the context of an assertive, across-the-board market-based strategy on the part of the Commission. After ten years of controversial debates, the EU adopted Directive 96/92/EC,[5] initiating the gradual liberalization of the electricity market. The internal energy market created third-party access (at a certain level) to electricity networks and broke down monopolies with regard to the construction of power lines and power stations. The creation of this internal energy market was a clear shift away from the energy policies of the Member States towards a European energy policy (Eising and Jabko 2001: 745).[6] The Commission thus used both environmental and econcomic arguments to politicize energy issues.

2000s: Consolidating Internal Energy Markets and a Common (Foreign) Energy Policy

Around the turn of the millennium the Commission elaborated on the security aspect of its energy policy: *The Green Paper Towards a European Strategy for the Security of Energy Supply* drew on the context of growing energy consumption and structural weaknesses of energy supply in the EU as well as on rising oil prices to outline the need for an active European energy policy. It emphasized that achieving security of supply should not be aimed primarily at maximizing energy self-sufficiency or minimizing dependence on imports but more at reducing the attendant risks and hence striving to achieve balance and diversification in relation to the different sources of supply (by products and by geographical zones) (European Commission 2000: 2).

Within the context of climate change caused by a rising energy demand, the Commission pointed out that the growing energy demand carried a major risk for the security of supply and concluded that a long-term energy strategy needs to prioritize demand management. Five aspects for this demand side management are outlined: reducing consumption by a change in consumer behaviour, developing an alternative transport policy, investing in new and renewable energies, maintaining a degree of self-sufficiency, and finding common solutions for common problems.

Besides the emphasis on demand, the Commission made clear that energy policy is a Community issue (the interdependence of member states with regard to internal market and to combating climate change) and that the lack of political consensus on a Community energy policy limits the scope of action. Thus, it launched the debate about the potential extension of Community powers with regard to energy issues (European Commission 2000).

Following a wide consultation of stakeholders on the 2000 Green Paper, the Commission reiterated its insistence on a Community approach to energy security:

The debate on the Green Paper has shown the need to develop a Europe-wide security of supply concept which alone will enable Europe to control its energy future. As recently emerged from the Paris, Brussels and very recently Moscow summits, the dialogue the EU is entering into with Russia aims to create a new energy partnership. Projects have been launched on network security, protection of investments or identification of major projects of interest. Hopefully, this dialogue will make it possible to determine the best future use of long-term supply agreements and pro-duction sharing agreements, on which the representatives of industry ex-pressed some major concerns in the Green paper debate. (European Commission 2002)

The Commission points out that the EU has made progress with regard to securing supply by using instruments such as the approximation of laws to implement the internal energy market, the implementation of the internal energy market, environmental protection laws to promote renewable energy, or the chapter on trans-European networks to de-velop gas and electricity networks. But it emphasizes that 'at the very time when the European Union has the world's most integrated energy market, it is necessary to reinforce the co-ordination of the measures ensuring security of supply' (European Commission 2002).

Ten years after the publication of the energy policy White Paper, the Commission released another Green Paper entitled *A European Strategy for Sustainable, Competitive and Secure Energy*. In continuity with the 2000 Green Paper on energy security, it outlines the context of 'a new energy era' characterized by an urgent need for investments in infrastructure, a rising import dependency, increasing global demand, concentration of reserves, soaring oil and gas prices, a need for completion of competitive internal energy markets, and climate change (European Commission 2006).

As the title indicates, sustainable development, competitiveness, and security of energy supply had become equal energy policy objectives that had to be balanced. First, sustainability aims primarily at combat-ing climate change by the promotion of renewable energy and energy efficiency; second, the competitiveness goal comprises the upgrading of the European energy grid by the completion of the internal energy market; and, third, an improved coordination of the EU's energy sup-ply and demand within an international context is required (European Commission 2006).

More specifically, the objective of security of supply aims at tackling the EU's rising dependence on imported energy through an integrated approach – reducing demand, diversifying the EU's energy mix with greater use of competitive indigenous and renewable energy, and diversifying sources and routes of supply of imported energy, creating the framework which will stimulate adequate investments to meet growing energy demand, better equipping the EU to cope with emergencies, improving the conditions for European companies seeking access to global resources, and making sure that all citizens and business have access to energy. (European Commission 2006: 18)

The Commission calls attention to the need for solidarity among Member States to avoid energy supply crises as well as for effective mechanisms to create emergency stocks. In conformity with the 1995 Green Paper, it reiterates the importance of open markets as 'one way of guaranteeing a secure energy supply because it creates the stable, competitive environment in which companies invest.'

Among other things, the Commission proposes the creation of a European Energy Supply Observatory to monitor energy demand and supply at the EU level, thus complementing the activities of the International Energy Agency. Another institutional proposition is a more formal grouping of transmission system operators – which may evolve in a European Centre for Energy Networks – to increase network security (European Commission 2006: 8).

At the heart of these objectives and proposed institutional innovations is the Commission's concern for a common energy policy to regroup the domestic energy policies of its Member States. To ensure the security of supply, the Commission believes in the need for an international dialogue with producer countries. A condition for successful dialogue is however a common position with regard to the energy mix, new infrastructures, and partnerships with third countries. Being endowed with an external energy policy is seen as a key element to guarantee energy security, especially in a context where energy is high on the international agenda with regard to climate change and sustainable development (European Commission 2006: 14–16). Here the Commission is definitely trying to securitize energy issues by advocating the need for new procedures which go beyond the standard procedures.

Member States replied to the Commission's Green Paper at the 2006 Spring European Council and, in particular, agreed to establish a regular EU Strategic Energy Review; the Commission published the first one in 2007. As a follow-up, the 2007 Spring European Council agreed on the

EU's energy priorities set out in the European Action Plan. The Action Plan takes up the three objectives of the 2006 Green Paper: sustainability, competitiveness, and energy security. A second Strategic Energy Review was published in 2008 and focuses on security of supply and external aspects of EU's energy policy (European Commission 2008a).

In its second review, the Commission got back to its 2006 Green Paper proposals and presented an EU Energy Security and Solidarity Action Plan to secure sustainable energy supplies and to prevent energy crisis within the EU. Again the emphasis was on the need to support infrastructure projects, on the better use of indigenous energy resources, or on more solidarity through EU crisis mechanisms. Again it was highlighted that stronger coordination among Member States and with the Commission is required with regard to the EU's international relations (European Commission 2008a).

Finally, the three objectives – sustainability, competitiveness, and energy security – were also at the heart of the Green Paper *Towards a Secure, Sustainable and Competitive European Energy Network*, which was released for consultation in November 2008 (European Commission 2008b). The Green Paper details aspects with regard to infrastructure put forth in previous papers and underlines the Commission's concern that Europe's energy networks will no longer guarantee energy security in the future. If the EU is to meet the energy and climate objectives that it agreed on in 2007, new and modernized energy networks are needed. In this respect the 2008 Green Paper identifies several key projects (Baltic Interconnection Plan, North Sea offshore grid for wind energy, Mediterranean energy network, Southern Corridor for Caspian gas, etc.)

Discussion

Our overview of European discussions around energy security suggests that the notion of energy security has been ubiquitous since the late 1960s, but that it has been substantially reframed as a consequence of three external developments: the internal energy market as an economic attribute, the emergence of the climate change debate as an environmental attribute, and the search for a common European policy as a political attribute. These developments emerged in parallel to energy issues but were gradually integrated into the Commission's framing of energy security. They now give a specific content to the notion of energy security that is markedly different from the one that prevailed in the 1970s, when the security of oil supplies from Middle Eastern countries dominated the agenda. Each development has a potential for securitization, but most of the time they contribute to the politicization of energy issues.

The Economic Attribute

Starting with the 1995 Green Paper, the Commission began to define energy security as a matter of sharing internal energy resources. This new framing paralleled the Commission's push to open up first electricity and later gas markets. Its rationale was that the opening of markets and the creation of pan-regional grids helped secure supplies in case of a local disruption, but also lead to more investment in infrastructure. The consolidation of a liberalization policy at the European level ('completing the internal energy market') is promoted as a remedy to the failings of domestic approaches, which have resulted in underinvestment, higher prices, and public service concerns.

One reason behind the 'security through markets' logic might be the Commission's firmer legal grounds when it deals with the free circulation of goods and services than when it deals with energy policy, where its treaty competence is weak. This economic narrative is therefore embedded in an established institutional frame. In my opinion, another reason is related to the proclaimed success of the Single Market Program. The late 1980s saw unprecedented Commission activism under Jacques Delors, who launched a flurry of Community legislation with regard to the completion of the internal market for goods, services, capital, and persons. The Single Market Program brought together free-market liberals and social democrats around a common assumption, namely that the growth of trade should force the creation of European social and environmental rules. This golden age of European integration served as a template for energy policymakers because it showed a way in which market-based strategies could enhance the power of the Commission (Jabko 2006, Fligstein 2008).

Hence, from the mid-nineties on, the liberalization of energy markets became one of the pillars of the energy security discourse. But as Scharpf (1999) argues, the problem is that negative integration – market making and deregulation – does not automatically lead to positive integration – market correcting and reregulation. It is interesting to note that, in the past few years, the Commission has put forward notions such as *solidarity* and *common solutions*, for example in the 2006 Green

Paper: 'With respect to the physical security of infrastructure, two main
actions merit further consideration. Firstly, a mechanism could be developed to prepare for and ensure rapid solidarity and possible assistance to a country facing difficulties following damage to its essential
infrastructure. Secondly, common standards or measures might be tak-
en to protect infrastructure' (European Commission 2006: 9). The 2006
Green Paper also mentions a new legislative proposal concerning gas
stocks to 'ensure solidarity between Member States' (9). These examples illustrate the way in which the Commission attempts – alternating
between politicizing and securitizing discourses – to create European
rules and capabilities to strengthen European energy markets. One can
speculate whether this new emphasis on solidarity and common solutions suggests that market liberalization has reached its limit as the key
economic attribute of energy security.

The Environmental Attribute

The second development was the inclusion of an environmental dimension in the energy security agenda. The environment has been on
the political agenda of industrialized countries since the early 1970s. It
became a Community competence in the 1986 Single European Act.
Since then the EU has generated an increasing body of legislation and
programs, making of environmental policy one of the EU's unexpected
success stories (McCormick 2001). However, although the environment
was mentioned occasionally in official energy policy publications in the
1970s and increasingly in the 1980s, it was rarely explicitly associated to
energy *security*.

A change occurred in the late 1990s with the 'securitization' of environmental issues (Litfin 1999, Krause and Williams 1996). In particular the
debate on climate change increasingly grabbed the attention of decision
makers and the broader public. The EU took its first climate-related initiative in 1991, but launched the first European Climate Change Programme
(ECCP) in 2000, followed by ECCP II in 2005. The EU also played a leading role in the negotiations for the United Nations Framework on Climate
Change (1992) as well as the Kyoto Protocol (1997) (Schreurs, Selin, and
VanDeever 2009: 174–7). The securitization of the environmental issue –
or sustainable development as it has been called at least since the Earth
Summit in Rio in 1992 – within the energy security debate has been facilitated by the climate change issue: the sense of emergency and risk has
been progressively reinforced by scientific evidence and the fact that its

main causes are related to energy production and consumption (IPCC 2008). As in the case of the economic attribute, the Commission can fall back on an established institutional frame.

Juxtaposing environmental issues with energy security entails a relative shift of focus away from the concern with increasing supplies towards a better management of the demand, as the 2000 Green Paper *Towards a European Strategy for the Security of Energy Supply* illustrates. The traditional utility consensus, in which supply is supposed to adapt to unlimited demand and is ensured by the regional monopolies, is replaced by a series of objectives, which are more and more formulated on the EU level, to reduce demand (for example, energy performance of buildings: directive 2002/91/EC; eco-design requirements for energy-using products: directive 2005/32/EC). This demand management is presented as a means to simultaneously enhance energy security and combat climate change. But even the perception of what supplies are is altered, with a new emphasis on domestic alternative sources (for example, promotion for renewable energy sources: directive 2001/77/EC; biofuels for transport: directive 2003/30/EC) rather than external conventional sources (oil and gas).

The Political Attribute

Like market liberalization, adding an environmental attribute to energy security has the advantage of giving the European Commission a stronger treaty basis to intervene in domestic affairs. Unlike the economic and environmental developments, however, the third development occurred in an area where the Commission has weak legal competence, that is, the domain of external relations. There is no institutional frame here to rely on. Having already proclaimed it in previous Green Papers and Communications, the Commission is very explicit in the Energy Security and Solidarity Action Plan and the Green Paper about the need for a common energy policy and a single voice when it comes to external relations. The subtext of these proposals, which include 'crisis mechanisms' and new supply networks, is the perceived threat Russia poses to European gas supplies.

The framing of Russia as a key source of energy insecurity has had the effect of highlighting the energy security issue for governments and the broader public. Over the past few years, the energy security issue has increasingly been politicized through the prism of the 'Russian energy superpower' and its attendant risks for Europe.

Although Moscow's assertiveness is undoubtedly an important factor in this process, the Eastern enlargement has also transformed the energy security equation in Europe. Like some Western European countries, these newcomers are heavily dependent on Russian gas. But, for historical reasons, they take a much more intransigent position towards Russia's display of power. Now that they are members of the EU, Eastern countries force the EU to take a clearer stance vis-à-vis Russia. As a result of deteriorating EU-Russia relations, energy security has become one of the most visible topics in European debates, with the Commission arguing along with a number of Member States that a common external policy vis-à-vis Moscow is needed to ensure the security of supplies. In other words, only a supranational response can help the Europeans face the challenge of Russia's resurgent power. This is a new political attribute for energy security that is markedly different from the Middle East worries of the 1970s, which were then used as the major reason for developing a common foreign policy for Europe.

Conclusion: A Paradigm Shift?

The outline of the Commission's discourse as found in the Green and White Papers as well as in different Communications shows that priorities within energy policy, and therewith the understanding of energy security, have changed over time. I have tried to demonstrate that three external developments reframed energy security: the liberalization became an instrument for securing supplies in and of itself (economic attribute); the climate change issue was integrated as an environmental attribute of energy security; and new perceived threats, especially Russia, politicized the issue. But is there a true shift in the European energy policy? Does, for example, the move from a planned monopolized energy system to liberalized markets really impact on energy security?

In analogy with Kuhn's theory, Helm (2005) argues that a paradigm shift took place around the turn of the millennium: the energy policy debate shifted from liberalization and deregulation issues to energy security and climate change. In line with Helm's argument I tried to show that environmental and political attributes have been added to the energy policy debate, but, unlike Helm, I argued that energy security has been a constant energy policy item over the last forty years and, moreover, that issues of liberalization and deregulation remain relevant today. Rather than a paradigm shift, I would argue that an integration and reframing of different issues occurred, with a view that European energy policies and networks become 'secure, competitive and sustainable' at the same time.

For Helm, paradigm shifts in a policy domain imply new ideas and bring about new objectives and new policy instruments. My argument converges with his in this respect. The gradual liberalization of energy markets broke down the traditional electric consensus (Hirsh 1999), where the main objective of electric utilities – and, in association, of governments that backed the monopolies – was to meet the ever-growing demand. These objectives have shifted to more demand management in order to guarantee energy security. Because there is no implicit electricity consensus anymore and because no monopoly guarantees energy security anymore, there is a call for solidarity among different sectoral and national players. The fact that no monopolies are in direct command over technology choices any longer may also give another meaning to the diversification of supplies, especially with regard to renewable sources. Finally, it is interesting to note that there are also new actors within the energy policy domain, whether as a consequence of the liberalization of energy markets that increases the number of economic actors, or as a consequence of the enlargement of the EU and the environmental concerns which added political actors.

In sum, it remains ambiguous whether a genuine paradigm shift took place. What is certain is that energy security is an expansive concept that evolves over time. As the IEA recapitulates: 'In the 1970s and 1980s, the term meant reducing the level of oil imports and managing the risks associated with those imports still required. Today, the term includes other types of energy, and risks such as accidents, terrorism, under-investment in infrastructure and poorly designed markets, all of which might curtail adequate supplies of energy at affordable prices. Energy security does not stop at national borders, but goes all the way to the final consumer' (IEA 2002).

NOTES

1 The term 'European Union' (EU) replaced 'European Community' only in 1993; I will use EU throughout the text for ease of reading.
2 Liberalization is understood as the creation of conditions of competition in a given market, whereas deregulation refers to the reduction and abrogation of rules of the state (Vogel 1996).

3 The Brundtland Report, which elaborated on the notion of sustainable development, was published in 1987 and became the main reference on the international level.
4 The 1995 Green Paper thus takes up the major definitional elements quoted
   in the literature.
5 The directive 2009/72/EC abrogates the directive 96/92/EC and its follow-
   er directive 2003/54/EC. The first directive for the liberalization of the gas
   market was issued in 1998 (98/30/EC), replaced by the directive 2003/55/
   EC in 2003 and by the directive 2009/73/EC.
6 Eising and Jabko (2001: 746) point out that this shift was not 'a foregone
   conclusion at the outset in the energy sector. When the European Commission introduced a working paper on the IEM in 1988, it only set the relatively modest goal of achieving price transparency and freer transit of
   electricity across borders. In fact, the prospect of a European energy policy
   had initially appeared so utopian that the electricity sector was simply not
   mentioned in the original 1985 White Paper on the Internal Market.'

REFERENCES

Barton, Barry, et al., eds. 2004. *Energy Security. Managing Risk in a Dynamic Legal
    and Regulatory Environment*. Oxford: Oxford University Press.
Bohi, Douglas R., and Michael A. Toman. 1996. *The Economics of Energy Secu-
    rity*. Norwell, MA: Kluwer Academic Publisher.
Borenstein, Severin, and James Bushnell. 2000. 'Electricity Restructuring: De-
    regulation or Reregulation?' *Regulation* 23, no. 2: 46–52.
Buzan, Barry, Ole Waever, and Jaap de Wilde. 1998. *Security: A New Framework
    for Analysis*. Boulder, CO: Lynne Rienner.
Crooks, Ed. 2007. 'FT Report – Energy 2007: Delusional Dream of Indepen-
    dence.' *Financial Times*, 9 November.
Eising, Rainer, and Nicolas Jabko. 2001. 'Moving Targets: National Interests
    and Electricity Market Liberalization in the European Union.' *Comparative
    Political Studies* 34, no. 7: 742–62.
Energy Charter Secretariat. 2004. *The Energy Charter Treaty and Related Docu-
    ments. A Legal Framework for International Energy Cooperation*. Brussels: En-
    ergy Charter Secretariat.
European Commission. 1995. *Green Paper for a European Union Energy Policy*.
    COM/94/659.
– 1996. *White Paper on an Energy Policy for the European Union*. COM/95/0682.
– 2000. *Green Paper Towards a European Strategy for the Security of Energy Supply*.
    COM/2000/769.

– 2002. *Communication from the Commssion of 26 June 2002 to the Council and the European Parliament – Final Report on the Green Paper Towards a European Strategy for the Security of Energy Supply.* COM/2002/321.
– 2006. *Green Paper on a European Strategy for Sustainable, Competitive and Secure Energy.* COM/2006/105.
– 2008a. *Communication from the Commission to the European Parliament, the Council, the European Economic and Social Committee and the Committee of the Regions – Second Strategic Energy Review : An EU Energy Security and Solidarity Action Plan.* COM/2008/0781.
– 2008b. *Green Paper – Towards a Secure, Sustainable and Competitive European Energy Network.* COM/2008/0782.
European Communities. 1986. 'The History of Community Energy Policy – The Washington Conference: 11 February 1974.' *Energy in Europe* 5: 19–22.
– 1988. 'The Community's Oil Supplies.' *Energy in Europe* 11: 29–33.
– 1990. 'Energy for a New Century: The European Perspective (Report of the "Groupe des Sages").' *Energy in Europe,* special issue (July): 9–30.
Fligstein, Neil. 2008. *Euroclash.* Oxford: Oxford University Press.
Hajer, Marteen, and David Laws. 2008. 'Ordering through Discourse.' *The Oxford Handbook of Public Policy,* 251–68. Oxford: Oxford University Press.
Hancher, Leigh, and Sally Janssen. 2004. 'European Legal Framework for Security of Supply.' In Barry Barton et al. (2004), 83–119.
Helm, Dieter. 2005. 'The Assessment: The New Energy Paradigm.' *Oxford Review of Economic Policy* 21, no. 1: 1–18.
Hirsh, Richard F. 1999. *Power Loss. The Origins of Deregulation and Restructuring in the American Electric Utility System.* Cambridge, MA: MIT Press.
IEA. 2002. *Energy Security.* Paris: OECD/IEA.
– 2004. *Energy Outlook 2004 Edition.* Paris: OECD/IEA.
– 2007. *Energy Security and Climate Policy. Assessing Interaction.* Paris: OECD/IEA.
IPCC. 2008. *Climate Change 2007 Synthesis Report.* Geneva: IPCC.
Jabko, Nicolas. 2006. *Playing the Market: A Political Strategy for Uniting Europe.* Ithaca, NY: Cornell University Press.
Jegen, Maya. 2001. *Energiepolitische Vernetzung in der Schweiz.* Basel: Helbing and Lichtenhahn.
Kuhn, Thomas S. 1970 (1962). *The Structure of Scientific Revolutions.* Chicago: University of Chicago Press.
– 1992 (1977). *Die Entstehung des Neuen: Studien zur Struktur der Wissenschaftsgeschichte.* Frankfurt: Suhrkamp.
Krause, Keith, and Michael Williams. 1996. 'Broadening the Agenda of Security Studies: Politics and Methods.' *Mershon International Studies Review* 40: 229–54.

Litfin, Karen T. 1999. 'Environmental Security in the Coming Century.' In *International Order and the Future of World Politics*, ed. T.V. Paul and John A. Hall, 328–51. Cambridge: Cambridge University Press.

Martin, William Flynn, Ryukichi Imai, and Helga Steeg. 1998. *Maintaining Energy Security in a Global Context*. The Trilateral Commission. http://www.trilateral.org/library/maintaining_energy_security.pdf.

McCormick, John. 2001. *Environmental Policy in the European Union*. Basingstoke: Palgrave.

Scharpf, Fritz. 1999. *Governing Europe*. Oxford: Oxford University Press.

Schreurs, Miranda, Selin, Henrik, and Stacy D. VanDeever. 2009. 'Conflict and Cooperation in Transatlantic Climate Politics: Different Stories at Different Levels.' In *Transatlantic Environment and Energy Politics*, ed. Miranda Schreurs, Henrik Selin, and Stacy VanDeever, 165–85. Farnham: Ashgate.

Scott, Richard. 1994. *IEA – The First 20 Years. Policies and Actions*, vol. 1. Paris: OECD/IEA.

Vogel, Steven K. 1996. *Freer Markets, More Rules. Regulation Reform in Advanced Industrial Countries*. Ithaca, NY: Cornell University Press.

Waterloos, Christian. 1995. 'Emergence of a Community Energy Policy.' *Energy in Europe* 26: 54–9.

PART TWO

The Transformation of European Security Institutions

6 Global Europe: An Emerging Strategic Actor

SVEN BISCOP

The European Union (EU), and the European Economic Community (EEC) before it, has always been a global economic power. Its economic weight endowed it with the potential to also become a global actor in the realm of diplomacy and defence, but it was not until the Maastricht Treaty created the Common Foreign and Security Policy (CFSP) that Europe began to develop its own strategy, and even then very tentatively. This chapter will track, from the policy science point of view, how, during the fifteen-odd years since the entry into force of the Maastrict Treaty in 1993, the EU gradually evolved into a global strategic actor – that is, an actor that consciously and purposely defines long-term objectives, with regard to all dimensions of foreign policy, actively pursues these objectives, and acquires the necessary means to that end. I will demonstrate how, in the process, EU thinking incorporated the paradigm shift towards a holistic conception of security that took place in this same period.

The adoption of the *European Security Strategy* (ESS) by the December 2003 European Council is a landmark event in this regard. It is omnipresent – in EU discourse, in statements by European and other policymakers, and in the academic debate (Biscop and Andersson 2008). In December 2007 the European Council mandated High Representative Javier Solana to produce a report on its implementation by December 2008, launching a high-profile, full-year debate about the ESS. All of this proves its importance as the first ever strategic document covering the whole of EU foreign policy, from aid and trade, democracy and human rights promotion, to diplomacy and the military. It expresses the EU's ambition as an international actor and has become the reference framework guiding the EU's performance as well as the benchmark to

judge it. Through its performance, the EU at the same time is developing a strategic culture of its own, the maturation of which is helped forward by the ESS. Ultimately, however, what counts to assess whether
the EU is a strategic actor, and what determines the consolidation of the
EU's strategic culture, is whether the EU, through its policies and actions, is able to achieve results.

Strategic Indications

EU foreign policy until the adoption of the ESS was of course not completely ad hoc. Over the years, a distinctive European approach
emerged, characterized by a holistic, integrated, or comprehensive
understanding of foreign policy and a focus on cooperative security
and multilateralism.

Particularly revealing in this regard is the 2001 *Communication on
Conflict Prevention*, in which the Commission proposed to address the
'root causes of conflict' by promoting 'structural stability,' defined as
'sustainable economic development, democracy and respect for human
rights, viable political structures and healthy environmental and social
conditions, with the capacity to manage change without resort to conflict' (European Commission 2001). The EU Programme for the
Prevention of Violent Conflicts was adopted by the European Council
on 15–16 June 2001 based on this Communication. The EU subsequently developed the Country and Regional Strategy Papers, which outline
policy priorities, the Check-List for Root Causes of Conflict, and the
continually revised Watch List of Priority Countries (where there is a
serious risk of conflict). The holistic approach has been especially evident in EU policy with respect to its neighbours, which it attempts to
integrate in an encompassing network of relations: the Stability Pact for
the Balkans, the Euro-Mediterranean Partnership, the successful transition of Central and Eastern Europe, probably its most significant
achievement since the start of the European integration project itself,
and the European Neighbourhood Policy (ENP). Relations with the
African, Caribbean, and Pacific (ACP) countries as well as with strategic partners such as Russia and China have been expanding into a wide
range of areas too, leaving behind the exclusively economic focus.

For long-term policies, the holistic approach thus emerged as the predominant characteristic of what Keukeleire and MacNaughtan (2008)
call the 'structural foreign policy' of the EU. It is less visible than traditional diplomacy or 'high politics' but nonetheless represents a huge

and often very successful effort (see also Bretherton and Vogler 2006). This development did not happen overnight. Elements of the holistic approach were present in the earliest external policies of the EEC, and already in the 1980s the Western European Union (WEU), as it was gradually being reactivated, developed a broad conception of security. But the paradigm shift is real: by the EU, security, including 'hard' security, is now seen as an integral part of a holistic approach to foreign policy as a whole. Other actors – for example, NATO under the heading of the comprehensive approach – have even imported the holistic paradigm as propagated by the Union.

When the EU was confronted with acute crises, however, it often proved unable to translate the holistic approach into practice. '9/11' and its aftermath are a case in point. At first, the EU did react unanimously, focusing on the root causes of terrorism. The extraordinary European Council of 21 September 2001 called for 'an in-depth political dialogue with those countries and regions of the world in which terrorism comes into being' and 'the integration of all countries into a fair world system of security, prosperity and improved development' (European Council 2001). '9/11' was therefore not a turning point for EU policy but confirmed the view that a policy that focuses exclusively on military instruments cannot achieve long-term stability. But subsequent events, notably Washington's declaration of a 'war on terrorism' and the US-led invasion of Iraq, led to deep divisions between 'new' and 'old Europe,' as US Defence Secretary Donald Rumsfeld worded it, putting the motto *divide et impera* to good use. An explicit strategy does not guarantee the absence of such divides, but without it, 'belated reactions, decision-making paralysis and coalitions of the willing outside the EU framework are the likely outcome' (Meyer 2004: 3). Faced with a dominant global player, the US, that is both very determined and very powerful and does possess an explicit National Security Strategy – in its 2002 and 2006 versions under the Bush Administration, with the Obama administration publishing its own in May 2010 – the EU often cannot escape the American framework of thought.

Ironically, the divide over Iraq also enabled the decisive step to launch a strategic debate that was impossible until then. There may have been different motivations: defining a 'European way' for some, so as to distance themselves from a US policy with which they could not agree and highlight alternatives; or aligning European priorities with those of the US, to preserve a transatlantic partnership perceived to be threatened. At an informal meeting of the General Affairs and

External Relations Council on 2 and 3 May 2003, Solana was – rather unexpectedly – tasked with producing a draft strategic document. On 19–20 June the European Council welcomed the document submitted by Solana, *A Secure Europe in a Better World*, and charged him with taking the work forward. On behalf of the EU, the EU Institute for Security Studies then organized three seminars, in Rome (19 September), Paris (6–7 October), and Stockholm (20 October), bringing together officials from Member States, candidate States, and EU institutions, as well as the academic world, NGOs, and the media. This innovative process allowed input to be collected from a wide variety of actors and observers, a number of which found their way into the final *European Security Strategy*, which was duly adopted by the European Council on 12 December 2003. At the same time, by keeping the drafting firmly in the hands of his own staff, Solana avoided tenuous debates about points and commas between Member States and ensured a concise and readable final result.

In 2008 a similar process was used to debate the implementation of the ESS, at seminars in Rome (5–6 June), Natolin (27–8 June), Helsinki (18–19 September), and Paris (2–3 October), resulting in the adoption of a *Report on the Implementation of the European Security Strategy – Providing Security in a Changing World* (hereafter the Report) by the European Council on 11 December. French President Nicolas Sarkozy and Swedish Foreign Minister Carl Bildt, who were at the origin of the debate, envisaged a review of the ESS itself, but the European Council left the text untouched. Many Member States feared all-too-divisive debates, notably on Russia; hence the cautious – and grammatically slightly awkward – mandate of the December 2007 European Council: 'to examine the implementation of the Strategy with a view to proposing elements on how to improve the implementation and, as appropriate, elements to complement it' (European Council 2007). The Report 'does not replace the ESS, but reinforces it.' If the EU is not yet the global actor that it could have been, it is indeed not because its strategy is not valid, but because it has been half-hearted in implementing it. The question is, though, as will be seen below, whether actionable conclusions will be drawn from the Report in order to improve implementation.

Global Ambition and Mission Statement

The ESS unequivocally expresses the EU ambition: 'As a union of 25 states with over 450 million people producing a quarter of the world's Gross National Product (GNP), and with a wide range of instruments at its disposal, the European Union is inevitably a global player.' The politico-military dimension is included – 'Europe should be ready to share in the responsibility for global security and in building a better world' – but as an instrument of last resort. The emphasis is on the holistic approach, putting to use the full range of instruments, through partnerships and multilateral institutions, for a permanent policy of prevention and stabilization: 'The best protection for our security is a world of well-governed democratic states. Spreading good governance, supporting social and political reform, dealing with corruption and abuse of power, establishing the rule of law and protecting human rights are the best means of strengthening the international order.' This is the mission statement of the EU as an international actor. As Major and Riecke (2006: 44) say: 'If the constitutional treaty defines the European Union's *finalité intérieure*, then the ESS outlines its *finalité extérieure*, tackling not just security questions but also issues relating to the European Union's identity, values and political philosophy.'

This *finalité* can be conceptualized through the notion of global public goods (GPG). Physical security or freedom from fear; economic prosperity or freedom from want; political freedom or democracy, human rights and the rule of law; and social well-being or education, health services, a clean environment, and so forth: these 'goods' are global, or universal, because everybody is entitled to them; and public because it is the responsibility of public authorities to provide access to them. As the individual is the point of reference, there is an obvious link with 'human security,' mentioned for the first time in the Report: 'We have worked to build human security, by reducing poverty and inequality, promoting good governance and human rights, assisting development, and addressing the root causes of conflict and insecurity.' The gap between haves and have-nots in terms of access to the core GPG is indeed the root cause of economic instability, mass migration, frustration, extremism and conflict, thus creating a much more diffuse set of risks and challenges from the negative effects of which Europe cannot be insulated, even though Europe itself is no longer threatened militarily, the very fact which enabled the holistic paradigm shift. Ultimately therefore, in today's globalized world, Europe can only be secure if everybody is secure, as expressed by the ESS subtitle: *A Secure Europe in a Better World*. Because of this interdependence the core GPG are marked by non-excludability and non-rivalry. They are also inextricably related – one needs access to all in order to enjoy any one – and present in every foreign policy issue; hence the need for the holistic approach: all policies must address all dimensions simultaneously in order to achieve durable results rather than combat the symptoms of underlying issues. Working proactively to diminish inequality and increase access to GPG is the basis of prevention and stabilization, and because the EU does not want to impose, it does so through partnerships with other states and regions and through rule-based multilateral institutions.

Does this constitute a 'distinctive European approach to foreign and security policy,' as the Report has it, that makes the EU into a special type of power? Is the EU a power at all, a notion which the ESS itself actually does not mention (Whitman 2006: 9)? During the Cold War, the idea of Europe as a power was irrelevant, as all Allies fundamentally subscribed to NATO's strategy, in view of the overarching Soviet threat, while the EEC lacked the capacity anyway to play such a role. Implicitly the ESS certainly expresses the EU's ambition to be a global power, something which in 2001 the European Council had already done very explicitly in the Laeken Declaration: 'a power resolutely doing battle against all violence, all terror and all fanaticism ... a power wanting to change the course of world affairs in such a way as to benefit not only the rich countries but also the poorest. A power seeking to set globalisation within a moral framework, in other words to anchor it in solidarity and sustainable development' (European Council 2001b).

In reality the will to act on that is lacking all too often. Nevertheless, the EU does influence events and developments worldwide, certainly in the economic sphere, also in the sphere of norms and values, and less consistently but increasingly in the politico-military sphere. The comparison with the much more purposive American power hides the fact that after the US the EU is the world's second power – who else would that be? But it consciously uses its power differently, preferring persuasion over coercion, multilateralism over unilateralism, and diplomacy over the military. Different characterizations of the EU have been provided: a soft power, preferring non-military instruments; a civilian power, aimed at changing the international environment rather than expanding its interests (at 'milieu' rather than 'possession goals'); a normative power, a model in terms of norms and values; a transformative power, seeking to export its model; or a tranquil power ('puissance tranquille'), averse to power projection.

All of these characterizations catch part of the EU. The core of EU strategy is indeed to transform others by exporting its model. Linking together political, economic, and social reform and security cooperation through partnership and conditionality, this holistic approach, *if* it is effectively implemented, is proactive and intrusive; for Dannreuther and Peterson (2006: 181) the ESS signals that, like the US, the EU sees itself as a transformational and even revolutionary power. Being a model for others to emulate is not sufficient to be a power; as Telò (2006: 59) warns, Europe then runs the risk of ending up like 'something of a cultural beacon, fit only for ceremonial purposes, much like Greece's role within the Roman empire.' Power cannot be tranquil but implies the will to actively shape events. Furthermore, hard power, from sanctions to intervention, is part of the EU toolbox, as an emergency brake in case of grave human rights violations, the invocation of the 'responsibility to protect' (R2P),[1] and threats to peace and security. The EU's distinctiveness lies perhaps in the positive, indeed progressive, tone of its project. Rather than threat-based, aimed against somebody, it is aimed at achieving positive objectives, which by addressing the root causes of conflict and instability[2] are of course in the interest of the EU – that is what policy is about – but which also directly benefit others and thus express a feeling of responsibility[3] for and solidarity with the have-nots. In that sense, the EU could also be described as a positive power – to advance just one more label (Biscop 2005).

Benchmark and Reference Framework

More than a mission statement, the ESS is also a strategy in the broad, public management meaning of the term.[4] It is a policymaking tool which, on the basis of EU values and interests,[5] outlines the long-term overall objectives to be achieved and the basic categories of instruments to be applied to that end, serves as a reference framework for day-to-day policymaking, and guides the definition of the means – that is, the civilian and military capabilities – that need to be developed. One should not be misled by the semantic confusion created – consciously or unconsciously – by strategic studies in the realist school.[6] The ESS is not a strategy in the narrow, military sense of the term; nor was it meant to be: in spite of its misleading – and perhaps mistaken – title, it is an international or foreign policy strategy that addresses the whole of external action. This is very clear from the Report, which even more than the ESS itself devotes attention to issues such as climate change and the Doha Round. Strategic studies too ought to adapt their vocabulary to the holistic paradigm shift. Such a foreign policy strategy is not an operational document, but has to be translated into sub-strategies, policies, and actions – including a military strategy – which for that matter also applies to the US National Security Strategy. It has an inspiring function vis-à-vis policymaking (Bailes 2005: 14). In fact, in the ESS, combined with the many existing sub-strategies[7] and policies, the EU has a much more explicit strategic concept than most Member States.

As stated above, the choice for the holistic approach is not a new, let alone a revolutionary, one. Rather the ESS is the codification of a strategic orientation that had already emerged through the practice of the CFSP, which in turn had its roots in European Political Cooperation (EPC) of the 1970s–1980s. Herein lies the strength of the ESS: it represents a fundamental consensus, the roots of which go much deeper than the temporary circumstances surrounding its adoption. Nevertheless there was a chance that the ESS would soon disappear: a one-off demonstration of regained unity after the divide over Iraq, of high symbolic value but with little impact on policymaking. A stratagem rather than a strategy ... The ESS has proved too evocative for that to happen. It is one of the most circulated EU documents among the general public and frequently appears on reading lists at universities around the world. Many EU decisions, especially those relating to the CFSP and its military dimension, the European Security and Defence Policy (ESDP), refer to the ESS, as do Solana and EU representatives generally. The ESS is the connecting thread throughout the courses for practitioners from Member States organized by the European Security and Defence College (ESDC). Edwards (2006: 9) speaks of a genuine '"agitation architecture" geared to "mainstreaming" ESS issues.'

That does not mean that the ESS is always first on policymakers' minds. In many cases, its presence is implicit and it is de facto being implemented, precisely because it is an expression of continuity in EU foreign policy. But even though it is not always explicitly referred to, the codification of this strategic orientation is important because it strengthens its status and makes it more difficult – though not impossible – to transgress its boundaries and thus promotes coherence and consistency. Because the ESS has remained so present, it has effectively become the benchmark to judge EU performance. This certainly holds true for third states and organizations: even if it would want to, the outside world would not allow the EU to forget the ESS, which it reads as a binding statement of what the Union aims to achieve and which therefore generates demands and expectations. The ESS has thus very much become part of the identity of the EU. The significance attributed to the debate on its implementation in 2008, and the expectations for a strategic review generated by it, are proof of that.

Naturally, the ESS is not perfect. Its drafters could only build on consensus in areas where that existed. On a number of issues it remains particularly vague because consensus was absent or not yet strong enough. Often it tells us more about *how* to do things than about *what* to do, about the instruments rather than the objectives. But a strategy it is.

Strategic Culture

If the EU is a global power, equipped with a foreign policy strategy, one might ask whether an EU strategic culture is developing. The ESS stresses that 'we need to develop a strategic culture that fosters early, rapid, and when necessary, robust intervention.'

Again there is an issue of definition.[8] If strategic culture is understood as concerning only the use of hard power in the implementation of strategy, it is easy to deride the EU, for this is indeed its least developed dimension. Some almost make it appear as if only a strategic culture emphasizing force can be strong or 'good.' But the EU is more than a military actor and the ESS explicitly puts strategic culture in the context of the holistic approach: 'This applies to the full spectrum of instruments for crisis management and conflict prevention at our disposal, including political, diplomatic, military and civilian, trade and development activities.'[9] Therefore, as stated above, the concept of strategy must be adopted to the holistic paradigm shift, and accordingly that of strategic culture too. Surely a concept shaped by the study of Cold War nuclear strategy must be updated to remain a useful tool of analysis. Building on Snyder's definition as amended by Gray (2006: 9), strategic culture can be defined as 'the sum total of ideas, conditioned emotional responses, and patterns of habitual behaviour that members of a [strategic community] have acquired through instruction or imitation and share with each other with regard to [strategy].'

In the case of the EU, the strategic community is very diverse. It comprises various actors at the EU level, political and administrative, individuals and collective entities, the latter intergovernmental as well as supranational, including: Solana; the Policy Unit; the Political and Security Committee (PSC), the Military Committee (EUMC) and their subsidiary working groups; the Council Secretariat, including the Military Staff (EUMS); the Commission, notably the Relex group of Commissioners; and various Commission directorates-general. The constant interaction in, for example, the PSC is very important in forging a strategic culture. Because a substantial part of EU foreign policy remains intergovernmental the strategic community also includes relevant actors in the capitals. Some Member States have strong national strategic cultures, while those of others are less developed; EU strategic culture is an additional layer and both layers mutually influence each other. The ESDC actively diffuses EU strategic culture.

The heterogeneity of the EU strategic community leads to the expectation that a strategic culture will develop more slowly. Yet when assessing the discourse and especially the practice of the actors involved, it seems fair to say that a collective EU strategic culture is developing. There is a 'European way' of responding to foreign policy issues, while it is perhaps even more clear that some responses are not expected from the EU or even contradictory to its nature. That does not mean that the EU always responds to every issue it is confronted with: alas, the Member States all too often do not find consensus. Then it is up to each Member State to wage a national policy. But if consensus is found and the EU as such makes policy, there is an increasingly clear idea of *how* it can and should act. To some extent, the EU even exports this strategic culture; NATO, for example, has adopted part of the discourse on the holistic approach (see Gheciu's chapter in this volume).

EU strategic culture is strongest when it comes to the long-term policy of stabilization and prevention, the most supranational dimension of EU foreign policy. It is much less strong when it comes to the application of coercive instruments, especially military force. This is probably the issue on which national strategic cultures differ the most. Arguably, however, what impedes the development of a strong strategic culture is not so much that Member States have different views about when and how to use force, but rather that they remain very much divided about *who* should use force. Because Atlantic-oriented Member States feel that high-intensity military operations should remain the prerogative of NATO or ad hoc coalitions, consensus often cannot be found to act as EU.[10] The case of Iraq can illustrate this. The real intra-European divide over Iraq did not concern the substance and principles of policy. It can safely be argued that all Member States agree that in principle the use of force is an instrument of last resort which requires a Security Council mandate. The real issue at stake was the nature of the transatlantic partnership. If the US reverts to the use of force in a situation in which the EU would not, or not yet, what then has priority for the EU: following its own principles or supporting its most important ally? The subsequent case of Iran, in which the EU has taken the lead, demonstrates that *au fond* Member States very much agree about how to deal with proliferation.

The *Paper for Submission to the High-Level Panel on Threats, Challenges and Change*, approved by the Council for transferral to the Panel in May 2004, provides an interesting summary of the European approach. The EU first reaffirms its commitment to the holistic approach, stressing the need for 'economic, political and legal instruments, as well as military instruments, and close cooperation between states as well as international organizations across a range of sectors.' When crisis management is in order, a gradual and comprehensive process of intervention is outlined, from 'the reinforcement of institutions, the security system, and the promotion of economic and social development,' through 'the mandating of a civilian mission,' to 'carefully targeted sanctions,' and finally, 'if warranted by ongoing security conditions and crisis management needs, the mandating of a rapid reaction force and/or a military peacekeeping mission.' This would particularly apply in case of 'actual or threatened failure of state institutions' and in an R2P scenario. Even the hard end of security is thus fitted into the holistic paradigm.

Meyer's (2006: 141) impressive empirical research concludes that there is 'a new European consensus that the use of military force abroad can be legitimate for the purpose of protecting vulnerable ethnic groups against massive violations of their human rights.' Other elements of this consensus, which Meyer dubs 'humanitarian power Europe,' are the need to obtain Security Council authorization and to avoid 'collateral damage,' and the view of the use of force as a last resort. Howorth (2004: 212) too finds that Member States are shifting towards 'a common acceptance of integrated European interventionism, based not solely on the classical stakes of national interest, but also on far more idealistic motivations such as humanitarianism and ethics.' Freedman (2006: 39) describes this as 'a move from defensive to offensive liberal wars,' which reflects 'the growing importance of the norms of human and minority rights,' that is, human security (Haaland Matlary 2006). Clearly, interventions for these reasons have become increasingly acceptable including for Member States that are less inclined to use force. If the EU would continue to develop an activist strategic culture along these lines, that would fit in with the idea of a 'positive' or 'responsible' power that assumes its part of the responsibility for global security.

In spite of the divide between 'Atlanticists' and 'Europeanists,' and highlighting the growing consensus on 'European interventionism,' the EU is 'doing' more and more. It is therefore far too early to speak of EU strategic culture as something definite. Each time the EU undertakes a new type of task, in new regions of the world, this is incorporated into its strategic culture, which is very much developing by doing. This is especially true in the field of military and civilian ESDP operations. The adoption of the ESS can be seen as the codification of strategic culture as it had developed up to that point. At the same time, it promotes its consolidation, because it enhances the strategic community's awareness of strategic issues and thus promotes debate.

If strategic culture is developing by doing, it is but one of the factors that determines what is being done. First and foremost, the Member States have to find the political will to act, and to act as EU. Many other factors play a role: the availability of financial means and military and civilian capabilities, the degree to which EU interests are directly at stake, and the position of other relevant actors. Neither the adoption of the ESS nor the development of a strategic culture, but its degree of activism and the results of its policies, determine whether the EU is an effective strategic actor. The proof of the pudding is in the eating – not in drawing up the recipe.

A Mixed Performance

The ESS offers a sound concept and an ambitious agenda, but judging by the EU's performance, as the Report states, 'despite all that has been achieved, implementation of the ESS remains work in progress. For our full potential to be realised we need to be still more capable, more coherent and more active.' The Report did not meet expectations for a thorough strategic review, however: it confirms the holistic and multilateral approach, provides a concise overview of implementation, and ends with a firm call to action – 'To build a secure Europe in a better world, we must do more to shape events. And we must do it now' – but it offers little in terms of concrete recommendations. Nor did the European Council provide a follow-up mechanism to ensure that implementation of the ESS would be stepped up and the linkages between the ESS and decision making enhanced. That would require more political courage, more and better capabilities, and, in a number of areas, the definition of clearer 'sub-strategies' to the ESS. As it is, the strategic objectives have – rightly – been reaffirmed in the 2008 Report, but a number of questions remain as to how to achieve them.

Global Crisis Management

EU Member States are certainly not averse to deploying their forces, but the large majority is deployed on the Balkans, in their backyard where they logically assume responsibility, and in Afghanistan and Iraq, as a follow-up to the interventions – one rather more controversial than the other – initiated by the US and a number of EU Member States themselves. The 7,000–8,000 European blue helmets in Lebanon (since 2006) are a positive exception. But they contrast sharply with the 1,000 troops reluctantly deployed in the Congo in 2006 and the apparent unwillingness to launch a new bridging operation in the east of the DRC in late 2008 (after Operation Artemis in 2003) in order to avert a humanitarian catastrophe. The same applies to Darfur: only after the African Union (AU) took on the operation did the reluctance to intervene give way to intense EU-NATO competition to gain visibility through second-line support for the AU. Only in January 2008, after a very long force generation did the EU launch a bridging operation to protect refugees in neighbouring Chad, until March 2009. Clearly, the EU's strategic culture in itself is not strong enough to stimulate intervention in every situation that requires it. Participation in UN operations other than UNIFIL, notably in Sub-Saharan Africa, remains minimal: in late 2008 the EU27, Lebanon set aside, accounted for less than 2,700 out of nearly 90,000 'blue helmets' or just under 3 per cent.

Most Member States do put their forces in harm's way in national, NATO, or coalitions-of-the-willing operations. Yet although legally the EU's Petersberg Tasks include operations at the high end of the spectrum of violence, politically the Member States, as stated above, are still extremely divided over the use of force under the EU flag. It is striking that in a *Declaration on Strengthening Capabilities*, also adopted by the December 2008 European Council, when setting out what the EU should actually be capable of in the short term – 'in the years ahead' – alone of all 'illustrative scenarios' elaborated by the EUMS, 'separation of parties by force' is not mentioned – the only scenario for significant operations at the high end of the spectrum. Battlegroup-size rapid response operations of limited duration are the only high-intensity target listed. Even though the EU has proved that it can mount high-risk operations, most EU-led operations are of lower intensity and of smaller scale. The still young ESDP needs to legitimize itself; hence the tendency to select operations with a large chance of success. To some extent therefore the criticism is justified that the EU takes on important but mostly 'less difficult' operations, in the post-conflict phase, in reaction to the settlement of a conflict – a criticism which can of course be applied to the international community as a whole. Nevertheless one must question whether Member States are willing to accept the implications of the strong EU diplomatic support for R2P, which if it comes to military intervention by definition implies high-intensity operations; not mentioned in the ESS, R2P is included in the Report – a positive signal.

There are positive examples of EU engagement: UNIFIL, as already mentioned; the EU Monitoring Mission in Georgia, deployed at record speed on 1 October 2008 after President Sarkozy successfully brokered the Six-Point Agreement between Moscow and Tbilisi; EULEX Kosovo, deployed in December 2008 in spite of Member States' divisions about the recognition of Kosovo independence; and EU NAVFOR Somalia, deployed in the same month in order to safeguard trade routes against the threat of piracy off the Somali coast. But in spite of the global ambitions expressed in the ESS, Member States are reluctant to commit to long-term, large-scale operations outside their immediate periphery or where no direct strategic interests are at stake – where the risks are too high and the stakes are too low. There is more appetite for rapid reaction operations, of smaller scale and limited duration, or lower-intensity operations; but for high-intensity operations Member States still habitually look to other frameworks than the EU.

Interestingly though, even when EU Member States deploy forces for non-EU operations, the EU increasingly sells this as an EU contribution. This was clearly the case for UNIFIL, which politically was decided upon in the Council, a fact which was acknowledged by then UN Secretary-General Kofi Annan, who explicitly welcomed the EU contribution. The Report also mentions Afghanistan, where 'EU Member States make a major contribution to the NATO mission.' This reflects the trend that the *political* centre of gravity has increasingly shifted away from NATO in particular to what are in effect the Alliance's two main pillars, the US and the EU, which are the 'complete' foreign policy actors, covering everything from aid and trade to diplomacy and the military. The EU has increasingly become the political centre and the primary decision-making level for European states: it is here that they decide whether or not to act in a given situation; if their decision entails military action, the secondary step is to select the organization through which to act – NATO, ESDP, the UN, the OSCE, an ad hoc coalition. This will always be an ad hoc decision, in function of which partners want to go along and which organization is best suited for the case at hand.

The Elaboration of a Military Strategy?

If the EU's engagement for global peace and security can be stepped up, there are, sadly, too many conflicts for the EU to deal with all of them, certainly in a leading role. Therefore, as the Report states, 'We need to prioritise our commitments, in line with resources.' Because the ESS is not clear on the priorities for ESDP, there is a missing link between the overall objective in the ESS – 'to share in the responsibility for global security' – and ESDP operations and capability development. Quantitatively, ESDP is based on the 1999 Helsinki Headline Goal of 60,000 troops. Not only has this objective been overshadowed by the much more limited battlegroup project – although renewed emphasis is put on it in the above-mentioned *Declaration on Strengthening Capabilities* – but the actual availability of the forces declared cannot be assessed, as they are not pre-identified and Member States have declared similar numbers to NATO as well. If all ongoing ESDP, NATO, UN, and national operations in which EU Member States participate are counted, Europe today deploys more than 80,000 troops but obviously cannot mobilize 60,000 additional troops. It is equally obvious that even the combined ESDP and NATO ambition still falls far short of the total combined armed forces of the EU-27: 2 million troops. Even if collective defence is taken into account, there is no grand vision about how many of these 2 million Europe really needs.

What is required is a unified vision on the level of ambition, cutting across organizational divides; whether operations are conducted through ESDP, NATO, the UN, or an ad hoc coalition, is secondary. The EU as the political expression of Europe must decide on a military strategy for ESDP, a 'white book' which would function as a sub-strategy to the ESS: How many forces should the EU-27 be able to muster for crisis management and long-term peacekeeping? for which priorities? What reserves does that require, and which capacity must be maintained for territorial defence? In all probability the conclusion will be that Europe does not need 2 million uniforms.

Elaborating an ESDP strategy will require a thorough debate, but some outlines can already be discerned. The EU is obviously very committed to the region which it dubs its 'Neighbourhood,' in which it seeks to promote political, economic, and social reform; it should also be a priority for ESDP if peace and security in the region are threatened, as in Lebanon and Georgia. Sub-Saharan Africa has been an important area of focus for ESDP, and should probably remain so, for few other outside actors appear willing to contribute to crisis management on the African continent. Securing Europe's lines of interaction with the world, of which the operation off Somalia is an example, seems another priority. Importantly, the collective security system of the UN, and therefore the EU itself, as its main supporter and with two permanent members

of the Security Council in its ranks, can only be legitimate if it addresses the threats to *everyone's* security – too much selectivity undermines
the system. Even though it cannot always play a leading role, the EU
must therefore also shoulder its share of the responsibility for global
peace and security by playing an active role in the Security Council and
by contributing capabilities, notably if anywhere in the world the
threshold to activate the R2P mechanism is reached.

Permanent Prevention and Conditionality

The EU is very active in prevention and stabilization, via 'positive conditionality,' for which the 'sub-strategies' are already available, notably
the ENP. Yet, if 'positive conditionality' as a theory seems sound
enough, practice is often lagging behind, certainly in countries that do
not immediately qualify for EU membership. The proverbial carrots
that would potentially be most effective in stimulating reform, such as
opening up the European agricultural market or legalizing economic
migration, are those that the EU is not willing to consider, in spite of im-
perative arguments suggesting that Europe would actually benefit. At
the same time, conditionality is seldom applied very strictly. The impression is that the EU favours stability and economic – and energy –
interests over reform, to the detriment of Europe's soft or normative
power. Surprisingly perhaps, in the Mediterranean public opinion
mostly views the EU as a status quo actor.

This lack of soft power should not be underestimated. Rather than
the benign actor which the EU considers itself, in many southern countries it is seen as a very aggressive economic actor. For many countries,
the negative consequences of dumping and protectionism – which
often cancel out the positive effects of development aid – are far more
important than the challenges of terrorism and proliferation that dominate the Western agenda. In the current difficult international climate,
the EU model urgently needs to enhance its legitimacy. The EU must
muster the courage to effectively apply conditionality. Admittedly, this
requires an extremely difficult balancing act, especially vis-à-vis countries with authoritarian regimes and great powers like Russia and
China: maintaining partnership and being sufficiently critical at the
same time. But in that difficult context, the EU could notably show
more resolve in reacting to human rights abuses, which should visibly
impact on the relationship with any regime. A much enhanced image
will follow, which is a prerequisite for the gradual pursuit of more far-
reaching political, economic, and social reforms.

But has the EU solved the dilemma of stability versus democracy? A debate seems in order on the desired end state of the ENP. The Report mentions that the Mediterranean has still seen 'insufficient political reform' and that instability is rampant, but does not indicate the way ahead. Is the aim incremental progress while maintaining the existing regimes, or full democratization? And if the latter, are EU instruments sufficient or is there an upper limit to what can be achieved via consensual tools such as the ENP? These are questions which the new Union for the Mediterranean (although the further institutionalization of the Barcelona Process which it entails is positive) does not answer, and which the projected Eastern Partnership will have to address as well.

Implementing the Holistic Approach

The ESS advocates a holistic approach, but have its objectives really been incorporated by all parts of the EU machinery? Is there sufficient coordination between the different strands of foreign policy, across and within pillars, or is 'stove-piping' still the order of the day? The very progressive agenda of the ESS risks a loss of credibility if the EU does not draw the full conclusions from it, notably for external trade, agriculture, and migration. If an exclusive focus on hard security undermines effectiveness and legitimacy, so does a one-dimensional focus on trade. The holistic approach cannot be efficiently implemented without changes in the EU machinery. The personal union of the High Representative and the Commissioner for External Relations and the European External Action Service provided in the Lisbon Treaty would allow for the integration of the security, political, social, and economic dimensions in all foreign policies, from the creation to the implementation and evaluation of policy. A High Representative with a stronger mandate would also strengthen the capacity for preventive diplomacy.

Implementing the holistic approach also requires the active cooperation of all global powers. The UN collective security system can only work if all permanent members actively subscribe to it and refrain from paralysing or bypassing the Security Council. Conditionality can only work if it is not undermined by actors that disregard human rights. How can the EU persuade strategic partners like Russia and China, but also India, Brazil, Mexico, *and* the US, that 'effective multilateralism' is in their long-term interest, to arrive at 'inter-polarity' (Grevi 2008: 14) or cooperation between poles to share the advantages and address the common challenges of globalization? Specific but concrete joint interests can perhaps function as building blocks to give substance to the politico-military dimension of these strategic partnerships. For example, in the negotiations with Iran, Russia and China have been difficult but not impossible partners, given that sanctions have been adopted by the Security Council. At the same time, the growing importance of these bilateral strategic partnerships must be reconciled with the other EU objective of promoting regional integration in other parts of the world.

Finally, and perhaps most importantly, the ESS can only move from a concept to consistent and resolute action if the EU acts as one. As long as the EU remains divided between 'Atlanticists' and 'Europeanists' neither the EU nor NATO can be effective actors. In a multi-polar world, only a united EU-pole has the weight to deal with the challenges facing it and to become a consistent and decisive actor in an equal partnership with the United States.

Conclusion

Without any doubt, Europe has the potential to be a global power – a power in its own distinctive way, but a power nonetheless. In the economic sphere and in the realm of norms and values, it already is. In the politico-military sphere, its commitment is much less consistent, but gradually increasing. When the EU does not act, most of the times it is not so much because the Member States differ fundamentally on the course of action to be followed but because some Member States prefer to act through other institutions, notably NATO, or to act alone. Of the three features that mark a great power – i.e., (1) the scale of its resources, (2) 'a sense of responsibility for milieu-shaping, system-management and providing collective goods,' (Hyde-Price 2007: 38), and (3) the willingness to act – it is the latter which is often missing in the EU. Pragmatism in view of the poignant fact that increasingly only a united EU can face the challenges of a globalized world *should* make the Member States mend their ways. Whether they will depends on the political leadership.

NOTES

1 Endorsed at the UN Millennium+5 Summit in September 2005, R2P implies that if a state is unable or unwilling to protect its own population, or is itself the perpetrator of genocide, ethnic cleansing, war crimes, or crimes against humanity, national sovereignty must give way to a responsibility to protect

on the part of the international community. In such cases, the Security Council must mandate intervention, if necessary by military means.

2 Whereas too strong a focus on threats can induce a lack of attention for 'challenges' or underlying causes, as well as fear and introspection (Grevi 2008: 9).

3 On responsibility, see Mayer and Vogt (2006).

4 Which, the author feels, is not so broad as to validate Strachan's (2005: 34) view that 'the word "strategy" has acquired a universality which has robbed it of meaning, and left it only with banalities.'

5 It is often argued that national interests block the emergence of a truly European foreign and security policy, yet in reality most Member States no longer have national interests at all, that is, interests that are different from those of the other Member States. Interests are too often confused with attention: if Belgium pays more attention to Central Africa than to the Caucasus, that does not mean that objectively it has less of an interest in a stable Caucasus than Poland, and vice versa.

6 See, for example, Heisbourg (2004), Toje (2005), and Wyllie (2006).

7 Sub-strategy does not refer to a specific or new category of documents, but to documents that elaborate on one aspect of the ESS and thus de facto function as sub-strategies to it, for example, the strategies on WMD, on terrorism, on Africa etc.

8 Gray (2006: 9) remarks that 'the ability of scholars to make a necessarily opaque concept like strategic culture even less penetrable is truly amazing' or, as worded more positively by Booth (2005: 26), applying the concept is 'an art rather than science.'

9 Howorth (2007: 178) prefers the term 'security culture,' 'because it is more neural politically and … is more appropriate as a label for whatever collective mindset is in fact taking shape in the EU.'

10 Giegerich (2006: 84–5) makes the point with regard to the UK: 'The most striking feature has to be the high degree of overlap between the norms of British strategic culture and ESDP … The only clear clash … exists on the dimension of preferred areas of cooperation … the traditional position of British policy-makers is to favour NATO.'

REFERENCES

Bailes, Alyson. 2005. *The European Security Strategy – An Evolutionary History*. Policy Paper no. 10. Stockholm: SIPRI.

Biscop, Sven. 2005. *The European Security Strategy – A Global Agenda for Positive Power*. Aldershot: Ashgate.

Biscop, Sven, and Jan Joel Andersson, eds. 2008. *The EU and the European Security Strategy – Forging a Global Europe*. Abingdon: Routledge.

Booth, Ken. 2005. 'Strategic Culture: Validity and Validation.' *Oxford Journal on Good Governance* 2, no. 1: 25–8.

Bretherton, Charlotte, and John Vogler. 2006. *The European Union as a Global Actor*. 2nd ed. Abingdon: Routledge.

Council of the EU. 2004. *Paper for Submission to the High-Level Panel on Threats, Challenges and Change*. Brussels.

Dannreuther, Roland, and John Peterson. 2006. 'Conclusion: Alliance Dead or Alive?' In *Security Strategy and Transatlantic Relations*, ed. Roland Dannreuther and John Peterson, 178–91. London: Routledge.

Edwards, Geoffrey. 2006. 'Is There a Security Culture in the Enlarged European Union?' *The International Spectator* 41, no. 3: 7–23.

European Commission. 2001. *Communication on Conflict Prevention*. Brussels.

European Council. 2001. *Conclusions of the Extraordinary European Council Meeting, 21 September 2001*. Brussels.

European Council. 2001b. *Conclusions of the European Council, 14–15 December 2001*. Brussels.

European Council. 2003. *European Security Strategy. A Secure Europe in a Better World*. Brussels.

European Council. 2007. *Conclusions of the European Council. 13–14 December 2007*. Brussels.

European Council. 2008. *Report on the Implementation of the European Security Strategy. Providing Security in a Changing World*. Brussels.

Freedman, Lawrence. 2006. *The Transformation of Strategic Affairs*. Adelphi Paper no. 379. London: International Institute for Strategic Studies.

Giegerich, Bastian. 2006. *European Security and Strategic Culture. National Responses to the EU's Security and Defence Policy*. Baden-Baden: Nomos.

Gray, Colin S. 2006. *Out of the Wilderness: Prime Time for Strategic Culture*. Fort Belvoir, VA: Defense Threat Reduction Agency.

Grevi, Giovanni. 2008. 'Framing the European Strategic Debate.' *Studia Diplomatica* 61, no. 3: 5–18.

Haaland Matlary, Janne. 2006. 'When Soft Power Turns Hard: Is an EU Strategic Culture Possible?' *Security Dialogue* 37, no. 1: 105–21.

Heisbourg, François. 2004. 'The "European Security Strategy" Is Not a Security Strategy.' In *A European Way of War*, ed. Steven Everts et al., 27–39. London: Centre for European Reform.

Howorth, Jolyon. 2004. 'Discourse, Ideas and Epistemic Communities in European Security and Defence Policy.' *West European Politics* 27, no. 2: 211–34.

– 2007. *Security and Defence Policy in the European Union*. Basingstoke: Palgrave.

Hyde-Price, Adrian. 2007. *European Security in the Twenty-First Century: The Challenge of Multipolarity.* London: Routledge.

Kaldor, Mary, and Andrew Salmon. 2006. 'Military Force and European Strategy.' *Survival* 48, no. 1: 19–34.

Keukeleire, Stephan, and Jennifer MacNaughtan. 2008. *The Foreign Policy of the European Union.* Basingstoke: Palgrave.

Major, Claudia, and Henning Riecke. 2006. 'Europe's Little Blue Book. More Strategic Debate in the European Union.' *Internationale Politik. Transatlantic Edition* 7, no. 3: 44–51.

Mayer, Hartmut, and Henri Vogt, eds. 2006. *A Responsible Europe? Ethical Foundations of EU External Affairs.* Basingstoke: Palgrave.

Meyer, Christoph O. 2004. *Theorising European Strategic Culture: Between Convergence and the Persistence of National Diversity.* Working Document no. 204. Brussels: Centre for European Policy Studies (CEPS).

– 2006. *The Quest for a European Strategic Culture. Changing Norms on Security and Defence in the European Union.* Basingstoke: Palgrave.

Strachan, Hew. 2005. 'The Lost Meaning of Strategy.' *Survival* 47, no. 3: 33–54.

Telò, Mario. 2006. *Europe: A Civilian Power? European Union, Global Governance, World Order.* Basingstoke: Palgrave.

Toje, Asle. 2005. 'The 2003 European Union Security Strategy: A Critical Appraisal.' *European Foreign Affairs Review* 10, no. 1: 117–33.

Whitman, Richard. 2006. 'Road Map for a Route March? (De-)civilianizing through the EU's Security Strategy.' *European Foreign Affairs Review* 11, no. 1: 1–15.

Wyllie, James H. 2006. 'Measuring Up. The Strategies as Strategy.' In *Security Strategy and Transatlantic Relations*, ed. Roland Dannreuther and John Peterson, 165–77. London: Routledge.

7 European Defence: Functional Transformation Under Way

HANNA OJANEN

The post–Cold War European Union is in many respects a different entity from the European Communities of the Cold War times. One of the differences is that the European Union now deals with security and defence policy. Security and defence did not figure in the Treaty of Rome of 1957. It was indeed only after the end of the Cold War, in the Maastricht Treaty, that foreign and security policy were added to the Union's remit. It took several years still before the actual development of European Security and Defence Policy (ESDP) started, in practice with the Saint-Malo Summit of France and the United Kingdom in 1998. The decade to follow consolidated the EU as an actor in security and defence in the realm of crisis management, while also strengthening its legitimacy as a forum for security and defence political consultation and decision making between Member States. Thus, Mérand defines ESDP as first and foremost a decision-making structure that enables the EU to launch crisis management operations and pursue its foreign policy objectives, and also as a strongly institutionalized transgovernmental field (Mérand 2008: 29, 42).

The new security and defence dimension of the EU is manifest in the twenty-two different civilian and military crisis management missions that were ongoing or achieved by July 2009. Among these, the EU has been active outside the coast of Somalia for at least two years with more than twenty vessels and aircraft, and more than 1,800 military personnel (*ESDP Newsletter* 8, Summer 2009). It also shows in the European Defence Ministers' – who meet in the Steering Board of the European Defence Agency – decision of November 2008 to establish a European Air Transport Fleet (EDA website). Finally, it can also be seen in outsiders' reactions: that the NATO Secretary General speaks of the importance of improving EU-NATO cooperation says a lot of the new role the EU has come to play (*EUobserver*, 4 August 2009).

Thus, the EU now makes use of its Member States' military capabilities for its own operations, and both the defence ministries and the armed forces of the Member States have been given a role in the Union. The Member States' Chiefs of Defence form the EU Military Committee, and the European Defence Agency has been established to help the Member States develop their military capabilities. This means that the nature of the EU has quite profoundly changed. Yet, it is not only the EU that has changed: also the Member States have gone through a major change. Many of them were cooperating on defence matters during the Cold War; now, however, they do so also within the framework of the EU that combines traditional intergovernmental cooperation with supranational elements, and the traditional outlook of an international organization with that of a political union.

Why did this all happen? Would the end of the Cold War itself lead to such a development? The end of the Cold War put the continued need for defence alliances in doubt, leading to a debate on NATO's future. It also made the bloc-related conventional existential threat disappear from Europe. Security and defence were widely redefined. While the threat at the EU's external borders disappeared, its internal borders were demolished.

Howorth (2007: 52–7) sees the exogenous forces deriving from the end of the Cold War among the underlying drivers behind the ESDP, notably the diminishing importance of Europe for the United States, the start of crisis management, and the new norms outweighing sovereignty. He would see endogenous drivers, too, referring to the needs of correlation between different sides of the integration process, and to the needs of European defence industry.

Similarly, while mapping the various explanations for the ESDP and for the EU foreign and security policy, Strömvik (2005) would list the effect of EU institutions on Member State behaviour, changing threats, and the EU's new desire for global influence as driving forces. Forsberg (2006) finds that the three most common explanations of the ESDP pertain to the nature of the integration process, the United States, and the need to respond to crises.

Overall, however, the existing layer of theoretical work on the European Security and Defence Policy is still rather thin. The ESDP was not expected to happen. For a long time, it seemed as if there was no urgent need to predict the integration of security and defence in any 'foreseeable future.'[1] Rather, it was assumed that integration would not happen in the fields of security and defence, which were seen as closest to the core of national sovereignty. Some early integration theorists had devised theories that predicted a steady progress of the process of integration from one field to another. Notably the neofunctionalists delineated such spillover, but even they made a deviation for security and defence as a field exempt from inclusion. Ernst B. Haas came up in 1961 with the idea of special different functional contexts to explain why some fields, such as security, were 'immune' to the forces of spillover.

It would still seem as if the ESDP was for many a mere anomaly. In other words, there is still a tendency not to give much weight to this transformation of the EU into a security and defence political actor. It is frequently belittled, either by comparing it with the more traditional defence alliance, NATO, or by referring to the Member States' unwillingness to relinquish their decision-making autonomy to the EU on these issues. There is resistance to new ways of seeing; the old models are defended. National interest is still referred to, and the factual importance of the ESDP is questioned. While the spiralling development of the ESDP did eventually wake up the theorists to revise their views and to start explaining why security and defence entered the EU – rather than explaining why they did *not* do so – the explanations have still more often than not stemmed from traditional paradigms.

The resistance to seeing the ESDP as a major change might be a sign of resistance to a paradigmatic shift in the making. The paradigmatic shift here, to refer back to table 1.1, would in ontological terms be about the ability to observe and take seriously entities other than the independent, unitary state. Indeed, the independence of the state would be reduced in security and defence; instead, the Union as a new kind of entity enters the field not only as a security community between its members but also as an actor within the international system. Second, when it comes to the question of what counts as evidence, again, the traditional emphasis on material capabilities would still show in the reluctance to take ESDP seriously, while a new emphasis on ideational resources and practices would lead the observer to look at the specificities of the EU as an actor or as a model, and at the new practices within the Union that may change the way security and defence policy are made – such as the role of the European Defence Agency or of the Political and Security Committee.

This chapter aims at showing that the ESDP transforms both the Union and its Member States. The transformation is in this chapter understood and analysed as a transfer of tasks or functions, primarily from the Member States to the Union, but also between organizations. In practice, the ESDP means that security and defence, traditionally a central part of the functions of a state, come to be seen also as functions of the Union, first perhaps more nominally so, but later predominantly as functions of the Union and not of Member States. Accordingly, the Member States' autonomy – for instance to use their military capabilities outside of its borders – would gradually be tied to consultation or cooperation with other members and the EU institutions.

To conduct such an analysis, the obvious tool is functionalist theory. Functionalism, or perhaps more often neofunctionalism, does appear regularly in the literature, but mainly in minor roles. Having never returned to the role of hero it still played in late 1960s, neofunctionalism has had the pitiful, lineless role of the less worthy option compared with the better and more powerful theory. Indeed, neofunctionalism has been described as probably the most heavily criticized integration theory, objected to because of its grand theoretical pretensions and determinism, but also for its systematic (and naive) underestimating of the continued impact of sovereignty consciousness and nationalism (Niemann with Schmitter 2009: 51–2). In security studies, a typical criticism of neofunctionalism would be to disregard it because of lack of evidence: for neofunctionalism to be right, there should by now be supranational defence institutions; as, however, unanimous decision making still prevails and national armies have been preserved, other theories fit the reality better (e.g., Forsberg 2006: 15).

The problem with (neo)functionalism might in the end be paradigmatic in character. If the very paradigm was to change, the relevance of sovereignty and the nature of what counts as evidence would be reassessed.

In this chapter, functionalism is seen as a most useful way of explaining what has taken place in the ESDP, and potentially as one that opens up for a new research paradigm, too. Functions are a simple, straightforward way of understanding what is going on in security and defence integration in Europe. Thus, security and defence are seen as a function that someone has to take care of, or a series of functions such as crisis management, territorial defence, border management, defence policy, and armaments industry and trade.

The explanation of the ESDP based on functionalism sees the ESDP as a process whereby security and defence-related functions are relocated, shifted between the EU Member States and the Union, but also between states (including between the United States and European states) and between international organizations (in particular NATO and the EU).

At the same time, the repertoire of functions gradually changes, reflecting the changes in how security is perceived in Europe. The traditional basic defence function of defending the territory gives place for crisis management. Crisis management, then, is increasingly becoming a mixed civilian-military endeavour: there is increasing need to sketch a comprehensive approach to crisis management, including both civilian and military means. Further, external and internal security tend to get blurred. Even more fundamentally, and perhaps as a cause of these changes, the relationship with territoriality changes in the Union. Free movement of people leads to a need for integrated border control policies. And, fourth, in a world of increasing cross-migration, there are changes even in the question of citizenship and how the citizens are served, or want to be served, and who in the first place these citizens are.

Fundamentally, then, the functions of the state change, and at the same time what is expected of a state in the field of security changes. The provision of security has certainly been a core part of the functions of the state. The state may even legitimize its existence by providing security to its citizens. Moreover, by fulfilling certain functions, the states also play their role both in the international system and in its subsystems, such as the European Union.[2] If a state is not able to fulfil its functions, someone else has to do it, which is a burden for the other actors and the whole system. Notions such as 'responsibility to protect' are gaining ground, implying that judging the citizens' best interests would thus no longer be a monopolistic right of the state in question. Were the state not capable of protecting its citizens, other states might have the right to intervene.

In the end, a functional view on the ESDP not only sheds light on what the ESDP is about, but also helps understand the more profound changes in the European system. It brings up a tandem evolution: that of European integration and that of state functions. Eventually, such evolution leads to two large questions. First is the question about change or even dissolution of state legitimacy, if no longer based on security functions, and the accompanying increase in the legitimacy of other actors taking over. Second is the question about decreasing similarity between the states in the international system as a result of functional differentiation between states in the EU and states outside of it. Put together, these might be seen as a paradigm shift in the making.

Functionalism: About Conferring Tasks

Functionalism as a theory of integration is best described directly through David Mitrany's work. For Mitrany, it was important to break away from the link between authority and territory. The essence of functionalism was to confer the management of practical tasks, previously functions of the state, to explicitly created functional organizations. There would be a gradual surmounting of territorial and ideological divides through an inconspicuous and partial transfer of authority. As a process, this is naturally expansive and leads to further cooperation within similar functions – the transfer is both logical and natural. It would not go against the interests of the states, either. National agencies might even derive fresh life and scope from such cooperation. Gradual fading off of frontiers would also imply less frontier-related conflicts (Mitrany 1943, as quoted in Ojanen 1998: 36–7, 91fn7).

While federalists would stress territory, functionalists would stress functions. As Andreatta (2005: 21) puts it, functionalists 'believed that modern society was increasingly dominated by matters of "low politics" such as the welfare of the citizens and economic growth and criticised federalists because of their neglect of such issues.' The fundamental motive for integration would thus stem from the inability of nation-states to provide essential services to their citizens. Individuals would thus be in a primary position to pose requirements, to articulate expectations, even to compare alternative agencies' ability to provide certain services, under the general understanding that political functions must be performed at the most efficient level.

If we look at Haas's definition of integration from 1958, it tells us that in the process, national political actors are persuaded to shift their loyalties, expectations, and political activities towards a new centre whose institutions possess or demand jurisdiction over the national states. This is how a new political community is subsequently formed, superimposed over the existing ones (Haas 1968: 4–5, 16).[3]

What is important to note in Haas's early theorizing is the centrality of calculation of advantage. In the later preface of 1968 (Haas 1968: xxxii–xxxv), Haas argues that in the process of integration, national governments seek to secure a maximal position for themselves, but without obstructing the process. In the long run, they refer to federal decisions as they recognize a point beyond which attempts to sidestep, ignore, or sabotage them are unprofitable. There is something called 'integration threshold': beneficiaries of earlier integrative steps have achieved such vested position in the new system as not to permit a return to an earlier mode of action (Haas 1968, quoted in Ojanen 1998: 54).[4] Governments, thus, not only experience loss of power, but they also gain. The state may, for example, come to see supranationalism as the method to secure maximal welfare (Haas 1963: 67–73.)

Integration is, thus, rational for the governments. As Wessels puts it, the long-term growth trend in integration can be explained by rational choice of national governments and administrations, but also of other public and private actors: the growing demands for welfare and public services – for efficient performance of such functions – combined with increasing interdependence and globalization lead to a situation in which developments are outside their realm of direct control (Wessels 1997: 273), while joining forces through integration seems to help them regain some of that control.

Integration would, in other words, be about conferring tasks to the Union, in a way that benefits the Member States. These tasks might even come to include those related to security and defence.

In addition to governments, and demanding citizens, other actors might step in to further the integration process, too. As Andreatta notes, neofunctionalists would put emphasis on the supranational agencies. These might exploit the increasing difficulty in dealing with technical issues at the national level, as well as the tendency of integration to create 'spillovers,' to further integration from above. Neofunctionalists would stress the endogenous character of the process of integration but also point to unintended consequences as well as the spontaneous and incremental character of the process. Technical spillovers, for instance, may create political spillovers in the sense that formal control is necessarily transferred from the national level (Andreatta 2005: 21–2.)

When thinking about integration in security and defence, then, we see that these same conditions would apply. Thus, integration in security and defence would be incremental. It would have causes both internal and external to the states. Internally, governments might seek increased efficiency through integration. Above them, there would be the supranational institutions, be it old ones that aim at getting a role in the process – the European Commission and the European Parliament – or new ones expressly created for the new field, here typically the European Defence Agency (EDA). Such institutions might then further promote integration, or, as a minimum, they might lock in existing levels of cooperation and thereby account for continuity (Strömvik 2005: 116–18, 178). At the same time, below the state level, both the general public and specific groups may take an active role in furthering integration. Citizens might also be behind an eventual shift of functions from one actor to another. For them, the state's efficiency might be linked with its legitimacy: the state's role in security might become more difficult to legitimize if it were to fulfil security functions less effectively than expected.

In the context of security and defence, European public opinion has quite consistently been in favour of a larger role for the European Union in these matters, and can thus be counted as a factor furthering it. When asked what people expect from the EU, Eurobarometer polls bring forward security, even defence (Howorth 2007: 58–60). There are also specific sectors or groups that have an interest in the process and see their interests better served through integration (the Union) than through the state: these may include industrial interests, but also defence administrations, and defence forces. There might be state or state-related actors that are active in the process but more for their professional interests than in terms of national interest (Mérand 2008: 139; cf. Ojanen 2006 on the broadening of the circle of participants).

Also experts might play a role in the development of the ESDP. Already Haas has emphasized the importance of the role of experts and of learning in his criticism of Mitrany (Haas 1964). To this, one might add the impact of socialization that affects those involved, as emphasized by Øhrgaard (2004: 39–40), also putting forward the idea that the process of integration can be led by unforeseen consequences of previous decisions, not necessarily being consciously and strategically mastered by anyone in particular.

Externally, a state outside the process can also provide a stimulus for integration: non-members may exert pressure towards deeper integration to be able to negotiate with a single partner rather than with all Member States individually (Schmitter, quoted by Andreatta 2005: 22). But the external stimulus can also be opposite: instead of pushing the Member States closer together, it may pull the Member States further apart. It may be in the interests of third states to keep them divided in order not to let them grow stronger together. Furthermore, successful cooperation with external actors may decrease the need to cooperate internally. As an example, Strömvik (2005) notes the influence of the United States: the EU Member States feel more need to cooperate with each other when they disagree with the US, and conversely.

Finally, the third actors need not be third states: other organizations may also have an effect on the integration process. Organizations might mould and shape each other, notably if and when active in the same domains. In the end, therefore, transfer of functions would not be about transfer of functions only from the EU Member States to the Union, but also from other organizations to the EU. It could take place for instance from the United States to European states, or from NATO to the EU. Being able to perceive this, however, may necessitate a paradigm change whereby organizations are taken as real, independent actors, instead of their activities being reduced to the will of their Member States.

State Functions

What, then, are the functions that governments may want to shift or that for other reasons might be shifted from one actor to another? David Mitrany started practical. It would be above all technical questions where the profit of such functional shift would be felt. For quite some time, the research community also stopped at this, excluding, by so doing, defence-related functions from the equation. Here, the starting point is different. To understand defence integration is to see defence as one among the functions, not as essentially different from the others. Importantly, thus, the process of shifting or transferring functions, described above, would in principle include all state functions, without distinction.

What, then, are the functions of a state? There is no universally accepted view of what the functions of a state are. One could list security, welfare, and social justice, or, as Wallace (1994: 64) states, preserving internal order, maintaining national borders, defending national territory, providing legitimate government, services, and welfare, and promoting national prosperity. Further, Schmitter (1991: 2–3) would define the state as a political organization that uniquely controls the concentrated means of coercion within a given contiguous territory, that exclusively claims the right to control the movement of people and goods across its boundaries, and that is formally centralized and differentiated from society.

Susan Strange argued in 1989 that states have growing difficulties in fulfilling their functions, for instance those linked to keeping up and improving living standards. States are becoming defective, hollow in the middle though still growing new shoots. Authority over society and economy is increasingly diffused, having leaked away and evaporated to become shared with, sustained by, or constrained by others (Strange 1995). She also points out that industrial and trade policies have become more important than defence and foreign policy (Strange 1989).

One of these 'others' with which functions are shared or that constrains the states' autonomy is the European Union. The EU has noticeably broadened its scope: it is not only about internal market or trade, as, since the Maastricht Treaty, citizenship, monetary autonomy, defence, and internal security are at least touched upon. More is to come: Wessels saw ten years ago environment and consumer protection as the next fields for the EU (Wessels 1997: 278.)

Wessels does not see this as simple transfer of competencies, though. While transfer of competencies takes place, there is also increasing incorporation of national actors in EU processes, something that Wessels calls 'engrenage' (Wessels 1997: 279–81). Similarly, loyalties might not be transferred as in Haas (above), but multiple loyalties do emerge (Wessels 1997: 291). Wessels also uses the term 'fusion.' The fusion thesis means essentially the merger of public resources. This is something that may have both positive and negative consequences. The rationale might be efficiency; yet fusion also implies diffused responsibilities and less accountability. It is also difficult to reverse the trends (Wessels 1997: 274). The decision-making forums change and are populated somewhat differently. In Brussels, there is an increase of 'other presences,' too, including local authorities, and third countries (Wessels 1997: 282–3). In all, the states remain and see themselves as 'masters of the treaty,' but this can be seen as compensation for loss of national competence (Wessels 1997: 287).

Whether transferred or shared, state functions are changing. Such functions as Schmitter's 'unique control' and exclusive claims (see above) seem highly theoretical in today's Europe, where the functions of control of individuals and of territory seem increasingly shared with the European Union. When applied to the field of defence, Wessels's fusion thesis helps to see the degree to which national decision-making processes are affected by the ESDP (Mérand 2008: 149) and interlinked with it.

Changing Security Functions

In terms of the state's security functions proper, the traditional view would be that the state ensures the security of its territory and of its citizens on that territory. In other words, the state defends its territorial integrity against external aggression or invasion, and has for that a right to self-defence in international law. Territorial defence would be the classic task of the state's military force. States may also conclude more or less permanent defence alliances with each other, where the right to self-defence also applies.[5] The state also takes care of the surveillance of its territorial borders. Finally, the state ensures the security and safety of its citizens through appropriate police forces and emergency services. In all these cases – territorial defence, border control, and policing – force may be used. In Weber's classic definition, the state has the monopoly of the *legitimate* use of force within the society.

In time, however, security functions have changed. A first change takes place when defending the territory is no longer seen as the most important task, or a priority when resources are allocated. This may be because the likelihood of aggression diminishes; that is, threat perception changes: there is no existential threat. What follows is a twofold development. On the one hand, the state is increasingly seen as ensuring the security of its citizens, and of its own 'vital functions' (as defined in Finland) and infrastructure, more than that of the territory. On the other hand, the state may be defending its own interests somewhere else than on its own territory. Defence becomes crisis management, the aim of which may be, for instance, to impede a regional conflict from spreading closer to one's own territory. In some cases, the capacity to defend the territory falls somewhat back in importance, giving precedence to the capacity of taking part in international tasks (Sweden).

Crisis management may also be a new formula for defence. As a notion, it is less menacing and more neutral than 'defence' proper. Furthermore, when acting together in a concerted way, instead of acting alone, states diminish the possibility of third countries' interpreting their action as defence of their national interest only, and increase their legitimacy.

A second change takes place when the state is no longer capable of ensuring the security of its citizens. Increasing movement of people means that one's citizens are not necessarily any longer at home, but they would still expect something from their home country. Citizens can expect their state to help them in faraway places (the tsunami of 2006 would be a case in point). Citizens, on the other hand, are no longer citizens of their home country alone: EU citizenship is there, too,[6] with possible consequences when it comes to who ensures the citizens' security. Other countries' citizens are present on one's own territory. Similarly, territory becomes shared as internal frontiers are abolished. Border guarding gets done not on the border but instead on the territory: it shifts locus in a similar way as defence does when it takes place outside one's own territory, in the form of crisis management. As internal and external security get mixed, the police and the military would also change functions and roles. The traditional roles of the military and the police get mixed, as do the environments in which they act: the military finds internal duties, notably in disaster relief, while the police are sent abroad on various missions. Both 'citizens' and 'territory' are, thus, no longer unambiguous.

The EU increasingly takes part in all these activities: crisis management, defence, border guarding, internal security or safety. The functions get to be organized following a certain pattern – for example, the Member States committing themselves to sending a certain number of persons to operations at a short notice. This would include military crisis management, civilian crisis management, and emergency units (e.g., firemen), but also frontier guards. The EU countries agreed in 2007 on committing to send frontier guards to help member countries at the Schengen external border in case of urgent crisis. FRONTEX would coordinate these so-called rapid frontier intervention groups.

On a deeper level, the EU is transforming the state. It might even seem to take away the very essence of the state: its territory, its citizens, and its security functions. It takes away the territory by making the external borders shared and dissolving the internal ones. But there might also be cases in which the EU compels a state to consider as its own territory something much wider or more than what the map would tell. Of this, the mutual assistance clause would be an example, as is the European Security Strategy from 2003 that literally says that 'With the new threats, the first line of defence will often be abroad.' Second, the EU takes away from the state its citizens – the European External Action Service might mean new practices in helping citizens in need in third countries. Third, the EU takes away the security functions: it becomes an influential actor in the framing of the internal security of its Member States, and obviously in external security. What is important is that it is a legitimate actor, perhaps even a legitimate user of force, in both contexts. In the international arena, the Member State's own legitimacy in the use of force might already be contested.

These changes might be summarized as a trend of low politicization of security and defence (Ojanen 2002), which implies that security and defence are less than before seen as an essential part of statehood or state sovereignty. Mérand speaks about denationalization of defence policy: its transgovernmental character gets more pronounced, and defence is being Europeanized as it is no longer seen as a fundamental part of state identity (Mérand 2008: 13, 16). Sovereignty and defence can be transferred under certain conditions to other actors. The number of possible actors grows; the state no longer has the monopoly position.

Functionalist Explanation of the Development of the ESDP

Long (1999) stands out in the existing literature as a rare case in which Mitranian functionalism is explicitly applied to EU security policy. Yet, Long does not look closer at various security functions. Instead, he delineates a functional criticism of the Common Foreign and Security Policy as confrontational, premised on territorial exclusion and ultimately military force. He then proposes a functional alternative, based on variable geometry, community-oriented and integrative in nature, and premised on giving each organization a narrow focus of its own. For the EU, this would mean concentrating on the economic aspects of security, highlighting the link between welfare and security already present in Mitrany's thinking.

Others have arrived at similar conclusions from different starting points: the EU should have a properly defined role in security that does not overlap with that of other organizations and that reflects its general nature and its strengths. What we see happening in ESDP, however, is something different: a constant expansion of functions and increase of overlap. Yet this does not make a functionalist account obsolete: a functionalist account does not need to take us in the direction Long indicates, but can help us understand this very expansion through a better understanding of changing security functions.

We can also ask what function the ESDP serves. The building up and further strengthening of the ESDP has been motivated in several different ways, and these motivations can also be seen as the ESDP's functions. Witney (2008) lists the need for the Union to tackle the real threats to its citizens' security and to make a significant contribution to maintaining international peace. Thus, the functions would be related to the Union's international image and to the security of its citizens. However, Witney continues to add that developing the ESDP is actually functional from the point of view of the Member States: it helps them provide for their citizens' security, defend their humanitarian values in the wider world, and keep the Atlantic alliance in good shape (Witney 2008: 9). Another function of the ESDP would thus be bolstering certain capabilities of the Member States, while a third function would be, somewhat surprisingly perhaps, maintaining another organization, NATO, in good condition.

Using these broad categories, we can also described the ESDP as a list of functions divided in three groups. There are, first, functions related to international peace and security, where we would place crisis management, the planning of related military and civilian capability, capability improvement, related training, and related strategies. Second are functions related to the security of the citizens, including border and territorial security. Third, an offshoot of capability development is the bolstering of other organizations, notably NATO.

We can also map the development of the ESDP in terms of how these functions have been (partially) transferred to the Union or become shared with it. Crisis management as a function became 'popular' after the end of the Cold War. It is also typically something that has been defined as a collective function, rather than a function of a single state, also because of reasons of legitimacy: an intervention by a single state may be seen as less legitimate than that by an organization. Similarly, framing European defence as a capability-enhancement process aimed at enabling Europe to prevent crises on the continent is a rationale that has helped overcome controversies on ESDP (Mérand 2008: 124).

The first stage in the creation and transfer of functions thus becomes the Amsterdam Treaty, whereby the crisis management tasks, or the Petersberg tasks, were conferred to the Union – not from the Member States, which incidentally would not have seen crisis management as their function, but from the Western European Union, which had defined these tasks as its own in 1992 in an attempt to reinvigorate itself with something concrete and useful to do. These tasks originally included humanitarian and rescue tasks, peacekeeping tasks, and tasks of combat forces in crisis management, including peacemaking. Subsequently, the crisis management tasks have expanded: the Lisbon Treaty (and already the draft Constitutional Treaty of 2003) adds joint disarmament operations, military advice and assistance, conflict prevention, and post-conflict stabilization. The explicit expansion of these functions is interesting as such.

Related to the acquisition of a new function, crisis management, opens a second stage: the function of gathering and improving crisis response capacity to be able to take care of the new functions. Here, some collective decisions were made and common goals set in 1999. The Helsinki Headline Goal set as a goal a force catalogue of 60,000, 100 ships and 400 aircraft to be deployable in sixty days for the duration of one year. It was followed by the Headline Goal 2010. Goals also included improving European military capacity through ECAP, the European Capacity Action Plan. Some of the initiatives were originally aimed at a smaller group of Member States, for example, the EU Battle Groups (EUBGs), even though in the end all but two countries took part in them. The European Gendarmerie Force, an initiative by Spain, Italy, the Netherlands, Portugal, and France, is limited to countries with a gendarmerie tradition. Further, the European capabilities are complemented by single Member States' so-called niche capabilities, for instance the Cypriotic medical group or the Athens Sealift Coordination Centre (Howorth 2007: 103–8). On the civilian side, the Civilian Headline Goal 2008 was set, and discussions on different forms of civilian rapid reaction capability have been ongoing (see also Witney 2008). Not all of these have been put in action; the EUBGs, for instance, have not been deployed yet.

As a new institutional framework, the European Defence Agency (EDA) was created in 2004 to help improve the military capabilities and to strengthen European defence capability. Interestingly, these common-sensical-sounding aims hide more profound novelties. First, member governments are now committed to purchasing defence equipment from each other if the tender is the best available, rather than from a national supplier; thus, the original exclusion of armaments from trade liberalization is ending. Second, qualified majority voting is used, which is still not common in ESDP (Howorth 2007: 111; Mérand 2008: 34).

On a third stage, two more related European functions, capacity planning and training, emerge and come to mix with national planning and training. Originally, it was thought that the EU would use in its crisis management operations the planning and command assets of either NATO or any of the five Operation Headquarters (OHQs) currently available in European Member States (France, the UK, Germany, Italy, and Greece). Since 1 January 2007, the EU has a third option for commanding missions and operations of limited size from the EU Operations Centre within the EU Military Staff that uses some EUMS core staff, as well as some extra 'double-hatted' EUMS officers and so-called 'augmentees' from the Member States (Council of the European Union). The ESDP structures and instruments now also include the Civilian Planning and Conduct Capability (CPCC).

Joint operations lead to the need to train together and to ensure interoperability, perhaps specialization. A concrete manifestation would be the Revolving European Security and Defence College, established in July 2005, that is a network for enhancing European security culture and providing Member States with knowledgeable persons on the EU (Howorth 2007: 114).

While Member States might feel they profit from shared planning and joint training, there can be friction with NATO. Strategic and operational planning – as well as command – has been regarded as a central sign of autonomy, a limit for what the EU can do, and a basis for the EU-NATO complementarity. Yet, the EU has at least started to cross that limit.

Fourth, the need for a shared overall view appears, and thus a need for a common strategy. The European Security Strategy of 2003 was, as Forsberg (2006: 17) notes, driven by the logic of practical needs of crisis management. A logical next step would be the emergence of a European strategic culture.

Fifth, other security functions linked to territory surface, including the question of common defence policy and common defence. A clause on military assistance, similar to but not identical with the WEU article V, was inserted in the draft Constitutional Treaty and found its way to the Lisbon Treaty, too. The Treaty encompasses the duty to assist a Member State under attack by a third country, yet with reference made to NATO as the foundation of collective defence and the forum for its implementation for its member countries.

Stage six brings in the EU's borders and links ESDP with non-ESDP related matters of internal security and border security. The creation of common external Schengen borders and the concomitant abolition of internal borders has led to a necessity to integrate the function of border control. The EU itself refers to the 'European model of integrated border management.' The European Agency for the Management of Operational Cooperation at the External Borders of the Member States of the European Union, FRONTEX, established in 2004, is one of the implementers of this model, as well as a facilitator and coordinator among the various actors. What is interesting about the role of FRONTEX is that border management does not start or end at the border: it includes measures taken elsewhere, on the Member States' territory, in that of the neighbouring states, even in third states (Laitinen 2008). FRONTEX's role in carrying out risk analysis adds to the emerging shared threat perception, while its orbit of actions shows the blurring of the internal-external divisions.

Finally, as stage seven, the solidarity clause and the practical measures taken to monitor security threats internally within the EU complement the EU's role in internal security, or in what used to be seen as the states' internal security. The solidarity clause was adopted in March 2004 after the Madrid bombings. It implies that all Union instruments, including the military provided by the Member States, have to be available to prevent terrorist threats, to protect democratic institutions and the population, and to assist a state at the request of its political authorities, in the event of a terrorist attack or a natural or man-made disaster.

In practice, this may also imply helping fellow Member States with sending the military to operate on their territory and getting help from other states' militaries on one's own territory. Also included are a specific Community civil protection mechanism; advance identified intervention teams; joint preparation and planning; the Monitoring and Information Centre (MIC) that takes part in monitoring and coordination; and a rapid alert network which has been employed several times – for instance, after the earthquake in Morocco in February 2004 and in Greek forest fires in 2007.[7]

When looking at how and why the ESDP has been developing, one notices that different aspects of security might be developing at different paces, or unevenly. To date, it would seem that internal security is more advanced, and also gives the EU a larger role, than the external security side, where older models are still recurred to. The solidarity clause of the Lisbon Treaty is an example of the new developments, while the mutual defence or assistance clause represents the past. According to the mutual defence clause, the Member States are to use all the means in their power to help another member country that has been attacked by a third state. This is an article from the 1940s in spirit, with roots in a world where territorial threat still exists, where the states are the only real actors, and where their cooperation takes place mainly in military alliances: the article refers to NATO as the forum for the implementation of common defence for its members. The formulation of the clause might be logical in the sense that it needs to fit the existing institutional framework, that is, not overlooking NATO. Yet, compared with the solidarity clause, there is a difference: the EU does not exist for this article: it does not have a role defined for itself – even though the Union institutions would hardly remain inactive in reality if there was such a threat. The solidarity clause, on the contrary, does bring in the EU, mentioning as it does 'all Union instruments.' Including the military provided by the Member States, that have to be available in cases of terrorist threat and natural and man-made disasters. In the long run, this internal security role of the EU might increase its overall legitimacy, bolstered by its more straightforward and less caveat-laden approach, but also responding better to the perceived security threats and needs of European citizens.

Thus, the growth and development of ESDP can be explained in functionalist terms as a process in which EU Member States transfer (parts of) certain security and defence-related functions to the EU. The reasons for these can be both political and economic – which in turn implies that they are no longer as high-political as before.

What one needs to note, however, is the uneven nature of this transfer. The true role of the EU remains contested. The Member States still remain the ultimate decision makers, or can still claim that role because of the prevailing unanimity rule in decision making and treaty change, as Wessels pointed out.

Yet, there is a tendency towards an increasing Europeanization of decision making in this domain, too. Elements of transgovernmentalism (if not supranationalism) do emerge, the Political and Military Committee (PSC) being one interesting example. Indeed, one might consider the decision making on security and defence as a separate function that is increasingly shared with other Member States or increasingly takes places within new EU agencies and institutions.

The PSC, permanent since January 2001, monitors and gives opinions, exerts political control and strategic direction of crisis management operations, meets two to three times a week, and consists of permanent representatives in Brussels. It can be under a very strict control of Member States in important matters (Howorth 2007: 69–70) but has been said to be 'unusually cohesive,' pioneering and consensus-seeking, with a high esprit de corps. Howorth (2007: 73) quotes Meyer (2006) characterizing the PSC as one of the most important ideational transmission belts of a gradual Europeanization of national foreign, security, and defence policy.

Compared with what existed before PSC, the direction of change becomes visible. Earlier on, under the General Affairs Council (renamed in 2003 as General Affairs and External Relations Council), meetings were prepared by COREPER (permanent representatives), and the role of the Political Committee, composed of the political directors of the Ministries for Foreign Affairs, thus, the capitals, was relatively greater. At its most, one could speak about 'intensive transgovernmentalism' (Howorth 2007: 63–6).

There are two other relatively new ESDP institutions that bring in new kinds of expert constituencies and also concentrate decision making in Brussels. The Military Committee (EUMC) and the Military Staff (EUMS) have implied a considerable investment for the Member States in terms of placing military personnel at the EU. In the EUMC, the Chiefs of Defence Staff meet twice a year, usually through military representatives (and mostly double-hatted with NATO) to give advice and recommendations. The EUMS, a General Directorate with the Council General Secretariat, takes care of early warning, situation assessment, and strategic planning (Howorth 2007: 74–5, Mérand 2008: 32–3).

The Council of Defence Ministers does not exist as such but meets regularly and informally since 2002 under the aegis of the General Affairs Council. As Howorth points out, 'in democratic systems, defence ministers are generally kept strictly subordinate to foreign ministers.' In their informal setting, they have, however, become significant security policy shapers. They also meet as the Steering Board of the European Defence Agency (Howorth 2007: 75–6).[8]

Finally, the functionalist account of the development of the ESDP would not be complete if restricted only to transfer of functions – including decision making – from the Member States to the EU. One also needs to take into consideration the transfer of functions that takes place from other organizations. Indeed, the EU has taken over functions from other organizations, not only from its Member States. This might be because of its hybrid nature as an entity resembling both a state and an organization (or becoming so because of transfer of competencies). The EU first 'inherited' the Petersberg tasks from WEU. It has then assumed a larger role in European security, sharing functions with NATO, perhaps at some point even replacing NATO in some functions related to security and defence in Europe. Finally, it has assumed, or been given, certain tasks by the United Nations in the framework of peace support operations, as a regional organization of particularly well-developed crisis management capacities. Both types of transfer of functions, from states and from organizations, may also lead to friction, to inter-organizational rivalry, and to a more diffused picture of who is responsible for which functions (see also Wessels above).

Conclusion: Paradigm Shift with New Deal in Legitimacy?

In explaining integration, and security and defence integration in particular, there might be windows of opportunity for various actors to mark the process, to influence the outcome; but to build the entire account or explanation of security integration on their role would obviously not be fair. Yet, this is what they tend to do themselves. The actors, be it governments, interest groups, individuals, attempt to explain ESDP as having resulted from their efforts. It may be one of the central elements of a functional account that the state is still able to claim a role for itself. If it has lost the real ability to take care of some functions attributed to it, switching these over to a European level is still in a way keeping them at home if the state at the same time argues that it is in control of the European process as a whole. In other words, a functional view on integration would not be the direct opposite of intergovernmental explanations.

In the end, the functions of the state are changing. In particular, security-related functions are undergoing transformation. So is citizenship and territory. Immigration becomes a security issue, as shown in the document on the implementation of the ESS (European Council 2008). Security and defence are entangled; internal and external security are mixed. This also implies that new actors come into play: private security enterprises, international organizations, alliances.

Security and defence are traditionally seen as the field that is closest to state sovereignty. Now, there can be a gap between rhetoric and capability. It can lead to legitimacy problems: if the state no longer can or does provide these functions or services, why would one then need the state? Today, the EU is needed in several sectors, including security.

Within the EU Member States, there might in the future be a growing difficulty in finding new descriptions, new ways of legitimizing the state's diminishing role in security and defence. The military, then, might legitimize its existence with new arguments, new functions: international tasks and internal security, even nation-building, may become new ways of legitimizing existence and budgetary claims in a situation where territorial defence no longer gives such a legitimization (Edmunds 2006; Mérand 2008: 100).

While an EU Member State may lose legitimacy as a security actor internationally, it may acquire new legitimacy as a security actor internally, on other Member States' territory. In other words, a single Member State of the EU may have practically surrendered parts of its monopoly over legitimate violence: it is almost impossible for national authorities to launch procurement programs or to deploy military contingents without taking into account the EU and their counterparts in it (Mérand 2008: 148). Yet, on the territory of the EU, the presence of 'foreign' – and now by definition no longer foreign but European – armed forces would no longer be objected to for the purposes of disaster relief, border control–related operations, and the like.

The EU's own legitimacy in the field of ESDP seems strong. There are great expectations for its role in international peace and security, notably in crisis management. The EU's legitimacy as an international actor is often attributed to its multilateral and inclusive nature, but also on the perception that it 'acts differently' and does achieve results (see de Vasconcelos 2009: 21–2). An important constituent of the growing legitimacy is the success of the EU in strategic and operational planning and capability improvement. Here, a basic argument has been that of efficiency gains in defence spending. Seen from the point of view of the EU as a whole, it has been pointed out that the national defences become quite a spending dilemma as the EU spends \$230 billion to fund 25 armies, 21 air forces, and 18 navies, 'for no reason that is any longer obvious or clear,' and yet most Member States would be in no position even to defend their own territory from a serious existential threat (Howorth 2007: 117). As a way of getting rid of inefficient spending, ESDP would appear a quite welcome improvement, if not an alternative, to traditional national defence. It might also be an improvement to similar processes within NATO if the EU were to be relatively more successful in getting its Member States to comply. Finally, the EU's role in the security of its citizens might be growing.

The whole ESDP development has greatly benefited from benign public opinion. This was seen in the work of the European Convention, where various far-reaching security- and defence-related initiatives were explicitly motivated by public opinion. Similarly, the fact that parts of the then Lisbon Treaty were enacted without waiting for the treaty to enter into force relied on a strong belief of shared acceptance by the Member States and their population. Being one of the successful initiatives of the EU, ESDP did become the engine of the whole integration process in the early 2000s, perhaps even reversing the traditional relationship between foreign, security, and defence policy: integration could in fact start from defence, and then move to foreign policy, instead of first having to wait for a common foreign policy to emerge, as had been assumed earlier.

The division of tasks and the attribution of roles in security and defence are not clear, however. The way Nick Witney (2008) pamphlets for the future strengthening of ESDP – mentioned above – tells a lot about the lack of clarity as to who in the end is doing what. Witney lists both the motives for the Union to develop ESDP and those for the Member States to do so. He implies that ESDP helps both the Union and the Member States tackle the threats and provide for their citizens' security, while at the same time helping the Union to make a significant contribution to maintaining international peace, and the states to defend their humanitarian values in the wider world, while also seeing to it that NATO keeps functioning well (Witney 2008: 9). Following this line of argument, more ESDP would be in the interests of both organizations. Yet, there might also be an issue of shifting legitimacy there: the perceived ability of the two in fulfilling the security functions may alter in time.

Still, a considerable part of the literature on the ESDP seems to fall back on traditional frameworks of analysis. In a volume entitled *What Ambitions for European Defence in 2020?* de Vasconcelos (2009) emphasizes questions such as how to improve the operational capabilities of the Union or generate more political will among the Member States. Notions such as 'European army' are used only in sentences saying that such a thing will not materialize or is not the goal. The occasional glimpses at an alternative future, such as Moustakis and Violakis's (2008: 431) idea of including the European army and rapid reaction forces with their operational roles in every member country's constitution, are readily dismissed as unrealistic.

Paradigms are very resistant, indeed. Yet, the case of the ESDP shows how the Member States are giving up certain security functions and how security and defence have become more easily transferable as functions. If defence has ever really been a borderline that the process of integration would not cross, it has now been crossed. A paradigm change that lessens the importance of states as actors, of security and defence as the core functions of the state, and of traditional capabilities as assets would seem to be de rigueur.

Whether or not state legitimacy suffers from this depends on the availability of other sources of legitimacy, for instance, the role of the state as the provider of social security and welfare.

What matters for the international system as a whole is that states are giving up functions in an unequal way: EU Member States more than non-EU states, some EU Member States more than other EU Member States. This means, first, increasing diversification among the states, and potentially more difficulties in mutual understanding and cooperation. Second, while increasing the need to take organizations seriously as actors, it also means less diversification among the organizations: there is, indeed, increasing functional overlap among international organizations in the security sector. This may make the identification of responsible and accountable actors in security policy more difficult than before.

NOTES

1 To borrow a curious and paradoxical notion that political scientists seem very fond of.
2 The importance of the capacity of a state to fulfil these functions is underlined by the fact that the EU Security Strategy (European Council 2003) lists state failure as one of the major security threats of the European Union.

3 Here, Haas is taken as a functionalist, as he called himself. In 1970, he explicitly noted that he did not see himself as a neofunctionalist; in his article
   of 2001, however, he states that he would be happy with being called the father of neofunctionalism.
4 One should also note here the juxtaposition of nationalism and supranationalism – rather than of supranationalism and intergovernmentalism.
5 Even though restricted; see the UN Charter.
6 Except for the Danes who have an opt-out.
7 It is noteworthy that this element of the EU's security functions encompasses a broader community than the EU. Assistance to the MIC is also provided by member countries of the European Economic Area, as well by other
   countries such as Turkey, Serbia, and Israel. This may affect the EU's external legitimacy.
8 Such institutions are often seen as places of socialization. There might even
   be peer pressure of some kind, reinforced by the possibility to use mechanisms that let some countries advance faster than others, like the permanent
   structured cooperation.

REFERENCES

Andreatta, Filippo. 2005. 'Theory and the European Union's International Relations.' In *International Relations and the European Union*, ed. Christopher
   Hill and Michael Smith, 18–38. Oxford: Oxford University Press.
Council of the European Union. EU Operations Centre. http://www.consilium
   .europa.eu/cms3_fo/showPage.asp?id=1211&lang=en&mode=g (accessed
   10 August 2009).
Duke, Simon, and Hanna Ojanen. 2006. 'Bridging Internal and External Security: Lessons from the European Security and Defence Policy.' *Journal of European Integration* 28, no. 5: 477–94.
EDA website. http://www.eda.europa.eu/newsitem.aspx?id=422 (accessed
   10 August 2009).
Edmunds, Timothy. 2006. 'What Are Armed Forces For? The Changing Nature
   of Military Roles in Europe.' *International Affairs* 82, no. 6: 1059–75.
ESDP Newsletter 8, Summer 2009. Council of the European Union; Operation
   Atalanta, fact sheet. http://www.consilium.europa.eu/uedocs/cms_data/
   docs/missionPress/files/090622%20Factsheet%20EU%20NAVFOR%20
   Somalia%20-%20version%208_EN.pdf (accessed 10 August 2009).
EUobserver. 'New Nato Chief Pledges to Fix Relations with EU,' by Valentina
   Pop. http://euobserver.com/9/28518 (accessed 10 August 2009).

European Council. 2003. A Secure Europe in a Better World. European Security Strategy. Brussels, 12 December 2003. http://www.consilium.europa. eu/uedocs/cmsUpload/78367.pdf (accessed 10 August 2009).

– 2008. Report on the Implementation of the European Security Strategy: Providing Security in a Changing World. Brussels, 11 December 2008. S407/08. http://www.consilium.europa.eu/ueDocs/cms_Data/docs/pressdata/ EN/reports/104630.pdf (accessed 10 August 2009).

Forsberg, Tuomas. 2006. 'Explaining the Emergerce of the ESDP: Setting the Research Agenda.' Paper prepared for the British International Studies Association Meeting, Cork, 18–20 December.

Haas, Ernst B. 1961. 'International Integration. The European and the Universal Process.' *International Organization* 15, no. 3: 366–92.

– 1963. 'Technocracy, Pluralism and the New Europe'. In *A New Europe?* ed. Stephen R. Graubard, 62–8. London: Oldbourne Press.

– 1964. *Beyond the Nation-State. Functionalism and International Organization.* Stanford, CA: Stanford University Press.

– 1968. *The Uniting of Europe. Political, Social, and Economic Forces 1950–1957.* Stanford, CA: Stanford University Press. (Originally published by Stevens and Sons Limited, London, 1958.)

– 2001. 'Does Constructivism Subsume Neo-functionalism?. In *The Social Construction of Europe*, ed. Thomas Christiansen et al., 22–31. London: SAGE.

Howorth, Jolyon. 2007. *Security and Defence Policy in the European Union.* Basingstoke: Palgrave Macmillan.

Laitinen, Ilkka. 2008. Presentation of Brig. Gen. Ilkka Laitinen, Executive Director of FRONTEX, at a seminar organized by the Finnish Institute of International Affairs together with the Stefan Batory Foundation in Helsinki, 15 September 2008.

Long, David. 1999. 'The Security Discourses of the European Union: A Functional Critique.' In *New Perspectives on International Functionalism*, ed. Lucian M. Ashworth and David Long, 120–36. Houndmills, Basingstoke, and London: Macmillan Press.

Mérand, Frédéric. 2008. *European Defence Policy. Beyond the Nation State.* Oxford: Oxford University Press.

Meyer, Christoph O. 2006. *The Quest for a European Strategic Culture: Changing Norms on Security and Defence in the European Union.* Basingstoke: Palgrave Macmillan.

Mitrany, David. 1943. *A Working Peace System. An Argument for the Functional Development of International Organization.* London: The Royal Institute of International Affairs.

Moustakis, Fotios, and Petros Violakis. 2008. 'European Security and Defence Policy Deceleration: An Assessment of the ESDP Strategy.' *European Security* 17, no. 4: 421–33.

Niemann, Arne, with Philippe C. Schmitter. 2009. 'Neofunctionalism.' In *European Integration Theory,* 2nd ed., ed. Antje Wiener and Thomas Diez, 45–66. Oxford: Oxford University Press.

Øhrgaard, Jakob C. 2004. 'International Relations or European Integration: Is the CFSP *sui generis?*' In *Rethinking European Union Foreign Policy,* ed. Ben Tonra and Thomas Christiansen, 26–44. Manchester: Manchester University Press.

Ojanen, Hanna. 1998. *The Plurality of Truth: A Critique of Research on the State and European Integration.* Aldershot: Ashgate.

– 2002. 'Theories at a Loss? EU-NATO Fusion and the "Low-Politicisation" of Security and Defence in European Integration.' UPI Working Papers 35. Helsinki: Finnish Institute of International Affairs.

– 2006. 'Explaining the ESDP: Theoretical Grips on Recent Developments.' In *European Security and Defence Policy: A European Challenge,* ed. Bo Huldt, Mika Kerttunen, Jan Mörtberg, and Ylva Ericsson, 1–16. Strategic Yearbook 2006 of the Swedish National Defence College and the Finnish National Defence College. Stockholm: Swedish National Defence College.

Schmitter, Philippe C. 1991. 'The European Community as an emergent and novel form of political domination.' Estudio/Working Paper 1991/26. Madrid: Centro de Estudios Avanzados en Ciencias Sociales, Instituto Juan March de Estudios e Investigaciones.

Strange, Susan. 1989. 'Toward a Theory of Transnational Empire.' In *Global Changes and Theoretical Challenges. Approaches to World Politics for the 1990,* ed. Ernst-Otto Czempiel, and James N. Rosenau, 161–76. Lanham, MD: Lexington Books.

– 1995. 'The Defective State.' *Dædalus* 124, no. 2: 55–74.

Strömvik, Maria. 2005. *To Act as a Union. Explaining the Development of the EU's Collective Foreign Policy.* Lund Political Studies 142. Lund: Lund University, Department of Political Science.

Vasconcelos, Álvaro de, ed. 2009. *What Ambitions for European Defence in 2020?* Paris: The European Union Institute for Security Studies.

Wallace, William. 1994. 'Rescue or Retreat? The Nation State in Western Europe, 1945–93.' *Political Studies* 42: 52–76.

Wessels, Wolfgang. 1997. 'An Ever Closer Fusion? A Dynamic Macropolitical View on Integration Processes.' *Journal of Common Market Studies* 35, no. 2: 267–99.

Witney, Nick. 2008. *Re-energising Europe's Security and Defence Policy.* Policy paper. London: European Council on Foreign Relations.

8 Geopolitics and the Atlantic Alliance

STEN RYNNING

'In war,' wrote Sun Tzu some 2,500 years ago, 'prize victory, not a protracted campaign' (Sun Tzu 2003: 13). It would seem that we here encounter a diagnosis of the ills of the Atlantic Alliance. NATO as a whole as well as its leader, the United States, is tied up in protracted campaigns far from its home territory: NATO in Afghanistan, the United States in both Afghanistan and Iraq.

Yet analysts disagree on what this turn of events portends for the Alliance. One school of thought holds that NATO is a relic of the past bipolar distribution of power and now must fade as American primacy matures and perhaps evolves into a new pluralist world order. This school of thought is dominated by realists. Some realists initially proclaimed NATO's rapid demise (Mearsheimer 1990) but later explained its durability with reference to the uncertainty of the balance of power in Europe: the United States will withdraw, and so NATO will come to an end once American policymakers are secure in their belief that Germany will not rise again to dominate Europe (Mearsheimer 2001). Other realists disagree that the problem lies with balances of power in Europe and instead argue that American policymakers are wedded to imperialist visions that de facto undermine the American national interest (Layne 2006). However, all these realists agree that changes in the international distribution of power undermine NATO and account for NATO's travails in Central Asia and elsewhere.

Another school of thought sees NATO as a critical component in the evolving international effort to provide order amid globalization. The threats that justified NATO's status as a defensive alliance are gone but new and ambiguous 'risks' prevail, and NATO is one of several important instruments in the collective management hereof. The Atlantic

Alliance must rebalance the transatlantic partnership and enable a new type of global concert (Calleo 2003). The task for American policy-makers in particular, Calleo continues, is to turn away from 'unipolar illusions' and undertake the construction of a type of Asian Union akin to the one realized in Europe (2007a and 2007b). Other analysts concur: the problem is not globalization and global governance but the inadequate efforts by Western governments to align politically and address globalization's challenges (Dufourq 2006, Schori 2005). Still other analysts perceive a greater danger underneath globalization and see no real remedy in management in concert or otherwise. The ability of rogue actors to exploit globalization – to communicate, coordinate, and network, and target any of the numerous critical points of the global and Western infrastructure – means that the West can win only by turning back the clock on globalization (Robb 2007).

These schools of thought are insightful but raise questions. If realists are right that the changed distribution of power is a threat to NATO, why is NATO still around? If the answer is, as Mearsheimer indicates, that NATO is the United States' instrument to control affairs in Europe, then why is NATO the operational lead agent in Afghanistan? The mobilization of European power and purpose simply does not square with the minimalist role accorded to NATO in Mearsheimer's framework. Conversely, if the globalization analysts are right that NATO is responding to the globalization's logic, why is NATO stubbornly clinging to its regional and defensive raison d'être – as illustrated with the invocation of Article 5 in September 2001?

In this chapter I will suggest that we must grasp both international power and globalization if we are to understand NATO but that this story in itself is incomplete. That which ties power and globalization coherently together in an account of NATO's strengths and weaknesses is geopolitics. NATO is a geopolitical phenomenon embodying the United States' engagement in Eurasia. The Atlantic allies all support this engagement for a variety of geopolitical reasons: one has to do with Russia's position vis-à-vis Western Europe; another with the fate of the global institutions erected in the post–Second World War era and which today support Western interests; yet another with the ability of the allies to manage these tasks while also responding to the threats that do emerge from globalization, such as international terrorism. Ultimately, NATO is a wedding between one part of Eurasian landmass (Western Europe) and a Eurasian periphery (the United States), and their political project comes under the heading of the West and is concerned with sustaining an international order favourable to their interests.

Geopolitics adds value to our understanding of NATO. First of all, geopolitics is as focused on international power and changes therein as are realists, but geopolitics explains – via global geography – why power continues to be a glue and not a dissolvent in Atlantic relations. Second, geopolitics is concerned with the threats inherent in globalization but sharpens our understanding of why the response to these threats cannot simply be global: it would run counter to the logic of the Western project. Finally, geopolitics provides an antidote to the pervasive idea of a paradigm shift in security studies that has taken root following the end of the Cold War and globalization's growth. Issues of the day, key policymakers, military instruments, and diplomacy's vocabulary – these all change, but the basic issue of managing Eurasian power relations remains.

Geopolitics

The confluence of international politics and geography was famously analysed by Thucydides in the Peloponnesian War, where the relative growth of a maritime power (Athens) caused a land power (Sparta) to 'break the peace and begin the war' (1998: 15). Land and sea; relative power; and alliances – these remain the basic conceptual tools of geopolitical analysis.

Not surprisingly, there are two positions in the debate over geopolitics, with one favouring land and the other favouring sea. Both positions were established in the late nineteenth century when geopolitics emerged as a sort of integrated field of study. Alfred T. Mahan emphasized the sea because of its significance in military history: Roman sea power denied the Carthaginians the secure lines of communication on which an attack on Italy depended (Mahan 1987: 20). Alfred Mackinder equally looked to history and observed quite to the contrary the operation of a 'heartland' in Eastern Europe, the control of which would enable control of Eurasia and ultimately the world (1904 and 1942). This debate should be treated as a matter of emphasis, and the decision to weigh land relative to sea must follow from an assessment of international power: does modern power depend on secure territories or, conversely, the ability to project itself across oceans?

John Mearsheimer (2001) brings both land and sea into his sophisticated framework but then denies historical evolution any major role in the story. There is a constant pattern, in other words, which is unaffected by technological, economic, political, or other kinds of changes. The pattern consists first of the durable primacy of 'land power' ('a state's power is largely embedded in its army') and moreover, considering water's 'stopping power,' the division of world politics into regional games of primacy. 'Specifically, the presence of oceans on much of the earth's surface makes it impossible for any state to achieve global hegemony ... Thus, great powers can aspire to dominate only the region in which they are located' (2001: 83–4).

In contrast, historical evolution is everything to Daniel Deudney, whose historical gaze finds that power is gradually becoming so penetrating and destructive that the world has become 'violence interdependent' (2007: 29). As violence interdependence ceaselessly grows, the world must become one – by which Deudney understands a type of global restrained-power Republicanism. Mahan, Mackinder, and other classical geopolitical theorists were path-breaking, Deudney acknowledges, but yet they failed to look beyond the technologies of their time. In thus reviving historical evolution (though Deudney's History must come to an end with the advent of Republicanism), Deudney curiously discards the relevance of the land-sea distinction: what matters are only the military technologies (essentially nuclear-tipped rockets) that transcend land and sea.

Mackinder may have fathered heartland theory but he also prefaced his 1904 article (in which the 'heartland' was labelled 'pivot') with the observation that the past 400 years – the Columbian epoch – were marked by sea power and open space. By 1900, as space had become global and finite, land power regained its pivotal role. Rather than choosing between a fixed geopolitical framework à la Mearsheimer and a transcendent one à la Deudney, I will invoke Mackinder and the argument that we are better able to grasp NATO if we remain open to historical evolution in power's make-up and the relative weight of land and sea. At this point I will therefore outline some conceptual tools; the subsequent analysis will discuss how they apply to distinct historical contexts.

- World islands: the world consists of five great landmasses, the biggest of which is Eurasia. The other four are North and South America, Africa, and Australia.
- Core and periphery: in geographical terms Eurasia is the core landmass. North America, like the other three, is a peripheral landmass.
- Hegemony: a great power will seek to dominate the international order by virtue of its own power and its ability to divide the remainder of the world.

- Power: power is based on latent power and military power (Mearsheimer 2001: 55). Latent power refers to socio-economic factors that can be located anywhere on the five world islands. Military power concerns the military forces that a hegemon and its allies command.

These are the essential conceptual tools for understanding NATO – past, present, and future. In the sections that follow I will interpret first NATO's Cold War history, its continuity into the post–Cold War decade of the 1990s, and its current effort to transform itself into continued relevance past the turn of the century.

Controlling the Rim: NATO's Cold War Past

The United States' entry into the Second World War in 1941 marked its transition to global power. The Spanish-American War of 1898 along with a more assertive Monroe doctrine signalled an end to the continentalism that defined much of the nineteenth century and marked the onset of global politics. The United States participated in the First World War, as we know, but then withdrew from the League of Nations because domestic opponents saw it as an 'international enforcement system' that would get the United States involved in faraway battlefields (Claude 1962: 99). It is therefore ironic that the League's architect, President Wilson, was later accused of naivety. The rise of great Eurasian powers – Germany and the Soviet Union – and the growing inability of the British Empire to check them meant that the United States would have to involve itself in Eurasian power politics in spite of its dislike precisely for power politics. The solution lay in a kind of collective security scheme that promised to manage power differently from the balance-of-power model associated with Europe's dreaded past. The solution lay partly with the United Nations (UN) and its 'policemen' – the permanent members of the Security Council – partly with regional arrangements under the UN umbrella. NATO became one such arrangement. Thus the United States in 1944–5 engaged globally under the banner of collective security. However, the engagement emptied collective security of its clarity because NATO was after all a collective defence alliance, as Inis Claude noted (1962: 116–22). Collective security was the politically appealing image for policymakers seeking to break a tradition of isolationism, but the outcome was a balance-of-power commitment to defend Western Europe against a continental Eurasian power.

Geopolitics tells us that the United States could no longer expect to be safe in North America if a single power dominated Eurasia. The geopolitically peripheral power needed to engage in Eurasia in order to divide it. American war planning logically took aim at defeating the power that occupied the 'heartland' – which meant Germany (it had invaded the Soviet Union in 1941 and thus occupied Mackinder's heartland). Defeating a heartland power required a massive effort to 'outbuild' Germany, transport the new army across the Atlantic, and to get it ashore at Germany's nearest frontier. And so the United States began in 1941 to build an army of armoured divisions and infantry divisions that would be 'suitable for only one sort of operation: large-scale, tank-infantry battles on the continent of Europe' (Keegan 1992: 32). Unlike the indirect strategies favoured by Britain, the United States wanted a direct strategy – a war of attrition – and the result was the Normandy invasion in 1944 and the drive to Berlin coordinated with the Soviet Union.

At this point collective security dominated political thinking, but military thinking was onto a different path. The 'strategic perimeter' of hemispheric defence needed expansion following not only the Pearl Harbor attack (of December 1941) but the development of nuclear weapons. Fearing a surprise attack that would bomb the United States into strategic submission, the Department of Defense saw overseas bases as necessary to enable the United States 'to interdict an attack from *any* source far from American shores' (Leffler 1992: 56). As a minimum, the United States needed to dominate the Atlantic and Pacific oceans in a military sense and gain air transit rights along a corridor running from Morocco across the Middle East and India to South-East Asia. The United States was de facto developing a containment doctrine and this prior to George Kennan's Long Telegram of 1946 (Leffler 1992: 61).

The political doctrine of containment developed in 1946–7 and culminated in the creation of NATO in April 1949. Lord Ismay, NATO's first Secretary General, once famously noted that NATO was there to 'keep the Soviets out, the Germans down, and the Americans in.' Ismay's remark made sense: the presence of the United States ensured that none of the power pretenders – the Soviet Union and Germany – could lay claim to the heartland. However, it is remarkable that NATO never covered the area that Mackinder labelled the heartland, and this in spite of NATO incorporating West Germany in 1955 and Mackinder having pushed his heartland westwards in the course of his writings. Nicolas Spykman provided a different geopolitical assessment that ultimately may tell us more about NATO during its Cold War years. NATO effectively covered the European rim, and rims were on the mind of Spykman. 'The great coastal regions of the world are interdependent,' wrote Spykman (1942: 165), and 'there has never really been a simple land power-sea power opposition (1944: 43). Spykman scorned the heartland concept, which in his view referred to a large and barren region of the world. Real power was to be gained in the coastal regions, and critical alignments in world politics have therefore involved combinations of sea and landpower. NATO was such an alignment.

The United States had certain advantages in the race to secure control of the Eurasian rims, notably its alliance-like relations to Europe, its South-East Asian access (the Philippines and occupied Japan), and its unharmed socio-economic infrastructure and thus muscle. However, the Soviet Union was in geographical proximity to the rim; it had secured control of satellite states; it demobilized considerably slower than the United States; and data on Soviet strategic policy was scarce (Krieger 1992: 101–3). The push and pull of these uncertainties resulted in US military commitments along most of the Eurasian rim: NATO (entered 1949) in Europe and ANZUS (1951) in Asia were multilateral alliances; Japan and the Philippines had bilateral security treaties (from 1951); SEATO (1955) added Thailand and Pakistan to US commitments (SEATO involved other already existing allies); and South Korea and Taiwan gained bilateral treaties (in 1953 and 1955 respectively). As John Lewis Gaddis notes, US policymakers at this time vacillated between essentially two positions – a selective policy of defending 'strongpoints' and an offensive policy of defending the entire Eurasian 'perimeter.' President Eisenhower's Secretary of State John Foster Dulles was allegedly susceptible to 'pactomania,' but the matter of fact is that the Truman administration, though initially in favour of the selective policy that George Kennan helped outline, became more expansive over time and put in place the basic perimeter architecture that characterized the Cold War of the 1950s (Gaddis 2005: 150).

It was simply too controversial to refer to geopolitics when this architecture fell into place, which partly had to do with the discredited German geopolitical tradition, partly with the need to mobilize US opinion with the aid of collective security rhetoric. The onset of a nuclear arms race early in the 1950s offered an opportunity to channel intellectual energies in new directions void of controversial geopolitics and its association to balance-of-power politics: nuclear deterrence. A golden era of nuclear deterrence theory and modelling followed in which geopolitics and history were almost completely sidetracked. It took the Sino-Soviet split in the 1960s and the ascent of Richard Nixon and Henry Kissinger in 1969 to bring geopolitics back, this time in the shape notably of the Nixon-Kissinger policy of 'triangular diplomacy' (see Kissinger 1994: chap. 28). The basic geopolitical idea was to take advantage of the new split running through the Eurasian landmass, and this opened a more dynamic era of great power politics compared with the prior nuclear stand-off. NATO in this new era was not always a clear priority, which resulted in European allies' frustration with superpower condominium and the US promise to patch up relations during the Year of Europe in 1973. The Ottawa Declaration of June 1974, celebrating the Alliance's twenty-fifth anniversary, promised continuity in terms of cohesion and determination to prevail, but the promise really underscored the malaise brought to NATO by Eurasian changes. These changes could portend a transformation of world politics: while scholars began studying new worlds of cobwebs, interdependence, and North-South relations, Atlantic policymakers cultivated distinct versions of détente policy that threatened to clash. The renewed Cold War of the 1980s helped restore NATO's sense of cohesion by freezing the geopolitical changes that had become visible in the late 1960s. NATO was as always fraught by politically tense questions – now related notably to intermediate nuclear weapons – but NATO once again embodied a vital strategic partnership.

Heartland Redux? NATO in the 1990s

John Mearsheimer argues that NATO, contrary to the expectations of his own and other analysts, did not collapse following the Cold War because US policymakers realized that they needed to stick around in Europe to ensure that the European Union effectively would absorb newly united Germany (Mearsheimer 2001). This argument is appealing in some ways. The G.H.W. Bush administration did focus sharply on the German question in the early 1990s and insisted on Germany's continued participation in both the EU and NATO when faced with Soviet demands for a looser organization of Central Europe. In crude terms, the fact that the Soviets soon were no longer around to be 'kept out' did not mean that Germany should not be 'kept down.' The question remains, though, whether Germany and German power are the answer to the question why US policymakers wanted the United States 'kept in.'

The American push to enlarge NATO into Eastern Europe and NATO's decision to go out-of-area in the early to mid-1990s testify to a greater geopolitical rationale. First of all, NATO's enlargement brought the Alliance into the heartland for the first time in its history, thus effectively checking Russian power. The United States faced a unique opportunity to benefit from a vacuum in the heartland and they exploited it. Moreover, NATO going out-of-area – in addition to enlarging – made the Atlantic Alliance the foundation for Europe's operational security architecture. France at one point entertained the idea that NATO should remain as an Article 5 organization while the EU should deal with new security challenges short of a territorial threat. US policy ensured the faltering of this vision: NATO became the vehicle for managing the European part of the Eurasian rim.

The American preoccupation with both the heartland and the rimland is indicative of policy that looks beyond the question of German power: the heartland involves notably Russia in addition to Germany, and the rimland involves EU operational capacity and autonomy. This is also to say that it was not clear whether the new era was one of Mackinder or Spykman: did power reside inside Eurasia in the heartland, or was it located in the coastal zones? What was clear was the American ambition to remain engaged and assert hegemonic leadership. The United States focused on both the heartland and the rimland because it could and because it seemed a reasonable strategy of geopolitical pre-emption.

This was the outcome, which is not to say that US policymakers perceived geopolitical imperatives correctly. US policymakers differed on key policy points and pursued policies that in their own way imperiled NATO. Some policy advocates in the G.H.W. Bush administration favoured displacing formal alliances such as NATO with informal and ad hoc coalitions, the effect of which of course would be to leave NATO as a hollowed-out bureaucratic structure suitable only for diplomatic ceremony. Other policy advocates in the subsequent Clinton administration were enthused by the democratic peace and the scope for democratic action, the effect of which was to substitute NATO for the United Nations – at a regional level – and provoke conflict both within NATO and with non-NATO powers. By 1999–2000 these ideas had had their moment and NATO had survived, albeit with a role ambiguously divided between its heartland and rimland functions.

The push to downplay NATO in favour of coalitions of the willing came from some of the policymakers who would later play a leading role in the G.W. Bush administration that took office in January 2001: Richard Cheney as Secretary of Defense and below him people such as Paul Wolfowitz, Libby Lewis, and Zalmay Khalilzad. Following the chain of command, the three former had the latter write the 1992 Defense Planning Guidance that – as all such guidances – described the United States' military strategy and justified military structures. However, this time the forty-six-page classified guidance zeroed in on discouraging 'the advanced industrial nations ... from challenging our leadership' (*New York Times*, 8 March 1992). The proposed 'base force' of 1.6 million soldiers should convince 'potential competitions that they need not aspire to a greater role.' Void of references to the United Nations, it was, according to the *New York Times*, 'the clearest rejection to date of collective internationalism.' Subsequent controversy caused the Guidance to be watered down, but Charles Krauthammer made an important point when he asked what the alternative was: clearly it would have to be greater autonomy for one or several industrial great powers (Mann 2004: 211). This alternative stood in opposition to US post-Cold War security policy writ large: the goal was to sustain the world order that was beneficial to US interests and leadership.

The Gulf War of 1991 that preceded the 1992 Guidance was a triumph for the United States but it failed to clarify the principles of a new order. The Gulf War was a legitimate war of self-defence (UN Charter Article 51) backed by explicit authorization from the UN Security Council (adopted under Charter Chapter VII). As such it confirmed the idea of sovereign equality and international law in opposition to ideas of hegemony and geopolitical spheres of influence. However, the Security Council in itself is an expression of legalized hegemony (five great powers hold a veto), and the United States' scope for building a 'new world order' raised questions in respect to the relative weight of sovereign equality and interventionism and the hegemon's exceptional role in upholding one or the other of these principles (Simpson 2004: 194–8).

Interventionism gained the upper hand through the 1990s and this for a variety of reasons linked to the advance of human rights, good governance programs, and tenets associated with the democratic peace thesis. Interventionism signalled a shift of emphasis from what was legal to what was right, and this relative shift from order to justice emphasized the role and responsibilities of hegemons with the power to do right. The United States turned out to be willing to do right, first in the wake of the Gulf War with the decision to provide relief to the Iraqi Kurds, then in Somalia and elsewhere. European governments were equally willing. The newly created EU agreed to intervene in the former Yugoslavia where war was looming, though a combination of European mismanagement and US desire to work through NATO (as opposed to a US-EU relationship) brought NATO to the forefront of Balkan issues. Interventionism culminated in the 1999 NATO decision to bomb Serbia into submission on the issue of Kosovo – without a UN Security Council mandate.

The Kosovo intervention was a critical moment in NATO's history because it represented the Alliance's infatuation with its own values. Not surprisingly, NATO has been compared to the Holy Alliance of the early nineteenth century (Simpson 2004: 201–14). NATO was offering itself as an agent for collective security, which was a dangerous posture considering that the Alliance did not have the collective will to strategically challenge outside powers such as Russia and China who protested the Kosovo war, nor the collective ability to maintain unity when small actors such as Serbia succeeded in generating a drawn-out war of diplomatic and political stress (Rynning 2005). The result was a collective security backlash. A widely reached conclusion was that committees were ill suited to conduct wars. Moreover, value-based security policy became a topic of discord, which really concerned not the 'whether' but the 'how': the allies could as always agree to promote democracy but disagreed on the means, a disagreement that soon fed stereotypes of Mars and Venus.

Kosovo was the crest of the 'collective democracy' wave that had begun with President Clinton's 1994 national security strategy – Engagement in and Enlargement of the democratic community (En-En). The strategy represented a break with the unilateral Guidance of 1992, but it contained the same basic idea of the United States as an 'indispensable' power (Mann 2004: 214). Clinton thus pushed through NATO's first Eastern enlargement, which was also by far the most controversial of NATO's post–Cold War enlargements, and he helped father the NATO-EU accords (Berlin and Berlin Plus) that codify NATO's primary role in European security affairs.

Post-Kosovo, it was clear that changes imposed themselves. Continued pursuit of 'democracy' would imply the downgrading of 'collective' because strategic challenges (hostile relations and counter-challenges by outside powers) would have to be handled by determined coalitions, typically US-led. Conversely, if 'collective' was to be preserved, it meant the downgrading of 'democracy' in the dealings with non-Western countries. The first option pointed in the direction of the Holy Alliance;

the other option in the direction of Chartered order combining collective participation and a degree of hegemonic leadership (Simpson 2004). At the turn of the century the Atlantic compass thus wavered. A clarification had to await the new G.W. Bush administration and its reactions to geo-political circumstances.

Global Threats and Rim Management: NATO beyond 2001

The G.W. Bush administration ended up pursuing a unilateral policy that had little to do with a chartered order and which resembled the value-based offensive of the Holy Alliance, except, of course, that this was not an alliance. G.W. Bush's America was 'unbounded,' as some observers noted (Daalder and Lindsay 2003). The administration's em-phasis on good and evil, right and wrong, caused dissent and contro-versy also within the Atlantic Alliance, where the potent September 2001 Article 5 declaration was put to marginal use. Deputy Secretary of Defense Wolfowitz came to NATO headquarters that month to explain that US-led coalitions took precedence over regular alliances, and so NATO lingered as the Afghan campaign took off. The Iraq debacle of the fall of 2002 and spring of 2003 only worsened relations.

This policy turn and these controversies are well known: the ques-tion here is how we should account for them in a geopolitical perspec-tive, and how we can account for NATO's overcoming its marginalization in 2001–3. The answer to the latter has to do with Afghanistan. NATO runs the International Security Assistance Force (ISAF) and has become the *collective* backbone of the plan to revive Afghanistan as a function-ing and regular – as opposed to rogue – state. At the time of writing NATO commanded some 60,000 soldiers in the country. The United States provided 30,000 of these but had another 20,000 operating out-side NATO command in Operation Enduring Freedom (OEF) notably in the most difficult areas on the Afghan-Pakistan border. These num-bers have subsequently increased but the basic pattern has not: ISAF is growing because the US contribution is growing and is channelled through NATO's ISAF command. One must be clear on the issue of na-tional vs collective leadership: the United States provides most leader-ship in Afghanistan and NATO has struggled to provide even moderate doses of it. As NATO-ISAF by 2006 expanded to all of Afghanistan and as the counter-insurgency campaign toughened, the effort, and thus NATO, has been 'Americanized.' The United States and some allies have at different points toyed with the idea of pulling all troops in

Afghanistan under NATO command but NATO has not been robust enough for this turn of events. Instead, the United States is now in command of both ISAF and OEF (General S.A. McChrystal is the double-hatted commander at the time of writing), and NATO decided in June 2009 to reinforce ISAF command and control with a three-star headquarters in Kabul that effectively sidetracks the official NATO command structure and notably the German-led operational headquarters in Brunssum. It nonetheless remains significant that the United States has chosen to 'Americanize' the NATO-ISAF mission instead of bypassing NATO, as it did some years ago. Mobilizing international support for security operations in Afghanistan requires a collective mechanism, and NATO has proven to be the best option.

How, then, do we account for the G.W. Bush value-based security policy? The literature on the administration agrees overwhelmingly that 'neoconservative' ideas drove much of the policy, which is also to say that the sources were internal and to a great extent freed from geopolitical analysis. The ideas were cultivated by a new generation of neoconservative thinkers who early in the 1990s turned against the old generations' inclination to lay down the arms following the end of the Cold War: there were still battles to be fought to uphold democratic ideals (Halper and Clarke 2004). That the ideas and policies were internally generated is not to say that they were disconnected from an assessment of world politics: after all, the Iraq war was meant to resolve problems of radicalism in the Middle East (via a process of democratization), which went to the heart of the problem of addressing al Qaeda and the radicalism that struck on 11 September 2001. However, the neoconservative assessment of world politics began with a certain dose of idealism that ran in opposition to geopolitical thinking: democracy and freedom led policymakers to generalize policy and make prescriptions (i.e., spread democracy) that geopolitical thinking would not. Geopolitical thinking is concerned with the political control of land and resources and prescribes no solution in particular – democratic or otherwise.

Geopolitical thinking may not have left much of an imprint on the G.W. Bush administration but geopolitics eventually did as the superpower confronted Eurasian realities. China is a growing great power that has continental depth and a long shoreline and thus potential power to project into blue water. It was appropriate that the first foreign policy crisis of the G.W. Bush administration, in March-April 2001, concerned China following the collision between an American reconnaissance plane and a Chinese fighter. Southeast Asia and India are

growing fast in economic terms but are in demand of a regional security architecture. Russia is not in the ascent but it covers a great landmass
and has control of strategic resources – notably nuclear weapons and
oil and gas. Europe remains ambiguously wedded to both Atlantic
partnership and European Union and, though its political power is
fragmented, experiences increasing strength vis-à-vis neighbouring regions. These geopolitical trends have weighed in on the United States
because the G.W. Bush administration has failed to prioritize its engagements across the Eurasian board. The result has been an impressive range of controversial and difficult engagements:

- *The renewed enlargement of NATO.* Had G.W. Bush had his way at
  NATO's Bucharest summit in April 2008, NATO would have invited
  the Ukraine and Georgia for membership. This policy ignites
  Russian hostility (Russia and Georgia fought a small war in August
  2008) and divides the European allies, thus undermining Europe's
  essential cohesion. This lack of cohesion is not merely the fault of
  the G.W. Bush presidency: it must also be attributed to European
  disunity and Clinton's policy of US leadership, as well. Still, the fact
  of the matter is that Europe today lacks a potential leader or group
  of leaders and that institutional enlargement increases the problem.
  The EU-3 (France, Britain, and Germany) has sought to take the
  lead, most visibly in the nuclear negotiations with Iran, where they
  have come to realize the limits of their ability to move the negotiations forward (Rynning 2007).
- *Democracy in Asia.* The United States has supported its democratic
  allies – Japan, South Korea, and Taiwan; it has urged China to
  reform; and it has sought to punish North Korea for its rogue
  policies. The three democratic allies are vital to the United States:
  they – and especially Taiwan – are the geographic checks and
  balances that keep China's focus regional. However, US policy has
  yet to demonstrate that it can produce the kind of regional framework that eventually will absorb China's growth peacefully. Instead,
  the US confrontation with North Korea – and this in spite of signs of
  progress in the nuclear disarmament negotiations – has proven so
  intransigent that the United States has had to mobilize China in the
  search for a diplomatic solution. US regional allies are no doubt
  cognizant of the costs they had to bear nearly forty years ago when
  the United States, this time squeezed by Vietnam, sought out
  China's friendship (i.e., Nixon's 'opening' of China).

- *A new central axis and US commitment.* In between Europe and Asia
runs a new central axis, from the Horn of Africa over the Middle
East into Central Asia (essentially the Pentagon's Central
Command). Most of the United States' projectable military power is
engaged in this region for the official purpose of building states and
democracy in Afghanistan and Iraq (and thus solving US problems).
The task is difficult in and of itself: it is made even more difficult by
third players such as Iran, Syria, and also Russia and China that
perceive their own geographic encirclement by the United States,
whose official agenda concerns their internal affairs (i.e., democracy). It is also made more difficult by the unsettled allied relations
in Europe and Asia, where combinations of absence of local leadership and regional concerns result in the limited ability and willingness to help out the United States along this central axis.

The argument that the G.W. Bush administration has failed to prioritize its geopolitical engagements is *not* tantamount to arguing that the
United States today must choose between the heartland and the rim.
The course of events past the Cold War indicates that Eurasian power
relations must be managed in their entirety. One can debate whether
there is a centre of gravity: Zbigniew Brzezinski (1997) tends to focus on
the old heartland; however, more than half the world's population (3.4
billion) live within sixty kilometres of the coast, and the number is
growing. The important point is that the full set of Eurasian relations
must be taken into account now and managed simultaneously. By this
account, an integrated policy – whether American or otherwise – must
balance commitments. Particular problems in one region should be offset
by smooth relations in another; conversely, trouble in all regions, stretching even a hegemon's resources, is testimony to troubled leadership.

Thus we return to NATO's bounce back to relevance. The United
States' new willingness to work through NATO while, naturally, prod-
ding its allies to do more is born of necessity. At some level of military
planning and preparation, it is true that NATO is no longer terribly relevant to the United States: the Pentagon has pulled back most large
contingents and today operates a global infrastructure made up of various 'lily pads' that the domestically based and projectable forces can
utilize on a case-by-case basis (Kaplan 2008), and NATO is as noted undergoing a process of Americanization in Afghanistan. However, at a
diplomatic-strategic level, NATO remains a geopolitical bridgehead of
paramount importance. If NATO can be made to work, NATO will offer

support along the beleaguered central axis and ensure that Europe's security actors – from Russia to the EU – are drawn into an Atlantic orbit. This is then the question: how can NATO be made to work?

There are essentially two paths down which NATO can travel, and current affairs illustrate their relevance. One path can be labelled 'globalization' and follows the much heralded idea that as threats become more transnational and global, so should policy responses. Thus, to address global threats and protect the idea of democracy, a global idea par excellence, NATO should go global. US policy has since the 1990s sought to push NATO beyond its regional boundary, but the G.W. Bush presidency brought a new dimension: the policy of global partnerships. Introduced in 2006, it was partly a recognition of certain countries' extensive partnership with NATO in Afghanistan, but it was also partly a measure to deepen NATO's ties to the global democracy agenda. Japan, South Korea, and Australia were singled out for partnership, in addition to Sweden and Finland. NATO did not quite follow suit: in Riga, in 2006, it underscored that practical cooperation with so-called contact countries should be deepened, but it did not pay tribute to the democracy agenda. This remains NATO's position, as confirmed by the Bucharest summit of April 2008. Presidential hopeful John McCain planned to take the issue further with his proposal to set up a global 'league of democracies' (McCain 2007). McCain also intended to stay the course in Iraq, and so we can see via McCain's unsuccessful candidacy one geopolitical path: maintain US policy along the central axis and integrate Europe and Asia (the League) to mobilize the support needed to fight 'global' threats as they appear along the axis.

There is another option on the table. It consists of safeguarding NATO's regional identity and preserving its transatlantic rationale. The reason is essentially geopolitical: it is in the combined interest of the United States and Europe that their Western institutions continue to define the international order. We touched on this issue in the introduction. The argument is that global threats – for instance al Qaeda and related terrorist organizations – must be countered by effective means, of course, but effective means do not imply a single grand tool, the global league of democratic nations. Western governments can do much, and so they should. However, instead of going global the West should focus on reinventing itself, conclude five former NATO generals who in early 2008 urged NATO reform: referring to the political space from Finland to Alaska, they write that 'Building this space into a community with a sense of purpose in the world is both our most urgent and our long-term task' (Naumann et al. 2007: 116).

This other option – regional NATO – is rooted in a geopolitical logic that is almost the mirror image of that of global NATO. Europe and Asia, as opposed to the central axis, are the centres of gravity: Europe as the host of 'Western' interests; Asia as the host of a future security architecture similar to that in Europe, an Asian regional union that dampens local hostilities and includes the United States as an external power – at least if things turn out the way David Calleo envisages (2007a, b). The other option is thus premised on European and Asian primacy and the argument that policy along the central axis should be tailored to enable America's leadership in Europe and Asia, not vice versa.

Conclusion

NATO has been a geopolitical creature from day one, and so it remains. Globalization has not suddenly transformed NATO into a new institution geared to manage global risks. NATO represents a geopolitical compromise between European and North American allies who now must readjust their relationship to manage the current agenda of new and old security issues. Change – in the shape of threats and risks that transcend boundaries between domestic and international affairs – is thus important but it happens on the familiar chessboard of Eurasian geopolitics, where relations between North America, Western Europe, and Russia remain of essence.

NATO was originally a means with which the United States could exert influence along the European part of the Eurasian rim – the most vital part of this rim, it should be added. Other alliances followed elsewhere during the Cold War, but NATO remained the privileged alliance. The Soviet Union may have occupied Mackinder's heartland, but it was the development potential of the rims that ran the heartland into the ground in this contest, as Spykman might have ventured had he lived to witness the Cold War.

The balance between heartland and rim was ambiguously defined in the 1990s, and the United States, with its overwhelming power, chose to enhance its control of both. Neoconservatives within the G.H.W. Bush administration were frank about their ambitions; the Clinton presidency put a different face on the policy but at no point entertained the idea that Eurasia would benefit from power pluralism and that the US should reduce its relative power and influence. NATO remained an instrument of US influence – a hegemon's policy of Eurasian power management.

The G.W. Bush presidency's neglect of NATO and promotion of a global agenda of democracy promotion questioned this underlying geopolitical logic. However, the resulting clash between policy and power realities has brought about a crisis in American security policy. The United States is currently overstretched: it has troubled engagements along a new central axis and is unable to mobilize significant support from Europe and Asia. Geopolitical analysis cautions a policy revision, the implications of which for NATO were discussed. One option is to focus on the central axis and integrate other policies to strengthen the American engagement here: this would lead to global NATO. Another option is to focus on Europe and Asia and temper the axis engagement: this would lead to regional NATO.

The future is notoriously difficult to predict. Still, it appears that global NATO has dim prospects. Neither allies in Europe or Asia are likely to subject their interests to a design whose raison d'être resides in America's engagement along the new central axis. If the United States keeps up its engagement along the central axis, making this its Eurasian priority, NATO is in for a bumpy ride. NATO could prosper, but it requires a shift of priorities. The United States should recognize that the two most productive regions of Eurasia are Europe and Asia. Thus, these two regions should be America's geopolitical priority. Once functioning regional security arrangements that include the United States are up and running here, it will be comparatively easy to prioritize engagements along the central axis and mobilize international support for them. In conclusion we thus return to Sun Tzu, who wrote that to achieve victory one must 'know when to fight and when not to fight' (2003, 18).

REFERENCES

Brzezinski, Zbigniew. 1997. *The Grand Chessboard: American Primacy and Its Geostrategic Imperatives.* New York: Basic Books.
Calleo, David P. 2003. 'Transatlantic Folly: NATO vs. the EU.' *World Policy Journal* 20, no. 3 (Fall): 17–24.
– 2007a. 'The Atlantic Alliance in a Global System.' *Asia–Pacific Review* 14, no. 1 (May 2007): 72–89.

– 2007b. 'Unipolar Illusions.' *Survival* 49, no. 3 (Autumn): 73–7.

Claude, Inis L. Jr. 1962. *Power and International Relations*. New York: Random House.

Daalder, Ivo H., and James M. Lindsay. 2003. *America Unbound: The Bush Revolution in Foreign Policy*. Washington: Brookings.

Deudney, Daniel H. 2007. *Bounding Power: Republican Security Theory from the Polis to the Global Village*. Princeton: Princeton University Press.

Dufourcq, Jean. 2006. 'Les stratégies occidentales à l'épreuve de la mondialisation.' *Politique étrangère* 71, no. 3 (Fall): 623–32.

Gaddis, John Lewis. 2005. *Strategies of Containment*. Oxford: Oxford University Press.

Halper, Stefan, and Jonathan Clarke. 2004. *America Alone: The Neo-Conservatives and the Global Order*. Cambridge: Cambridge University Press.

Kaplan, Robert D. 2008. 'What Rumsfeld Got Right.' *The Atlantic Monthly*, July/August.

Keegan, John. 1992. *Six Armies in Normandy: From D-Day to the Liberation of Paris*. London: Pimlico.

Kissinger, Henry. 1994. *Diplomacy*. New York: Knopf.

Krieger, Wolfgang. 1992. 'American Security Policy in Europe before NATO.' In *NATO: The Founding of the Atlantic Alliance and the Integration of Europe*, ed. Francis H. Heller and John R. Gillingham, 99–128. New York: St. Martin's.

Layne, Christopher. 2006. *The Peace of Illusions: American Grand Strategy from the 1940s to the Present*. Ithaca, NY: CUP.

Leffler, Melvyn. 1992. *A Preponderance of Power: National Security, the Truman Administration, and the Cold War*. Stanford: Stanford University Press.

Mackinder, Harold. 1904. 'The Geographical Pivot of History.' *The Geographical Journal* 23, no. 4 (April): 421–37.

– 1942. *Democratic Ideals and Reality*. Washington DC: NDU Press.

Mahan, Alfred T. 1987. *The Influence of Sea Power Upon History, 1660–1783*. New York: Dover.

Mann, James N. 2004. *Rise of the Vulcans: The History of Bush's War Cabinet*. New York: Viking.

McCain, John. 2007. 'An Enduring Peace Built on Freedom: Securing America's Future.' *Foreign Affairs* 86, no. 6 (November/December): 19–34.

Mearsheimer, John J. 1990. 'Back to the Future: Instability in Europe after the Cold War.' *International Security* 15, no. 1 (Summer): 5–56.

– 2001. *The Tragedy of Great Power Politics*. New York: Norton.

Naumann, Klaus, et al. 2007. *Towards a Grand Strategy for an Uncertain World: Renewing Transatlantic Partnership*. Washington: CSIS/Noaber Foundation.

New York Times. 1992. 'U.S. Strategy Plan Calls for Insuring No Rivals to Develop.' 8 March.

Robb, John. 2007. *Brave New War: The Next Stage of Terrorism and the End of Globalization*. New York: John Wiley.

Rynning, Sten. 2005. *NATO Renewed: The Power and Purpose of Transatlantic Cooperation*. New York: Palgrave.

– 2007. 'Peripheral or Powerful? The European Union's Strategy to Combat the Spread of Nuclear Weapons.' *European Security* 16, no. 3–4 (September–December): 267–88.

Schori, Pierre. 2005. 'Pain Partnership: The United States, the European Union, and Global Governance.' *Global Governance* 11, no. 3: 273–81.

Simpson, Gerry. 2004. *Great Powers and Outlaw States: Unequal Sovereigns in the International Legal Order*. Cambridge: Cambridge University Press.

Spykman, Nicolas J. 1942. *America's Strategy in World Politics: The U.S. and the Balance of Power*. New York: Harcourt Brace.

– 1944. *The Geography of the Peace*. New York: Harcourt, Brace.

Sun Tzu. 2003. *The Art of War*. London: Penguin.

Thucydides. 1998. *The Peloponnesian War*. Indianapolis: Hackett.

9 The Transformation of European Armed Forces

ANTHONY FORSTER

In line with neorealist analysis, Moskos, Williams, and Segal have argued that broadly similar threats to transatlantic states have led to a common response to post–Cold War transformation of armed forces (Moskos, Williams, and Segal 2000: 2; Waltz 2000). Perhaps this is unsurprising given the priority they give to the structural level of analysis, the anarchic nature of international relations, and the overlap of international security institutions. Most (though not all) European states are members of the two leading European security institutions, NATO and the European Union. There is a high degree of overlap between these security institutions: of the 28 NATO states, 21 are EU members, and of the 27 EU states, 21 are NATO members. NATO in particular has been important in transmitting norms of professionalism, developing a corpus of military doctrine, promoting interoperability, and supporting multinational command structures (Cottey, Edmunds, and Forster, 2002; Forster, Edmunds, and Cottey, 2003).

However, this chapter argues that over the last twenty years there has in fact emerged a set of distinctive patterns of European civil-military relations, with different dynamics from those operating in North America and markedly dissimilar to the binary East-West divide that dominated Europe prior to the end of the Cold War.[1] Whether it be in terms of defence reform, difficulties in providing adequate resources to fund the defence structures, or the need to secure effective relations between armed forces and the societies they serve, this chapter argues that the transformation taking place in Europe is distinctive from that of the US. The analysis here thus challenges North American scholars who argue that the US model of armed forces is *the* hegemonic model of the twenty-first century (Waltz 2000).

Uniquely European institutions, notably the EU, the European Court of Justice, and the European Court of Human Rights, have had a very significant impact on the ability of the armed forces to regulate themselves (Forster 2006a: 100). As a result of the direct effect of the authority of these institutions, they have had significant 'reach' into armed forces, transcending the autonomy of the military to regulate itself and in key areas significantly affecting employment rights, the terms and conditions of service, and the duty of care (Forster 2006b). However, this chapter poses an equivalent challenge to Europeanist scholars who have been too quick to argue that there is a *single* European model of armed forces, or indeed a *single* European way of war, and it thus concurs with the findings of Venesson, Breuer, de Franco, and Schroeder in the next chapter (Wallace 2007; Kagan 2003). The armed forces of European states are surprisingly resilient in terms of their modernist foundations, structures, and purposes. Militaries remain quite firmly rooted in their national context and in all instances hold onto their role in the defence of national interests, albeit variously defined. The extent to which European governments now seek external validation for the use of armed force in international relations is striking, but it takes place in a context in which national governments remain the final arbiter. In analysing these issues further, this chapter focuses on two first-order issues of European transformation: the types of missions and role of armed forces and the different approaches European states have to the use of force in international relations. It highlights that while there has been a paradigm shift, it is from homogeneity to heterogeneity.

Models of European Armed Forces

The end of the Cold War removed the spectre of a major European land war between east and west, and this had a direct impact on the principal roles of armed forces. From an American vantage point, this led to the dominance of a single postmodern military, committed to the expeditionary warfare involving overseas deployments and power projection (Moskos, Williams, and Segal, 2000). This chapter argues that at least in Europe the reality is more complex – there does not appear to be a convergence along a single axis of transformation from a Cold War to an expeditionary model, nor is it a question of moving towards a single destination with different speeds of travel. As Table 9.1 illustrates, analysing the principal missions, military doctrines, defence reform philosophies, and reform challenges leads to the conclusion that wide-ranging

Table 9.1
Key models of European armed forces

Ideal type/ model	Spectrum of conflict	Principal missions	Force doctrine	Defence reform philosophy
Expeditionary warfare	Full range from high- to low-intensity operations	War fighting	Joint, combined, and multinational	Transformation with no end goal
Territorial defence	Ability to cover tasks in the medium to low spectrum of conflict	Defence of national territory with some limited international security missions, e.g., peacekeeping	Single service	Modernization
Late modern	Limited aspiration and capability to cover the full range	International security missions – principally peacekeeping	All arms with some limited joint and combined units	Transformation for some units to operate alongside exped. warfare armed forces
Post-neutral	Low-intensity operations	Defence of national territory with some very limited international security missions, limited to peacekeeping	Militia-based forces	Modernization

restructuring of Western and post-communist armed forces has in fact led to four distinct models of armed forces with different capacities to engage in the spectrum of conflict.

Expeditionary Warfare

In this model, armed forces are substantially oriented towards the rapid deployment of military power outside national territory with the armed forces organized around the purpose of undertaking expeditionary warfare. This includes joint and combined war-fighting operations often in a multinational context at brigade, division, and corps levels at the top end of the spectrum of conflict. These forces can undertake 'cosmopolitan tasks' such as traditional peacekeeping tasks and nation-building, but these are undertaken by default as a consequence of the armed forces being structured around and trained for high-intensity war fighting. While expeditionary warfare armed forces may continue to have the role of providing for defence of national territory if that is required, the defining feature of this type of military is that structure, equipment, and organization are primarily driven by the goal of projecting military power beyond the national territory of the state concerned and perhaps more importantly high-intensity military intervention.

The epitome of the expeditionary warfare model lies outside Europe in the United States, where expeditionary warfare has gathered pace during the last eight years to become the goal of US reform. The outline of this role change was established during the Clinton administration and set out in Joint Vision 2010, with the ideas further developed in President George W. Bush's National Security Strategy and in the last four years championed by Secretary for Defense Donald Rumsfeld. In this type of force structure, the reform process is conceptualized as a process of continual adjustment to ensure the armed forces are appropriately organized (Schulz and Reimer 2004: 42). European states that aspire to the expeditionary warfare model differ in how they interpret its features (Bratton 2002). For the UK, which explicitly aspires to the expeditionary warfare model, it is not a slavish application of the US model, but rather the creation of 'a new British way of warfare' that has as its centrepiece interoperability with 'first-wave' US forces, while for the French military direct interoperability with the US is a less prominent goal (Dorman 2004; Jackson 2004; Guthrie 2001).

Territorial Defence

In this model, relatively large armed forces are primarily oriented towards national territorial defence, but the aspiration is that forces are also capable of contributing in a very limited way to international security missions – in both peace enforcement and a variety of interventions at the lower end of the spectrum of conflict. The defining feature of this model of defence reform is that, while governments may contribute armed forces to international security missions, force structure, equipment, and organization are primarily driven by the goal of maintaining forces capable of defending national territory from ground or air attack. Armed forces in this model are also generally based on relatively large and 'heavy' armoured formations, rather than more lightly armed joint and combined ground forces. The reform philosophy is based around developing an all-arms concept rather than wholesale transformation of armed forces, with a small component of the armed forces capable of participating in low- to medium-level operations within the spectrum of conflict.

Late-Modern

In this model armed forces are relatively small in size and share a dual commitment to national defence and a contribution to international security missions. To sustain a national defence role, many states retain a commitment to conscription and mobilization of a large number of reserves in time of war. In terms of the international security role, armed forces are trained to contribute to more 'cosmopolitan' missions such as traditional peacekeeping operations and stabilization operations (Elliott and Cheeseman 2004). Unlike the expeditionary warfare model, governments of late-modern states do not plan for military contributions to international security missions at the very highest end of the spectrum of conflict, notably full-scale war fighting operations. The key distinction between the territorial defence model and late-modern model armed forces is the latter's reliance on quality rather than quantity of armed ground forces. The key difference between late-modern forces and the expeditionary warfare model is the limited capability and intention of engaging in war fighting. However, in terms of the military reform process, transformation is the predominant reform philosophy.

Post-Neutral

Under this ideal type, armed forces are almost entirely oriented towards national defence. Post-neutral armed forces also rely on more lightly armed ground forces and mass mobilization in the event of war, but in contrast to the late-modern model they make no – or only very limited – contribution to international peacekeeping or intervention operations beyond national territory and have no aspiration to include peace enforcement in the missions of the armed forces. In this ideal type the defence reform philosophy is modernization rather than transformation. Table 9.2 assigns the armed forces of European states to each of the ideal types/models.

The Challenges of the Transformation of European Armed Forces

Different perceptions of threat within Europe have been the key factor in shaping different roles and force structures. While almost all European

Table 9.2
Typology of armed forces in Europe

Ideal type/model	Country
Expeditionary warfare	France, UK
Territorial defence	Albania, Belarus, Bosnia-Herzegovina, Bulgaria, Croatia, Czech Republic, Estonia, Finland, Georgia, Greece, Hungary, Latvia, Lithuania, Macedonia, Moldova, Norway, Poland, Romania, Russia, Serbia-Montenegro, Slovakia, Slovenia, Sweden, Turkey, Ukraine
Late-modern	Belgium, Denmark, Germany, Italy, Netherlands, Portugal, Spain
Post-neutral	Austria, Ireland, Switzerland
Outliers	Andorra, Cyprus, Holy See, Iceland, Liechtenstein, Luxembourg; Malta, Monaco, San Marino[1]

1 These states have either no armed forces or very small armed forces that exclude them from the typology set out above.

armed forces to some degree contribute to international security missions, the extent to which this has led to major mission redefinition and reorientation of force structures varies widely. In the two expeditionary warfare states (France and the UK), power projection and war fighting at the highest level of the spectrum of conflict are the avowed goals – and while these forces undertake traditional peacekeeping tasks, they have clearly been structured and organized around the application of deadly force beyond national borders. In the twenty-five territorial defence armed forces, concern about the integrity of territorial borders remains the core organizational purpose. Participation in overseas deployments is an important and prestigious, but essentially supplementary, activity. In seven states with late-modern forces, governments have embraced relatively low-intensity security missions in support of international peace and security and have reorganized their force structures accordingly. Perhaps most telling in understanding the relative priorities of different missions is the weak response to deploy troops to Iraq and more recently Afghanistan. As this indicates, where there is war fighting, governments with late-modern forces lack both significant capacities and (as will be seen below) the will to commit their forces. Likewise the post-neutral group of three states has embraced low- to medium-level peace support operations, but not as a replacement for the defence of national territory function, and all of these states have a complex post-neutral relationship with multinational organizations.

In regard to the nature of the reform process, Timothy Edmunds has suggested that most European militaries have been persuaded through the passage of norms in NATO and the EU – and to which we can add a demonstration effect of the US military – that 'modern' armed forces are now synonymous with the expeditionary warfare type. For Edmunds similar reform processes will ultimately lead to the dominance of an expeditionary warfare model, even if this will take considerable time to achieve, and in practice for some militaries this will remain an unobtainable goal (Edmunds 2004). However, close examination of European states indicates that the direction and impact of military reform are not similar across European states, with highly 'selective emulation' depending on the type of national defence model they have.

In France and the UK, the aspiration to create forces capable of warfighting operations marks out the scale and depth of an ongoing reform process from other European states. In the late-modern, territorial defence, and post-neutral groups, developing forces capable of contributing to international security missions involves numerically less forces. In addition it requires a different mix of lower-level technologies, training, and attitudinal change because it is aimed at a lower level in the spectrum of conflict, typically peace support operations and peacekeeping rather than war fighting. In this regard it is important to highlight the different challenges governments face in delivering a military force 'fit for purpose.' In the late-modern group three states – Denmark, Germany, and the Netherlands – have reoriented their armed forces to enable them to participate in overseas operations, through the introduction of a two-tier structure. However as the German case indicates, this has only been made possible by targeting a small proportion of forces with investment alongside and a cash-starved majority. In the case of the UK government, it remains committed to ensuring all its land forces are capable of operating alongside US forces and invested in network-enabled technologies to facilitate this. However in France and the UK the levels of investment required to create forces capable of operating at the highest level of the spectrum of conflict have led these governments to trade force size for capabilities. Both governments have redirected investment to equipment and reduced the number of troops to increase the overall levels of spend per troop (UK Ministry of Defence 2003: 1; *Guardian* 2003).

Another striking feature of the transformation of European armed forces is that all governments are struggling to support the ambitions they have set out for their armed forces. In most states, defence budgets have declined from a Cold War high point, with the impact of the September 2001 attacks at best stabilizing rather than significantly increasing defence budgets. In addition, for most states operating costs of international security deployments come out of the overall defence budget, creating a widespread tension between the immediate commitments governments have made to international security missions and the medium- and long-term need to invest resources in military reform to create the force structure which governments would like. For example, in the UK deployments in Iraq and Afghanistan have created a significant shortfall in expenditure of around £2 billion and led to consultation on a new defence review, the first in over a decade (Fox 2008). In addition, military reforms in the expeditionary warfare states – especially network-enabled warfare and full interoperability – are more expensive and ambitious, involving defence reform across the whole of the armed forces compared with other defence models. Investments of a different kind are necessary for other defence models. For example, while the post-neutral structure is financially the least expensive to maintain, as Haltiner and Hirt (2000) show, they are highly dependent on conscription and societal support, which demand a sustained commitment over a long period of time to nurture this support (Haltiner and Hirt 2000).

In terms of recruitment, in all four models a competitive marketplace requires improved terms and conditions of service to attract and retain military personnel; within a context of declining birth rates across Europe, this makes the task even more challenging. However a clear distinction lies between those European states that have abandoned conscription and those that have chosen to retain it. For expeditionary warfare states, a focus on high-intensity war fighting has made conscription too expensive and the use of conscripts in war fighting impracticable and has removed the need for large quantities of troops at the expense of high-technology equipment (Jehn and Selden 2002: 95). However, in both Britain and France problems of retention are leading to significant under-staffing. In a study carried out by the UK Ministry of Defence in the last quarter of 2005, almost 25 per cent of members of the armed forces wanted to leave at the earliest opportunity. The army is also finding it difficult to recruit soldiers, and by the end of 2008 the army had an overall shortfall of 5,790 personnel, with none of the three services at full strength (Ministry of Defence 2008; HCPAC 2007: 7). The difficulties of retention have also been reflected by the increasing speed with which women and ethnic minorities are being wooed to join the armed forces, although the British and French governments have as yet shied away from formally deploying women in front-line combat roles. Reflecting personnel shortages, British recruiters have been very active in 'new' commonwealth countries (Miller 2001). By 1998 there were 6,600 serving in the armed forces with predictions Commonwealth citizens would comprise 10 per cent of the army by 2012 and, unless unchecked, 20 per cent by 2020 (Norton-Taylor 2008).

The issue and pattern of recruitment are more complex in the three other models, with the majority of late-modern states abandoning conscription (the exceptions are Germany and Denmark). In most of the territorial defence states and in two out of three of the post-neutral states (Austria and Switzerland), it has been retained. Where conscription remains it is a system under stress, and almost all states that have retained it have reduced the proportion of conscripts within their armed forces (Haltiner and Szvircsev Tresch 2007) (see table 9.3). For those states that have suspended conscription, the challenge of sustaining an all-volunteer force is similar to that in the expeditionary warfare states. Recruiting in a competitive job market and the rigours of military service have put a severe strain on the ability of the armed forces to recruit and, as important, to retain highly trained personnel. For those states that retain conscription both within the late-modern and territorial defence models, the move in Germany and Denmark towards what might be termed 'professional conscripts' has been an innovative means to square the circle of maintaining some form of conscription (often on a selective basis) while providing personnel for international operations, albeit with limited rules of engagement. The sustainability of this practice in terms of expense and the financial opportunity cost remain open questions, as does societal support for it, with some predicting its impending demise (Haltiner and Szvircsev Tresch 2007) and others noting its resilience and capacity for adaptation within some defence models (Forster 2006a: 70).

In sum, while some observers have anticipated the emergence of a single post-modern model of armed forces following the US lead (Moskos, Williams, and Segal 2000), there is considerable evidence to challenge this contention. Twenty years after the fall of the Berlin Wall, analysis of European armed forces challenges the notion that any model is dominant. Indeed, the two states developing expeditionary warfare forces that echo US defence transformation remain stubbornly in the minority. The extent to which armed forces are legitimized, sustained,

Table 9.3
Plans to retain or end conscription, 1989–2008*

Country	Conscription?	Plans to phase out conscription?	Date of AVF	Max. service (months)
Albania	Y	N	n.a.	12
Austria	Y	N	n.a.	8
Belarus	Y	N	n.a.	12
Belgium	N	n.a.	1992	n.a.
Bosnia-Herzegovina	Y	N	n.a.	12
Bulgaria	Y	Y	2008	9
Croatia	Y	Y	2008–9	6
Czech Republic	N	n.a.	2004	n.a.
Denmark	Y	UC	n.a.	4
Estonia	Y	N	n.a.	12
Finland	Y	N	n.a.	12
France	N	n.a.	2002	n.a.
Germany	Y	N	n.a.	9
Georgia	Y	N	n.a.	18
Greece	Y	UC	n.a.	12
Hungary	N	n.a.	2004	n.a.
Iceland	n.a.	n.a.	n.a.	n.a.
Ireland	Never introduced	n.a.	n.a.	n.a.
Italy	N	n.a.	2005	n.a.
Latvia	Y	2005	n.a.	12
Lithuania	Y	N	n.a.	12
Luxembourg	N	n.a.	1967	n.a.
Macedonia	Y	N	n.a.	6
Moldova	Y	N	n.a.	12
Netherlands	N	n.a.	1996	n.a.
Norway	Y	N	n.a.	12
Poland	Y	Y	2010	9
Portugal	N	n.a.	2004	n.a.
Romania	Y	2007	N	12
Russia	Y	N	n.a.	24
Serbia – Montenegro	Y	N	n.a.	9
Slovakia	Y	2006	N	6
Slovenia	N	n.a.	2003	n.a.
Spain	N	n.a.	2002	n.a.
Sweden	Y	Y	2010	n.a
Switzerland	Y	N	n.a.	4.5
Turkey	Y	N	n.a.	15
UK	N	n.a.	1962	n.a.
Ukraine	Y	UC	N	18

*Excludes Andorra, Cyprus, Holy See, Liechtenstein, Malta, Monaco, San Marino.
Y: Yes; N: No; n.a.: Not applicable; UC: Under consideration.
Source: Adapted and updated from Jehn and Selden (2002: 94); International Institute for Strategic Studies (2007).

and supported by the societies they serve is clearly a key issue of armed forces–society relations, since without societal support, being 'fit for purpose' serves little value. It is this issue which is the focus of the next section.

Legitimizing the Use of Force

Since the end of the Cold War electorates have themselves become far more questioning of the role of violence in the contemporary security environment – especially in wars of choice that are more contested and often seem more partisan, serving political party rather than national interests. The changing nature of military operations since the end of the Cold War therefore poses significant challenges in terms of how such missions are legitimized by European governments and their parliaments and societies. This is particularly so given the move away from a consent-based approach to intervention, so dominant during the Cold War, to one that does not necessarily require the approval of the parties to a conflict (Finnemore 2003; Gazzini 2003; Thym 2004).

In no European state does the constitution expressly prohibit operations outside national boundaries (Stein 2002: 34). Belgium, Denmark, Finland, Germany, Hungary, Ireland, and Sweden all require parliamentary assent for participation in peacekeeping and peace enforcement missions, while most other European states to varying degrees locate this responsibility with the political executive (Thym 2004: 14; Stein 2002: 37; Barder 2004). However, over the last twenty years a key variable which has emerged in legitimating the use of force in international security missions is the degree to which the UN Security Council is viewed as the authority in determining where and under what circumstances military intervention should take place. Once again there is no single European view (see table 9.4) For some governments under no circumstances will they participate in peacekeeping operations of all forms without UN authorization; a second group are willing to act unilaterally in this area; a third group would prefer to operate with UN approval but will in exceptional circumstances operate without its authorization.[2]

For a first group of 'Westphalian' states, no military intervention beyond state boundaries is legitimate without the explicit authority of the UN and the agreement of the parties concerned.[3] This statist view of intervention is based on the centrality of state security, the inviolate nature of a state's authority and borders, and the authority of the state (Paris 2003: 444); in practice for these states intervention should be limited to traditional peacekeeping and managing transition tasks based on consent.

Table 9.4
Use of military forces by European regional organizations and UN approval

Missions	UN Security Council approval	Formal post-hoc UN approval[1]	Informal post-hoc approval[2]
European Union missions			
Peacekeeping			
Macedonia (FYROM) 2003	Yes (1345)	n.a.	n.a.
Dem. Republic of Congo, 2003	Yes (1484)	n.a.	n.a.
BiH 2004	Yes	n.a.	n.a.
Post-conflict stability			
Croatia, 1996–	No	Yes (1145)	n.a.
BiH, 1996–	Yes (1144/1088)[4]	n.a.	n.a.
Kosovo 1999–	No	Yes (1244)[5]	n.a.
BiH 2004–	Yes	n.a.	n.a.
Peace enforcement			
No operations as of 1 Jan. 2005			
NATO missions			
Peacekeeping			
BiH (no-fly zone; implementation of parts of Dayton Agreement air protection UNPROFOR)	Yes (1031)	n.a.	n.a.
Post-conflict stability			
BiH 1995–	Yes (1031)	n.a.	n.a.
Kosovo 1999–	Yes (1244)	n.a.	n.a.
Macedonia 1999–2003	No	Yes (1371)	n.a.
Afghanistan, 2003–	Yes (1510)	n.a.	n.a.
Iraq 2004–	No	Yes[4]	n.a.
Peace enforcement			
Kosovo, 1999	No	Yes (1371)	n.a.

1 Through reference to UN Security Council resolutions and attempts to operate under UN umbrella.
2 No UN Security Council veto of actions or UN follow-on association with a mission.
3 EU not named, but members called to act, so can be considered informal approval.
4 Since July 2004.

Specifically, the arguments of this group are that without the UN as the arbiter of the circumstances in which military intervention should take place, decisions are less likely to be made on the basis of universal rights and obligations, though specific concerns vary quite widely (Roberts 2003: 42). Some fear intervention will rest on leaders' views about responsibility to their citizens and the geopolitical costs and benefits of taking action (Bellamy 2003: 338; Ramsbotham and Woodhouse 1996). Others fear that a humanitarian justification will be used to validate the use of violence to pursue the interests of the rich against weaker states, what Noam Chomsky terms 'new military humanism' (Chomsky 1999; Ignatieff 2001; Booth 1994).

A Westphalian viewpoint has been particularly promoted by the Russian government (except concerning its own actions in what it considers to be its sphere of influence), SFRY, and the four EU post-neutral states (Austria, Finland, Ireland, Sweden), and Switzerland, which have opposed intervention without UN authority (Gazzini 2003: 238, 250; Bergman 2004: 176). This position has been articulated comprehensively in the Swiss *Report on Neutrality in Practice* (RNP), published in 2000, which disagreed with NATO's intervention in Kosovo without the explicit authorization of the UN, an intervention that led to a Swiss refusal to allow NATO access to its airspace. It stated that 'as a neutral country, Switzerland will only support future military measures by the international community if these measures are in compliance with the valid provisions of generally recognised international law' (Swiss Federal Department of Foreign Affairs 2000).

For a second group of 'post-Westphalians' states, of which the most prominent are the United Kingdom and France, but which also includes Denmark and Poland, the inviolability of state borders and centrality of consent should be put aside if circumstances require action from outside (Bellamy 2003: 334; Wheeler 2000).[4] In June 1998 the UN Secretary General advanced the idea that state frontiers 'should no longer be seen as watertight protection for war criminals or mass murderers. The fact that a conflict is "internal" does not give the parties any right to disregard the most basic rules of human conduct' (Connaughton 2000: 74). In 1999 in his 'Doctrine of the International Community,' Tony Blair further developed these points by arguing there is an obligation on the international community to prevent genocide and ethnic cleansing and set out five 'tests' to determine when and whether to intervene where 'values' rather than a direct threat to national territory were involved (Blair 1999; Daalder and O'Hanlon 1999).[5]

The 'post-Westphalian' states have therefore been willing to deploy military force without explicit UN approval and have done so on quite a frequent basis over the last decade. Examples of recent such international security missions include the British deployment of forces in a peace enforcement role outside UN control in Sierra Leone, Operation Allied Force in Kosovo in 1999, Operation Veritas in Afghanistan in 2002, and Operation Telic in Iraq in 2003–4, alongside Danish (naval) and Polish forces. Given the willingness of these governments to operate without UNSC approval they would rather avoid seeking a UNSC mandate than to run the risk of attempting to secure a mandate and failing.[6] However, in most instances where failure to secure a resolution is likely, governments prefer to claim that action is authorized under previous resolutions, and though they claim humanitarian interventions are exceptional, their willingness to undertake these types of missions is well established (Gazzini 2003: 238).

In a third grouping of 'solidarist' states, European governments generally accept the post-Westphalian argument concerning the need to intervene in situations within as well as between states and have generally embraced and promoted the need for intervention on humanitarian grounds (Wheeler 1997; Bergman 2004: 176). However, this group of states has a strong preference to see the UNSC as the arbiter of when and where intervention is legitimate and to seek UN authority whenever possible. Almost all European states refused to participate in the first phase of the US-led invasion of Iraq because this action was not seen as a legitimate action explicitly sanctioned and authorized by the UNSC. This group have also generally been reluctant to allow NATO and the EU to be used for non-UN-authorized missions, and where this has occurred many governments have disassociated themselves from decisions and exempted themselves from missions. Likewise these states have often only engaged in military deployments as part of post-conflict reconstruction once missions have been taken under the umbrella of the UN and associated with it. This was the case in ISAF in Afghanistan in 2003 (Gazzini 2003: 261), the EU's mission in the DRC in 2003, and after some delay in Iraq in 2004 (Roberts 2003: 53; Bellamy, Williams, and Griffin 2003: 223). However NATO's intervention in Kosovo in 1999, which took place without an explicit UNSC authorization, requires some comment, since a number of states in this solidarist group participated in this mission. Here the Belgian, German, Italian, and Greek governments were very hesitant about endorsing and participating in Operation Allied Force for fear of the precedent this would set in terms of justifying any intervention on humanitarian grounds and thus side-stepping UN Security Council authority (Caplan, 2001). As Nicholas Wheeler comments, for these states, Kosovo should genuinely be viewed as an exceptional humanitarian case, which is not seen as setting a precedent for future action outside the authority of the Security Council (Wheeler 2001: 118).

Much of the conceptual difference between the second and third groups revolves around two issues. First, the nature and frequency of exceptionalism, and second, whether missions have been explicitly or implicitly endorsed by the UN, the latter of which is inevitably a matter of interpretation. In terms of the mandate issue, states in the post-Westphalian group seem generally less concerned by the absence of a UN Security Council resolution and more willing to claim a greater authority for preserving international security as the justification for intervention. These states have also been more willing to claim that action is authorized under previous resolutions – what Adam Roberts calls 'continuing authority' (Roberts 2003: 51). By contrast, European governments in the solidarist group hold to the notion that where there is no UNSC resolution there should be no intervention. However this presents some practical policy challenges for solidarist states that want to participate in operations which have not received formal authorization. Rather than discard its commitment to the authority of the UN, the Belgian government (which provided troops and led one of the five NATO task forces) preferred to claim the legal base for intervention in Kosovo in 1999 as the 1998 Security Council Resolution 1203, which was sufficient to legitimate action (Gazzini 2003: 238; Weller 1996); likewise some solidarist states argued that NATO's Operation Deliberate Force in Bosnia-Herzegovina in 1995 was mandated under an existing Resolution 836 rather than accept that it was an unauthorized action (Weller 1996: 161). To what extent this becomes a frequent rather than an exceptional occurrence will determine whether specific governments move from solidarist to the post-Westphalian group, as has Denmark.

Since the end of the Cold War, the number of peacekeeping missions undertaken by European armed forces has increased, but they have also evolved in nature to cover an increasingly wide spectrum of activities. In particular, the presence and role within such operations of the 'holy trinity' of consent, impartiality, and minimal use of force have become not just ambiguous, but often entirely lacking once missions start, and this has presented European states with serious normative and practical challenges. A key variable is the extent to which UN authorization is viewed as the touchstone of legitimacy, but the situation is further complicated by the often fluid nature of peacekeeping missions, the parameters of which frequently proved extremely difficult to define and maintain. Equipped with its own European Security Strategy and its own Battle Groups, the EU may appear to offer an attractive alternative multilateral framework within which to undertake these types of missions (EU 2003). However one enduring feature of the post–Cold War era is the distinctive normative approach that each state brings to permitting the use of lethal force as a tool of international relations.

Conclusion

In combination, the fragmentation of the defence model and changing attitudes towards the use of force have created distinctly European patterns of military transformation, especially when compared with the United States. These patterns are one of complexity, with fundamentally different approaches within Europe to the missions and roles of national armed forces and the use of force in international relations. This is posing challenges for military and political partnership with the United States, for example, concerning the appropriate role of technology within defence reform and the value of an all volunteer force, as well as the merits and demerits of particular types of missions. However it is also important not to overlook the fact that it is also raising key issues about the possibilities for the further integration of defence within Europe. While some might argue there is a 'European way of war,' if European states are unwilling or unable to wage war, in practice such claims will lack real meaning (Wallace 2007). Twenty years after the end of the Cold War, an inescapable conclusion is that in Europe there is heterogeneity rather than homogeneity in contemporary European civil military relations and ambiguity rather than certainty about the use of force. This poses fundamental questions for the US about who might be an appropriate partner in international operations, but also questions about future models of European defence integration addressed in other contributions in this volume.

NOTES

1 Parts of this chapter draw on and develop arguments in Forster (2006a).
2 It may be possible to argue that a fourth category may emerge: states willing to use regional organizations to justify intervention.

3 Missions undertaken with host nation consent fall within the Charter framework even if they are not expressly authorized by the UN since nothing prohibits a state from inviting external intervention.

4 While the French government has argued with regard to NATO that any non–Article 5 missions have to be placed under the authority of the Security Council, it has systematically intervened in third countries without a UN mandate and has not been as keen on constraining the EU in this way, which suggests the French government can be included in this category notwithstanding its position regarding NATO.

5 These tests are: (1) Are we sure of our case? (2) Have we exhausted all diplomatic options? (3) Are there military operations we can sensibly and prudently undertake? (4) Are we prepared for the long term? and (5) Do we have national interests involved? Interestingly there was only one passing reference to the UN as part of a list of international institutions created after the Second World War (Blair 1999).

6 This group of states has a soft preference for using the authority of the UN to endorse actions and avoid sanction of a particular course of action. Adam Roberts argues it was precisely the fear of a Security Council veto that prevented the US from tabling a resolution before the UN on Kosovo, to which one could also add Iraq in 2002 (Roberts 2003: 52).

REFERENCES

Barder, B. 2004. Ephems, 1 March. http://www.barder.com/brian/1pointofview/K1Mar04.htm (accessed 8 January 2005).

Bellamy, A. 2003. 'Humanitarian Responsibilities and Interventionist Claims in International Society.' *Review of International Studies* 29, no. 3: 321–40.

Bellamy, A., P. Williams, and S. Griffin. 2003. *Understanding Peacekeeping*. Oxford: Polity.

Bergman, A. 2004. 'The Nordic Militaries: Forces for Good?.' In *Forces for Good*, ed. L. Elliott and G. Cheeseman, 168–86. Manchester: Manchester University Press.

Blair, T. 1999. 'Doctrine of the International Community.' Speech at Economic Club of Chicago, Hilton Hotel, Chicago, USA, 22 April. http://www.number-10.gov.uk/output/Page1297.asp (accessed 8 January 2005).

Booth, K. 1994. 'Military Intervention: Duty and Prudence.' In *Military Intervention in European Conflicts*, ed. L. Freedman, 56–75. Oxford: Blackwell.

Bratton, P. 2002. 'France and the Revolution in Military Affairs.' *Contemporary Security Policy* 23, no. 2: 87–112.

Caplan, R. 2001. 'International Diplomacy and the Crisis in Kosovo.' *International Affairs* 74, no. 4: 745–61.

Chomsky, N. 1999. *The New Military Humanism: The Lessons from Kosovo*. Monroe, ME: Common Courage Press.

Connaughton, R. 2000. *Military Intervention and Peacekeeping: The Reality*. Aldershot: Ashgate.

Cottey, A., T. Edmunds, and A. Forster. 2002. 'The Second Generation Problematic: Democratic Civilian Control of the Armed Forces.' *Armed Forces and Society* 29, no. 1: 31–56.

Daalder, I., and M.E. O'Hanlon. 1999. 'Unlearning the Lessons of Kosovo.' *Foreign Policy* 116 (Fall): 128–40.

Dorman, A. 2004. 'Defence Transformation: Does One Size Fit All? The Experience of America's European Allies.' Paper presented at the International Security Studies Section, ISA Annual Meeting, Washington, DC, 29–30 October.

Edmunds, T. 2004. 'What Are Armed Forces For? The Changing Nature of Military Roles in Europe.' Paper presented to the Research Seminar, Department of Politics, University of Bristol, November.

Elliott, L., and G. Cheeseman, eds. 2004. *Forces for Good*. Manchester: Manchester University Press.

EU. 2003. *A Secure Europe in a Better World, European Security Strategy*. Paris: EU Institute for Security Studies.

Finnemore, M. 2003. *The Purpose of Intervention: Changing Beliefs about the Use of Force*. Ithaca, NY: Cornell University Press.

Forster, A. 2006a. *Armed Forces and Society in Europe*. Basingstoke: Palgrave.

– 2006b. 'Breaking the Military Covenant: Governance and the British Army in the Twenty-First Century.' *International Affairs* 82, no. 6: 1043–57.

Forster, A., T. Edmunds, and A. Cottey, eds. 2003. *Soldiers and Societies in Postcommunist Europe: Legitimacy and Change*. Basingstoke: Palgrave.

Fox, R. 2008. 'Hutton Slashes Defence Spending across the Forces.' *Standard Online*, 11 December. http://www.thisislondon.co.uk/standard/article-23600045-hutton-slashes-defence-spending-across-forces.do (accessed 18 December 2008).

Gazzini, T. 2003. 'NATO's Role in the Collective Security System.' *Journal of Conflict and Security Law* 8, no. 2: 231–63.

Guardian. 2003. 'Minister: Troop Deployment Is No Stunt.' *Guardian Unlimited*, 12 February. http://www.guardian.co.uk/terrorism/story/0,12780,894086,00.html (accessed 8 January 2005).

Guthrie, C. 2001. 'The New British Way in Warfare.' Annual Liddell Hart Centre for Military Archives Lecture, King's College London, 12 February. http://www.kcl.ac.uk/lhcma/info/lec01.htm (accessed 23 Feb. 2004).

Haltiner, K., and E. Hirt. 2000. 'Switzerland: Between Tradition and Modernity.' In *The Postmodern Military*, ed. Moskos, Williams, and Segal, 205–23.

Haltiner, K and Szvircsev Tresch. 2007. 'New Trends in Civil-Military Relations: The Decline of Conscription in Europe.' Paper presented at the Inter-University Armed Forces Seminar on Armed Forces and Society, The Palmer House Hotel, Chicago.

House of Commons Committee of Public Accounts Committee (HCPAC). 2007. *Recruitment and Retention in the Armed Forces,* July 2007. Norwich: The Stationery Office.

Ignatieff, M. 2001. *Human Rights as Politics and Idolatry.* Princeton, NJ, and Chichester: Princeton University Press.

Jackson, M. 2004. 'Interview with Gavin Esler.' *Newsnight,* BBC2, 20 July.

Jehn, C., and Z. Selden. 2002. 'The End of Conscription in Europe.' *Contemporary Economic Policy* 20, no. 2: 93–100.

Kagan, R. 2003. Of *Paradise and Power. America and Europe in the New World Order.* New York: Alfred A. Knopf.

Miller, C. 2001. 'The Death of Conscription.' BBC News, 29 June. http://news.bbc.co.uk/1/hi/world/europe/1414033.stm (accessed 5 August 2004).

Ministry of Defence. 2003. *Delivering Security in a Changing World.* Defence White Paper, December. Cm 6041-I. London: The Stationery Office.

– 2008. *UK Armed Forces Quarterly Manning Report.* http://www.dasa.mod.uk/applications/newWeb/www/index.php?page=48&thiscontent=20&date=2008-11-27&pubType=1&PublishTime=09:30:00&from=home&tabOption=1 (accessed 19 December 2008).

Moskos, C., J. Williams, and D. Segal, eds. 2000. *The Postmodern Military: Armed Forces after the Cold War.* Oxford: Oxford University Press.

Norton-Taylor, R. 2008. 'MoD May Halt Surge in Commonwealth Recruits to Army.' Guardian Online, http://www.guardian.co.uk/uk/2008/apr/05/military.defence (accessed 30 January 2009).

Paris, R. 2003.'Peacekeeping and the Constraints of Global Culture.' *European Journal of International Relations* 9, no. 3: 441–73.

Ramsbotham, O., and T. Woodhouse. 1996. *Humanitarian Intervention in Contemporary Conflict.* Cambridge: Polity.

Roberts, A. 2003. 'Law and the Use of Force After Iraq.' *Survival* 45, no. 2: 31–56.

Schulz, G., and Reimer, H. 2004. 'Transformation der Bundeswehr – Der Weg in die Zukunft.' *Europäische Sicherheit* 53: 31–7.

Stein, T. 2002. 'Kosovo and the International Community. The Attribution of Possible Internationally Wrongful Acts: Responsibility of NATO or of Its Member States?' In *Kosovo and the International Community: a Legal Assessment,* ed. C. Tomuschat, 243–85. The Hague and London: Kluwer Law International.

Swiss Federal Department of Foreign Affairs. 2000. *Report on Neutrality in Practice.* http://www.eda.admin.ch/eda/e/home/recent/rep/neutral/neut00.html (accessed 8 January 2004).

Thym, D. 2004. 'Reforming Europe's Common Foreign and Security Policy.' *European Law Journal* 10, no. 1: 5–22.

Wallace, W. 2007. 'Is There a European Approach to War?' In *The Price of Peace: Just War in the Twenty First Century*, ed. C. Reed and D. Ryall, 37–54. Cambridge: Cambridge University Press.

Waltz, K. 2000. 'Structural Realism after the Cold War.' *International Security* 25, no. 1: 5–41.

Weller, M. 1996. 'Peace-Keeping and Peace-Enforcement in the Republic of Bosnia-Herzegovina.' *Zeitschrift für Ausländisches öffentliches Recht und Völkerrecht* 56, no. 1–2: 70–177.

Wheeler, N. 1997. 'Humanitarian Intervention and World Politics.' In *The Globalisation of World Politics: An Introduction to International Relation*, ed. J. Baylis and S. Smith, 391–407. Oxford: Oxford University Press.

– 2000. *Saving Strangers: Humanitarian Intervention in International Society.* Oxford: Oxford University Press.

– 2001. 'Humanitarian Intervention after Kosovo: Emergent Norm, Moral Duty or the Coming Anarchy?' *International Affairs* 77, no. 1: 113–28.

10 Is There a European Way of War?

PASCAL VENNESSON, FABIAN BREUER,
CHIARA DE FRANCO, AND URSULA C. SCHROEDER

Military Role Conceptions and Ways of War in Europe

Europe has the most dense network of security institutions in the world. Since the Second World War, the North Atlantic Treaty Organization, the Western European Union, and the Organization for Security and Cooperation in Europe, and increasingly the European Union have played a significant security role. Yet, while these institutions contributed to a major shift in the use of force within the region, they did not erase differences about conceptions of force employment among European countries and between European countries and the United States. Why have concepts of military power and force employment remained distinct and varied in Europe, and what facilitates their convergence at the European Union level into the ambiguous notion of crisis management? We argue that the answers to these questions are endogenous to the military: both role conceptions and organizational frames of military institutions are key underlying aspects of the differences at the national level and of the common ground at the European Union level.

Our chapter has two objectives. First, we contribute to the debate opened by Stephen Biddle on the sources of variations in the meaning of military power and in military effectiveness (Biddle 2004: 5–9). Military forces do many things, and proficiency in one or several tasks does not imply proficiency in others. If no single, undifferentiated concept of military power can apply to all states in all places and times, what are the sources of variations in force employment in an international system which does not dictate a unique response? Biddle's suggestion is to examine the domestic environment of the military, especially its relations with political leaders, as well as its domestic politics and its societal and budgetary constraints (Biddle 2004: 48–51). Specifically, in the case of Europe there has been a growing interest in the alleged development of a European strategic culture through a socialization process accelerated by the institutional arrangements put in place by the European Union (Cornish and Edwards 2001, 2005; Howorth 2002; Everts et al. 2004; Giegerich 2006; Meyer 2006; Wallace 2007).[1] Our proposition is that military institutions themselves, out of their own history and memory, develop enduring ideas about themselves and their roles. These endogenously generated ideas have an impact on conceptions of military power and force employment which previous works on the transformation of European security have neglected. In contrast to the European strategic culture literature, we focus on the military and its conceptions of force employment instead of the broad and often vague notions of 'strategy' and 'culture.' Using the notions of role conception and organizational frame, we suggest one way to conceptualize military doctrines sociologically. We recognize that military institutions, especially in the European Union, are formally controlled by civilian authorities and do not make military strategy in isolation. Partisan politics, for example, might play a role in European governments' decisions to get involved in peace enforcement (Rathbun 2004: 153–85). However, the complexity of force employment and the military monopoly on operational expertise suggest that even when military advisers do not prevail, the relatively autonomous logic of military power constantly influences the political choices related to the use of force, in the initial decision on whether to use force (and what kind of force) during the conduct and at the end of the operation (Posen 1991: 16–19; Legro 1996). The political end can only be reached by coming to terms with the specific logic of the military system: the political and military dimensions constantly interact with each other (Poirier 1985: 17, 476, 473–7; Mearsheimer 1983: 61).

Second, this focus allows us to explore more directly and deeply whether there is a European way of war, that is, an approach to force employment that might be common to the Member States of the European Union. We argue that while there has been an overall shift from territorial defence to crisis management, the ways of war of these military institutions remain distinct and do not lead to a single 'European' way of war. This argument is coherent with the work of comparativists, who do not draw a sharp line between institutional reproduction and institutional change as resilience and innovation in military role conceptions often go together in intriguing patterns (Thelen 2004; Streeck and Thelen 2005).

We explore and compare empirically the main role conceptions and organizational frames of the armed forces in France, Germany, Italy, and the United Kingdom. While an examination of these four countries cannot be a substitute for an analysis of the military organizations and doctrines of the twenty-seven Member States of the European Union, there are good reasons to select them. In the European Union, these four countries spend the most on defence in absolute terms; they also have the largest force in numbers, and are heavily involved in various military deployments abroad (IISS 2007, 406). In short, because of their comparatively strong military capability, these countries are highly relevant to European security. Whatever common ground and convergence there might be in the field of European defence and security, through NATO or through the EU, it is unlikely to be at odds with the defence capabilities and intentions of these countries.

In the first part of the chapter, we focus on the military's role conceptions and organizational frames. In the second part, we examine the ways in which military institutions in France, Germany, Italy, and the UK define their preferred roles.

How Military Institutions Think about the Uses of Force

Military Role Conceptions and Organizational Frames

Force employment is the central challenge confronting military organizations. The command and control of operations conducted by a complex organization whose main goal is to use force is the main distinctive skill of the officer corps (Huntington 1957: 11). In *On War*, Clausewitz underlined the remarkable complexity of force employment and the conditions under which military organizations and military leaders can keep and improve their problem-solving capacity despite the general friction that characterizes warfare (Clausewitz 1989: 112, 586; Biddle 2004: 48–51; Holmes 2007). Why do military organizations face the problems associated with the use of force in different ways?

In order to get a better sense of a military organization's comprehension of the use of force, we need to examine its overall role conception, as well as its organizational frame, that is, its approach to solving the problems associated with force employment. Drawing on the 'national role conception' approach that originated in the 1970s and 1980s following Holsti's pathbreaking essay, and Krotz's more recent reformulation, we define the military's role conception as a shared view, shared within one service or by all the services, regarding the proper purpose of the military organization and of military power in international relations (Holsti 1970; Walker 1987; Krotz 2002: 6–10). In the study of the military, this approach is best exemplified by Shy (1993; see also Johnston 1996). A military organization's role conception is shaped by its history and memory and is used to socialize military personnel. It may evolve over time, become blurred and even contested, partially or entirely, at certain periods (which might temporarily make the notion less useful analytically), but it is not a transient attitude. Military organizations, however, do not all have the same willingness, or the same capacity, to assert and define their own role, and this is in itself an intriguing phenomenon. Finally, the military organization's role conception affects policy because, as Krotz notes, it prescribes certain goals and action, and also because it rules out some policy options, making them implausible or even unthinkable (Krotz 2002: 9).

Embedded in a role conception also is a preference for particular processes of policymaking related to the use of force. The notion of organizational frame, introduced by Lynn Eden, usefully complements the notion of role conception because it focuses on the ways in which organizations attempt to solve problems. Drawing on Wiebe E. Bijker's definition of technological frame, Eden defines organizational frame as the approach used by an organization to solve problems (Eden 2004: 3, 37–60; Bijker 1995: chap. 2). These frames incorporate central ideas and values regarding how the organization chooses and represents problems, how the organization develops strategies to solve them, and how it places constraints and requirements on possible solutions (Eden 2004: 3).

Operationalizing Military Organizations' Role Conceptions and Organizational Frames

To uncover military organizations' role conceptions and organizational frames we draw from a variety of sources, including defence ministries and services' official publications and statements, speeches, military journals, and memoirs. To the extent that they are publicly available, which is not always the case, we especially use the services' internal documents and field manuals, an important source to uncover the services' role conception and organizational frame. These sources, especially the services' documents, publications, and manuals, define the service's military doctrine. A military doctrine is a set of principles, authoritative but requiring judgment in application, which provides the military organization with guidelines about when, and how, to employ military force to reach specific goals. These principles reflect the judgment of professional military officers, and to a lesser but important extent of civilian leaders, about what is and is not militarily possible and necessary (Posen 1984: 13). A military doctrine is the military institution's preferred mode for employing force. It embodies the military institution's conception of how force ought to be employed and provides the frame of reference with which military institutions approach the employment of military power. Military doctrines specify what means should be employed and how, and serve as a broad guide to action. Military doctrine is the sub-component of grand strategy (or foreign policy) that deals specifically with military force. It is 'a set of prescriptions … (about) how military forces should be structured and employed to respond to recognized threats and opportunities' (Posen 1984: 13). Military doctrines notably answer two questions: What type of force shall be employed? How shall they be employed? But, in defining common conceptions and standard operating procedures, doctrines encapsulate common knowledge and explanations of events, conceptions of the history and memory of the organization, lessons learned, myths, and language (Biddle 2002; Hull 2005: 92, 97–8).

Waging War or Managing Crisis? The Military's Role Conceptions in France, Germany, Italy, and the UK

France: Mastering Violence and Beyond

Since the end of the Cold War, the French military, especially the army, has engineered a doctrinal revival. During the 1990s, the army leadership, which saw itself less constrained by the rigidities of France's nuclear deterrent doctrine and involved in numerous and heterogeneous missions abroad, developed ideas about the use of force and the army's operational identity as it was shifting to an all-volunteer format and redefining its core values. On 1 January 1999 the army created the Command for Doctrine and Superior Military Education, an effort to revisit its doctrinal thinking since the beginning of the twentieth century and develop a new approach to force employment (CDES 2000, 2001; Marill 2001).

In light of its missions, the military recognized the diversity of ways in which force is, and should be, employed in a changing international environment.[2] The repeated involvements of French troops in a variety of crises since the end of the Cold War led military leaders to perceive conventional war, like the 1990–1 first Gulf War, as the exception rather than the rule. They estimated that what was usually asked of them was less to defeat a military adversary in a conventional battle than to mobilize the resources of the military art to control spaces (ground, air, military) in which the political leadership could implement a complex political action (DAS 1998). To them, the military should not see itself as having only one exclusive type of mission, but as being capable to accomplish a set of different tasks including war, peace support, security, or urgent help. In this perspective, the main role of conventional forces is to contribute actively to the prevention, limitation, or, if need be, the forceful resolution of crisis and regional conflicts (EMA 1997: 10). The joint doctrine on force employment, as well as the Army doctrine, emphasize that the main goal of the armed forces is no longer the destruction of an enemy (EMA 2001: 4; *Armée de terre* 2007: xviii, 1). Rather, the use of force is designed to preserve balance, to bring back peace and stability, or to save lives. The army doctrine considers that, more than in the past, force employment is deeply shaped by political logics and influenced by a wider variety of constraints.

The Army's combined arms 901 Manual adopted in April 1999 defined two main roles for the army (Veyrat 2003: 12–19). On the one hand, the armed forces should be able to control the ground in a durable way and hence the various situations that can occur in that environment. On the other, the armed forces should also be able to impose the decision in an air-land combat (*combat aéroterrestre*). Furthermore, the armed forces contribute to bringing life back to normal after the fighting (facilitate the reconstruction of civilian infrastructure, for example). In order to reach political objectives, ground forces can be used in two ways, depending on the nature of the conflict: to coerce the armed forces of the adversary or to control violence (Veyrat 2003: 15; Francart 1999: 115–44). The coercion of enemy forces is a direct strategy that seeks a military victory by targeting the enemy's centres of gravity, taking into account deception, the enemy's morale, and the public perceptions of the events. The mastering-of-violence type of force employment seeks to ensure or to restore security in a territory through an indirect strategy. The military leadership does not see these two modes of operations as mutually exclusive. They are instead two poles of a continuum with actual force employment usually located in between and borrowing elements of each. In both cases, the tactical action of the force is organized into four clusters: offence, defence, securitization, and assistance. Beyond the traditional offensive and defensive modes of action, the 1999 doctrine added securitization and assistance, which were both practised before but not self-consciously formalized. Securitization refers to the control of an area and assistance refers to an effort to help a population. The army doctrine emphasized not only the need for a controlled use of the force, but also the need for several principles of action (decision, multi-nationality, information, etc.) and some specific knowledge and capacity to use force in an efficient way in a new context (Francart 1999; CDES 2000). This approach to war is close to the indirect approach logic, as defined by Basil Liddell Hart, and it is often accompanied by a critique of Clausewitz's ideas (Cot 2000: 13–15). The mastering of violence is presented as a way to stop the logic of violence prevalent in internal conflicts without resorting to armed combat (CDES 2000: 49). The level of force should be strictly dependent on the effect envisioned. In some situations, the army's doctrine mentions that it might be possible to give to the adversary the possibility, materially and psychologically, to disengage. Furthermore, the force is expected to conduct civil-military operations and to participate in stability operations.

In this doctrinal formulation, especially regarding the notion of mastering violence, the army leadership relied on its own memory and interpretation of colonial conquest and the wars of decolonization (Marill 2001: 45–68, 78).[3] The history and memory of colonial wars are deeply contested.[4] Army planners notably emphasized the heritage of key military figures of colonial wars, like Galliéni and Lyautey, who insisted that pacification meant a careful combination of limited uses of force and society-building. The 2007 version of the army's doctrine distinguishes three phases in force employment: intervention, stabilization, and normalization and does not give the same importance to the mastering of violence. The mastering of violence still plays an important role, however, and the army doctrine confirms that the defeat of the enemy is insufficient to the success of the operation and is not the main objective of force employment (*Armée de terre* 2007: 19).

In sum, the French military, and especially the French army's role conception and its organizational frame, are not bounded by one exclusive, or even privileged, mode of action, like mid- to high-intensity warfare. On the contrary, the military acknowledges the limits of such a way to use force, even its partial irrelevance. It favours instead the possibility of tackling a broader range of problems, which include the deterrence and isolation of an adversary, the creation of a secure environment, and the improvement of the daily life of the population.

Debates and disagreements persist within the military, however, regarding the relative emphasis given to the war-fighting missions and to the control of violence (see, for example, Decrok 2006; Sentinelles de l'agora 2007).

The UK: Minimum Necessary Force and Potential for Escalation

Since the early 1990s, the British armed forces have capitalized on what they identified as their historical expertise in robust counter-insurgency operations and imperial policing. Nevertheless, extensive force reductions and the general willingness to 'trade force size for capabilities' (Forster 2006: 48) have resulted in the overstretch of armed forces personnel, particularly in light of the high level of commitments to forces during the multiple parallel missions of the 1990s and the 2000s. These burdens on the armed forces result from the shift in long-term defence planning initiated by the 1998 Strategic Defence Review. It changed the focus from 'stability based on strategic deterrence and fear' to 'stability based on the active management of risks' through an expeditionary strategy (UK Ministry of Defence, 1998; UK Ministry of Defence 2002; McInnes 1998). While retaining a small strategic deterrence capability, 'frequent, smaller operations are becoming the pattern' (UK Ministry of Defence 2002: 32). In these operations, the British military deploys a medium-weight expeditionary force with counter-terrorism and robust peace support mandates and focuses on 'conflict prevention and stabilisation, rather than the defeat of opposing forces' (UK Ministry of Defence 2003: 11).

Moving away from earlier lightly armed UN-style peacekeeping missions, the most recent British military doctrine for peace support operations draws attention to the growing need for coercive force and counter-insurgency-type operations in crisis management: 'The game has become more violent, and thus needs some referees to control it (for example, ice hockey rather than cricket)' (Joint Doctrine and Concepts Centre 2004: section 3-1). In complex crisis management operations that are 'being conducted in a far less certain, and potentially more volatile international environment' (Joint Doctrine and Concepts Centre 2004: v), the British armed forces thus increasingly prepare for the coercive use of military force, a trend we also found in the French military. The British armed forces' understanding of force employment in these operations is characterized both by its predilection for using minimal force where possible and by its ability to escalate the level of force if necessary. Similar to the French notion of 'mastering violence,' the UK employs military power in peace support operations not as a primarily destructive and lethal force to destroy an enemy, but as a coercive means to foster conflict management through military presence. Hence, British armed forces are held to restrain their use of force in peace support operations, since 'an unduly heavy-handed approach with excessive use of force is unlikely to aid in the promotion of consent' (Joint Doctrine and Concepts Centre 2001a, section 6-4; Kennedy-Pipe, McInnes 1997; Thornton 2004).

Nevertheless, this strategy of using minimal force in peace operations is carried out on the assumption that the UK armed forces can overmatch any potential opposition. In the words of the British Defence Doctrine, the nature of peace support 'must not be allowed to divert the Armed Forces from the reality that their success in them has been based on their ability to escalate the level of force they deliver when the circumstances demand it' (Joint Doctrine and Concepts Centre 2001a: section 3-4). The ability to 'apply lethal force in a measured and deliberate fashion when necessary' (Joint Doctrine and Concepts Centre 2001a: iii) not only extends to crisis management missions, but is central to the British approach to the use of force across all types of operations. The core of the UK's military doctrine is thus a 'warfighting ethos': The British armed forces' war fighting skills 'must remain the key to their credibility and effectiveness' (Joint Doctrine and Concepts Centre 2001a: iii) and give them the ability to fight and win in warfare. Even in non-war operations, the Navy operational concept concluded, the British Armed Forces' 'ability to discharge functions at the lower end of the conflict spectrum will derive principally from our capability to fight at high intensity. The reverse must not be assumed' (UK Minister of Defence-Navy 2001: 2). These concepts of using minimal force and escalating it only when necessary combine with a specific approach to force protection. Assuming that excessive force protection inhibits the successful execution of military missions, the British armed forces manage the risk to the force, rather than seeing force protection as an ultimate goal in itself. As a result, the British armed forces visibly behave differently during deployments than for instance German or US troops. In recent operations in Iraq or on the Balkans, British troops actively engaged with local authorities and tried to establish good relations with the population 'by establishing headquarters in central urban areas; by avoiding body armour and carrying weapons slung where possible; by discouraging the wearing of sunglasses; by permitting vehicles to travel alone if threat conditions warrant' (Cornish 2003: 122).

The main aspects of the military's organizational frame are the notions of mission command and the manoeuvrist approach to operations that the British armed forces adopted in the late 1980s (Kiszely 2005). The latter approach is based on the principle of 'shattering the enemy's overall cohesion and will to fight, rather than his materiel' (Joint Doctrine and Concepts Centre 2001a: section 3-5). Manoeuvre warfare is thus based on the idea that 'wars are ultimately won or lost in the hearts and minds of men and women' (Joint Doctrine and Concepts Centre 2001b, section 2-1). Defeat and disruption of an enemy are brought about by destroying his centre of gravity with considerable strength through 'taking the initiative and applying constant and unacceptable pressure at the times and places the enemy least suspects' (Joint Doctrine and Concepts Centre 2001a: section 3-5). In contrast, attritional warfare reduces the effectiveness of enemy forces by destroying enemy forces and their materiel. The concept of mission command is the second central tenet of British defence doctrine. It refers to a decentralized style of command that delegates responsibility for military action down to the lower levels, while the commander retains the overall direction. Commanders use a 'minimum level of control so as not to limit unnecessarily his subordinate's freedom of action' and ensures that 'his subordinates understand his intentions, their own missions, and the strategic, operational and tactical context' (Joint Doctrine and Concepts Centre 2001a: section 3-7).

Italy: The Military Prestige of Humanitarian Interventions

Before the end of the Cold War, Italy's armed forces have had less exposure to questions of the use of force than the United Kingdom and France. While the British and French armed forces have a long and diverse history of military operations, including during the Cold War, the Italian military's role conception has been shaped by article 11 of the 1948 Italian Constitution: 'Italy rejects war as an instrument of aggression against the freedoms of others peoples and as a means for settling international controversies; it agrees, on conditions of equality with other states, to the limitations of sovereignty necessary for an order that ensures peace and justice among Nations; it promotes and encourages international organizations having such ends in view' (Vergottini 2004: 32–69).[5] Throughout the Cold War, NATO and Atlanticism, more than operational deployments abroad, shaped the Italian military's role conception and organizational frame.[6] However, two missions in Lebanon, in 1982 and 1984, altered this tradition and initiated a period in which Italian armed forces would be employed beyond national borders. Even more frequently and significantly throughout the 1990s, the Italian armed forces participated in a variety of missions conducted mostly within multilateral frameworks, like NATO and/or the UN, but also on its own (Nuciari 2000: 137; Rusconi 2002). The Kosovo intervention in 1999, in particular, was a turning point and led to the publication of a new military doctrine (Italian Ministry of Defence 2001, 2002; Chief of the Italian Defence Staff 2005). The Kosovo conflict has been perceived by both the military and public opinion as proof of the expertise the Italian armed forces had obtained after their twenty years of experience in the field. These military interventions became a salient element of Italy's foreign policy and a source of pride and prestige for the armed forces. This was not an easy transition, however, and domestic factors, as well as the relationship with the United States, continue to shape the decision-making process before and during the conduct of these operations (Cremasco 2000).[7] A key characteristic of the military's evolving role conception is that the use of military force is firmly embedded in multilateral operations and that the armed forces are dependent on NATO for the formulation of their doctrine.

To respond to the challenges of the evolving strategic context, the chief of the Italian Defence Staff published in 2005 the *Strategic Concept*, which outlines 'the conceptual reference frame for the planning, predisposition and employment of the Armed Forces, as the concrete technical-military implementation of the political-military guidelines contained in the ministerial directives' (Chief of the Italian Defence Staff 2005: 4). The first version of the *Strategic Concept* was published in 2000. The *Strategic Concept* addresses 'the national military instrument transformation process coherently with the current evolution in the Atlantic Alliance environment and with the building process of European Union Common Security and Defence Policy' (Chief of the Italian Defence Staff 2005: 4). The armed forces' role conception is shaped by three main principles. First, since defence and security capacity are no longer limited to the national territory but projected abroad, the armed forces must be capable of sustaining various engagements related to the support of diplomatic action, crisis management, and low- to mid-intensity post-conflict management on a global level in support of national interests and within the context of coalitions or alliances. Second, the armed forces must adopt a holistic approach (global, integrated, interdisciplinary), aimed at developing operational capabilities suitable for carrying out a wide

spectrum of missions, from humanitarian operations to crisis prevention and management to high-intensity conflict (Chief of the Italian
Defence Staff 2005: 31; see also Corneli 1998: 191–206).

Third, for the prevention or management of high-intensity conflicts,
the military is influenced by the revolution in military affairs approach
coming from the US and from NATO. The Italian military does not exclude the necessity of partial or full-blown high-intensity operations in
order to safeguard vital or strategic interests. Similarly, from the military's point of view, the recurrence, in the longer term, of traditional military threats to Italian or to NATO territory cannot be excluded. For these
reasons, even though responding to asymmetric threats, managing crises, and conducting post-conflict stabilization activity will represent the
most frequent forms of intervention, the Italian armed forces seek to
maintain the capability to conduct, within the framework of coalitions,
high-intensity operations with forces capable of facing – in quantity and
quality – significant threats. This conception is based on the idea that a
surveillance capability, combined with command and control and flexible expeditionary forces will favour 'effect-based' operations. The military sees the development of such capability, and notably the adoption of
a network-centric conception of force employment, as an important contribution to national security.[8]

The crisis management missions have been considered by the military leadership as proof of the military's rapid and effective adaptation
to a changing international environment which contributed to Italy's
external influence. Neither the military leadership nor military personnel consider that these interventions threaten their institutional identity
(Battistelli 1996; Ammendola 1999; Ammendola 2003). Quite the opposite: the army leadership presents the service as a good illustration of the
shift of the Italian military to a force that is actually employed and not
only held in reserve. The army has in various contexts emphasized its
specialization in stabilization and reconstruction tasks intended to restore normal social and political conditions of life in the areas of crisis
(Agnetti 1999; Nativi 2004; Loi 2004).[9] In the military doctrine, as well
as in several articles published in the various services' magazines and
books, a strong emphasis is put on peacekeeping and humanitarian for-
cible interventions, as well as on political and social considerations
linked to force employment (Gaiani 2005; Fraticelli 2004; Casari 2004;
Maggi 2005). Furthermore, the Strategic Concept underlies the overrid-
ing necessity of extending military action to the most recent forms of

asymmetric conflict, with particular reference to international terrorism and the proliferation of weapons of mass destruction.

Due to the deployment of the Carabinieri, a mixed police/military force, Italian peacekeeping is also characterized by the relevance given to security functions and activities. The Carabinieri deployed abroad represent more than 10 per cent of the total number of Italian soldiers in missions. Moreover, they hold responsibilities within multinational missions that no Italian force had obtained before. In Sarajevo, for example, they had the leadership of the SFOR, the first time Italy received such an important role and recognition (Agnetti 1999: 85). In sum, since the beginning of the 1990s, the Italian military has moved from a tradition of non-intervention to a cautious interventionism into international crises.

Germany: Force beyond Territorial Defence

The German military's approach to the use of force has been undergoing a far-reaching change since the end of the Cold War. During the Cold War and particularly since the German rearmament in 1955, force employment for the Bundeswehr meant a territorial self-defence posture focusing on high-intensity warfare within NATO. Because of its traumatic past and the international context, Germans have been sceptical about the use of military force and the deployment of the Bundeswehr abroad. With the end of the bipolar system, however, the role conception of Germany's armed forces, embedded in the civilian power identity and the culture of restraint, evolved within that framework (Berger 1998: 167–92; Longhurst 2004; Breuer 2006). Foreign and security policy, and also the armed forces' approach towards the use of force, were adapted to the new international challenges: 'Germany has shifted to a security posture which in principle includes the need for German participation in military interventions outside the traditional NATO context of collective defence' (Maull 2000: 56–80). Landmarks in this development were the wars in the former Yugoslavia, the judgment of the Federal Constitutional Court concerning the deployment of the Bundeswehr in 1994, the participation of Germany in air strikes against Serbia in 1999, and the threat of international terrorism and the fight against terrorism after the 9/11 attacks. As of today, the German armed forces take part in several peacekeeping and crisis management operations, and more than 7,500 Bundeswehr soldiers are deployed around the globe.[10]

The beginnings of German military interventions abroad were ac-companied by a long and tempestuous public debate about the legitim-acy of these 'out-of-area' interventions (Philippi 2004). This conflict was settled by the 1994 decision of the Federal Constitutional Court that al-lowed the German armed forces to operate outside the NATO-area.[11] Ever since this historic verdict, German participation in multilateral crisis management operations has mushroomed and the tasks and the mission spectrum of the Bundeswehr has changed accordingly. The Bundeswehr is currently undergoing a major reform, and the German security policy is being adjusted to the new character of the internation-al environment. In this regard, the 2003 'Defence Policy Guidelines' is a central document concerning the transformation of the German armed forces. They underline that German defence includes crises prevention, management and reconstruction. The goal of defence is to contribute to safeguard Germany's security wherever it is in jeopardy and not only within the limits of national boundaries. It is made very clear that no conventional threat to the German territory is to be expected in the near future and that the Bundeswehr's spectrum of operations has accord-ingly changed in a fundamental way.

To transform the Bundeswehr from a defensive, heavily mechanized force into a power projection force allowing the political and the mili-tary leadership to fulfil its international obligations, an important re-form was put into place. The *Grundzüge der Konzeption der Bundeswehr* of August 2004 underlines the flexible character of the transformation in order to adapt constantly and to make force usable in a variety of contexts (GKB 2004). Despite the ongoing reform, which does not sup-press conscription, and despite the military's new approach of force employment, the political, social, and military framework within which the military role conception is embedded has not been turned upside down. Military force is not perceived as an efficient instrument of secu-rity policy, its legitimacy is questioned, and the notion that it can only be a very last resort is prevalent. The majority of the German public is convinced that the Bundeswehr should not take part in high-intensity ground combat operations (Meiers 2000).

The 'White Paper on German Security Policy and the Future of the Bundeswehr,' published in 2006, puts forward that 'the Bundeswehr's "raison d'être" and core function continue to be the defence of Germany against external threats. Additional responsibilities include the defence of allies in the event of attack and assistance in crises and conflicts that might escalate into actual threats. Thus, the central task of the Bundeswehr continues to be national and collective defence in the classical sense. However, the White Paper acknowledges that the Bundeswehr is an instrument of German foreign and security policy and that 'for the fore-seeable future, the most likely tasks will be the prevention of international conflicts and crisis management' (White Paper on German Security Policy and the Future of the Bundeswehr: 9). Peace enforcement and crisis management operations are at the top of the task list of the armed forces, and these expected functions and operational needs decide on the structure of the capabilities, command and control systems, avail-ability, and equipment of the Bundeswehr. The ongoing reform of the Bundeswehr is influenced by these operational scenarios, and to meet the current challenges the German armed forces are being reorganized into the categories of response, stabilization, and support forces that are trained and equipped according to their respective functions. Further-more, the armed forces are supposed to keep available an adequate contingent composed of forces from all services as a contribution to coping with contingencies in the event of conflict. Finally, the reform stresses the need of adequate military capabilities and weapons in the context of joint 'network centric' high-intensity operations, inspired by the revolution in military affairs promoted through NATO. This in-cludes the improvement of operational readiness across the entire mis-sion spectrum and better joint force thinking and interaction between land, air, and maritime forces.

Conclusion

There are both significant differences and similarities in the ways in which military institutions in France, Germany, Italy, and the UK envi-sion the use of force. On the one hand, military institutions in the UK and in France draw on their colonial heritage (however contested and controversial) and have been involved in different interventions abroad before the end of the Cold War, value roles which go beyond conven-tional high-intensity warfare. The French armed forces, in particular, see conventional wars as exceptions and emphasize their role in ensur-ing or restoring security in a territory through the mastering of violence (*maîtrise de la violence*). In the field of peace operations and crisis man-agement, both the British and the French armed forces perceive the direct defeat of an adversary as only a secondary goal and focus instead on the control and stabilization of specific territories. The British military accordingly emphasizes the use of minimal force wherever possible, although its 'expeditionary' role conception highlights the need for a high escalation potential whenever necessary.

On the other hand, military institutions in Italy and Germany expanded their role beyond territorial self-defence. In contrast to the Cold War period, both militaries prepare for interventions abroad, particularly for peace operations in multilateral settings. The Italian armed forces continue to draw mainly on NATO for their doctrine formulation but see their role as contributing to a wide spectrum of both high-intensity and lower-spectrum multilateral operations. The German Bundeswehr's transformation during the last decade has been striking. Moving away from its former strict orientation towards territorial self-defence, the German armed forces deploy worldwide within different multilateral peacekeeping missions. Nevertheless, its ingrained culture of restraint and its role conception as the defender of a civilian power give it a predilection for low-end peacekeeping and stabilization missions rather than for high-intensity ground operations.

Overall, the ways of war of these military institutions remain distinct, and these differences are not residual: there is no single 'European' way of war (our results are coherent with other research using the same units of analysis, but employing a different approach; see Forster's chapter in this volume and Forster 2006). Military institutions' preferred ways of war in France and in the UK appear to be closer to each other, while military institutions in Germany and Italy also share preferences in the ways they approach force employment. It is also easier to find a clear-cut position of the armed forces on ways of war in France and in the UK than it is in Italy or, especially, in Germany. Despite these differences in organizational frames and role conceptions, military institutions in all four states have converged towards doctrines that emphasize crisis management and peace operations tasks, albeit through different trajectories. Coming from the opposite spectrum of role conceptions, French and British military institutions moved away from a former emphasis on stability based on deterrence towards an expeditionary role conception based on risk management. German and Italian role conceptions moved from territorial self-defence to cautious forms of multilateral interventionism. This convergence of role conceptions around a 'crisis management core' has facilitated the joint deployment of French, British, German, and Italian forces in the European Union's multilateral crisis management missions. Yet the notion of crisis management has remained conveniently ambiguous: since 'its meaning has not been clearly defined at the EU level' (Nowak 2006: 16; see also Bono

2004, Kaldor, Martin, and Selchow 2007), EU crisis management operations remain a one-size-fits-all notion that can incorporate distinct military role conceptions and understandings of the use of force.

NOTES

An earlier version of this chapter appeared as 'Is There a European Way of War? Role Conceptions, Organizational Frames, and the Utility of Force,' *Armed Forces and Society*, 35 (4) (July 2009), 628-645. We thank the editor and the publisher for their authorization to publish this revised version.

1 For a sceptical view, see Rynning (2003). For different perspectives, see Smith (2004) and Jones (2007).
2 For a personal experience of this transformation, see De Giuli (2006).
3 On French colonial warfare, see Porch (1986) and Frémeaux (2006).
4 For different styles of colonial warfare, see Charnay (1984). For critical appraisals, see Maspéro (1993: 169–218, 219–62) and Le Cour Grandmaison (2005: 137–99).
5 On the post–Second World War trauma, see Crainz (2007).
6 On Italy's foreign and defence policies during the Cold War, see d'Amore (2001) and Panebianco (1997: 227–51). On the military see Ceva (1999) and Labanca (2002).
7 On the difficult relation between national identity and military identity in Italy, see Battistelli (2004, 69–78) and Mini (2007).
8 For a sceptical view see Bellinzona (2007).
9 For a critical assessment, see Gaiani (2007).
10 For current numbers of German personnel deployed on the various missions, see http://www.bmvg.de (accessed 5 December 2007).
11 Decision of the *Bundesverfassungsgericht* of 12 July 1994; BVerfG AZ 2 BvE 3/92 u.a. http://www.juris.de/jportal/index.jsp (accessed 5 December 2007).

REFERENCES

Agnetti, Pino. 1999. *La Forza e la Pace*. Milano: Istituto Geografico De Agostini e Stato Maggiore della Difesa.
Ammendola, Teresa, ed. 1999. *Missione in Bosnia. Le caratteristiche sociologiche dei militari italiani*. Milano: Angeli.
– 2003. 'L'Esercito italiano e il peacekeeping: un caso di incrementalismo culturale.' *Quaderni di Sociologia* 47, no. 32: 37–62.

Armée de terre, Les forces terrestres dans les conflits aujourd'hui et demain. 2007. Paris: Economica.

Battistelli, Fabrizio. 1996. *Soldati. Sociologia dei militari italiani nell'era del peacekeeping.* Milano: Angeli.

– 2004. *Gli italiani e la guerra. Tra senso di insicurezza e terrorismo internazionale.* Rome: Carocci editore.

Bellinzona, Carlo. 2007. 'Le nozze con i fichi secchi.' *Limes. Rivista Italiana di Geopolitica* 3: 107–14.

Berger, Thomas U. 1998. *Cultures of Antimilitarism. National Security in Germany and Japan.* Baltimore: Johns Hopkins University Press.

Biddle, Stephen. 2004. *Military Power. Explaining Victory and Defeat in Modern Battle.* Princeton, NJ: Princeton University Press.

Biddle, Tami Davis. 2002. *Rhetoric and Reality in Air Warfare. The Evolution of British and American Ideas about Strategic Bombing, 1914–1945.* Princeton, NJ: Princeton University Press.

Bijker, Wiebe E. 1995. *Of Bicycles, Bakelites, and Bulbs: Toward a Theory of Sociotechnical Change.* Cambridge: MIT Press.

Bono, Giovanna. 2004. 'The EU's Military Doctrine: An Assessment.' *International Peacekeeping,* 11, no. 3 (Autumn 2004): 439–56.

Breuer, Fabian. 2006. 'Between Ambitions and Financial Constraints.' *German Politics* 15, no. 2: 206–20.

Casari, Enzo Gasparini. 2004. 'Al di là della forza e della violenza.' *Rivista Militare* 4: 32–43.

CDES (Commandement de la doctrine et de l'enseignement militaire supérieur de l'armée de terre). 2000. *L'action des forces terrestres au contact des réalités. Une nouvelle approche doctrinale.* Paris: CDES.

– 2001. *La pensée militaire, hier et aujourd'hui.* 1st ed. 1990. Paris: CDES.

Ceva, Lucio. 1999. *Storia delle forze armate in Italia.* Torino: Utet.

Charnay, Jean-Paul. 1984. *Technique et géosociologie. La guerre du Rif, le nucléaire en Orient.* Paris: Éditions Anthropos.

Chief of the Italian Defence Staff. 2005. *Concetto Strategico.* Rome.

Clausewitz, Carl von. 1989. *On War.* Edited and translated by Michael Howard and Peter Paret. Princeton, NJ: Princeton University Press. (Orig. pub. 1832.)

Corneli, Alessandro. 1998. *L'Italia va alla guerra. La cultura militare dall'Unità a oggi.* Rome: Ideazione Editrice.

Cornish, Paul. 2003. 'Myth and Reality: US and UK Approaches to Casualty Aversion and Force Protection.' *Defence Studies* 3, no. 2: 121–8.

Cornish, Paul, and Geoffrey Edwards. 2001. 'Beyond the EU/NATO Dichotomy: The Beginnings of a European Strategic Culture.' *International Affairs* 77, no. 3: 587–603.

- 2005. 'The Strategic Culture of the European Union.' *International Affairs* 81, no. 4: 801–20.

Cot, Jean (General). 2000. *La paix du monde. Une utopie réaliste*. Paris: Castelles Labor-Quartier libre.

Crainz, Guido. 2007. *L'ombra della guerra. Il 1945, l'Italia*. Rome: Donzelli editore.

Cremasco, Maurizio. 2000. 'Italy and the Management of International Crises.' In *Alliance Politics, Kosovo and NATO's War. Allied Force or Forced Allies?* ed. Pierre Martin and Mark R. Brawley, 165–80. New York: Palgrave.

d'Amore, Ciro. 2001. *Governare la difesa. Parlamento e politica militare nell'Italia repubblicana*. Milano: Franco Angeli.

DAS. 1998. 'Introduction. L'action militaire dans l'après guerre froide: orientation des réflexions stratégiques (Jean-Claude Mallet – DAS),' Colonel Patrice Sartre, 'La 'maîtrise des espaces de crise': un mode opératoire de l'action militaire dans l'après-guerre froide', 23 July.

Decrok, Jean-Philippe (Chef de bataillon). 2006. 'La crise des otages en Bosnie: dix ans déjà!' *Inflexions. Civils et militaire : pouvoir dire* 2 (February): 172–82.

De Giuli, Jean-Marc (General). 2006. 'Témoignage.' *Inflexions. Civils et militaires: pouvoir dire* 2 (February): 45–61.

Eden, Lynn. 2004. *Whole World on Fire. Organizations, Knowledge, and Nuclear Weapons Devastation*. Ithaca, NY: Cornell University Press.

EMA-État-major des armées-Division emploi. 1997. 'Concept d'emploi des forces' (October).

- 2001. 'Doctrine interarmées d'emploi des forces en opération.' Instruction 1000 (September).

Everts, Steven, et al. 2004. *A European Way of War*. London: Centre for European Reform.

Forster, Anthony. 2006. *Armed Forces and Society in Europe*. Houndmills, Basingstoke: Palgrave.

Francart, General Loup, with Jean-Jacques Patry. 1999. *Maîtriser la violence. Une option stratégique*. Paris: Economica-'Bibliothèque Stratégique.'

Fraticelli, Giulio. 2004. 'L'esercito Italiano nella funzione di stabilizzazione e ricostruzione.' *Rivista Militare* 2: 12-24.

Frémeaux, Jacques. 2006. *Intervention et humanisme. Le style des armées françaises en Afrique au XIXème siècle*. Paris: Economica.

Gaiani, Gianandrea. 2005. 'Sudan Meridionale. Nuova Missione per l'ONU e per l'Italia.' *Rivista Aeronautica* 4: 4–6.

- 2007. *Iraq-Afghanistan: Guerre di pace Italiane*. Venezia: Studio LT2.

Giegerich, Bastian. 2006. *European Security and Strategic Culture: National Responses to the EU's Security and Defence Policy*. Baden-Baden: Nomos.

GKB. 2004. *Grundzüge und Konzeption der Bundeswehr* by Minister of Defence Peter Struck, August.

Holmes, Terence M. 2007. 'Planning versus Chaos in Clausewitz's *On War.*' *The Journal of Strategic Studies* 30, no. 1: 129–51.

Holsti, Kalevi J. 1970. 'National Role Conceptions in the Study of Foreign Policy.' *International Studies Quarterly* 14, no. 3 (September): 233–309.

Howorth, Jolyon. 2002. 'The CESDP and the Forging of a European Security Culture.' *Politique Européenne* 8: 88–108.

Hull, Isabel V. 2005. *Absolute Destruction. Military Culture and the Practices of War in Imperial Germany.* Ithaca, NY: Cornell University Press.

Huntington, Samuel P. 1957. *The Soldier and the State. The Theory and Politics of Civil-Military Relations.* Cambridge, MA: The Belknap Press of Harvard University Press.

IISS (International Institute for Strategic Studies). 2007. *The Military Balance 2007.* London: Routledge.

Italian Ministry of Defence. 2001. *Nuove Forze per un nuovo millennio.* Rome.

– 2002. *Libro Bianco.* Rome.

Johnston, Alastair Iain. 1996. 'Cultural Realism and Strategy in Maoist China.' In *The Culture of National Security. Norms and Identity in World Politics,* ed. Peter J. Katzenstein, 216–68. New York: Columbia University Press.

Joint Doctrine and Concepts Centre. 2001a. *Joint Warfare Publication 0-01. British Defence Doctrine,* 2nd ed. October. Shrivenham.

– 2001b. *UK Doctrine for Joint and Multinational Operations.* Joint Warfare Publication 0-10, 2nd ed. October. Shrivenham.

– 2004. *Joint Warfare Publication 3-50,* 2nd ed. *The Military Contribution to Peace Support Operations.* June. Shrivenham.

Jones, Seth G. 2007. *The Rise of European Security Cooperation.* Cambridge: Cambridge University Press.

Kaldor, Mary, Mary Martin, and Sabine Selchow. 2007. 'Human Security: A New Strategic Narrative for Europe.' *International Affairs* 83, no. 2: 273–88.

Kennedy-Pipe, Caroline, and Colin McInnes. 1997. 'The British Army in Northern Ireland 1969–1972: From Policing to Counter-Terror.' *The Journal of Strategic Studies* 20, no. 2: 1–24.

Kiszely, John. 2005. 'Thinking about the Operational Level.' *RUSI Journal* (December): 38–43.

Krotz, Ulrich. 2002. 'National Role Conceptions and Foreign Policies: France and Germany Compared.' Program for the Study of Germany and Europe – Working Paper 02.1. Cambridge, MA: Harvard University–Minda de Gunzburg Center for European Studies.

Labanca, Nicola, ed. 2002. *L'istituzione militare in Italia. Politica e società.* Milano: Unicopli.

Le Cour Grandmaison, Olivier. 2005. *Coloniser, Exterminer. Sur la guerre et l'État colonial.* Paris: Fayard.

Legro, Jeffrey W. 1996. 'Culture and Preferences in the International Cooperation Two-Step.' *The American Political Science Review* 90, no. 1 (March): 122–3.

Loi, Bruno. 2004. *Peace-keeping, pace o guerra? Una risposta italiana: l'operazione
Ibis in Somalia*. Milano: Vallecchi.

Longhurst, Kerry. 2004. *Germany and the Use of Force: The Evolution of German
Security Policy 1990–2003*. Manchester: Manchester University Press.

Maggi, Giuseppe. 2005. 'Riconfigurare l'Esercito.' *Rivista Militare* 4: 46–55.

Marill, Colonel. 2001. *De la Grande Guerre à la chute du mur de Berlin. Ruptures et
évolutions de la doctrine militaire française*. Paris: CDES-Document d'étude.

Maspéro, François. 1993. *L'Honneur de Saint-Arnaud*. Paris: Plon.

Maull, Hanns W. 2000. 'Germany and the Use of Force: Still a "Civilian Power"?' *Survival* 42, no. 2: 56–80.

McInnes, Colin. 1998. 'Labour's Strategic Defence Review.' *International Affairs*
74, no. 4: 823–45.

Mearsheimer, John J. 1983. *Conventional Deterrence*. Ithaca, NY: Cornell University Press.

Meiers, Franz-Josef, 2005. 'Germany's Defence Choices', *Survival* 47, no. 1:
153–65.

Meyer, Christoph O. 2006. *The Quest for a European Strategic Culture: Changing
Norms on Security and Defence in the European Union*. Basingstoke: Palgrave-
Macmillan.

Mini, Fabio. 2007. 'A che (chi) servono le missioni.' *Limes. Rivista Italiana di
Geopolitica* 3: 25–43.

Nativi, Andrea. 2004. *Esercito Italiano. Le nuove Frontiere del Peacekeeping*. Milano: Mondadori.

Nowak, Agnieszka. 2006. *Civilian Crisis Management: The EU Way*. EU ISS
Chaillot Paper no. 90. Paris.

Nuciari, Marina. 2000. 'Italy: A Military for What?' In *The Postmodern Military:
Armed Forces after the Cold War*, ed. Charles C. Moskos, J.A. Williams, and
David R. Segal, 137–55. Oxford: Oxford University Press.

Panebianco, Angelo. 1997. *Guerrieri democratici. Le democrazie e la politica di po-
tenza*. Bologna: Il Mulino.

Philippi, Nina. 2004. 'Civilian Power and War: The German Debate on Out–
of–Area Operations 1990–1999.' In *Germany as a Civilian Power? The Foreign
Policy of the Berlin Republic*, ed. Sebastian Harnisch and Hanns W. Maull, 49–
67. Manchester: Manchester University Press.

Poirier, Lucien. 1985. *Les voix de la stratégie. Généalogie de la stratégie militaire,
Guibert, Jomini*. Paris: Fayard-Géopolitiques et stratégies.

Porch, Douglas. 1986. 'Bugeaud, Galliéni, Lyautey: The Development of French
Colonial Warfare.' In *Makers of Modern Strategy, from Machiavelli to the Nuclear
Age*, ed. Peter Paret, 376–407. Princeton, NJ: Princeton University Press.

Posen, Barry R. 1984. *The Sources of Military Doctrine. France, Britain, and Germany between the World Wars.* Ithaca, NY: Cornell University Press.

– 1991. *Inadvertent Escalation. Conventional War and Nuclear Risks.* Ithaca, NY: Cornell University Press.

Rathbun, Brian C. 2004. *Partisan Interventions. European Party Politics and Peace Enforcement in the Balkans.* Ithaca, NY: Cornell University Press.

Rusconi, Gian Enrico. 2002. 'Guerra e intervento umanitario. L'Italia alla ricerca di una nuova affidabilità internazionale.' In *Storia d'Italia, Annali 18, Guerra e Pace,* ed. Walter Barberis, 797–838. Torino: Einaudi.

Rynning, Sten. 2003. 'The European Union: Towards a Strategic Culture?' *Security Dialogue* 34, no. 4: 479–96.

Sentinelles de l'agora. 2007. 'Incidences des opérations de paix sur l'emploi de l'Armée française.' *Défense nationale et sécurité collective* 4 (April): 56–66.

Shy, John. 1993. 'The American Military Experience: History and Learning.' In *A People Numerous and Armed. Reflections on the Military Struggle for American Independence,* rev. ed., 265–94. Ann Arbor: University of Michigan Press. (Orig. pub. 1971.)

Smith, Michael E. 2004. *Europe's Foreign and Security Policy. The Institutionalization of Cooperation.* Cambridge: Cambridge University Press.

Streeck, Wolfgang, and Kathleen Thelen, eds. 2005. *Beyond Continuity: Institutional Change in Advanced Political Economies.* Oxford: Oxford University Press.

Thelen, Kathleen. 2004. *How Institutions Evolve. The Political Economy of Skills in Germany, Britain, the United States, and Japan.* Cambridge: Cambridge University Press.

Thornton, Rod. 2004. 'The British Army and the Origins of Its Minimum Force Philosophy.' *Small Wars and Insurgencies* 15, no. 1: 83–106.

UK Ministry of Defence. 1998. *Strategic Defence Review. Modern Forces for the Modern World.* July. London: UK Ministry of Defence.

– 2002. *The Strategic Defence Review. A New Chapter.* Cm 5566. July. London: UK Ministry of Defence.

– 2003. *Delivering Security in a Changing World. Defence White Paper.* Cm 6041-I. December. London: UK Ministry of Defence.

UK Ministry of Defence–Navy. 2001. *Future Navy Operational Concept.* Navy Board Paper 13/2001. London: UK Ministry of Defence–Navy.

Vergottini, Giuseppe de. 2004. *Guerra e costituzione. Nuovi conflitti e sfide alla democrazia.* Bologna: Il Mulino.

Veyrat, General Jean-Marie (CDES Deputy for Doctrine). 2003. 'Land Forces Employment.' *Objectif Doctrine* 39: 9–16.

Walker, Stephen G., ed. 1987. *Role Theory and Foreign Policy Analysis.* Durham, NC: Duke University Press.

Wallace, William. 2007. 'Is There a European Approach to War?' In *The Price of Peace: Just War in the Twenty-First Century*, ed. Charles Reed and David Ryall, 37–54. Cambridge: Cambridge University Press.

White Paper on German Security Policy and the Future of the Bundeswehr. 2006. Berlin.

PART THREE

Regional Challenges: Change and Continuity

11 The Year NATO Lost Russia

VINCENT POULIOT

It is often assumed in the media as well as in the specialized literature that the fast-increasing assertiveness of Russia's foreign policy with regards to Western countries is a recent phenomenon that owes much to the rise of Vladimir Putin's team of *siloviki* at the Kremlin, including current president Dmitri Medvedev. According to this storyline, it is the present government's autocratic tendencies that best explain Moscow's mounting resistance to Western policy in Europe and the rest of the world, from Kosovo to Ukraine through Iran, and now Georgia. While there certainly has been a crackdown on Russia's fragile democracy in recent years, this chapter seeks to debunk the myth that it is at the root of contemporary Russian-Atlantic disputes. This view, this chapter argues, is a convenient way for NATO Member States to overlook their own responsibilities in the current stalemate. The following pages demonstrate that the contemporary spiral toward renewed confrontation has a much earlier origin: the double enlargement policy launched by NATO in 1994, which set Russian-Atlantic security relations on the uneasy tracks that they still ride to this day. Many of today's problems, it will be shown, are the logical extension of Brussels's practices starting in the mid-1990s.

Twenty years after the fall of the Berlin Wall, and after much shifting, Russia now appears to have left the Euro-Atlantic orbit for good. For instance, Moscow staunchly opposes ballistic shield plans in Eastern Europe; it has suspended its obligations under the CFE treaty; it vigorously fights any NATO rapprochement with Ukraine, Georgia, and other colour-revolution countries; and it actively contests the Alliance's self-arrogated, global security mandate. The revival of mild confrontation in NATO-Russia relations is a stark reminder of the missed opportunity of the end of the Cold War for European security. After all, in the early 1990s Moscow seemed on the way to integrate the Euro-Atlantic security community, sparking high hopes for a new peaceful order in the northern hemisphere. In this context, it is absolutely crucial for students of international security to understand what went wrong and why. Given the extraordinary authority that NATO Member States enjoyed over Russia in the aftermath of the end of the Cold War, how did they manage to spoil the relationship to that extent? The chapter demonstrates how NATO's double enlargement practices progressively alienated the Russians, in large part by re-empowering the ingrained narrative of Great Power-ness in Moscow. While, from the Western point of view, enlargement is the natural widening of a democratic zone of peace and of its security responsibilities abroad, for Russia it has always been an exclusionary policy whereby the Alliance unilaterally arrogates new territories and duties. As a result, today's Russian-Atlantic disputes – for instance, over the American BMD project, the CFE treaty, the globalization of NATO, and a looming third wave of enlargement – all stem somewhat directly from the critical juncture of 1994. The chapter concludes by making the case for a shift in NATO's policy toward Russia.

In terms of the 'paradigm shift' that Mérand, Irondelle, and Foucault describe in the Introduction to this book, this chapter throws light on how localized the epistemic change remains twenty years after the fall of the Berlin Wall. After a short-lived hiatus that lasted until the mid-1990s, the Great Power narrative, which is closely related to realpolitik thinking, made a progressive comeback in Moscow to the point that it now forms a strong and pervasive consensus among policymakers and leaders. In fact, not only do most Russian elites discount human security and liberal peace talk as cheap, they also consider it duplicitous insofar as it has been used, from their perspective, to cloak much colder calculations on NATO's part throughout its double enlargement process. Western countries tried hard to get the Russians to buy into the new, benign security paradigm, but to no avail, largely because it proved exclusionary for Moscow. In sum, as much as security may have transformed from a European perspective, in Russia this new discourse was and remains construed as a façade hiding a timeless power politics.

At the theoretical level, this chapter builds on a relational approach inspired by Pierre Bourdieu's structural constructivism (Bourdieu 1990; Pouliot 2008). To Bourdieu, political order results from the homology between the positions that agents occupy in a given field and the dispositions that they embody as part of their 'habitus.' So long as people desire what is structurally 'theirs' and never contemplate what cannot be obtained given the distribution of social, cultural, economic, and symbolic resources, the orchestra can play without a conductor, as Bourdieu liked to say. However, conflict and disruption erupt when a mismatch emerges between agents' positions and the reflection of these social locations inside agents' bodies and mind. The theoretical narrative that informs the empirical case study that follows is precisely one of a growing mismatch between Russia's fairly junior position in the post–Cold War field of international security and the key disposition of Great Power-ness that Russian policymakers have increasingly expressed as NATO proceeded with its double enlargement. As a result of this 'hysteresis,' the symbolic order of NATO-Russia relations has been slowly but surely eroding over the last decade and a half (see Pouliot 2010).

The Turning Point in Post–Cold War NATO-Russia Relations

The end of the Cold War constituted a watershed in the history of the field of international security. After decades of bipolar confrontation, the whole structure of political interaction underwent radical changes prompted in large part by the demise of the USSR. At the intersubjective level, the rules of the game of international security underwent significant changes, away from power balancing and toward the cooperative security model born out of the CSCE process. From the 1990 Paris Charter to the EU's 2003 Neighbourhood Policy, traditional realpolitik has become second to democratic peace and human rights in the post–Cold War pursuit of European security.

NATO was particularly instrumental in effecting this intersubjective transformation toward cooperative security (De Wijk 1997; Adler 2008). Not only was the shift promoted by the Alliance, it also contributed a lot to consolidate NATO's growing dominance in the field (Williams 2007). In the new rules of the international security game defined by Brussels, talk about power balancing was replaced with the promotion of democracy and human rights as the best means of ensuring security. With the USSR still alive, NATO's Secretary General Manfred Woerner (1991: 8) promoted 'a more diffuse concept of security in which economic integration and assistance and the internal democratization of states become as important as traditional military defence in maintaining security.' At the London summit (1990), allies explicitly embraced the idea of indivisible security and launched, one year later, the North Atlantic Cooperation Council (NACC) with former Warsaw Pact enemies.

In its first years as an independent country, Russia enthusiastically embraced the internal mode of pursuing security, even to the point of supporting NATO's transformation in that direction. When the Alliance proposed to establish military contacts with former Warsaw Pact countries, in 1992, reactions in Moscow were generally positive (Sychov 1992; Kovalenko 1992). In a similar way, at first the Russians were quite supportive of NATO's functional transformation toward peacekeeping. For instance, the Charter of Russian-American Partnership and Friendship, signed in October 1992, asserted that Russia and the United States support 'the creation of a rather strong Euro-Atlantic peacekeeping potential, based on the CSCE's political authority, that would allow for use of the possibilities of the [NACC]' (quoted in *Rossiskaya Gazeta* 1992; see Yusin 1992). While it is true that a few Russian officials expressed concerns, overall the new Russian elites showed a strong disposition to support the new rules of the international security game, in line with Gorbachev's New Thinking. For instance, Russia's sanguine attitude toward NATO's functional transformation did not immediately darken when it became obvious that by taking up new functions of partnership and peacekeeping, the Alliance was giving itself a new lease on life. An echo of the CSCE's cooperative security approach, the inclusive and cooperative spirit of the NACC seemed to suit Russian interests quite well. Still in October 1993, when the Americans first floated the idea of the Partnership for Peace (PfP) with the Russians, the initial reaction was quite favourable: Yeltsin was reported to approve the outreach initiative toward the post-communist world insofar as it included Russia too (Erlikh 1993; Talbott 2002, 115). The Russians looked eager to enter in an ever closer partnership with NATO whatever it took.

Similarly, the most striking aspect of NATO-Russia dealings over involving the Alliance in the Bosnian civil war is the explicit support the Russian government offered in the beginnings. Until February 1994, confirms one expert, Russia shared 'the predominant Western interpretation of events in Bosnia: that Serb expansionism and aggressive ethnic nationalism was directed against the legitimate government of a sovereign and independent state' (Headley 2003: 211). This supportive approach was translated into deeds, as demonstrated by Russia's alignment with the Western members of the UNSC. In May 1992, Russia supported Resolution 757 imposing sanctions on the Federal Republic of Yugoslavia

(Serbia and Montenegro). It is noteworthy that Russia voted in favour while China and Zimbabwe both abstained. The most significant gesture demonstrating Moscow's support for the Atlantic approach came in early June, when Russia agreed to UNSC Resolution 836, authorizing the deployment of peacekeepers to protect Bosnian safe areas and threatening Serbia with 'tougher measures, none of which is prejudged or excluded from consideration.' This crucial vote implicitly supported NATO's repeated threats to strike if violations continued. In total, throughout 1992 and 1993, more than fifty resolutions on Yugoslavia were jointly adopted by Russia and the NATO countries at the UNSC. To be sure, Russia's support was not unequivocal, and some differences remained: for instance, Moscow systematically opposed the use of force and was critical, at times, of what it perceived as the West's anti-Serb bias. But overall, in practice the alignment remains striking.

Russia's accommodative foreign policy started to change in 1994, as the Alliance became militarily involved in Bosnia and talk of geographical expansion began. The real turning point came in December, when NATO issued a communiqué initiating 'a process of examination inside the Alliance to determine how NATO will enlarge, the principles to guide this process and the implications of membership' (NATO 1994: par. 6). This decision took the Russians by surprise, as the Alliance had just launched the PfP with Moscow's support. According to Goldgeier and McFaul (2003: 195), the 'Russians had good reasons to be confused about America's real intentions.' Kozyrev, who was in Brussels on that very day to sign an Individual Partnership Program (as part of the PfP) as well as a document fostering Russia-NATO dialogue, consequently refused to sign any document and, under Yeltsin's direct instructions, froze all further progress in institutionalizing cooperation with the Alliance. For the usually soft-spoken minister of foreign affairs, the unilateral decision to expand reflected a NATO pattern 'to offer Russia a fait accompli, a final position of the "take it or leave it" type' (Kozyrev 1995: 9). Within a few days, this about-face led to one of the most emblematic moments of the post–Cold War Russian-Atlantic relations. Until NATO's 1 December communiqué, Moscow had hoped that the Budapest C/OSCE summit would consecrate an inclusive European security architecture based on a strong pan-European institution. Instead, the new security order premised on the Alliance's functional and geographical enlargement relegated Russia to the margins of Europe. Lamenting the rise of a 'cold peace.' In Budapest Yeltsin denounced the exclusionary consequences of the Alliance's double enlargement, accusing it of 'sowing the seeds of mistrust.' With the benefit of hindsight, we know that it is precisely from this defining moment that Russia became, slowly but surely, a much more difficult partner with regards to NATO Member States. Recall that only days after the OSCE summit, Russian troops began invading Chechnya.

How can we ascertain the causal link between NATO's double enlargement practices and Russia's more difficult foreign policy? The chapter substantiates this correlation with two kinds of evidence. First, data show that between 1993 and 1995, an unprecedented consensus among Russian security elites emerged, largely away from integration into the West. In a detailed survey study, Zimmerman (2002: 93) observes that 'Russia's orientation to the world had changed considerably in the two years between 1993 and 1995. The era dominated by those sometimes termed the Atlanticists in Russian foreign policy had passed.' As the author continues, 'NATO expansion both in numbers and in role has very likely deterred those Russian elites who from a Western perspective warranted being deterred *and* has disabused Russian elites who would have been likely to respond favorably to policies designed to reassure' (206). An insider to these debates, Dmitri Trenin (2000: 13–14) confirms that 'the turning point came in 1994 with the decision in principle by NATO to admit new members. Most groups within the Russian elite, otherwise deeply divided on the issues of policy, were suddenly united in portraying this decision as essentially anti-Russian.' Significantly, this view is corroborated by many Western practitioners who similarly portray the double enlargement as 'the real culprit' in the deterioration of Russian-Atlantic relations (Blacker 1998: 179). Building on dozens of interviews with American diplomats and politicians, Goldgeier and McFaul (2003: 356) also conclude that although 'it is hard to measure the negative impact of NATO enlargement for U.S.-Russian relations on other security concerns [but] it is true that the cooperative pattern of problem solving on issues like Baltic troop withdrawal and the India rocket deal established in 1993–94 were not repeated after the NATO enlargement process began to move forward for subjects like Iran or START.' All in all, both Russian and non-Russian insiders agree in locating the turning point in Russian-Atlantic relations precisely in late 1994.

Second, the correlation is also apparent when we look at the precise sequence of events. For one thing, the Alliance took its crucial decisions *before* Moscow reverted to a more difficult foreign policy. For example, the Russian invasion of Chechnya – the first genuinely praetorian practice enacted by the post-communist Kremlin – was decided *after* NATO had announced its study on enlargement. It is mistaken, then, to argue that some prior aggressive practices on Russia's part motivated the Alliance's decision. For another thing, for one full year Moscow resisted popular pressures to take a more assertive stance toward NATO. Recall that at the Duma elections of 1993, nationalistic forces won a clear victory over pro-Western forces. Yet Moscow did not become more assertive immediately after that. During the first half of 1994, on the contrary, Russian officials were still taking a conciliatory tone toward NATO, supporting much of its diplomacy in the Balkans as well as its partnership initiatives. The real change in Russian foreign policy came only after NATO had announced its enlargement. Nothing better illustrates the change in Russia's foreign policy than the nomination, in January 1996, of Yevgeny Primakov as foreign minister in replacement of Kozyrev. At his very first press conference, the new minister summarized the newly empowered narrative quite clearly: 'Despite the current difficulties, Russia has been and remains a Great Power, and its policy toward the outside world should correspond to that status' (quoted in *Moskovskiye Novosti* 1996). From then on, Russian foreign policymakers appealed to the historical notion of 'derzhava,' which Tsygankov (2004: 93) translates as 'the holder of international equilibrium of power.' As a result, the main constitutive elements of Russia's narrative became calls for equality, multipolarity, spheres of interest, and balance of power (see Lo 2002: 98 ff.) – all elements of the Cold War rules of the international security game centred on power balancing and alliance making.

Given that for a little less than a decade, this traditional Russian narrative had been remarkably tamed inside the Kremlin to the benefit of cooperative security, how can we explain its resurgence in the mid-1990s? This chapter argues that despite all the Alliance talk to the contrary, the double enlargement appeared to Moscow to breach the three basic CSCE principles that had been so fundamental in putting an end to the Cold War – that security is indivisible, mutual, and cooperative. It looked as though the NATO-professed rules of the post–Cold War international security game were scorned by the Alliance itself, whose actions, as Moscow understood them, smacked more of realpolitik than cooperative security. First, from a Russian perspective, expanding NATO created new dividing lines in the European security system. So long as Russia remained on the margins of a tightly knit alliance that,

on top of it, was arrogating to itself the central role in European security, it could only cause its exclusion. 'What Russia seeks,' argued one
Russian pundit, 'is an arrangement that would assure its full participation in European affairs, rather than its isolation from, or marginalization in, Europe' (Pushkov 1997: 2). But instead, for Moscow, the
geographical enlargement of the Alliance was bound to lead to 'the creation of a buffer zone in reverse, a means to isolate the new Russia from
continental Europe' (Black 2000: 8). For sure, expansion seriously undermined the chances of developing a pan-European security institution with teeth in which Russia could exert influence.

In a similar logic, for the Russians, NATO's February 1994 ultimatum
to Bosnian Serbs contradicted the very essence of the new rules of the
international security game premised on inclusiveness and mutuality.
For instance, one official from the Ministry of Defence wrote in Kraznaya
Zvezda: 'Russia has a right to ask why it was included in the [NACC]
and why it should approve the [PfP] initiative if, when an ultimatum
was prepared – in a matter that affects it directly – Moscow was ignored' (Sidorov 1994). Gorbachev (1994), certainly no hawk, expressed
a similar complaint: 'Russia was confronted with a fait accompli. It was
treated as a junior partner that is expected only to nod its head and support the choice made by others, contenting itself with a pat on the shoulder.' In late August 1995, when NATO's Operation Deliberate Force
began, Yeltsin went even further, denouncing the Alliance for breaking
with the cooperative security discourse it was simultaneously preaching: 'In proclaiming its "peacekeeping mission," the North Atlantic alliance has essentially taken upon itself the role of both judge and jury'
(quoted in *Rossiskiye Vesti* 1995). For the Russians, NATO was guilty of
duplicity: while claiming to include Russia in diplomatic talks through
the Contact Group, it was simultaneously making unilateral decisions
to use force without Russia's participation. As a result, many in Moscow
came to construe NATO's functional enlargement not in terms of the internal mode of pursuing security, but as a very cold-blooded strategy
intended to strengthen the Alliance's profile in the post–Cold War era.

Space constraints make it impossible to pursue this interpretive analysis of NATO-Russia dealings beyond the mid-1990s. Suffice it to say
that the deteriorating trends that were just described further accentuat-
ed in the wake of the Alliance's intervention in Kosovo, of its new
Security Concept adopted in 1999, and of its post-9/11 decision to enlarge again (including to the Baltic states). As far as Russia was concerned, NATO's practices turned out to be profoundly self-defeating for
the new order of international security things premised on cooperative

security principles. As the next section demonstrates, twenty years after the fall of the Berlin Wall the Alliance is now forced to pick up the pieces for its short-sightedness.

Picking Up the Pieces: Current Disputes between Russia and NATO in Light of the Past

This section argues that the main disputes that currently plague Russian-Atlantic security relations are all related, more or less directly, to NATO's double enlargement practices. Four key bones of contention are discussed in turn: the CFE treaty, the American BMD project in Central Europe, a looming third wave of enlargement (including to Georgia), and the globalization of NATO. This list is obviously not exhaustive, as it leaves out Kosovo, Iran, Iraq, and so on, but it supplies a good *tour d'horizon* of the contemporary Russian-Atlantic relationship.

The CFE Moratorium

Russia's moratorium on the CFE treaty illustrates particularly well the extent to which NATO's double enlargement has jeopardized even the strongest *acquis* of the end of the Cold War. The CFE treaty was signed in late 1990 by the NATO and Warsaw Pact countries, setting limits on conventional forces and equipment on the European continent with solid verification and information exchange mechanisms. Under Russia's request, an adapted version was agreed upon in 1999 in order to allow more flexibility in Moscow's troops movements in the Caucasus, notably. In the OSCE Istanbul Final Act, Russia also agreed to withdraw its military from bases in Georgia and Moldova. In the ensuing weeks, NATO countries conditioned the ratification of the Adapted CFE treaty on Moscow's fulfilment of what has come to be known as the 'Istanbul commitments' (NATO 1999). On its part, the Russian Duma ratified the treaty in June 2004 while urging those new NATO Member States not covered by the original CFE to sign the treaty. In April 2004, at their very first NRC meeting, Slovenia and the Baltic states stated their intention to join the arms control regime (NATO 2004a). That was never done, however, and Moscow did not fully withdraw its forces from Georgia and Moldova either. In his presidential address in April 2007, President Putin proposed to suspend Russia's commitments under CFE, a decision that came into effect in December that year. In late 2007, the most far-reaching symbol of the end of the Cold War seemed doomed to oblivion.

The CFE stalemate is related to NATO's double enlargement in two main ways. First, throughout the tense negotiations over the Founding Act during the mid-1990s, Moscow repeatedly requested that some armament ceilings be put on the Alliance's new members. The goal was to avoid large deployments close to Russia's borders. Recall that among the ten new allies, six were part of the Warsaw Pact in 1990 (Bulgaria, the Czech Republic, Hungary, Poland, Romania, Slovakia) while the remaining four (the three Baltic states and Slovenia) were not independent states in 1990 (they are not covered by the CFE arms limitations). At the time, in December 1996 NATO responded with a non-binding declaration to the effect that it had 'no intention, plan or need to introduce substantial forces onto the territory of the new members' (quoted in Goldgeier and McFaul 2003: 205). That pledge was subsequently breached, for instance, when in early 2004 NATO's Allied Command Europe began patrolling the Baltic states' airspace and policing the border with Russia. This zealous and somewhat provocative operation profoundly irritated Moscow, who responded in kind by sending airplanes do similar reconnaissance missions on the border with the Baltic states (see Nechayev 2004; Safronov 2004).

Second, the CFE stalemate also stems from NATO's active courting of candidate countries such as Georgia. This issue will be specifically addressed below; suffice it to say here that from the Russian perspective, there seems to be no other means to slow down Tbilisi's admission than nurturing the frozen conflicts in Abkhazia and South Ossetia. The Alliance has systematically overlooked Moscow's objections in the past and nothing suggests that this time it will be different. In this context, Russia sharply contests NATO's conditioning of Adapted CFE ratification to the 1999 pledge as an 'artificial linkage,' to use General Yuri Baluyevsky's words (quoted in *Izvestia* 2004). As the general continued, 'the expansion of NATO, the changed military and political status of six CFE signatory countries and the resulting changes in the structure and composition of the groupings – all these things supposedly have nothing to do with the CFE Treaty, while Russia's bilateral relations with Moldova and Georgia have a direct bearing on the treaty and are preventing its ratification!' For the Russians, fulfilling the Istanbul commitments is out of question so long as NATO keeps seducing Tbilisi and other former Soviet capitals.

When he announced the moratorium, then-president Putin made it clear that he was reacting in large part to NATO's double enlargement. As he declared:

It turns out that NATO has put its frontline forces on our borders, and we continue to strictly fulfil the [CFE] treaty obligations and do not react to these actions at all. I think it is obvious that NATO expansion does not have any relation with the modernisation of the Alliance itself or with ensuring security in Europe. On the contrary, it represents a serious provocation that reduces the level of mutual trust. And we have the right to ask: against whom is this expansion intended? And what happened to the assurances our western partners made after the dissolution of the Warsaw Pact? (President of Russia 2007)

Russia's suspension of its CFE commitments seemed to take NATO by surprise although the idea had been floated several times since 2004. The many negotiations that have taken place since has not delivered any compromise. In an unprecedented show of impotence, NATO (2007a) announced its decision 'not to respond in kind at this stage to the Russian Federation's political decision to "suspend" its legal obligations [while] NATO Allies will continue to meet theirs, without prejudice to any future action they might take.' Meanwhile, it is now Moscow that conditions implementation of the CFE treaty on its ratification by all NATO members.

The American BMD Project in Central Europe

In May 2006, the Bush administration announced its plans to install a limited set of missile interceptors as well as a radar station on the territory of Poland and of the Czech Republic by 2011. The declared rationale for this Central European location was to intercept eventual Iranian missiles on their way to the US and Europe. The new interceptors will add to those already built at Fort Greely (Alaska) and the Vanderberg Air Force Base in California, while the proposed radar station would complement the modernized facilities in Fylingdales (UK) and the American Thule Air Base in Greenland. Had President Obama not decided, in September 2009, to scale back the earlier plan, the BMD project would have given way to the first permanent American deployment on Polish and Czech soil. The Russian reaction was as harsh as immediate. Yury Baluyevsky, the chief of the Armed Forces General Staff, declared that 'plans to make Eastern Europe a forward region in the US missile defense system are intended to neutralize Russia's strategic potential' (quoted in Litovkin 2006). Defense Minister Sergei Ivanov similarly claimed that 'the choice of location for the deployment of those systems is dubious, to put it mildly' (quoted in Gordon 2006). From the outset, the Russians rejected the American plan as designed against their nuclear deterrent, as if the Cold War had never ended: how can we make sense of this seemingly abrupt return to deterrence logics?

There are many reasons why the Russians are troubled by the American BMD project – including of course Washington's unilateral withdrawal from the ABM treaty – but two are particularly noteworthy as they pertain to NATO's double enlargement. First, the project breaks the political pledge taken by NATO and Washington in 1996 neither to station nuclear forces on the territory of new members nor to revise nuclear policy. As the communiqué reads: 'NATO countries have no intention, no plan, and no reason to deploy nuclear weapons on the territory of new members nor any need to change any aspect of NATO's nuclear posture or nuclear policy – and we do not foresee any future need to do so' (NATO 1996). For Moscow, this is just one more broken promise in a long series that started in 1990, when Gorbachev was told by several Western politicians that the Alliance would never move eastward. Second, as will become clear below, since the Kosovo intervention Moscow has been particularly wary of NATO's interventionist tendencies in the various conflicts of our time. Nuclear forces are one of the few resources that still promise Russia some semblance of influence over Brussels and Washington. In this context, Russia is particularly sensitive to any infringement on its nuclear deterrent because of its startling weakness on the conventional level. After more than fifteen years of decay addressed only recently, the Russian army has become a shadow of its former self and must rely on nuclear forces for territorial defence.

As late as 2006, two eminent Russian experts with insider connections wrote that 'since the end of the Cold War, nuclear deterrence between Russia and the United States had been receding into the background in terms of day-to-day foreign policy and official public relations' (Arbatov and Dvorkin 2006: 3). For several years, the only nuclear talk one could hear or read about was related to disarmament (START I, START II, and SORT, for instance) or to the cooperative management of old stockpiles (e.g., CTR, CIS denuclearization). In 1994, in a symbolic gesture Clinton and Yeltsin pledged to retarget all their nuclear forces away from their mutual territories. Even after 9/11, the major financial commitment of the 2002 Global Partnership (US$20 billion over ten years) to help Russia manage its nuclear arsenal partook in this generally cooperative climate in which nuclear deterrence did not seem the primary preoccupation on either side. To be sure, in both American and Russian defence strategies nuclear deterrence has always remained a central component after the end of the Cold War, but it had somehow receded into the background. Now it is back in the open, and with NATO possibly taking a stake in the American BMD project, the issue has started to grip the relationship between the Alliance and Moscow. For instance, in June 2007 Foreign Minister Sergey Lavrov enticed European capitals to cooperate on developing a joint defence missile with Moscow on the same day that then-president Putin threatened to retarget Russian nuclear bombs at EU countries (von Twickel 2007). Clearly, NATO's advance toward Russia's territory and its readiness to take unilateral action anywhere in the world have significantly contributed to revaluing nuclear deterrence in Moscow.

A Looming Third Wave of Geographical Enlargement

A third contemporary Russian-Atlantic dispute that flows directly from the double enlargement policy kick-started in 1994 regards the looming new wave of geographical enlargement, including to countries such as Georgia and Ukraine. Throughout the Bush presidency the Alliance publicly confirmed its 'open-door policy' (NATO 2004b: par. 25). 'In 2009 I would like to see more countries in NATO,' said Secretary General De Hoop Scheffer; 'I would like to see a NATO of 26 plus. I would like to see Serbia firmly on the road to NATO and I would like to see us coming closer to honouring the ambitions of Ukraine and Georgia' (NATO 2007b). NATO's double enlargement practices, which have significantly contributed to the re-emergence, sustenance, and consolidation of the Great Power narrative in Moscow, have not changed whatsoever since 1994. In 2007, Foreign Minister Lavrov (2007) publicly compared NATO's limitless expansion to Cold War containment.

After the colour revolutions in Tbilisi and Kyiv in November 2003 and 2004, the NATO bureaucracy took several steps to actively court Ukraine and Georgia despite Russia's strong reservations. As for the former, the Alliance offered an Intensified Dialogue process in April 2005 in order to prepare the country for eventual membership. When Kyiv held joint exercises with the Alliance in June 2006, however, major popular demonstrations took place for seven days in the Crimea seaport of Feodosia. As a result, then–prime minister Viktor Yanukovych told NATO in September 2006 that membership would be put on hold. At the time of writing the Ukrainian membership remains a hotly debated topic inside the Alliance as no decision could be made at the April

2008 Bucharest summit (NATO 2008). On the Russian side, Defense Minister Sergei Ivanov warned from the outset that there would be 'an inevitable impact one way or another on our relations, particularly on cooperation in the military-industrial sector and some other spheres' if and when Ukraine joins NATO (quoted in Associated Press 2006). Given the very close historical and cultural ties with Ukrainians, this issue is probably the toughest that Russia and the Alliance have faced since the end of the Cold War.

Russia's opposition is also intense with respect to Georgia, as the diplomatic crisis of September 2006 and the open war of August 2008 demonstrated. US President Bush had long declared his intention to invite Tbilisi inside the Alliance: 'I'm a believer in the expansion of NATO. I think it's in the world's interest. Georgia has got work to do, but we'll do all we can to make it easier for it to become a member of NATO' (quoted in Simonyan 2006). Given the frozen conflicts in Abkhazia and South Ossetia, however, the situation remains extremely tense. As with Ukraine, there is no consensus inside NATO about admitting Georgia. Nonetheless, the Alliance offered an Intensified Dialogue on Georgia's membership aspirations in September 2006 – that is, only days before Tbilisi expelled several Russian officials on spying accusations. The diplomatic row that ensued between the two countries was unprecedented and gave birth to hostile reactions on both sides. For Russia's foreign minister, Georgia's 'provocation' was the direct consequence of NATO's expression of interest in its candidacy: 'The latest escapade involving the seizure of our officers occurred immediately after NATO's decision to adopt a plan for intensified cooperation with Georgia and after the visit that Mikhail Nikolayevich paid to the US ... Here's how it all unfolded in chronological order: the trip to Washington, the NATO decision, the taking of hostages' (quoted in Solovyov and Sidorov 2006). As NATO's open-door policy reaches the post-Soviet space up to its very borders, Moscow is growing increasingly nervous and rigid in its opposition.

There should be no doubt that Russia's very harsh response to Georgian military operations in South Ossetia in August 2008 derived in part from the larger fight for influence in the Caucasus that NATO's endless enlargement sparks. As they powerlessly witness Russia's ruthless actions in South Ossetia, Alliance members are reaping what they sowed. Moscow's defiant assertiveness and, more to the point, its new deafness to Western criticisms and objections are testimony to the fact that twenty years after the fall of the Berlin Wall, NATO has lost its symbolic authority and as a result is not in a position to 'punish' Russia or steer its foreign policy anymore. While Moscow peacefully watched the train of enlargement pass in front of its eyes twice, this time, with Georgia and Ukraine in the cargo, it looks like its resistance will be much more active and resolved. Since the change of guard in Washington, however, the push for further NATO enlargement has considerably weakened.

The Globalization of NATO

The Russians are no more heartened by the Alliance's apparently limitless expansion at the functional level – the fourth contemporary dispute in line with the 1994 turning point. Recall that in 1999 at the Washington summit, NATO adopted a new Concept providing for out-of-area missions. That trend deepened in the wake of the 2001 terrorist attacks. At the Prague summit in 2002, NATO (2002: par. 4a) created the Response Force, a body of approximately 20,000 troops to be available on short notice for deployment around the world and across the full spectrum of military operations. By October 2006, the force was operational with 25,000 troops ready for operations of up to thirty days anywhere on the planet (more if re-supplied). As far as functional expansion is concerned, however, the real headway took place at the Istanbul summit in June 2004. There, the Alliance unambiguously affirmed that 'we are determined to address effectively the threats our territory, forces and populations face from *wherever they may come*' (NATO 2004c; emphasis added). For the first time, NATO was explicitly granting itself the right and even the duty to intervene anywhere on the globe. It is also in Istanbul that the Alliance took the decision to expand its ISAF mission to the whole of Afghanistan.

In this context, a new narrative emerged among Atlantic officials and experts to the effect that NATO is now 'going global,' as Daalder and Goldgeier (2006) put it. Since the turn of the millennium, the Alliance has lent logistical support to the African Union's mission in Darfur; assisted tsunami relief efforts in Indonesia; ferried supplies to victims of hurricane Katrina in the US; and airlifted food after a massive earthquake in Kashmir. For experts like Daalder and Goldgeier, the next logical step would be to enlarge membership to any democratic state in the world. Though this conclusion remains far from consensual, since the November 2006 Riga summit, the new name of the game for the Alliance is *functional* security – meaning that geography is no more a constraint on its action (NATO 2006). In the wake of the Kosovo precedent, Russian officials fear that in becoming a global policeman, NATO could eventually mingle in conflicts that are of direct concern for (and in close vicinity of) their country. Foreign Minister Lavrov put that feeling clearly:

> The parameters of our interaction largely depend on how the alliance's transformation will proceed. There are a number of aspects in this regard that evoke our concern. For example, it was agreed at the NATO Riga Summit in what cases military force could be used. The number of such hypothetical scenarios is increasing. But there is no clarity as to how this is going to correlate with the rules of international law, in particular, whether NATO will ask for permission from the United Nations, as it should be done under the Charter of the Organization. We cannot, of course, watch impartially the military structure of the alliance moving ever closer to our borders. It is worrying that since 1999 nothing has been done to advance arms control and military restraint. These tasks have a fundamental significance for our relations with the alliance. (Ministry of Foreign Affairs of the Russian Federation 2007)

Clearly, Moscow rejects the Alliance's self-attributed agenda on the global scale. For the Russians, a global NATO that intervenes anywhere in the world constitutes a very unwelcome development and a serious infringement on their capacity to influence the international order. Given the global economic crisis and the many problems faced by Allies in Afghanistan, though, the momentum in Brussels has switched to drawing limits to NATO's activities.

Conclusion: Shooting Oneself in the Foot

The story that this chapter told is the story of a missed opportunity. With the implosion of the USSR in the early 1990s, many new paths opened for Moscow and its former Atlantic enemy in building peace in and through practice. In 1992–3, everything was taking place as if a new security community was in the making. All the precipitating conditions had obtained (Pouliot 2007) and NATO could wield the power and organization to make diplomacy the 'self-evident practice' of Russian-Atlantic relations (see Pouliot 2008). That window of opportunity abruptly shut in 1994 when the Alliance decided to geographically enlarge and implement its functional expansion in Bosnia regardless of Russia's objections and requests. Since that turning point, the exclusionary consequences of the double enlargement for Moscow have led to the re-emergence of a foreign policy narrative suffused with realpolitik, which later consolidated over the Kosovo crisis, the globalization of

NATO, and a second wave of enlargement. Today, as the CFE controversy, the BMD row, and the persisting disputes over the double enlargement demonstrate, the Russian-Atlantic relationship has embarked upon a path of mild rivalry which, as non-violent as it may remain at this time, appears conducive to compounding security dilemmas. All in all, the promises of the end of the Cold War not only failed to materialize – a decade and a half later they also seem to have withered away.

The key policy lesson to be drawn should be clear: in hindsight, the policy of NATO's double enlargement was self-defeating as far as pacification with Russia was concerned. Of course, keeping alive the 'most successful military alliance in history' or 'welcoming back to the European family' countries that had been brutally occupied for decades cannot be said to be wrong in intent. Alliance officials cannot be completely blamed for being prudent with their former enemies in Moscow. The policy failure of the double enlargement rests not with its intent but with its effects, which were definitely not properly assessed with regards to Russia. As much as expansion made sense from the NATO point of view, it was plainly unpalatable to Moscow: exclusionary and delusionary, the policy corresponded to the realpolitik game of the Cold War far more than to the new rules of cooperative security simultaneously professed by the Alliance. The seeds of today's aggravating problems were planted back in 1994, and it is NATO Member States that bear the brunt of the blame for losing Russia at a time it was begging for inclusion. If, with the double enlargement, the Alliance was seeking to keep the Russians in their place and manage their transition away from confrontation, it achieved the unenviable feat of shooting itself right in the foot.

In the mid-1990s, proponents of enlargement put forward a seemingly irrefutable (but how fallacious) argument. If Russia were to remain cooperative despite expansion, then NATO could overlook its objections without consequences. This is the scenario that took place until Russia got back on its feet at the turn of the millennium. If, however, Moscow were to revert to praetorian tactics in response, then enlargement made sense to guard former satellites against it. In hindsight, this selling line turned NATO into a protection racketeer – create insecurity to justify security measures (Tilly 1985) – and brought about a dangerous self-fulfilling prophecy of confrontation. In the wake of the South Ossetian conflict, for instance, NATO's further enlargement to Georgia and Ukraine is now justified by Russia's resurging assertiveness in its neighbourhood – itself largely a consequence of the Alliance's expansion, geographical and functional. This is exactly the kind of vicious spiral that took the world into four decades of pointless nuclear confrontation. It is sad beyond words how little decision makers have learned from past mistakes.

REFERENCES

Adler, Emanuel. 2008. 'The Spread of Security Communities: Communities of Practice, Self-Restraint, and NATO's Post-Cold War Transformation.' *European Journal of International Relations* 14, no. 2: 195–230.

Arbatov, Alexei, and Vladimir Dvorkin. 2006. *Beyond Nuclear Deterrence: Transforming the U.S.-Russian Equation*. Washington: Carnegie Endowment for International Peace.

Associated Press. 2006. 'Ivanov Warns Ukraine Joining NATO Comes with Big Price.' *Moscow Times*, 8 December.

Black, Joseph Lawrence. 2000. *Russia Faces NATO Expansion: Bearing Gifts or Bearing Arms?* Lanham, MD: Rowman and Littlefield.

Blacker, Coit. 1998. 'Russia and the West.' In *The New Russian Foreign Policy*, ed. Michael Mandelbaum, 167–93. New York: Council on Foreign Relations.

Bourdieu, Pierre. 1990. *The Logic of Practice*. Stanford: Stanford University Press.

Daalder, Ivo, and James Goldgeier. 2006. 'Global NATO.' *Foreign Affairs* 85, no. 5: 105–13.

De Wijk, Rob. 1997. *NATO on the Brink of the New Millennium: The Battle for Consensus*. London: Brassey's.

Erlikh, Pavel. 1993. 'Eastern Europe Moves toward Cooperation with NATO.' *Sevodnya*, 26 October. Translated in *Current Digest of the Post-Soviet Press* (hereafter *CDPSP*) 45, no. 43.

Goldgeier, James M., and Michael McFaul. 2003. *Power and Purpose: U.S. Policy toward Russia after the Cold War*. Washington: Brookings Institution Press.

Gorbachev, Mikhail. 1994. 'The NATO Ultimatum Was the Worst Possible Way of Handling the Bosnian Crisis.' *Nezavisimaya Gazeta*, 22 February. Translated in *CDPSP* 46, no. 7.

Gordon, Michael R. 2006. 'U.S. Is Proposing European Shield for Iran Missiles.' *New York Times*, 22 May.

Headley, Jim. 2003. 'Sarajevo, February 1994: The First Russia-NATO Crisis of the Post-Cold War Era.' *Review of International Studies* 29, no. 2: 209–27.

Izvestia. 2004. 'Yury Baluyevsky, First Deputy Chief of the Russian General Staff: "NATO Expansion Will Strike a Fatal Blow to the Treaty on Conventional Armed Forces in Europe."' 3 March. Translated in *CDPSP* 56, no. 9.

Kovalenko, Yury. 1992. 'NATO and Former Warsaw Pact Countries under Blue Flag.' *Izvestia*, 21 December. Translated in *CDPSP* 44, no. 51.

Kozyrev, Andrei V. 1995. 'Partnership or Cold Peace?' *Foreign Policy* 99: 3–15.

Lavrov, Sergey. 2007. 'Beyond the Cold War: "Containing Russia: Back to the Future?"' *Global Research*, 20 July. http://www.globalresearch.ca/printarticle.php?articleid=6373 (accessed 20 July 2007).

Litovkin, Dmitri. 2006. 'Intercept at Any Costs.' *Izvestia*, 30 May. Translated in *CDPSP* 58, no. 22.

Lo, Bobo. 2002. *Russian Foreign Policy in the Post-Soviet Era*. New York: Palgrave Macmillan.

Ministry of Foreign Affairs of the Russian Federation. 2007. 'Transcript of Remarks and Replies to Media Questions by Russian Minister of Foreign Affairs, Sergey Lavrov Following Ministerial Meeting of Russia-NATO Council.' Oslo, 26 April. http://www.ln.mid.ru/brp_4.nsf/e78a48070f128a7b43256999005bcbb3/a0e7d8a140e816c (accessed 3 June 2007).

Moskovskiye Novosti. 1996. 'Primakov Starts with the CIS.' 14 January. Translated in *CDPSP* 48, no. 2.

NATO. 1994. 'Final Communiqué.' Communiqué NATO M-NAC-2(94)116, Brussels, 1 December. http://www.nato.int/docu/comm/49-95/c941201a.htm (accessed 11 October 2007).

– 1996. 'Final Communiqué.' Press communiqué M-NAC-2 (96)165, Brussels, 10 December. http://www.nato.int/docu/pr/1996/p96-165e.htm (accessed 26 September 2007).

– 1999. 'Final Communiqué.' Press release M(NAC) (99)166, Brussels, 15 December. http://www.nato.int/docu/pr/1999/p99-166e.htm (accessed 14 December 2007).

– 2002. 'Prague Summit Declaration.' Press release (2002)127, 21 November. http://www.nato.int/docu/pr/2002/p02-127e.htm (accessed 24 January 2005).

– 2004a. 'Chairman's Statement, Informal Meeting of the NATO-Russia Council at the Level of Foreign Ministers.' Brussels, 2 April. http://www.nato.int/docu/pr/2004/p040402-nrc-e.htm (accessed 14 December 2007).

– 2004b. 'Istanbul Summit Communiqué.' Press release 2004(096), 28 June. http://www.nato.int/docu/pr/2004/p04-096e.htm (accessed 4 July 2005).

– 2004c. 'The Istanbul Declaration: Our Security in a New Era.' Press release 2004(097). 28 June. http://www.nato.int/docu/pr/2004/p04-097e.htm (accessed 24 January 2005).

– 2006. 'Comprehensive Political Guidance Endorsed by NATO Heads of State and Government.' Riga, 29 November. http://www.nato.int/docu/basictxt/b061129e.htm (accessed 5 December 2007).

– 2007a. 'Alliance's Statement on the Russian Federation's "Suspension" of Its CFE Obligations.' Press release (2007) 139, 12 December. http://www.nato .int/docu/pr/2007/p07-139e.html (accessed 14 December 2007).

– 2007b. 'Speech by NATO Secretary General, Jaap de Hoop Scheffer, at the Munich Conference of Security Policy.' Munich, 9 February. http://www .nato.int/docu/speech/2007/s070209d.html (accessed 14 February 2007).

– 2008. 'Bucharest Summit Declaration.' Bucharest, 3 April. http://www .nato.int/docu/pr/2008/p08-049e.html (accessed 3 June 2008).

Nechayev, Gennady. 2004. 'Spies Fly to Russia's Borders.' *Noviye Izvestia*, 26 February. Translated in *CDPSP* 56, no. 8.

Pouliot, Vincent. 2007. 'Pacification without Collective Identification: Russia and the Transatlantic Security Community in the Post-Cold War Era.' *Journal of Peace Research* 44, no. 5: 603–20.

– 2008. 'The Logic of Practicality: A Theory of Practice of Security Communities.' *International Organization* 62, no. 2: 257–88.

– 2010. *International Security in Practice: The Politics of NATO-Russia Diplomacy*. New York: Cambridge University Press.

President of Russia. 2007. 'Speech and the Following Discussion at the Munich Conference on Security Policy.' Munich, 10 February. http://www.president .kremlin.ru/eng/text/speeches/2007/02/10/0138 (accessed 4 April 2007).

Pushkov, Alexey K. 1997. 'Don't Isolate Us: A Russian View of NATO Expansion.' *The National Interest*, 3 January. http://www.nationalinterest.org/ General.aspx?id=92&id2=11164 (accessed 4 October 2007).

Rossiskaya Gazeta. 1992. 'Charter of Russian-American Partnership and Friendship.' 19 June. Translated in *CDPSP* 44, no. 24.

Rossiskiye Vesti. 1995. 'Abandon Reflexive Resort to Force in Favor of Considered Approach.' 8 September. Translated in *CDPSP* 47, no. 36.

Safronov, Ivan. 2004. 'Russia Answers NATO with a "Flight of the Bumblebee."' *Kommersant*, 28 February. Translated in *CDPSP* 56, no. 8.

Sidorov, Sergei. 1994. 'Russia's Position Is Clear: No NATO Air Strikes against the Bosnian Serbs.' *Kraznaya Zvezda*, 19 February. Translated in *CDPSP* 46, no. 7.

Simonyan, Yury. 2006. 'US Promises to Smooth Tbilisi's Path to NATO.' *Nezavisimaya Gazeta*, 7 July. Translated in *CDPSP* 58, no. 27.

Solovyov, Vladimir, and Dmitry Sidorov. 2006. 'Sanction Master.' *Kommersant*, 4 October. Translated in *CDPSP* 58, no. 40.

Sychov, Aleksandr. 1992. 'NATO and Warsaw Pact Set Course for Closer Ties.' *Izvestia*, 2 April. Translated in *CDPSP* 44, no. 13.

Talbott, Strobe. 2002. *The Russia Hand: A Memoir of Presidential Diplomacy*. New York: Random House.

Tilly, Charles. 1985. 'War Making and State Making as Organized Crime.' In *Bringing the State Back In*, ed. Peter Evans, Dietrich Rueschemeyer, and Theda Skocpol, 169–91. New York: Cambridge University Press.

Trenin, Dmitri. 2000. 'Russia's Security Relations with the West after Kosovo and Chechnya.' *Notes de l'IFRI* 19, April.

Tsygankov, Andrei P. 2004. *Whose World Order? Russia's Perception of American Ideas after the Cold War*. Notre Dame, IN: University of Notre Dame Press.

von Twickel, Nikolaus. 2007. 'Putin Warns of Missiles Pointed at EU.' *Moscow Times*, 4 June.

Williams, Michael C. 2007. *Culture and Security: Symbolic Power and the Politics of International Security*. New York: Routledge.

Woerner, Manfred. 1991. 'The Atlantic Alliance in a New Era.' *NATO Review* 39, no. 1: 3–8.

Yusin, Maksim. 1992. 'Yeltsin and Bush Propose the Creation of International Armed Forces with Contingents from Russia and the U.S.' *Izvestia*, 19 June. Translated in *CDPSP* 44, no. 24.

Zimmerman, William. 2002. *The Russian People and Foreign Policy: Russian Elite and Mass Perspectives, 1993–2000*. Princeton, NJ: Princeton University Press.

12 Explaining EU Foreign Policy towards the Western Balkans

EVA GROSS

EU engagement in the Western Balkans since the end of the Cold War has been significant in military, political, and economic terms. While the 1990s were marked by foreign policy failures, the past decade has witnessed not only the growth of European security institutions but also the application of EU foreign and security policy instruments in the Western Balkans – including the perspective of EU membership. The security environment in the region has changed significantly over the past two decades, and renewed military conflict is no longer an urgent concern. In this more benign security environment the focus remains on political obstacles to the continued integration of the countries of the Western Balkans into the EU. While the process of integration has turned out to be longer and more complicated than had been initially assumed, the nature of the EU-Balkans relationship has been fundamentally transformed over the past two decades.

EU engagement in the Balkans illustrates the changing conceptualization of security from military security to political and societal security, with an underlying aim to embed the Balkans in the European security community. This chapter adopts a constructivist approach to analyse the transformation from military to societal security, the limits of enlargement as a foreign policy tool, and the continued securitization of aspects of EU policy towards the Balkans. The advantages of adopting such an approach is that it makes explicit assumptions of (in-)security that continue to inform policy towards the region. Such an approach also allows for a critical engagement with the continued blurring of internal and external security and the resulting practices of exclusion in a region that is to a large extent already firmly embedded in the Euro-Atlantic structures.

This chapter argues that notions of security in the Balkans have shifted significantly since the end of the Cold War and identifies four specific time periods in which these shifts have taken place. The period of the break-up of Yugoslavia, and in particular the violent conflict in Bosnia, saw a change in position among EU Member States that led in no small part to the creation of European security institutions able to act independently from NATO. Conflict in close proximity to the EU's borders also forced Member States to re-evaluate their views on the continued utility of military force in the post–Cold War era. The end of the conflicts in Bosnia and Kosovo, but also the successful EU intervention in the crisis in Macedonia in 2001, coincided with an evolving membership perspective for the region as a means to anchor the Western Balkans in the European security community. Much of the security discourse gave way to arguments in favour of 'membership-building' despite the fact that the EU simultaneously deployed a number of civilian and military crisis missions in Bosnia and Macedonia under the European Security and Defense Policy (ESDP).

Growing tensions between the integration and stabilization perspectives in the years that followed, as well as an increasing concern over organized crime, have shown that notions of security continue to be attached to the region. Contemporary security concerns no longer focus on 'high' military security but rather on 'low' political and societal security, particularly concerns over migration and organized crime. In conjunction with a restrictive visa regime for a number of countries in the Western Balkans, contemporary securitization practice points to the reproduction of the inside-outside divide, albeit to a lesser degree than was evident throughout the 1990s. Current challenges leave EU foreign policy towards the Balkans on a continued, if increasingly difficult, path towards integration and show divergence among EU Member States, particularly over the recognition of Kosovo. Despite the successful launch of EULEX, the EU rule-of-law mission in Kosovo, these divergences underline the fact that significant political challenges remain and that EU unity on these broader political questions is not a given.

The European Union Meets Theories of Securitization

The concept of security – how to define it, whom to apply it to, what policy instruments to employ in pursuit of it, and whether labelling something as 'security' is helpful in the first place – has preoccupied scholars of international relations for some time. The end of the Cold

War and the development of the EU foreign policy machinery have given rise to renewed debates on this subject. Perceptions of the EU's role and notions of security in the Balkans represent an illustrative case study of these conceptual concerns, which question notions of sovereignty and security traditionally understood as that of state security. The EU, clearly, is not a state even if it possesses state-like qualities;[1] and its foreign policy tools include enlargement and the inclusion of additional members. Indeed, the process of EU enlargement also constitutes a policy of conflict resolution by internalizing and over time resolving pre-existing conflicts or tensions (see Coppieters et al. 2004). Rather than merely expanding the European single market by widening Europe's borders, or reacting to the pressures of outsiders wanting to join the EU, enlargement as a foreign policy tool (see Sjursen and Smith 2004) has clear security implications by anchoring new and potential Member States in the European security community.

Buzan, Waever, and de Wilde (1998) have proposed the division of security into five sectors – military, environmental, economic, societal, and political – in order to account for the wider sense of security beyond traditional realist notions of the survival of the state. In addition to dividing security into sectors, work on securitization is also useful in highlighting the way in which an issue or problem reaches the level of security in policy discourse – how it is 'securitized.' This also has implications for how urgent a policy issue becomes and how it is then approached by policymakers. Buzan and Waever (2003: 491) accordingly conceptualize securitization as a speech act 'through which an inter-subjective understanding is constructed within a political community to treat something as an existential threat to a valued referent object, and to enable a call for urgent and exceptional measures to deal with the threat.' With respect to the Balkans, the emergence of border security and organized crime on the policy agenda shows that aspects of relations with the Balkans remain securitized. Through these contemporary securitization moves the Balkans remain 'outside' Europe, even if past military security challenges, such as the conflict in Bosnia or the crisis in Macedonia, have been resolved.

Applying a Security Framework: Analysing Two Decades of EU Engagement in the Balkans

EU political preoccupation with the Balkans has moved from military security concerns – traditionally focused on the defence of the nation-state, but in the case of the EU centred on maintaining European order, stability, and a negation of war – to concerns over political security. This largely concerns the preservation of the constituting principle of the state or, in the case of the EU, a supranational regime. A focus on political security includes sovereignty but also legitimacy – including circumstances that 'undermine the rules, norms, and institutions that constitute those regimes' (Buzan, Waever, and de Wilde 1998: 22). Military means may be used to preserve political security, as the ongoing military ESDP missions in Bosnia demonstrate, but concerns over physical security have largely disappeared from the security agenda. Current issues over border security exhibit concerns over both political and societal security – and threats posed by migration, ethnic politics, and secessionist movements – and have different consequences for the formulation of policy towards the region.

Two different contexts can be observed in the securitization of borders: one is the emergence of organized crime as a key threat to Europe, much of which enters the EU through the Balkans and thus represents a transnational security threat that emanates from more than one country in the region; the other is the practice of visa restrictions for citizens of individual Balkan countries. The inside-outside divide is thus reproduced at both the citizen level and the state level between the EU and countries outside its borders, including those with a EU membership perspective. Rather than a continued de-securitization following the end of military conflict in the Balkans since 1999, then, aspects of EU-Balkan relations have remained securitized. The continued reproduction of the inside-outside divide when it comes to the Balkans indicates that European self-identification has not fully embraced the Balkans as being inside Europe but retains a notion of a potential threat to the coherence (although certainly not the survival) of the European community.

The development of EU engagement in the Balkans since the end of the Cold War illustrates the evolving notions of security with respect to the Balkans. Four distinct time periods correspond to particular stages in the evolution of EU foreign policy instruments, the growth and the limitations of enlargement policy as a means to transform conflict in the region, and generally the EU's growing foreign policy ambitions and instruments.

1991–1999: Cracks in the European Peace Project

The end of the Cold War and the violent disintegration of Yugoslavia, followed by ethnic conflict in Bosnia and the war in Kosovo, caught

Europe unprepared as far as European security institutions, the EU foreign policy machinery, and European self-conceptualization were concerned. The violent conflicts that unfolded just outside Europe's border seemed to herald a return of Europe's past: a history of interstate war, which until this point had served as 'the other' to modern post–Second World War Europe (Waever 1996). As a result, Europe had to confront the limits of its own identity and its post–Second World War foreign policy posture: in short, its own securitizing moves by which a European identity as a peace project had been constructed. Not only had war become unthinkable, but the use of military force in one Member State – Germany –had become anathema to foreign policy. Having lived under the security umbrella of the United States and NATO for the duration of the Cold War, Europe was simply not prepared for the re-emergence of violent conflict, even if individual EU leaders were quick to call for a European lead in the management of the emerging conflicts. Partly as a result, European approaches to conflict resolution were out of step with respect to the use of military force required to end the conflict and the united political decision-making process and institutional development that would have been required for the EU to make a decisive impact on the conflict. A second significant factor in how Europe approached the conflicts in the Balkans in the first period was that the countries of the former Yugoslavia were regarded as essentially outside Europe rather than part of the European project.

The shock to long-held European perceptions of the nature of European identity and the role of the military (or absence thereof) in this identity gradually led to institutional adjustments that made future EU foreign policies towards the Balkans possible. First, it reinforced a change in previously held British attitudes with respect to the need for a European defence capability that made possible the creation of ESDP. Second, it induced a change in German attitudes towards the use of military force and pushed Berlin to take seriously its political and security role in the EU. Third, it made the EU more determined to show united leadership towards the Balkans rather than expose differences among the Member States,[2] and be seen as incapable of assuming responsibility for Europe's immediate neighbourhood. US military and political predominance in the resolution of the conflicts in Bosnia and Kosovo, as well as the primacy of NATO as the only security provider in Europe, slowly gave way to the realization that Europe needed its own foreign, security, and defence institutions and instruments, and that it needed to apply those instruments towards stabilizing its immediate neighbourhood (see Gross 2009). The conflict in the Balkans and the European response to it thus came to instil in the EU and its Member States an awareness that Europe bore responsibility for pacifying its backyard and that the Balkans were to be seen as part of Europe. The shift in the inside-outside divide – who was 'in' and who was 'out' – became evident in the emerging enlargement perspective as a way to bring the Western Balkans closer to Europe. 'Europeanizing' the Western Balkans thus became a foreign policy goal for the EU.

1999–2003: All's Well That Ends Well?

The second period of EU engagement in the Western Balkans shows the gradual disappearance of the inside-outside divide as the enlargement perspective came to be institutionalized in European foreign policy towards the region. At the same time, the growth of EU foreign and security instruments, including a military dimension, moved the EU closer to assuming military functions in the Balkans and beyond. The end of the war in Kosovo, coupled with the evolution of the emerging ESDP and improvement in the Common Foreign and Security Policy (CFSP), changed the potential long-term character of the EU's foreign policy institutions, as is evident in the debate over whether the acquisition of military instruments represented an end to Europe as a civilian power (see Smith 2000, Whitman 1998). With respect to the Balkans, however, emphasizing matters of military security was not a way of approaching the region in the aftermath of nearly a decade of conflict. Rather, the EU and the broader international community recognized the need for sustained political and economic engagement: after all, left to itself the Balkans might end up descending into conflict again. The EU membership perspective, which had been granted to the former countries of the Warsaw Pact, came to be seen as a solution for the Western Balkans as well, and by the time of the Thessaloniki summit in 2003 the EU confirmed for the countries of the Western Balkans the prospect of eventual EU membership as a way of integrating them into Europe and bringing about domestic change through the successive acceptance of and socialization into European norms and standards.

EU membership is linked to the implementation of a number of steps. The Stabilization and Association Process (SAP) was proposed to the five countries – Croatia, Macedonia, Albania, Bosnia and Herzegovina, and Serbia and Montenegro – in 1999. The SAP includes trade concessions, economic and financial assistance, and contractual relationships with the EU through the Stabilization and Association Agreement (SAA), which provides the framework for relations between the EU and countries of the Western Balkans; in return, the countries of the region have to meet a number of political and economic requirements. Progress by the individual countries has been uneven. At the time of writing, the six countries – following the secession of Montenegro from Serbia in 2006 – are at different stages on the way to membership: Croatia opened accession negotiations in 2005; Albania signed the SAA in 2006; Macedonia was given candidate status in 2005 without a date for the start of accession negotiations; Bosnia and Herzegovina as well as Serbia signed the SAA in 2008; and Montenegro signed in 2007.

Concurrent to the formulation of the policy goal of eventual EU accession, the same period also witnessed the successful launch of EU crisis management in Macedonia and the establishment of the EU as a crisis actor in its own right in the region (see Chivvis 2008; Piana 2002). The crisis had a strong symbolic character for EU crisis management. For the first time the EU made use of crisis management tools located in CFSP and later ESDP, including Secretary General/High Representative Javier Solana's role in the political resolution of the crisis. Furthermore, the EU and NATO worked together on a practical level, and an EU military crisis mission was eventually launched under the emerging ESDP. It was also the first time that the EU membership perspective was explicitly used as a conflict prevention tool: Macedonia signed the SAA in April 2001 during a lull in the fighting, before the signing of the Ohrid Peace Accord in August 2001.

In Bosnia, a dense network of EU instruments was put in place that included two ESDP missions, the European Commission Delegation, and the Office of High Representative, which came to be double-hatted with the office of the EU Special Representative. However, given the EU's past performance during the conflict in the 1990s as well as a more complex political landscape with high decentralization and ethnic politics, Bosnia represented a more difficult political environment than Macedonia.

Nevertheless, the path towards EU membership for the individual countries in the Balkans had come to be perceived as essentially unproblematic despite lingering security concerns – after all, economic assistance and association agreements with the EU were to pave the way to economic and political reform, which would make a European security presence unnecessary over time. The two potentially conflicting policy orientations – moving the Balkans from outside to inside while at the same time acquiring and deploying military and civilian crisis in-struments in the Balkans – were not regarded as mutually exclusive. Tensions between the two were to emerge only at the next stage, when the enlargement perspective alone was not seen as sufficient in effecting domestic change and resolving lingering ethnic conflicts and resent-ments. As a result, the two principles upon which EU policies towards the Balkans were formed – integration through EU membership and stabilization through ESDP missions coupled with political pressure exerted by the EU and its Member States – moved from being regarded as mutually reinforcing to being seen as increasingly at odds. This emerging tension was also worsened by internal political develop-ments inside the EU, notably the Dutch and French rejection of the EU Constitutional Treaty in 2005. 'Enlargement fatigue,' questions over the EU's capacity to integrate new Member States after the most recent round of enlargement of Bulgaria and Romania in 2007, and delays in the ratification of the Lisbon Treaty and concomitant institutional re-forms continue to present obstacles to future enlargements.

2003–2007: Facing the Stabilization-Integration Dilemma

With the launch of ESDP operations in Bosnia and Macedonia, the EU had achieved the reputation as a security actor in its own backyard, one of the goals that had originally been formulated with respect to the EU's policy towards the Balkans at the start of the 1990s. The EU there-fore signalled to its international partners that it was in fact taking re-sponsibility for its neighbourhood. Although the EU still faced a credibility problem in Bosnia – due to the fact that the EU had to rely on the US for an end to the fighting, coupled with the failure of individual EU Member States to prevent the massacre in Srebrenica or to consent to military strikes – 2003 nevertheless seemed to mark a turning point in EU-Balkan relations.

Emerging tensions between the stabilization and accession perspec-tive in Bosnia, coupled with enlargement fatigue in the EU Member States particularly in the aftermath of the failed constitutional referen-dum in 2005, show that the road to Brussels was not as simple and straight as had been assumed. This did not so much affect Croatia, which had obtained membership status and opened accession negotia-tions in 2005, or Macedonia, which was also seen as firmly on the way to Europe. By 2005, the two ESDP missions had given way to Commission-led projects to reform the police and the wider rule-of-law system.

Macedonia had also been granted candidate status, even if ongoing efforts to implement the Ohrid agreement and the long-standing name dispute with Greece prevented the start of accession negotiations. However, the cases of Bosnia and Kosovo suggested a more difficult path towards EU membership. As for Serbia, the prospect of the loss of Kosovo and a weak government that contained strong nationalist elements seemed to put into doubt the country's willingness to join the EU or to proceed with accession negotiations. Growing tensions over Kosovo's final status, and the determination by the EU to take over at least part of the security functions from the UN, reinforced the notion that, as in Bosnia, the political goals of integration and stabilization had come to be increasingly at odds. This also suggested to some that the balance between these two policy goals would have to be readjusted in favour of stabilization, in view of the threat of organized crime and the failure to adopt police reform in Bosnia (Batt 2007). The use of political conditionality on the part of the EU became increasingly accepted as a result, and the accession perspective was used as a means to effect domestic political change: only by April 2008, when Bosnia adopted two police reform laws, did the country resume the path towards signing the Stabilization and Association Agreement (SAA).

In general, then, compliance with EU norms and rules was found to be lacking, as the accession perspective induced less political transformation in Bosnia than it had in the countries of Central and Eastern Europe (Noutcheva 2007) – despite the fact that the institutional network of EU actors had become increasingly dense, with the post of the Office of the High Representative double-hatted with that of the EU Special Representative. Despite having been granted a clear membership perspective, then, Bosnia, rather than moving towards accession, seemed to remain in a protectorate stage, a notion that is reinforced by the political and security EU presence in domestic politics (see Merlingen and Ostrauskaite 2005). The challenge for the EU to succeed in the region and to 'build Member States' thus remains, as does the choice between soft foreign policy tools to effect a gradual adaptation towards European norms and practices and harder foreign policy instruments to impose stability. The logic underlying these two choices is starkly at odds and contain different conceptions of security and securitization practices.

For the EU, the threat of organized crime (see European Council 2000) necessitates increasing internal cooperation alongside a hardening of its external borders. Organized crime has come to be viewed as a foreign policy matter on account of its transnational nature. The 2000 UN Convention against Transnational Organized Crime defines crime as transnational if it is: committed in more than one state; committed in one but prepared/planned/directed/controlled in another state; committed in one state but involves an organized criminal group that engages in criminal activities in more than one state; committed in one state but has substantial effects in another state (United Nations 2000).

The emergence of organized crime – the trafficking of arms, narcotics, and human beings – as a security threat further shifted security concerns downward from military to political, societal, and economic: political, because organized crime structures, embedded in patterns of corruptions that permeate state security structures, challenge political order and legitimacy; economic, because profits from organized crime challenge economic policymaking and the established market; and societal due to the detrimental effects of trafficking on European societies. As a result, the focus on 'organized crime' can be interpreted as a securitizing device to label aspects of EU-Balkans relations that impact the way Europeans – citizens and policymakers alike – view their relationship to the countries in the region (see Berenskoetter 2006).

Focusing on organized crime in the Western Balkans has further increased the inside-outside divide and reinforced the stabilization-integration dilemma the EU has grappled with when it comes to the region. EU policies, but also individual domestic efforts to combat organized crime, have to date been less than effective in tackling this security threat: ESDP missions tasked with security sector reform face an uphill battle on account of limited jurisdiction coupled with local corruption, and individual countries themselves seem unable to rid their public administrations of corruption. The lack of economic development throughout the region – but particularly in Kosovo, Bosnia, and Macedonia, where unemployment rates are 41.3, 31.1, and 36 per cent, respectively (2006 figures cited in Balfour 2008) – further undercuts efforts and sets back political attempts to move these countries closer to the EU.

The practice of imposing visa restrictions, in the meantime, indicate that rather than moving towards inclusion, the inside-outside divide has been reproduced at the citizen level, with the EU applying specific conditions and timelines for removing visa requirements. Although visa regimes have been reassessed and visa-free travel has been granted to Macedonia, Montenegro, and Serbia (see European Commission 2009), visa-free travel for citizens of Albania and Bosnia at the time of writing continues to be contingent on the respective governments meeting criteria set by Brussels. This in turn reinforces the notion that, rather than being viewed as soon-to-be-members of the European club, parts of the Balkans remain excluded from certain aspects of EU practice, and that this extends to citizens and thus societal aspects of security.

2008: The Long and Winding Road … Back to the Future

The final period roughly started with Kosovo's declaration of independence and featured concerns over the EU's role in stabilizing Kosovo but also fears over Serbia turning away from Europe to a policy of isolation or closer cooperation with Russia. It was characterized by a continued rocky road towards EU membership but not a break with the enlargement perspective or a return to open conflict in the region. The EU remains the key actor in the Balkans, and stabilization and state-building rather than peacekeeping have taken over as security priorities. Importantly, Kosovo remains the one Balkan country where NATO continues to play a key military deterrent role: the EU, while having taken over the UNMIK mission from the United Nations, has no immediate plans for assuming the role of NATO. This indicates that, while in the long term the EU is certain to take over these functions from NATO, at present it is playing a stabilizing role that focuses on organized crime and military deterrence in Bosnia, a mission that has been reduced in size since the original takeover from NATO in 2004. Despite the securitization of 'organized crime' as a threat to European order that requires border controls and close supervision of Balkan compliance with European norms and standards, the EU so far has not seemed to be prepared to assume a security function in the Balkans that would suggest a return to a predominantly military conception of its role. When it comes to the diplomatic recognition of Kosovo there also has been a marked departure from the past: whereas the early 1990s featured acute EU disagreements over recognition of Croatia, 2008 saw agreement to disagree on the question of recognition but agreement that the EU would launch an EU crisis mission (see Emerson 2008). Bosnia and Serbia both seemed to have responded to EU conditionality, as witnessed by the arrest of Karadzic and Bosnia's signing of the police reform laws that same year.

While the path to accession continues, somewhat laboriously, in Bosnia as well as in Serbia, Kosovo's protectorate status means that the EU is engaged in outright state-building in a new country that is not quite independent. Through the EU Rule of Law Mission in Kosovo,

EULEX Kosovo, with its contingent of roughly 1,200 judges, administrators, customs and police officers to Kosovo territory, the EU retains executive powers over the management of borders, judicial competences, and the deployment of an international police force. The tension between holding executive powers over aspects of Kosovo sovereignty and Europeanizing the Western Balkans, including Kosovo, has thus become further apparent with the EU's latest state-building endeavour in the Western Balkans.

Conclusion: Shifting Notions (and Subjects) of Security?

By dividing the EU's engagement with or in the Western Balkans into four distinctive time periods, this chapter has traced a number of important shifts in European self-understanding in terms of both its borders and its role as a security provider. It has also traced shifting notions of security, from that of physical/military security in the 1990s to political and societal security since the turn of this century. Despite all the progress made in the region, fuzzy areas in the EU's conception of security and borders remain, and these, too, are visible in the EU's security discourse. Although the countries in the region are seen as potentially inside Europe, arguments informed by a security logic continue to be made that privilege stabilization. This indicates that the Western Balkans are not yet fully perceived as 'inside' by all Member States – at least not until a number of political conditions have been met. Rising concerns over 'border security' also suggest that security concerns have entered the policy discourse, creating implications for how the Western Balkans are viewed in relation to Europe and its citizens. Although aspects of relations with the Western Balkans continue to be securitized, however, they are no longer securitized to the point where politics in the Western Balkans are perceived as a threat to European order or self-understanding.

NOTES

1 For a discussion of the nature of the EU's presence, see Allen and Smith (1990).
2 As had been the case over the recognition of Slovenia and Croatia in 1991 (see Crawford 1996).

REFERENCES

Allen, David, and Michael Smith. 1990. 'Western Europe's Presence in the Contemporary Political Arena.' *Review of International Studies* 16, no. 1: 19–37.

Balfour, Rosa. 2008. *The Balkans in Europe: Containment or Transformation? Twelve Ideas for Action*. EPC Working Paper no. 31. Brussels: European Policy Centre.

Batt, Judy. 2007. *Politics of 'War by Other Means': Challenge to the EU's Strategy for the Western Balkans*. Institute Note IESUE/COPS/INF(07)-09. Paris: EU Institute for Security Studies, 19 November.

Berenskoetter, Felix. 2006. *Under Construction: ESDP and the Fight against Organized Crime*. CHALLENGE Working Paper.

Buzan, Barry, and Ole Waever. 2003. *Regions and Powers*. Cambridge: Cambridge University Press.

Buzan, Barry, Ole Waever, and Jaap de Wilde. 1998. *Security: A New Framework of Analysis*. London: Lynne Rienner.

Chivvis, Christopher. 2008. 'The Making of Macedonia.' *Survival* 50, no. 2: 141–62.

Coppieters, Bruno, et al., eds. 2004. *Europeanization and Conflict Resolution: Case Studies from the European Periphery*. Gent: Academia Press.

Crawford, Beverly. 1996. 'Explaining Defection from International Cooperation: Germany's Unilateral Recognition of Croatia.' *World Politics* 48, no. 4: 482–521.

Emerson, Michael. 2008. 'The Kosovo Decisions, Not So Bad after All.' Editorial. *CEPS European Neighbourhood Watch* Issue 35. Brussels: Center for European Policy Studies.

European Commission. 2009. *Commission Proposes Visa Free Travel for Citizens from the Western Balkans*. Brussels, 15 July.

European Council. 2000. *The Prevention and Control of Organized Crime: A European Union Strategy for the Beginning of the New Millennium*. Brussels, 3 May.

Gross, Eva. 2009. *The Europeanization of National Foreign Policy: Continuity and Change in European Crisis Management*. Basingstoke: Palgrave.

Merlingen, Michael, and Rasa Ostrauskaite. 2005. 'Power/Knowledge in International Peacebuilding: The Case of the EU Police Mission in Bosnia.' *Alternatives* 30, no. 3: 297–323.

Noutcheva, Gergana. 2007. *Fake, Partial and Imposed Compliance: The Limits of the EU's Normative Power in the Western Balkans*. CEPS Working Document. Brussels: Center for European Policy Studies.

Piana, Claire. 2002. 'The EU's Decision-Making Policy in the Common Foreign and Security Policy: The Case of the Former Yugoslav Republic of Macedonia.' *European Foreign Affairs* Review 7, no. 2: 209–26.

Sjursen, Helene, and Karen Smith. 2004. 'Justifying EU Foreign Policy: The Logics Underpinning EU Enlargement.' In *Rethinking European Union Foreign Policy*, ed. Ben Tonra and Thomas Christiansen, 126–41. Manchester: Manchester University Press.

Smith, Karen. 2000. 'The End of Civilian Power EU: A Welcome Demise or Cause for Concern?' *The International Spectator* 35, no. 2: 11–28.

United Nations. 2000. *The Convention against Transnational Organized Crime and Its Protocols (A/55/383)*. 2 November.

Waever, Ole. 1996. 'European Security Identities.' *Journal of Common Market Studies* 34, no. 1: 103–32.

Whitman, Richard. 1998. *From Civilian Power to Superpower? The International Identity of the European Union*. London: Macmillan.

13 European Security and the Middle East Peace Process

COSTANZA MUSU

Twenty years after the fall of the Berlin Wall, it is worth analysing the long history of Europe's involvement with the Middle East peace process (MEPP). The Arab-Israeli conflict in fact, and the subsequent peace process, have been among the most strongly debated issues by EU Member States, not only since the creation of the Common Foreign and Security Policy (CFSP) in 1991, but since the establishment of European Political Cooperation (EPC) in 1970, when bipolar rivalry still largely defined the conflict in the Middle East. The peace process has been the subject of innumerable joint declarations and joint actions on the part of the EU and has always remained a high-priority issue in the European foreign policy agenda (Musu 2010). Furthermore, it must be noted that the Middle East has often represented a problematic issue in EU-US relations, given on the one hand Europe's double dependence on the US as a security guarantor and on Middle East oil, and on the other the strategic American interests in the region and the United States' desire to maintain control over the development of the peace process, which has frequently clashed with Europe's attempts to cut a role for itself in the negotiations.

The events of the first years of the twenty-first century (such as the start of the Second Intifada, the election of Hamas, the Second Lebanon War, the take-over of power in the Gaza Strip by Hamas, the Gaza war) have once again underlined the importance of the issue for the European Union, while highlighting all the difficulties that the Member States face when attempting to elaborate a coherent – and effective – policy towards the peace process.

This chapter will evaluate to what extent the EU has been able to operate as an autonomous actor in the context of the Middle East conflict, and to what extent its action has been effective. A challenge to this analysis is posed by the fact that if on the one hand 'actorness' in the world is a quality the EU is often automatically assumed to possesses, on the other the intergovernmental nature of the CFSP suggests that European foreign policy might be viewed as no more then the sum of decisions taken by Member States. Two concepts are helpful to address this dilemma. The first is Sjostedt's (1977) notion of *actorness*, according to which an international actor might be defined as an entity delimited from others; with the autonomy to make its own law and decisions; and which possesses certain structural prerequisites for action on the international level (such as legal personality, a set of diplomatic agents, and the capability to conduct negotiations with third parties.)

A second concept, developed by Allen and Smith (1990), is that of *presence*. According to this notion, the EU has a variable and multidimensional presence in international affairs. A cohesive European impact on international relations must be accepted, despite the messy way in which it is produced. The EU's presence in the international arena can be characterized by two elements: first, the EU exhibits distinctive forms of external behaviour; and second, the EU is perceived to be important by other actors within the global system.

While the chapter will assume that the European Union is a genuine international actor in some respects (Hill 1993), it will however attempt to identify the limits to its 'actorness' and 'presence' in the Middle East. These limits, it will be argued, come both from within the European Union, namely from the inability of the Member States to go past the particularisms of national interests and elaborate a coherent foreign policy, and from without, mostly as a result of US interests in the region and its efforts to remain the main mediator between the conflicting parties.

The analysis spans a period of forty years in order to capture the trends of continuity and change in European policies towards the peace process. Particular attention is given to the shift that took place after the end of the Cold War, a shift that has affected not only the Arab-Israeli conflict, but also the formulation of European policy and the EU's perception of the threats emanating from the region.

If, in fact, the backbone of Europe's policy vis-à-vis the conflict took shape already in 1980 with the adoption of the principle of a two-states solution, important transformations took place with the end of the Cold War. As this chapter will argue, this phase saw an acceleration in the process of European political integration and in the transformation of the EU into a global actor, increasing its aspirations of playing a more relevant role in the Middle East. In this context the Middle East began to be viewed by the EU as a region of crucial importance in ways that go beyond the traditional concerns with regards to state security and integrity. Preoccupations with arms proliferation and the need to guarantee energy security were joined by concerns for the risk of uncontrolled migration flow and spill-over of political instability, in a blurring of the traditional distinction between 'external' and 'internal' security that has also been highlighted elsewhere in this volume.

While the Middle East and the Arab-Israeli conflict have ceased to be hostage to the dynamics of the Cold War and to superpower rivalry, the region has remained of crucial importance for the security of Europe. But the EU, it will be argued, has failed to cut for itself an independent role and to become a recognized, influential mediator in the peace process.

The Birth of a 'European' Policy towards the Middle East Conflict

Despite attempts such as the Fouchet plan (and before that the ill-fated European Defence Community), in the first years of its life the European Economic Community (EEC) made fairly small progress in the field of political integration. By 1967 economic integration was proceeding steadily, while a European common foreign policy remained little more than a project. In late May 1967, in the midst of an international crisis on the eve of the Six-Day War, an EEC Summit of the Six Heads of State or Government took place in Rome. The international situation called for a common Community declaration on the Middle East crisis, but positions were so irreconcilable that the Six went nowhere near such an achievement: 'I felt ashamed at the Rome summit. Just as the war was on the point of breaking out, we could not even agree to talk about it,' were German Chancellor Kiesinger's words following the summit (quoted in Greilsammer 1981: 64). But this failure to reach a common position was only a prelude to what would happen a few days later, when the war broke out. Indeed, the Six achieved the remarkable result of expressing each a different position, following their traditional national policy and privileging what was perceived to be the national interest. Attitudes ranged from France's strong condemnation of Israel and support for the Arabs, to Germany's support of Israel, disguised behind a formal neutrality. The Member States' different traditions and interests in the Middle East, the differing intensity of their ties with Israel and with the Arab world, and the inability to agree on a political role for Western Europe alongside the United States, all contributed to the failure to reach an agreement on that occasion.

The following two years saw hardly any attempt to harmonize the Member States' policies towards the Middle East conflict; however the inability of the EC to respond adequately and, if not unanimously, at least in harmonious coordination to major world crises, was becoming increasingly evident and was a striking contrast to the increasing economic weight of the Community. The Six increasingly felt the urgency to promote an enhanced political role for Europe in the world. Arguably their failure to adequately face the Middle East crisis in 1967 was one of the main triggers of the new developments that were to take place shortly thereafter in the process of European integration.

In December 1969 the foreign ministers of the six EEC members instructed the Belgian political director, Vicomte Davignon, to prepare a report which would serve as the basis for the future European foreign policy. The report, known as the Davignon Report, was finally presented and approved in October 1970. The Davignon Report sanctioned the official birth of European Political Cooperation (EPC) – the nucleus of what more than twenty years later would become the Common Foreign and Security Policy – and defined its initial structure. The rationale behind the creation of the EPC was 'to pave the way for a united Europe capable of assuming its responsibilities in the world of tomorrow and of making a contribution commensurate with its traditions and its mission' (European Community 1969: paragraph 3). The Member States, however, were torn between two different aspirations: on the one hand that of responding to international crises more adequately, trying to project in the international arena the combined political weight of all the Community members through foreign policy coordination; on the other hand, that of retaining national control over crucial foreign policy decisions that were perceived to be of a state's exclusive competence.

After 1969 EPC progressively developed and new instruments of political cooperation were slowly added, mainly in an informal and incremental fashion. In this framework the Middle East was very often used by the Member States as a testing ground for these instruments. The first EPC ministerial meeting took place in Munich in November 1970, and the Middle East conflict and the necessity to harmonize the Six's policy towards it was one of the topics chosen to be discussed. At the time of the meeting, though, the Member States' positions were still too divergent for an agreement over a common public document. What is of interest here, however, is the fact that since that first meeting in Munich, the Middle East conflict has been an almost permanent feature of EPC discussions, regardless of the very limited success obtained by the EC in dealing with the matter. It can be said that certain principles of today's European Union Middle East policy took shape as far back as in the years of EPC, and particularly between 1970 and 1980.

Since the Venice Declaration of 1980, in fact, the guidelines of Europe's policy have been constant: the centrality of the Palestinian question, the need to achieve a two-state solution, the importance attached to the UN's resolutions and to the principles of international law, and the insistence on the need for all the relevant issues to be taken on simultaneously through the convening of an international peace conference where regional actors could meet in a multilateral framework. These principles (particularly the centrality of the Palestinian question and the goal of achieving a two-state solution of the Israeli-Palestinian dispute) were embraced only years later by Israel and the United States, and it was only in 1991 that the first international conference on the Middle East peace process was convened in Madrid.

What became clear early on, however, were also the limits of European policy coherence, the contradictions of different Member States' positions, and the serious tensions that the development of an autonomous European stance in the Middle East created between Europe and the United States.

The Limits to Coherence

European countries are directly implicated in the Arab-Israeli conflict because of their geographic proximity, their dependence on oil and security needs, as well as the historical role played by several of them in the region. Harmonizing the EU's Member States' viewpoints on the Arab-Israeli conflict, however, is a task which has always proved difficult.

As a brief overview of some Member States' approach to the Middle East peace process demonstrates, the specific individual interests of the Member States are some considerable way apart despite the common interest and common efforts in finding a just and lasting solution to the conflict. It can be argued that very often policy coordination has been obtained not on the basis of policy convergence but rather on the basis of congruence – that is, of a sufficient compatibility of Member State preferences allowing the elaboration of a common policy.

French policy in the Middle East has privileged France's relations with the Arab world, even if it has tried at the same time to maintain good relations with Israel. Paris has often promoted an independent French policy in the area, and this independence has mainly implied conducting a policy that is different from that of the United States. At times, such a policy has gone so far as to cause tensions with other EU Member States, with autonomous French initiatives in the Middle East seemingly taken without any prior consultations with its European allies.[1]

For some European countries, such as Germany and the Netherlands, the sensitivities of relations with Israel are such that their governments have hesitated to criticize Israeli policy. For these countries the possibility of shifting national positions under the guise of a search for a common European position has proven attractive: it has allowed them to initiate a rapprochement with the Arab world while claiming this to be an 'unavoidable price' in striving for the superior objective of reaching a unified European position, and at the same time avoiding to upset their own internal public opinions.

Great Britain has tended to go along the lines of American Middle East policy: on the British foreign policy agenda, transatlantic relations are a much higher priority than Middle East policy, in spite of the long historical involvement of the United Kingdom in the area. London has been inclined to favour a policy that secures American approval and avoids direct confrontation with US policy in the name of Europe taking on an independent role in the peace process.

Italy's policy, on the one hand, has supported a European involvement in the peace process in the framework of a broader 'Mediterranean policy' which has to be, from the Italian point of view, one of the top European priorities and must not be neglected in favour of a policy more concentrated on enlargement problems and on the 'northern dimension'; on the other hand, Italy's internal political divisions tended to make its Middle East policy unsteady and unclear.

To summarize, it is fair to say that all EU Member States continue to have their own foreign policy agendas and to set their own priorities within these agendas with regard to their Middle East policy.

Transatlantic Relations and the End of the Cold War

In analysing EU policy towards the Arab-Israeli peace process, one cannot avoid the crucial problem: is EU Middle East policy *separable* at all from transatlantic relations?

The Middle East has indeed always been a highly controversial issue in transatlantic relations, sparking off some of the harshest instances of confrontation between the United States and Europe: this was the case during the oil crisis in 1973, when Europe's Arab policy in response to the oil boycott outraged the American administration, which considered it an interference both in its small-steps strategy towards the Arab-Israeli dispute and in its construction of an 'oil consumers front' by means of a new International Energy Agency. Contrasts arose again less than ten years later, in 1980, when the EC's Venice Declaration on the Arab-Israeli conflict caused discontent – to say the least – in Washington, where Europe's emphasis on the centrality of the Palestinian question and on the legitimacy of the PLO was seen as extremely untimely and potentially damaging to the peace process that had started in Camp David.

It may be argued that some of the patterns of US-European interaction in the Middle East began taking shape already at the time of the events mentioned above, with the United States progressively deepening its engagement in the region and becoming the main mediator in the Arab-Israeli conflict, and the EC confined to a subordinated role, constrained and conditioned in its action by internal divisions, institutional inadequacies, and a heavy dependence on Middle Eastern oil. Europe's role was also limited by American reluctance to share the 'driving seat' in the peace process and by the rigid dynamics of the Cold War – of which the Middle East was hostage – which allowed Europe very little leeway, caught as it was in the middle of a confrontation between superpowers.

The end of the Cold War changed the world's balance of power and security order: the United States emerged as the only surviving superpower, and the new Russia failed to fill the gap left by the Soviet Union (Gompert and Larrabee 1998, Gordon 1998). The Middle East was no longer viewed in the same perspective. Global intervention in the Middle East no longer projected bipolar superpower rivalry in the region, and the 1990–1 Gulf War transformed the dynamics of interregional relations, creating a window of opportunity for a resolution of the Arab-Israeli dispute and strengthening the role of the US as the only accepted mediator. Post–Cold War global intervention took on a unipolar form, with a dominant US using its influence in the region to protect its interests, which included: ensuring the free flow of oil at reasonable prices; achieving regional stability and prosperity, which would help protect oil supplies, create a market for American products, and reduce the demand for US military involvement in the area; guaranteeing the security of the state of Israel; and consolidating the Arab-Israeli peace process, which could guarantee Israel's security and at the same time contribute to the stability of the entire region.

EU interests and foreign policy priorities also underwent a deep change at this time: the fall of the Berlin Wall marked the dissolution of the political cement of the communist threat, and following the reunification of Germany integration became an even more important issue for European stability. With the Maastricht Treaty and the creation of CFSP, the European Union aimed to achieve a common foreign policy able to project onto the international arena the combined power of its Member States, whose weight and influence in international affairs was hoped to be stronger than that exercised by each state individually. The creation of the CFSP marked an acceleration in the process of European political integration and in the transformation of the EU into a global actor, increasing its aspirations – and also its chances – of playing a more relevant role in the Middle East.

Due to its geographical proximity and strong economic ties with the region in fact, the EU can be seriously affected by problems arising in the Middle East, such as an instability spill-over, uncontrolled migration flows, proliferation of weapons of mass destruction, and the spread of terrorism. The consolidation of the Arab-Israeli peace process is a crucial EU interest, as it aids stability and enhances the chances of resources and efforts being directed to the economic and political development of the region. On the other hand, Europe must balance its support for the search of a just and lasting solution to the conflict between the Arabs and Israel with its interests in the Arab world.

The changing dynamics in the Middle East created an opportunity for the EU to redefine EU-US interaction in the region and to promote its role as an important player in the conflict. The start of the peace process, however, saw the Unites States as the only accredited mediator (considering the inexorable decline of the Soviet Union) accepted by both the Arabs and the Israelis and able to exert a definite political influence, and Europe as a guest, invited as a normal participant to the peace conference and whose potential role as an additional mediator was refused by the main actors involved in the process.

Although initially excluded from the core negotiations and diplomatic efforts of the peace process initiated at Madrid,[2] the European Union nevertheless gradually expanded its role at least in its area of comparative advantage: the economic area. During the 1990s, the EU's economic role in the peace process increased progressively, to the point that the EU became the major single aid donor to the Palestinians. The logic of the peace process – in the EU's view – was that trade and cooperation were to underpin peace, Palestinian economic development being Israel's best long-term guarantee of security. This assumption was the justification behind the European Union's massive financial assistance to the consolidation of the peace process, the underlying logic being that this was a necessary precondition for keeping the peace process on track (House of Lords Report 2001). Together with direct aid to the Palestinians, the EU also promoted regional dialogue and cooperation through the so-called Barcelona Process – from which the United States were excluded – which saw the EU engaged in a political and economic relationship with twelve Mediterranean states (including Israel) in a context that, at least in the European intentions, was parallel and separated from the peace process itself.

On the other hand, Europe's enhanced economic role in the peace process for many years has not been matched by a similar increase of its political influence: the United States remained the only mediator between the parts and the EU played a diplomatically and politically complementary role to that of the US. In a way, it provided the basic economic foundation of the peace process, but for most of the 1990s it lacked the military instruments and security institutions to make a contribution on the front of security – which remained the domain of the United States – and also lacked that unitary dimension of action that in such negotiations necessarily qualifies an effective mediator.

The American position was ambivalent: on the one hand, the US wanted to keep its primary role in the peace process so as to protect its interests however it saw fit; on the other hand, it was happy to delegate a relevant part of the financial assistance to the Palestinians to the EU, as it was not willing to accept a free-riding European Union that exploits the security coverage offered by the US without offering at least the limited assistance it is able to provide (limited diplomatically speaking, but substantial in economic terms). The US was as well aware of the fact that an economic growth of the Palestinian Authority (PA) was a necessary precondition for the consolidation of the peace process and was willing to recognize a prominent role of the EU in this field, as long as it remained politically in line with US plans.

At a collective level, all EU Member States benefited from US presence in the region and the security guarantees that stemmed from that presence. The US keeps the Sixth Fleet stationed in the Mediterranean, has substantial military assets in the region, and provides enormous military assistance to friendly countries of the region (like Egypt and Israel); all this, while protecting US security interests, guaranteed a security coverage to Europe as well and at the same time contributed to deferring the problem of a European defence capacity. In other words, under the US security umbrella the EU was able to postpone tackling the potentially highly divisive issue of how Europe should protect itself from the dangers of an insecurity spill-over from the Middle East.[3]

Some Member States like Britain,[4] Germany, the Netherlands, and Italy remained highly aware of the risk that an EU move from a declaratory policy towards active diplomacy would risk a crisis in transatlantic relations: these countries were inclined to favour a low-profile EU policy, complementary to that of the United States and limited mainly to providing economic aid to the region, and particularly to the Palestinian Authority, a contribution that the US itself welcomes for its stabilizing effects. Some countries, however, particularly France, were not satisfied with a US-dominated peace process and continued to push for a more active EU policy.

From Camp David to the Creation of the Quartet: The Middle East in Flux

In July 2000 a summit took place in Camp David, involving Arafat, Barak, and US President Clinton. During the talks a number of crucial questions were discussed, including highly controversial issues such as the status of Jerusalem and the right of return of Palestinian refugees, but none of them were resolved.

The breaking down of the peace process also influenced the Barcelona Process negatively: Lebanon and Syria refused to attend the fourth Euro-Mediterranean conference of foreign ministers in Marseilles in September 2000, and the EU had to drop any attempt to sign a Charter of Peace and Stability for the Mediterranean as the Arab participants were not prepared to discuss the issue and no agreement was possible. Ultimately, economic cooperation could not prove conducive to a political settlement.

After the failure of the Camp David summit the situation between Israel and the Palestinians deteriorated rapidly. On September the Second Intifada – also called Al-Aqsa Intifada – started, and a vicious cycle of Palestinian violence and Israeli retaliation began. In October 2000 – in a last attempt to bring peace to the region before the end of his mandate – President Clinton convened a peace summit in Sharm-el-Sheikh, where he met with representatives of Israel, the Palestinian National Authority, Egypt, Jordan, the UN, and the EU. At the summit the decision was taken to appoint a fact-finding commission with the task of proposing recommendations to end the violence, rebuild confidence, and resume the negotiations. The commission was to be chaired by former US Senator George Mitchell and included EU CFSP High Representative Javier Solana.

The Sharm-el-Sheikh (or Mitchell) Committee presented its report in April 2001 to the new US president, George W. Bush, but the new administration (at least until 11 September) was showing relatively little interest in the Middle East and was deliberately disengaging from the previous administration's detailed involvement as main mediator between Arab states and Israel.

The Bush administration felt particularly strongly about differentiation on the Middle East, where – from their perspective – Clinton's overactive diplomacy had demeaned the presidency without achieving a settlement. They were committed to a much more 'selective engagement' in global diplomacy, to what Richard Haass, the new head of policy planning in the State Department, called in July 2001 'à la carte multilateralism.' The same month, after having vetoed a UN Security Council resolution to establish a UN observer mission, Bush dispatched CIA Director George Tenet to the Occupied Territories to negotiate a ceasefire plan. Hamas and the Islamic Jihad, however, rejected the plan, arguing that it failed to address the root of violence.

The terrorist attacks of 11 September 2001 forced a change in American policy. In order to secure the 'coalition against terrorism,' the US had once again to concentrate on the Arab-Israeli peace process: Bush declared his support for a Palestinian State, and in November 2001 retired Marine Corps General Anthony Zinni was appointed as senior adviser to work towards a ceasefire and to implement the Tenet plan and the Mitchell Committee Report. His mission, however, like the previous ones, failed, as violence continued to escalate.

The State Department decided to pursue a multilateral approach to the peace process, with cooperation with European governments as a key factor. On 10 April 2002, Colin Powell announced the formation of a Madrid 'Quartet,' reviving the agenda of the 1991 Madrid conference with the UN Secretary General, the EU High Representative for Common Foreign and Security Policy Javier Solana, and the Russian foreign minister. The cumbersome structures of EU diplomacy however also squeezed the Commissioner for External Relations and the foreign minister of the Member State holding the Council Presidency into the 'single' EU seat. The focus of this approach was on pursuing a two-state solution to the Israeli-Palestinian conflict, with the active engagement of outside actors (Musu and Wallace 2003). In a Communiqué issued in New York in September 2002, the Quartet announced that it was working with the parties and consulting key regional actors on a three-phase implementation 'roadmap' that could achieve a final settlement within three years (Quartet Communiqué 2002).

European Struggles in the Middle East

In 2001 tensions arose between the EU and Israel as the Israeli army, in retaliation for Palestinian terrorist attacks, proceeded to systematically destroy Palestinian infrastructures, most of which had been paid for by the EU, and as Israel continued to export to the EU goods manufactured in the Palestinian Territories (the so-called problem of the 'rules of origin'). When Israel halted the payments of tax revenues to the Palestinian Authority, the EU approved a series of replacement loans and, in response to the 'rules of origin' problem, threatened to withdraw the preferential tariffs that Israel enjoys. The threat, however, remained such,[5] and in general the EU's action did not show great incisiveness.

Arguably, the collapse of the peace process left the EU unable to react in a coordinated and effective fashion: notwithstanding High Representative Solana's participation in the October 2000 Sharm-el-Sheikh Peace Summit and in the Mitchell Committee, and the uninterrupted behind-the-scenes diplomatic activity of both the High Representative and the Special Envoy Moratinos, the EU's contribution to ending the violence in the area was not particularly effective. In 2002, after a number of clashes among Member States, who were unable to agree on a common strategy for the peace process, and after a failed diplomatic mission during which the CFSP High Representative and the Spanish presidency were not allowed by Israel to meet Arafat in Ramallah, the EU finally decided to renounce launching an independent peace plan and to back the US peace initiative that led to the creation of the Madrid Quartet. The EU hoped that participation in the Madrid Quartet would gain the EU more visibility and influence in the peace process and provide Europe with a tool for influencing American policies as they were formulated.

The Quartet has been praised for its 'multilateral' nature that officially brings other actors – particularly the European Union – into the peace process in addition to the 'old' ones (the Israelis, the Palestinians, and the US as mediators), but also despised for its inability to bring about a breakthrough in the negotiations. Surely the EU had played an increasingly important role in the peace process since the Madrid Conference, but participation in the Quartet arguably gave the European role a higher political relevance and resonance. The EU's presence was particularly welcomed by the Palestinians, who saw it as a potential counterbalance to an American position they perceived as permanently biased in favour of Israel. Conversely, the creation of the Quartet met with a less enthusiastic reception in Israel, where multilateralism is seen as a means to impose unwelcome decisions and the EU is perceived as a less-than-friendly actor.

In parallel with this multilateral approach the US administration elaborated new policy guidelines that favoured unilateralism in dealing with perceived threats from the region and from rogues states in light of the 9/11 attacks. The American approach to the region was set out by President Bush in his 'Axis of Evil' speech in January 2002, which linked the efforts of Iraq and Iran (and North Korea) to acquire weapons of mass destruction to their sponsorship of terrorism. Though there was no evidence linking any of these states directly to al Qaeda, this conceptual framework transmuted the war on terrorism into the pre-existing framework of rogue states and WMD, and thus into a potential war on Iraq. Iranian and Iraqi support for terrorist groups attacking Israel was an important part of their inclusion in this category, indicating how closely the Arab-Israeli conflict and the war on terrorism were linked in American minds. The priority for Western Middle East policy, in this formulation, was regime change in Iraq, combined with continued containment of Iran. The removal of a regime that encouraged Palestinian intransigence would in itself ease the Arab-Israeli conflict. The European allies would be invited to play supporting roles in the 'coalition of the willing' assembled to enforce disarmament – and/or regime change – on Iraq and to pay for subsequent social and economic reconstruction.

European governments, on their part, sympathized with the suffering and felt the outrage that the 9/11 attacks had generated in America. But they placed this new scale of transnational terrorism within the context of the lower level of transnational terrorism their countries had suffered in the past. As observers, too, of American strategy towards the region over previous years, largely without influence over that strategy and often critical of its sweep, there was an unavoidable undercurrent of differentiation: a feeling that the United States and the Muslim world were locked into a confrontation that both jeopardized European security and ignored European views.

In Europe's eyes, what was needed after 9/11 was a broad diplomatic approach to the region, including an active and concerted attempt to bring the Israel-Palestine conflict back to the negotiating table and a dialogue with 'friendly' Arab authoritarian regimes. In terms of power projection and political influence, however, European governments were acutely conscious of their limited capabilities in the face of American regional hegemony.

Competing Approaches to the Middle East's Crises

In 2002 the clash between the European approach to the Middle East, which traditionally favours multilateralism and negotiation, and the increasingly unilateral American approach, became more and more evident, bringing about a deterioration of transatlantic relations and generating mutual distrust.

The following passages, taken respectively from the 'National Security Strategy of the United States of America' adopted in September 2002, and from President Bush's 'Axis of Evil' speech of January 2002, while providing American political justification for the adoption of a pre-emptive approach to the war on terror, offer a measure of the United States' determination in pursuing their chosen strategy regardless of possible disagreements with their allies:

> For centuries, international law recognized that nations need not suffer an attack before they can lawfully take action to defend themselves against forces that present an imminent danger of attack … We must adapt the concept of imminent threat to the capabilities and objectives of today's adversaries. Rogue states and terrorists do not seek to attack us using conventional means … The United States has long maintained the option of pre-emptive actions to counter a sufficient threat to our national security.[6] To forestall or prevent such hostile acts by our adversaries, the United States will, if necessary, act pre-emptively.

> My hope is that all nations will heed our call, and eliminate the terrorist parasites who threaten their countries, and our own. Many nations are acting forcefully … but some governments will be timid in the face of terror. And make no mistake: If they do not act, America will.

These words indeed give a measure of the extent to which the United States had moved toward unilateralism and seem to confirm the view that Europe and America, while sharing the same value systems (i.e., humanitarian, liberal, capitalist systems), are different political cultures, and their preferences render it difficult for them to work together as they once did when it comes to instrumentalizing those values (Coker 2003: 50–1). America's decision to launch an attack against Iraq in 2003 (and the preceding diplomatic struggles at the UN) highlighted the rift between the transatlantic allies, while at the same time making painfully obvious Europe's own internal division and the persistence of national agendas that make the elaboration of a common foreign policy strenuous and at times impossible.

With the creation of the Quartet, however, EU and US approaches had formally converged, at least on the aspect of Middle East policy related to the peace process. It remained, however, unclear whether the US administration beyond the State Department was seriously committed to this exercise, or whether national governments within the EU were fully behind their collective representatives.

Since its creation the Quartet has been alternatively seen as protagonist of the peace process, mainly with the elaboration of the 'Roadmap to a Permanent Two-State Solution to the Israeli-Palestinian Conflict,' or given for dead, especially when the bilateral track of negotiations between Israel and the Palestinians – with the US as sole mediator or at least facilitator – seemed to be the only active track, or even more so in the numerous occasions in which violence escalated and the international community seemed unable, or unwilling, to play a constructive role in helping the parties to reach a settlement (Musu 2006).

In November 2005 the Quartet was instrumental in the conclusion of an 'Agreement on Movement and Access' between Israel and the Palestinian Authority, which included agreed principles for the Rafah crossing between Gaza and Egypt. On 21 November 2005, the Council of the EU welcomed the agreement and agreed that the EU should undertake the Third Party role proposed in the agreement. It therefore decided to launch the EU Border Assistance Mission at Rafah, named EU BAM Rafah, to monitor the operations of this border crossing point. The operational phase of the mission began on 30 November 2005 and was meant to have a duration of twelve months. It was then extended twice and was supposed to be operative until May 2008, but was instead suspended after the Hamas takeover of the Gaza Strip in June 2007.

This limited initiative was unprecedented in nature: for the first time EU military personnel, under the command of an Italian general, supervised an area of security concern for Israel. Only a few months before, such a proposal would have been unthinkable: the EU has long voiced its wish to be involved more directly in the security dimension of the peace process, but, as already underlined, both Israeli and American opposition had rendered this by and large unfeasible. In the particular circumstances created by Israel's withdrawal from Gaza, however, the EU was better suited to carry out the task of supervising the Rafah crossing, and American assurances contributed to convincing Israel to accept the EU's offer. Arguably, such a development was partly made possible by the EU's membership in the Quartet, which had created a formal framework for the EU's role tying it to the US one, thus easing Israel's deep-seated reservations with regards to the EU's involvement. It was also made possible by the significant changes that have taken place within the EU itself, with the creation of security and military institutions that contribute to reinforce Europe's credibility as a global actor. Both the EU's and the Member States' willingness to take part in military operations has undergone a notable transformation in the past few years, rendering the description of Europe as a solely 'civilian power' quite obsolete.

Whose European Policy in the Middle East?

If the creation of EUBAM can be seen as a – albeit limited – success in promoting the EU's role in the security dimension of the peace process, the difficulties that the EU faces remain enormous. The peace process and the Middle East as a whole pose challenges that the cumbersome structure of EU27 foreign policymaking has great difficulties in facing. Proof of this, arguably, is the tendency developed in the last few years by Member States of attempting to use a variable geometry of 'directoires' to address the problems arising from the region.

The EU3, for example, composed of the UK, France, and Germany, has been at the forefront of the diplomatic negotiations with Iran over its nuclear program (a window of opportunity opened partly by the absence of US-Iran diplomatic relations). In the summer of 2006, on the other hand, while the war between Israel and Hezbollah was raging in Lebanon, France and Italy took a leading role in attempting to resolve the crisis. In August, Israel accepted (and encouraged) the deployment of a large interposition force to reinforce the existing UN mission to Lebanon (UNIFIL) as a condition for a ceasefire. On 25 August 2006, EU foreign ministers met for a so-called troop-generating conference and agreed to deploy a total of almost 7,000 troops to Lebanon as a peacekeeping force.

The mission was to continue to be run under the aegis of the UN, but the most significant military presence was going to be European.

France had a central role in helping to negotiate the text of the UN Security Council resolution aimed at ending the conflict. Having initially committed to send up to 5,000 troops to Lebanon as a contribution to UNIFIL, France became very hesitant when the moment came to put 'boots on the ground.' Wariness of the unclear rules of engagement resulted in France changing its offer to only 200 troops. Only after several days, and lengthy diplomatic discussions with Italy, did France announce that it would send up to 3,000 troops. Italy also committed a large number of troops – between 2,000 and 3,000– and offered to take over from France the command of the operation in early 2007. This initiative was clearly in line with Italy's ambition to play an important role in the region with and efforts to ensure that the Mediterranean remains a high priority on the agenda of the EU's policymaking.[7]

Yet another example of the attempted use of alternative structures to the formal EU foreign policy mechanisms was the announcement by France, Italy, and Spain in November 2006 of a new Middle East peace plan. The proposal came after a major Israeli ground offensive in the Gaza Strip, which was aimed at ending militant rocket fire into Israel. In the words of Italy's President Prodi, 'Italy, France and Spain – taking their presence in Lebanon as a starting point – intend to develop the operational and concrete aspects of a wider initiative in the Middle East in order to give a real contribution to the pacification of the whole area.'[8] The initiative – which did not have the formal support of the Council – was short-lived and underlined once again the limits of EU's coordination.

Between a Rock and a Hard Place: The European Union and Hamas

In January 2006 the radical Islamist movement Hamas won the Palestinian elections by a large margin, creating for the international community a political dilemma very difficult to address: a by and large regular and democratic vote had brought to power a group that was included in the list of terrorist organizations of both the EU and the US and that rejected not only the principles of the Oslo Accords and of the Roadmap, but the notion in general of recognizing and making peace with Israel. The event heightened Israel's feeling of insecurity and its need to receive reassurances that the international community would not support the Palestinian Authority financially or diplomatically if this meant supporting an organization that organizes terrorist attacks on Israel's soil.

The victory of Hamas exposed the EU to a double set of pressures: on the one hand, the EU's policy has been long characterized by its preference for engagement rather than isolation of difficult interlocutors (as proved for example by EU's policy towards Iran); on the other, both the US and Israel insisted on the necessity to sabotage the government of an organization that had neither recognized Israel's right to exist nor renounced violence, and the EU was reluctant to create further occasions of friction with Washington after the difficult years in transatlantic relations following the rift over the war in Iraq.

The European Union decided to boycott politically the Hamas government, but at the same time it maintained – and even increased – its high level of economic support to the Palestinian Authority. What changed was that the money was given directly to the intended recipients through a Temporary International Mechanism[9] created ad hoc instead of being channelled through the Palestinian Authority. The mechanism was devised to prevent the flow of economic support from going through the hands of Hamas while at the same time avoiding a complete collapse of the Palestinian Authority.

The situation, however, worsened sensibly in the following months: Palestinian institutional reforms stalled, EU BAM became largely inoperable,[10] and the EU's other Civilian Crisis Management Mission, EUPOL COPPS,[11] met the same fate. Since Hamas's political victory, however, and even more since the organization violently seized control of the Gaza Strip in June 2007, numerous analysts, not only in Europe but also in the United States and in Israel, started suggesting that excluding Hamas from the peace talks meant attempting to achieve peace with only a part of the Palestinian Authority, a strategy that, according to many, would in no way bring the conflict to a resolution.[12]

By 2008, several European governments were making more openly the case for a policy change regarding Hamas, and France even admitted to informal contacts with the Islamist movement (*International Herald Tribune* 2008). In fact, the Quartet itself gradually moved away from its tough position. Its call for a 'new approach' for Gaza in May 2008 came close to admitting the failure of its strategy to weaken Hamas by boycotting it (Quartet Statement 2008; *The Independent* 2008).

At the time of writing the situation in Gaza appears on the verge of complete collapse: in December 2008 a six months' truce between Israel and Gaza came to an end, and, following the intensification of daily rocket launches from Gaza onto southern Israel, Jerusalem initiated a large attack, targeting the main centres of the Hamas government, the sites of the rocket launchers, and the tunnels between Egypt and Gaza used by Hamas to smuggle arms and explosives into the Gaza Strip. As the death toll rose and the unavoidable civilian deaths prompted calls for an immediate ceasefire, the reaction of the European Union has been less than coherent: if some countries (such as France and the UK) asked for an immediate cessation of Israel's incursions, others (Italy and the Czech Republic for example) underlined Israel's right to self-defence and have charged Hamas with the responsibility for the unfolding humanitarian disaster (*Haaretz* 2008). While the EU's foreign minister subsequently managed to issue a common joint statement, it is difficult not to notice how, once again, immediate Member States' responses have fallen short of a coherent 'European' response.

Conclusion

The objective of this chapter was to evaluate European policy towards the Arab-Israeli conflict in the period before and after the end of the Cold War. The starting point was the recognition that, while – as the editors to this volume have put it – 'the European security environment is … more benign than it was during the Cold War,' Europe's security is indeed closely linked to the stability and security of neighbouring regions. After the Cold War a transformation of the perception of what constitutes a security threat can be observed: beyond threats to the integrity of states' borders and institutions renewed attention is paid to the societal, economic, and political dimensions of security. In this respect the Middle East continues to be a region of crucial importance for Europe. The threats emanating from the region cover a vast spectrum, from more traditional ones such as arms proliferation to others that have only more recently been recognized as 'security threats,' such as uncontrolled migration flows and economic underdevelopment. The Arab-Israeli conflict contributes to the continued instability of the region and, by extension, affects negatively the security of Europe.

What has emerged from the analysis conducted is that some keys to understanding EC/European policy towards the conflict date back to the pre-1990 period, which saw the birth of an embryonic European foreign policy through EPC and Europe's first steps in the international arena as a new actor. In this period, despite several difficulties and false starts, members of the then EC managed to find an agreement on several basic points (e.g., the desire for a two-state solution, the deference to

UN resolution, and the wish for large international conferences to tackle all the contentious issues at the same time).

The early 1990s, however, brought increasing pressures on the EU to enhance its role as a relevant political actor on the international stage. In the Middle East, the end of the Cold War and the subsequent collapse of the Soviet Union created a political vacuum that could have become a political opportunity for the EU: theoretically there was a possibility to redefine EU-US interaction and the dynamics of burden-sharing in the region, and Europe had the possibility to increase its role and influence in the Middle East peace process, filling the gap left by the USSR. Yet, the EU did not manage to take full advantage of this opportunity, for a number of reasons that range from American reluctance to concede political space to other actors, to Israeli hostility towards the EU's involvement, to the EU Member States' inability and unwillingness to make full use of the mechanisms provided by the creation of the CFSP and to formulate a coherent common policy that could be taken seriously by all the other players.

Furthermore, a reluctance on the part of several Member States to endanger their relations with the United States by decisively promoting an independent European stance in the region has emerged clearly. Over the years it has become evident that effective and autonomous policy towards the Middle East unavoidably carries with it disagreement with the US – quite possibly involving active disapproval from Washington. This has proved to be a strong disincentive against attempting to develop a policy that is more than declaratory: in most Member States' foreign policy agendas transatlantic relations are indeed a much higher priority than the formulation of a distinct EU policy towards the Middle East.

Overall what has ultimately proven to be the driving force behind the formulation of a distinct EU policy towards the peace process is more congruence – defined as the compatibility of the policy actors' preferences as a basis for establishing a shared policy regime – rather than a real convergence capable of producing a truly collective policy, an expression of a unitary European political strategy.

EU Member States increasingly find that some of their national interests can be better protected through a common European action that is able to project into the international arena the combined weight of the twenty-seven members of the Union. As a consequence, more and more national governments, often prompted by totally different reasons and agendas, turn to the EU and encourage the formulation of common European policies. However the undiminished strength of specific national preferences and priorities continues to pose a challenge to the consolidation of political convergence among the Member States, and the intricacies of the Arab-Israeli conflict, with its local, regional, and global ramifications, have proved repeatedly to be one of the hardest tests for European harmony.

NOTES

1 See, for example, Mr Chirac's 1996 trip to the Occupied Territories.
2 While excluded from the bilateral negotiations, which were based on direct talks between the parties, the EU played a more relevant role in the multilateral negotiations, as gavel-holder of the Regional Economic Development Working Group (REDWG).
3 Author's interview with Sir Brian Crowe, Former Director-General for External and Politico-Military Affairs, General Secretariat of the Council of the European Union.
4 Author's interview with Sir Malcolm Rifkind, former British Minister of Defence and Secretary of State for Foreign and Commonwealth Affairs.
5 Until 2008 the official commission website offered an explanation of EU policy in the section 'The EU and the Middle East: Position and Background': 'The EU's policy is based on partnership and cooperation, and not exclusion. It is the EU's view that maintaining relations with Israel is an important contribution to the Middle East peace process and that suspending the Association Agreement, which is the basis for EU-Israeli trade relations but also the basis for the EU-Israel political dialogue, would not make the Israeli authorities more responsive to EU concerns at this time. It is also a well-known fact that economic sanctions achieve rather little in this respect. Keeping the lines of communication open and trying to convince our interlocutors is hopefully the better way forward.' http://ec.europa.eu/external_relations/mepp/faq/index.htm (last accessed in September 2008).
6 See, for example, Bill Clinton's 1999 National Security Strategy: 'America must be willing to act alone when our interests demand it' (iv); 'We will do what we must to defend these interests, including when necessary and appropriate, using our military might unilaterally and decisively' (1). http://www.globalsecurity.org/military/library/policy/national/nss-1299.pdf (last accessed in June 2010).

7 At the time of writing, France has 2,000 ground troops, including thirteen French Leclerc tanks. In addition, French Navy ships with 1,700 men are deployed off Lebanon in Opération Baliste, assisting UNIFIL operations. Italy has 2,500 ground troops and assumed charge of UNIFIL ground forces in February 2007.

8 See http://www.repubblica.it/2006/11/sezioni/esteri/medio-oriente-25/iniziativa-italia/iniziativa-italia.html (my translation) (last accessed in June 2010).

9 Known as PEGASE, Mécanisme Palestino-Européen de Gestion de l'Aide Socio-Économique.

10 See Youngs (2007). The Rafah crossing point was last opened with the presence of EUBAM Rafah on 9 June 2007. Since then, the mission has remained on standby, ready to re-engage but awaiting a political solution.

11 Coordination Office for Palestinian Police Support, a mission meant to provide enhanced support to the Palestinian Authority in establishing sustainable and effective policing arrangements.

12 In February 2008 a poll conducted by the Israeli newspaper *Haaretz* indicated that 64 per cent of Israelis favoured their government holding direct talks with Hamas in Gaza about a ceasefire and the release of captives. See http://www.haaretz.com/hasen/spages/958473.html (last accessed in June 2010). On the American side, see 'Failure Risks Devastating Consequences,' a letter to President Bush by Zbigniew Brzezinski, Lee H. Hamilton, Brent Scowcroft, Paul Volcker, and other former Washington officials from both parties published by *The New York Review* on 8 November 2007, just before the Annapolis conference.

REFERENCES

Allen, D., and M. Smith. 1990. 'Western Europe's Presence in the Contemporary International Arena.' *Review of International Studies* 16, no. 1 (January): 19–39.

Coker, C. 2003. *Empires in Conflict. The Growing Rift between Europe and the United States*. Whitehall Paper Series, no. 58. London: Royal United Services Institute.

European Community. 1969. *Communiqué of the Conference of the Heads of State and Government of the Member States of the European Community* (The Hague Summit Declaration), The Hague, 2 December.

Gompert, D., and S. Larrabee, eds. 1998. *America and Europe. A Partnership for a New Era*. RAND Studies in Policy Analysis. Cambridge: Cambridge University Press.

Gordon, P.H. 1998. *The Transatlantic Allies and the Changing Middle East*. Adelphi Paper 322. International Institute for Strategic Studies. Oxford University Press.

Greilsammer, I. 1981. *Israël et l'Europe*. Lausanne: Fondation Jean Monnet pour l'Europe, Centre des Recherches Européennes.

Haaretz. 2008. 'France, UK Aim to Impose Cease-fire to Halt Gaza Fighting.' 30 December. http://www.haaretz.com/hasen/spages/1051267.html.

Hill, C. 1993. 'The Capability-Expectations Gap, or Conceptualising Europe's Foreign Policy.' *Journal of Common Market Studies* 31, no. 3: 305–28.

Hill, C., and K.E. Smith. 2000. *European Foreign Policy: Key Documents*. London: Routledge.

House of Lords Report. 2001. Select Committee on European Union (Sub-Committee C), Ninth Report: *The Common Strategy of the European Union in the Mediterranean Region*. London.

International Herald Tribune. 2008. 'France Acknowledges Contacts with Hamas.' 19 May.

Musu, C. 2006. 'The Madrid Quartet: An Effective Instrument of Multilateralism?' In *The Monitor of the EU-Israel Action Plan*, ed. R. Nathanson and S. Stetter, n.p. Berlin/Tel Aviv: Israeli European Policy Network and Friedrich-Ebert-Stiftung.

– 2010. *European Union Policy towards the Arab-Israeli Process. The Quicksands of Politics*. Palgrave Studies in European Union Politics. Houndmills, Basingstoke: Palgrave Macmillan.

Musu, C., and W. Wallace. 2003. 'The Focus of Discord? The Middle East in US Strategy and European Aspirations.' In *Europe, America, Bush: Transatlantic Relations after 2000*, ed. J. Peterson and M.A. Pollack, 99–114. London: Routledge.

Quartet Communiqué. 2002. New York, 17 September. http://www.un.org/news/dh/mideast/quartet_communique.htm.

Quartet Statement. 2 May 2008. http://www.state.gov/r/pa/prs/ps/2008/may/104319.htm.

Sjostedt, G. 1977. *The External Role of the European Community*. Farnborough: Saxon House.

The Independent. 2008. 'Quartet Opens Door to Ending Hamas Isolation.' 3 May.

Youngs, R. 2007. *The EU and the Middle East Peace Process: Re-engagement?* FRIDE Comment, March. www.fride.org/download/COM_UEpazOr_ENG_mar07.pdf.

14 The Dynamics of European Security: A Research Agenda

MARTIAL FOUCAULT, BASTIEN IRONDELLE, AND FRÉDÉRIC MÉRAND

The preceding chapters have analysed a variety of European security issues, focusing on how they have evolved since the fall of the Berlin Wall. These issues range from classical ones in security studies (defence policy, armed forces, nuclear weapons) to emerging challenges such as energy security, transnational terrorism, and organized crime. Building on the notion that security is a shifting concept, our objective was to understand how the evolution of the European security environment since 1989 has been linked to changing social representations of security among people, practitioners, and theorists. In this concluding chapter, we try to gather the book's findings and propose an original research agenda that will help us begin to conceptualize the dynamics of European security.

The intensity of threats to the European continent has declined since 1989. This, we argued, suggests that Europeans live in a relatively more benign environment. Does this mean that Europe has become a completely pacified, stable security community? As Giegerich and Pantucci document in their contribution, terrorist acts in Madrid in 2004 and London in 2005 are good examples of the continuing existence of lethal risks. It is also striking that both the origin and the target of these threats have changed in a fundamental way. As Kirchner and Sperling (2007: 13) argue, security threats are no longer limited to the existential question of national survival or territorial integrity. To get a better sense of threat perceptions, we must consider two dimensions: the *origin* of the threat (producer) and the *target* of the threat (state and/or society). The combination of these two dimensions leads to a new architecture of security within Europe and in the European neighbourhood, one in which the visibility of threats is less clear and security risks are more diffuse because more threat producers target society as a whole. In this sense (in) security has become a transnational public good (bad), which, as Gheciu's chapter shows, enables actors to engage in a significant redrawing of the security field's boundaries. Among the main issues emphasized in this book, some relate to standard theories like realism while others lead us to look for new theories, for example securitization (energy, crime). As we argued at the outset, different theories may well be adapted to different security issues. But how do security issues become salient? Why did new ones appear after 1989 while others were marginalized?

These two questions point to the importance of analysing the (current and future) dynamics of European security. By dynamics, we mean the set of issues emerging both inside and outside the political scene that shape European decisions in the security domain. As Frank Baumgartner and Bryan Jones (2005) argue, a policy process is characterized by the 'dual and contrasting characteristics of stability and dramatic change.' Although the agenda-setting perspective developed by these two authors has never been applied to security studies, we believe it can generate insights into why security issues (in the form of policy agendas and scientific paradigms) are usually stable but sometimes undergo swift changes, what Baumgartner and Jones call 'punctuated equilibria.' We should try to understand why and to what extent political actors seek actively to bring issues onto the agenda if they are looking for a change of policy, or to keep them off the agenda if they want to defend the status quo. This could mean, for instance, studying the attention paid by parliamentarians to security issues through committees, question periods, special reports, and so forth, to improve our knowledge of security policymaking. By looking at security policy from a macro perspective, a research program based on the agenda-setting perspective may thus combine what security scholars observe in specific circumstances (peace, war, transition, etc.) with what scholars in comparative politics analyse at the sectoral level (law and order, health, environment, etc.). The basic idea, then, is to enlarge the analytical perspective and identify the dynamics of security agenda-setting in the past two decades. Did priorities vis-à-vis European security shift dramatically or not? How and under what conditions have such changes been put forward? What is the role of public opinion, media, policy actors, and academics in this process?

Although this task is too daunting to be taken up here, this chapter puts forward the first conceptual elements to account for paradigmatic changes in the European security agenda environment by looking more specifically at the security policy agenda of the European Union. The idea here is that agenda-setting dynamics will have a profound impact on theoretical developments in security studies. Gathering the main findings of the book, we would like to show how a policy agenda perspective may fit in European security studies and capture the dynamics of change in European security.

Five Trends in the European Security Environment

In this section we briefly summarize the book's main empirical findings. The various contributions to this book suggest that since 1989, five trends in European security dynamics have been taken into account and reflected in theoretical debates.

A defining feature of the post-1989 European security landscape is the *development of institutionalized security cooperation*. The continued existence of NATO following the demise of the Soviet threat and the development of ESDP have reinvigorated institutionalist approaches, which tend to show the self-reinforcing dynamics of European security cooperation (Wallander 2000; Mérand 2008; Howorth 2007). A parallel strand of research pays particular attention to the socialization effects of international security institutions given NATO enlargement, OSCE-based dissemination of human rights' norms, NATO-sourced military concepts and doctrines, or Europeanization (Schimmelfennig 2003; Gheciu 2005). To this we should add Moscow's standing offer for the creation of a pan-European security organization. We thus observe a proliferation of institutional arrangements, which results in fragmented but overlapping networks of actors, both public and private, managing European security issues (Krahmann 2008; Hofmann 2009).

The second trend is the *consolidation of Europe as a security community* dominated by a Kantian culture of anarchy (Adler and Barnett 1998, Cottey 2007). Europe and European states no longer face enemies in the international system, even though, as Pouliot's chapter shows, the opportunity to anchor Russia in this community was missed in 1994 and Islamist terrorism may be on the rise (see Gheciu's and Giegerich and Pantucci's chapters). Thus Europeans tend to privilege soft power and a comprehensive approach to international security rather than hard power and military force; they also support a judiciary and police approach to fighting terrorism rather than a military one. The transformation of Europe into a post-Westphalian security system, or a security community, was a challenge for European security studies (Kirchner and Sperling

2007). The normative and cultural transformation is twofold: on the one hand, as Biscop and Ojanen argue in this book, the emergence of a European strategic culture and the Europeanization of military policy; on the other hand, the study of the identity of Europe on the international scene and the debate over Europe's civil and normative powers (see Gross's chapter). This is the privileged domain of 'soft constructivism,' which preserves a positivist epistemology and attempts to foster dialogue with mainstream security studies approaches, namely realist ones.

The third trend we observe in the contributions is the *strategic marginalization of Europe* since 1989. Rynning illustrates this phenomenon through the geopolitics of NATO in Eurasia. Von Hlatky and Fortmann show that European security studies have seen the decline of the nuclear issue. Europe is no longer a key object of scholarship regarding nuclear deterrence, proliferation, or arms control and it rarely features as a future major player in realist analyses of the balance of power (for an exception, see Paul 2005). Much academic attention in recent years, evidenced in Forster's and Vennesson's chapters, has been paid to military transformation and military reforms involving the move from the large-formation force structures of the Cold War to joint modular expeditionary forces for crisis management (Dyson 2008). This research makes use of a cross-fertilization approach borrowed from sociology, military sociology, strategic studies, and political science. It suggests that, in the absence of major threats or external pressures, Europe is only slowly adapting its security institutions.

In parallel, European security studies are coming to terms with the gradual blurring of internal and external security, and the broadening of the notion of security to incorporate non-military issues such as organized crime, human migration, natural and technological disasters, health, or the environment. *Securitization* is the fourth trend of European security affecting, for instance, energy supplies (Jegen's chapter) or the EU's neighbourhood in the Balkans (Gross's chapter). Scholars are increasingly attentive to the logic of securitization pertaining to these social issues, often using a critical approach to address both securitization and its consequences for affected individuals (e.g., migrants) and civil liberties. This questions the classic boundaries between police forces and armed forces in a unitary state. A number of scholars are involved in mapping the field of (in)security professionals, analysing the emergence of the field of European police cooperation, anti-terrorism collaboration, and so on. This is the preferred field of critical constructivism (CASE Collective 2006).

Interestingly, the evolution of the European security environment has also generated a return to classical IR approaches. The latter, exemplified in Rynning's chapter, can be characterized by their positivist epistemology and a particular attention to material factors, notably unequal power relationships. This literature underpins public discourses on *Europe puissance* and multipolarity. The fifth trend is an *ongoing debate about Europe's role in the international system*, which goes some way towards explaining the prominence of institutional projects like the CFSP and ESDP. Realists emphasize the role of polarity in the international system to explain alliance formation, security cooperation, and foreign policy adaptation. The main issue for structural realists is evaluating the consequences of unipolarity within the European security architecture. From the unipolar structure of the international system, some realists infer that European security cooperation (i.e., ESDP) can be associated to hard balancing (Posen 2006) or soft balancing (Jones 2007, Paul 2005) by the Europeans vis-à-vis the US. A more convincing version of this argument asserts that European security cooperation patterns in NATO or ESDP represent a 'reformed bandwagoning for profit' or a 'leash-slipping' strategy. To wit: states form an alliance not to balance or constrain the unipole, but to reduce their dependence and increase their reputation as a credible partner for the unipole by pooling their capabilities (Press-Barnathan 2006; Walt 2009). More recently neoclassical realism, combining the causal primacy of international systemic variables and internal dynamics of states and domestics politics, has also scrutinized states' grand strategies to explain European security dynamics (Lobell, Ripsman, and Taliaferro 2009). The key, as Musu writes in her chapter, may be to distinguish the EU's actorness (or autonomy from member states) from its presence (or influence). In any event, this scholarship suggests that Europe's role in the international system remains a symbolically and politically powerful issue.

In sum, in spite of the erosion of the paradigmatic core of European security studies, it is possible to identify concrete developments in the European security environment since 1989. With the proliferation of overlapping security organizations, the blurring of the internal and external dimension of state security, and the ongoing debate about Europe's objective position in world affairs, we get the impression that the European security architecture lacks a clear structure of political authority. This lack of structure has been captured by the metaphor of 'security governance,' an approach that enjoys considerable currency even though it has failed so far to make very specific predictions about

the direction of European security. For reasons that we will expose below, we believe that an agenda-setting perspective would dovetail nice-
ly with security governance.

Security Governance and Dynamics

A growing number of scholars use the notion of governance, which em-
braces the multiplication of institutions and actors in an ever more unwieldy decision-making process, to analyse transformations in the
production of European security and to understand the specificities of
the EU as a security provider (Keohane 2001; Webber 2000; Webber et
al. 2004). In a context where risks are evolving, threat producers are no
longer only states, and the target of these threats become both state and
society, the emergence of EU as a security actor is not surprising.
Kirchner and Sperling (2007: 18) argue that 'the obsolescence of alliance
theory, with the possible exception of buck-passing and chain gangs
(which are in any case independent of the theory of alliances), calls for
an alternative method for understanding why the EU has become a security actor and, as such, how it goes about identifying and meeting
threats.' To some extent, the notion of security governance seems to fit
with the current panorama of European security. Webber and his colleagues (2004: 4) define security governance in a European context as
follows: 'Governance involves the coordinated management and regulation of issues by multiple and separate authorities, the interventions
of both public and private actors (depending upon the issue), formal and
informal arrangements, in turn structured by discourse and norms, and
purposefully directed toward particular policy outcomes.' This means
that there are more actors, more decision makers, more constraints, but
also a greater selection of options. How are we to make sense of this?
How or what influences security governance?

   Although the concept of security governance strikes us as a sensible
and accurate description of the challenges faced by European leaders, it
suffers from a lack of determinacy. While the traditional state-based, hier-
archical decision-making model clearly looks insufficient, the governance
image does not tell us which issues will come to the fore and wane, who
is more likely to influence security policy, or what institutions or solutions
will be used to tackle perceived security challenges. As such governance
analyses remain fairly static. Many trends we have identified in the book
– such as securitization – fit in with a dynamic perspective that the concept of governance does not capture comprehensively. The next section

proposes the main contours of a new research agenda that uses an agenda-setting perspective to analyse dynamic elements in European governance. Without showcasing this perspective as the holy grail that will reconcile all IR theories, we believe that it could prove a useful instrument for answering the questions left unanswered in the governance approach with a view to better understanding the present and future of European security.

Who Is the Agenda-Setter?

As briefly referred to at the beginning of this chapter, the agenda-setting framework was developed to analyse the dynamics of any kind of policymaking, but it has never been applied to security policy as such. Yet security (and even foreign policy) issues are often considered to be on top of domestic and EU agendas. How do these issues arise? Which social forces carry them? Let us take Jegen's example of energy security in this volume. The gas crisis that broke out twice, in 2006 and 2008, between Europe, Russia, and Ukraine provides an illustration of the irruption of a new issue within European institutions which quickly reshaped the security policy agenda. For a long time, energy security was not a salient issue, the public paid no attention, and national and EU institutions displayed no inclination to coordinate their policies (that is what Baumgartner and Jones call 'institutional friction'). All of this changed after 2006, with the result that energy security is now tightly linked to European foreign policy. Part of the reason is that energy policy was now associated with Russian power, which, as Pouliot documents, has been framed in an increasingly negative light since the mid-1990s in Europe. But what is also interesting in the 2006–8 critical juncture is the combination of different channels (print and TV media, national governments, Commission, European Parliament) that were forced to engage each other on that issue and, perhaps unwillingly, conspired to put this issue on top of the list of EU priorities. Not surprisingly, this sparked a flurry of academic writings on energy policy in the context of Russia-EU relations. Theorizing agenda-setting dynamics is key to understanding how 'agenda-setters,' be they governments, the media, or EU institutions, prioritize security challenges and the ways (or policies) to address them.

The agenda-setting framework offers three entry points for analysing European security dynamics: the *policy agenda*, the *public opinion agenda*, and the *media agenda*, which can be construed as the three blades that, together, move the European security propeller. The key insight is that issues, to become relevant, have to occupy more or less the same position in the respective agendas of policymakers, public opinion, and the media. The question, of course, is which agenda drives the others. To explore this, the agenda-setting perspective combines the analysis of the decision-making process (in particular the role of institutional and cognitive friction) with measures of attention (the salience of issues in policy, media, and public spheres). Although this framework has been up to now used to analyse domestic politics, we believe it could be fruitfully applied to EU security policy for two reasons. First, it enables us to conceptualize how security issues emerge in time and space, rather than taking their importance for granted. Given the pluralism that currently characterizes European security studies, the dynamics of agenda-setting should make specific theoretical approaches more relevant than others at different points in time. Second, because an agenda-setting perspective can generate a metatheory of security policy (seeing how the three blades of the propeller move together), it may help us consider and compare issues across institutional contexts.

The analytical value of this perspective is to measure systematically the attention received by security issues across the three main agendas (what we called the three blades). As the different contributions in this book suggest, European security decision makers regularly face new events that may (or may not) become new issues. Such issues do not automatically lead agenda-setters to react. For neorealists, for example, security issues are mostly driven by the international system and long-term strategic behaviour will almost always dominate, while for liberals, international cooperation is the only response to transnational threats. But, whether they act rationally or not, decision makers do react sometimes, at least in words if not in deeds, in ways that do not accord well with these theories. To understand why these issues come on the EU agenda, it is essential 'to look beyond external factors and delve into the process in which issues are defined and selected for decision-making' (Princen 2007).

A full research agenda would begin by distinguishing each component of the agenda-setting process. Indeed, the European elite media (e.g., *Financial Times*), EU-level opinion surveys (Eurobarometer), the European Parliament, the Commission and the Council, national government officials' 'utterances' as well as political parties' manifestos are some of the richest materials ignored by IR scholars. It is possible to develop quantitative measures for each of the three agendas (media, public opinion, and policy) on the basis of these and other sources. Tapping into them to understand European security dynamics better, of course, assumes that some of the agenda-setting with regards to security policy now takes place at the EU level, and not only at the domestic level. Not only is this congruent with the security governance literature, but it may also contribute to making its predictions more specific, for example by comparing the role of different institutions and actors in the agenda-setting process.

In particular, the agenda-setting perspective is premised on the argument that public opinion, media, and policy agendas are deeply interconnected. In terms of the public opinion agenda, the literature demonstrates the effect of public opinion attention on the weight policymakers give to certain issues (Baumgartner and Jones 2005). Agenda-setting describes the process by which public opinion signals to policymakers what is important by giving more salience to certain events and issues than others. The public, in turn, perceives the issues that receive the most media attention to be the ones of greatest importance (McCombs and Shaw 1972, Baumgartner and Jones 2005). This implies that heightened media attention to any issue will increase the likelihood that policymakers perceive this issue to be important.

While the precise nature and extent of the impact of public opinion on security policy remain contested at least since the so-called Almond-Lippmann consensus – which argued that the impact was modest at best (Holsti 2004) – we believe it is possible to infer such an impact at least on security policy at the EU level. In the implementation report of the *European Security Strategy*, issued in December 2008, the European Council states that 'Maintaining public support for our global engagement is fundamental. In modern democracies, where media and public opinion are crucial to shaping policy, popular commitment is essential to sustaining our commitments abroad' (European Council 2008: 12). This is more than a theorist on agenda-setting could hope for from an institution involved in a specific policy (security policy in this case). In fact, although there may be an element of window dressing here, European leaders concede that public opinion acts as a powerful medium that exerts a direct influence on the policy agenda. To better understand the contours of European security in the twenty-first century, we must therefore factor in public perceptions of strategic threats and solutions.

But the key for an agenda-setting perspective is to look at sudden changes. By comparing the results of a survey by the German Marshall Fund at different points in time, we observe in table 14.1 that Europeans and Americans follow the same evolution in their perceived or possible threats but with a different intensity for immigration issues (+25 per cent in Europe) and terrorism (–17 per cent in the US). The table shows evidence that energy dependence is a high-security concern and global warming a rising one. Immigration fears are also increasing: in that regard, the Europeans are catching up with the Americans. These results suggest that terrorism went through a peak in the public opinion agenda, but that attention then decreased or at least stabilized in Europe as in the US. With reliable policy agenda data, we could infer from specific trends that policy actors reacted to public attention by adopting, for example, effective counter-terrorism measures, which in turn lowered the tension in public opinion. We could also see whether attention to immigration or global warming went up. Here again, an agenda-setting perspective would suggest that, because policy actors adapt their own agenda to sudden changes in the public opinion agenda, there will likely be a policy response of the kind that EU leaders (German and French presidency, Commission, Parliament) have pushed forward towards the end of the 2000s, with the rapid development of Immigration Pact and the Energy and Climate Package, two initiatives that dominated the EU agenda in 2007–8.

Now correlation is not causation, and one of the main challenges in the agenda-setting literature is to disentangle the causal links among the three agendas. The role of the media in this story, in particular, is complicated because whether and how they influence public opinion agendas with regards to security policy remain open to question. On other issues, Soroka (2002) concludes that there is no direct link from the policy opinion to the public opinion agenda on the assumption that policymakers can affect the public through the media or real-world factors but not directly. Given the complexity with which public opinion delivers preferences on security issues, a research program on the relationships between public opinion and security would improve the framing of security agenda-setting.

Conclusion

Although the agenda-setting perspective was not developed to analyse theoretical paradigms, it is interesting to note in conclusion that the rise of public opinion attention to issues like climate change, immigration, and terrorism corresponds to the broadening, in security studies, of the concept of security, with the inclusion of soft, human, and environmental security as the kinds of questions that can legitimately be asked in security studies since the fall of the Berlin Wall (the epistemological

Table 14.1
Possible threats to vital interests in 2002 and 2007

	Europe	US	Evolution EU 2002–7	Evolution US 2002–7
International terrorism	65	91	−1	−17
Large numbers of immigrants and refugees coming into Europe/US	38	60	+25	+11
Iraq developing WMD	58	86	n.a.	n.a.
Global spread of a disease	57	57	n.a.	n.a.
Energy dependence	78	88	n.a.	n.a.
Major economic downturn	65	80	n.a.	n.a.
Global warning	50	46	+35	+24
Islamic fundamentalism	49	61	+4	+2

Note: Each cell corresponds to the percentage of people telling how likely or somewhat likely they are personally affected by each threat.
Source: German Marshall Fund, *Transatlantic Trends 2007*, www.transatlantictrends.org.

basis of security studies). They also correspond to the blurring of boundaries between internal and external security, and between state and societal security, that calls for security providers other than the sovereign state (the ontological basis of security studies).

Again, we are not arguing the case for replacing extant theoretical approaches to European security with an agenda-setting perspective. But the latter could help put these approaches into a richer macro-context where scientific paradigms tend to be correlated with more practical representations, such as public opinion, media, and policy agendas. Like the dynamics of European security, theoretical fashions come and go; concepts arise and are then discarded; research objects are deemed crucial and finally marginal. As of now, the theoretical landscape appears as fragmented as the security environment, with its diffuse risks, moving targets, and shifting cleavages. The challenge will be to explore how exactly (if at all) theoretical and practical representations are connected to each other.

REFERENCES

Adler, Emmanuel, and Michael Barnett. 1998. *Security Communities*. Cambridge: Cambridge University Press.
Baumgartner, Frank R., and Bryan D. Jones. 2005. *The Politics of Attention*. Chicago: University of Chicago Press.

CASE Collective. 2006. 'Critical Approaches to Security in Europe: A Networked Manifesto.' *Security Dialogue* 37, no. 4: 443–87.

Dyson, Tom. 2008. 'Convergence and Divergence in Post–Cold War British, French and German Military Reforms: Between International Structure and Executive Autonomy.' *Security Studies* 17, no. 4: 725–74.

European Council. 2008. *Report on the Implementation of the European Security Strategy. Providing Security in a Changing World.* Brussels, 11 December, S407/08.

Gheciu, Alexandra. 2005. *NATO in the New Europe. The Politics of International Socialization after the Cold War.* Stanford: Stanford University Press.

Hartley, Keith, and Todd Sandler. 1999. *Political Economy of NATO.* Cambridge: Cambridge University Press.

Hofmann, Stephanie. 2009. 'Overlapping Institutions in the Realm of International Security: The Case of NATO and ESDP.' *Perspective on Politics.* 7, no. 1: 45–52.

Holsti, Ole. 2004. *Public Opinion and American Foreign Policy.* Ann Arbor: The University of Michigan Press.

Howorth, Jolyon. 2007. *Security and Defence Policy in the European Union.* Basingstoke: Palgrave.

Jones, Seth. 2007. *A Rise of European Security Cooperation.* Cambridge: Cambridge University Press.

Keohane, R. 2001. 'Governance in a Partially Globalized World.' *American Political Science Review* 95: 1–13.

Kirchner, Emil, and James Sperling. 2007. *EU Security Governance.* Manchester: Manchester University Press.

Krahmann, Elke. 2008. 'Security: Collective Good or Commmodity?' *European Journal of International Relations* 14, no. 3: 379–404.

Lobell, Steven, Norrin M. Ripsman, and Jeffrey W. Taliaferro. 2009. *Neoclassical Realism, the State and Foreign Policy.* Cambridge: Cambridge University Press.

McCombs, Maxwell E., and Donald L. Shaw. 1972. 'The Agenda-Setting Function of the Mass Media.' *Public Opinion Quarterly* 36, no. 2: 176–85.

Mérand, Frédéric. 2008. *European Defence Policy: Beyond the Nation State.* Oxford: Oxford University Press.

Paul, T.V. 2005. 'Soft Balancing in an Age of US Primacy.' *International Security* 30, no. 1: 46–71.

Posen, Barry. 2006. 'The ESDP: Response to Unipolarity.' *Security Studies* 15, no. 2: 149–86.

Press-Barnathan, Galia. 2006. 'Managing the Hegemon: NATO under Unipolarity.' *Security Studies* 15, no. 2: 271–309.

Princen, Sebastiaan. 2007. 'Agenda-Setting in the European Union: A Theoretical Exploration and Agenda for Research.' *Journal of European Public Policy* 14, no. 1: 21–38.

Schimmelfenning, Frank. 2003. *The EU, NATO and the Integration of Europe: Rules and Rhetoric*. Cambridge: Cambridge University Press.

Soroka, Stuart. 2002. *Agenda-Setting Dynamics in Canada*. Vancouver: UBC Press.

Wallander, Celeste. 2000. 'Institutional Assets and Adaptability: NATO after the Cold War.' *International Organization* 54, no. 4: 705–35.

Walt, Stephen. 2009. 'Alliances in a Unipolar World.' *World Politics* 61, no. 1: 86–120.

Webber, M. 2000. 'A Tale of a Decade: European Security Governance and Russia.' *European Security* 9, no. 2: 31–60.

Webber, M., S. Croft, J. Howorth, T. Terriff, and E. Krahmann. 2004. 'The Governance of European Security.' *Review of International Studies* 30, no. 1: 3–26.

Contributors

Sven Biscop is Director of the Security and Global Governance Programme at Egmont – The Royal Institute for International Relations (Brussels) and Editor-in-Chief of its journal *Studia Diplomatica*. He is a Visiting Professor for European security at the College of Europe (Bruges) and at Ghent University and, on behalf of Egmont, co-organizes the Higher Studies in Security and Defence with Belgium's Royal High Institute for Defence. He sits on the Executive Academic Board of the EU's European Security and Defence College.

Fabian Breuer holds a PhD in Political Science from the European University Institute and an MA in International Relations from the University of Amsterdam. He also studied political sciences, international relations, and law at the Dresden University of Technology. He is Project Assistant at the European Union Democracy Observatory (EUDO) at the European University Institute, Robert Schuman Centre for Advanced Studies. He was Research Associate with the Global Public Policy Institute in Berlin and a postdoctoral fellow in the European Foreign and Security Policy Studies Program offered by the Volkswagen Foundation, the Riksbankens Jubileumsfond, and the Compagnia di San Paolo. He also worked for GPPi Consulting and the press office of Javier Solana at Council of the European Union and was project manager of the voting-advice application EU Profiler.

Chiara de Franco (PhD European University Institute, Florence) joined King's College London, Department of War Studies, in October 2008 as Research Associate. She has previously been Research Assistant at the European University Institute, Lecturer in International Relations

Theory and War Representations at the University of Florence, and Lecturer in European Affairs at the Florida State University (Florence Programme). At King's she is working in the framework of the FORESIGHT project research group, concentrating on the early warning-response problem, and she is teaching the course Media and War for MA students. She is also in the process of publishing an edited volume with Christoph O Meyer on *Forecasting, Warning, and Recognising Transnational Risks*, as well as her PhD dissertation, 'War by Images, from Kosovo to Afghanistan,' which examines the impact of international TV networks on foreign policymaking. The role of the media in postmodern conflicts is also the topic of her most recent article for the *International Studies Encyclopedia* (Blackwell, 2010). Other research interests include the use of religious discourses in conflict mediation. Her professional training also includes a working experience at the UNDPKO, Situation Center, NYC Headquarters, and the development of several documentary movies.

Anthony Forster is the Pro-Vice-Chancellor (Learning and Teaching) at Durham University. Anthony has also held posts at the University of Bristol, King's College London, and the University of Nottingham. His first degree was a BA in Politics from the University of Hull followed by service in HM Forces (Army) and postgraduate study at Oxford University. Anthony has held a number of visiting research posts at European universities. Between 1999 and 2002 he was a Special Advisor to the House of Lords Select Committee on Common Foreign and Security Policy. Anthony has written widely on British military politics and European defence issues. His most recent publication (with Tim Edmunds) is *Out of Step: The Case for Change in British Armed Forces* (London: Demos, 2007).

Michel Fortmann is Professor of Political Science at the University of Montreal. He is the director of the Research Group in International Security, which he founded in 1996. He is the co-editor, with T.V. Paul, of *Balance of Power: Theory and Practice in the 21st Century*, published by Stanford University Press in 2004. He also edits and contributes to *Les conflits dans le monde* published by Laval University each year. His areas of interest include nuclear strategy, proliferation issues, the evolution of modern warfare, theories about the causes of wars, and Canadian military history. His book on the impact of war on the evolution of the modern state, *Les cycles de Mars*, just came out with Economica.

Martial Foucault is Assistant Professor of Political Science at the University of Montreal. He joined the department in 2006 after a post-doctoral stay at the European University Institute in Florence. He defended his PhD thesis in economics at the University of Paris Pantheon-Sorbonne in 2004, where he has a continuing appointment as associate researcher. His current work focuses on international political economy, fiscal choices, agenda-setting, and comparative politics and has appeared in such journals as the *American Journal of Political Science, Public Choice, Political Studies, Journal of European Public Policy,* and *Social Science Quarterly.* His last research project funded by the National Bureau of Economic Research (USA) deals with strategic interactions and decentralization in Benin and was awarded the 2009 IIPF Young Economist Award by the International Institute of Public Finance for a paper co-authored with G. Rota-Graziosi and E. Caldeira.

Alexandra Gheciu is an Associate Professor at the Graduate School of Public and International Affairs, and Associate Director of the Centre for International Policy Studies, University of Ottawa. Her research interests lie in the fields of international security, international institutions, Euro-Atlantic relations, and international relations theory. Alexandra's recent publications include two monographs: *The Politics of International Socialization after the Cold War: NATO in the 'New Europe'* (Stanford University Press, 2005) and *Securing Civilization?* (Oxford University Press, 2008). Prior to joining the University of Ottawa, she was a Research Fellow at the University of Oxford and a Jean Monnet Fellow at the European University Institute, Florence. She continues to act as Senior Research Associate with the Changing Character of War Programme (Oxford University) and is also an Associate Editor of the journal *Security Studies.*

Bastian Giegerich is the Research Fellow for European Security at the International Institute for Strategic Studies (IISS), London, where he covers European security and defence issues. A graduate of the University of Potsdam, Germany, he was a Fulbright Scholar at the University of Maryland, College Park, MD. Bastian obtained his PhD at the London School of Economics and Political Science, where he is also teaching in the Department for International Relations. He is the co-author (with Alexander Nicoll) of *European Military Capabilities: Building Armed Forces for Modern Operations* (London: IISS, 2008) and author of *European Military Crisis Management: Connecting Ambition and Reality* (Abingdon: Routledge,

2008) and *European Security and Strategic Culture: National Responses to the EU's Security and Defence Policy* (Baden-Baden: Nomos, 2006). Bastian has published widely on European security issues in various journals and newspapers including *Survival, International Politics, Security Dialogue, Cambridge Review of International Affairs, Europe's World, International Herald Tribune,* and *Wall Street Journal.* He also contributes regularly to the IISS publications *Military Balance, Strategic Survey,* and *Strategic Comments.* Previously, he has worked at the Aspen Institute Berlin, Germany, and the National Defence University, Washington, DC.

Eva Gross is Senior Research Fellow for European Foreign and Security Policy at the Institute for European Studies, Vrije Universiteit Brussel, where she heads the research cluster 'European foreign and security policy.' Eva holds a PhD from the London School of Economics and has been a visiting fellow at the Centre for European Policy Studies (CEPS) in Brussels and the EU Institute for Security Studies and CERI Science Po, both in Paris. She has published on various aspects of European security in journals such as *Security Dialogue* and *International Politics.* She is the author of *The Europeanization of National Foreign Policy: Continuity and Change in European Crisis Management* (Palgrave, 2009); *Security Sector Reform in Afghanistan: The EU's Contribution,* Occasional Paper 78: EU Institute for Security Studies, April 2009; and editor (with Michael Emerson) of *Evaluating the EU's Crisis Missions in the Balkans* (CEPS Paperback, 2007).

Stefanie von Hlatky is pursuing postdoctoral research at Georgetown University. She is also a Junior Scholar at the Woodrow Wilson International Centre for Scholars in Washington, DC. She obtained her PhD in Political Science from Université de Montréal, where she was also the executive director for the Centre for International Peace and Security Studies. Her research interests focus on alliance theory and nuclear weapons policy. She recently published a chapter in *Complex Deterrence: Strategy in the Global Age* (University of Chicago Press, 2009), edited by T.V. Paul, Patrick Morgan, and James Wirtz.

Bastien Irondelle is Senior Research Fellow at the Centre for International Studies (CERI) and Lecturer at Sciences Po Paris, where he teaches international security, European security, and French defence policy. During the year 2009–10 he is Deakin fellow at St Antony's College and Research Visiting Fellow at the Changing Character of War

Programme, University of Oxford. His research interests are European security and ESDP, comparative European grand strategies after the Cold War, national security policy governance, and the transformation of European states. His articles appeared in *Politique Européenne, Revue Internationale de Politique Comparée, Journal of European Public Policy, French Politics, Security Studies,* and the *Journal of European Integration.* His book, *La fin du service militaire: Analyse décisionnelle d'une réforme radicale* is forthcoming with Presses de Sciences Po.

Maya Jegen is Professor of Political Science at the University of Quebec in Montreal (UQAM), where she teaches environmental policy. With a PhD from the University of Geneva, she has previously worked at the Federal Office for Energy and the Trudeau Foundation. Her research, funded by SSHRC and FQRSC, deals with energy security in the European Union and renewable energy policy in Canada. She is an expert on the Task 28 'Social Acceptance of Wind Energy' established by the International Energy Agency. Her work has been published in the *European Journal of Political Research,* the *Swiss Political Science Review, Energy Policy,* and the *Journal of Public Policy.*

Frédéric Mérand is Associate Professor of Political Science at the University of Montreal, Visiting Professor of European Studies at LUISS University in Rome, and Deputy Director of the McGill University–University of Montreal Centre for International Peace and Security Studies. He received his PhD in 2003 from the University of California, Berkeley. He was a policy adviser in the Canadian Department of Foreign Affairs and International Trade and a Research Fellow at the San Diego–based Institute on Global Conflict and Cooperation. He has published in *Cooperation and Conflict,* the *Canadian Journal of Political Science, Comparative European Politics, European Security, Acta Sociologica,* and *Security Studies.* His book, *European Defence Policy: Beyond the Nation State,* was published by Oxford University Press in 2008.

Costanza Musu is Assistant Associate Professor at the Graduate School of Public and International Affairs of the University of Ottawa. She obtained her PhD in International Relations from the London School of Economics and Political Science. Subsequently she was Jean Monnet Fellow in the Transatlantic Programme of the Robert Schuman Centre for Advanced Studies at the European University Institute (EUI) in Florence and Assistant Professor of International Relations at Richmond University

(London). She has been a consultant for the Military Center for Strategic Studies – Center for Advanced Defense Studies (CeMiSS-CASD), the think tank of the Italian Ministry of Defence, and the Book Reviews Editor of the journal *Mediterranean Politics* (Routledge). Her work focuses on the EU's foreign policy, transatlantic relations in the field of security and defence, and the Israeli-Palestinian conflict. Her latest book analyses European policy towards the Arab-Israeli peace process.

Hanna Ojanen works in the Swedish Institute of International Affairs as Research Director. She is also Adjunct Professor (Docent) in International Politics at the University of Helsinki. She holds a doctorate in political and social sciences of the European University Institute (EUI, Florence) and worked previously at the Finnish Institute of International Affairs. Her positions of trust include membership with the Board of the Trans European Policy Studies Association (TEPSA) and with the Foreign Affairs Committee of the Evangelical Lutheran Church of Finland. Her publications include 'Finland and the ESDP: "Obliquely Forwards"?' in *New Security Issues in Northern Europe. The Nordic and Baltic States and the ESDP*, ed. Clive Archer (Abingdon and New York: Routledge, 2008); 'Inter-Organisational Relations: The New Facet of European Security Policy,' in *Europe in Context: Insights to the Foreign Policy of the EU*, ed. Tuomas Forsberg et al. (Helsinki: Finnish International Studies Association, Publications N. 1, 2007); and, with Simon Duke, 'Bridging Internal and External Security: Lessons from the European Security and Defence Policy,' *Journal of European Integration* 28, no. 5 (2006).

Raffaello Pantucci is a Consulting Research Associate at the International Institute for Strategic Studies (IISS) in London. He has worked on counter-terrorism and European security issues at the Institute since 2006. Previously he worked for just under four years at the Center for Strategic and International Studies (CSIS) in Washington, where he worked in the Europe and Transatlantic Relations Program. While at CSIS he contributed to a number of reports on European security matters, including 'Test of Will, Tests of Efficacy' (Washington, DC: CSIS Press, May 2005) and 'Trusted Partners: Technology Transfers in the U.S.-UK Defense Relationship' (Washington, DC: CSIS Press, May 2006). Since working at IISS he has contributed to a number of reports looking at different aspects of counter-terrorism and counter-radicalization (including two reports examining what business can do to protect itself from terrorism in the UK and Southeast Asia). His work has been published in various academic outlets including *Democratization, Europe's World, Perspectives on Terrorism Journal, SAIS Review, Studies in Conflict and Terrorism,* and *Survival.* He is a regular contributor to the US magazine *Homeland Security Today* and the *Jamestown Foundation Terrorism Monitor.* His opinion-editorials have appeared in newspapers such as the *Wall Street Journal, Boston Globe, Moscow Times, Washington Times, Guardian, Baltimore Sun, New Statesman,* among others. He holds a Master's from King's College London in War Studies, and he previously read a BA in Literature at the University of Manchester. He is currently completing a book looking at the history of Islamist terrorism in the UK to be published in late 2010.

Vincent Pouliot is an Assistant Professor in the Department of Political Science at McGill University. His research interests lie at the intersection of international political sociology and the global governance of security, with ongoing research projects on NATO's transformation and the reform of the UN Security Council. His works have appeared in *International Organization, International Studies Quarterly, European Journal of International Relations, Journal of Peace Research, Global Governance, Canadian Journal of Political Science, Cooperation and Conflict, Journal of International Relations and Development,* and other scholarly outlets. His latest book, published by Cambridge University Press, is entitled *International Security in Practice: The Politics of NATO-Russia Diplomacy.*

Sten Rynning is Professor of International Relations at the Department of Political Science at the University of Southern Denmark. His main research areas are security studies, transatlantic security relations, NATO, and the EU. He is the editor with Antonio Marquina of *From the Hindu Kush to Lisbon: NATO, Afghanistan, and the Future of the Atlantic Alliance* (UNISCI, 2010), co-author with Jens Ringsmose of *Come Home, NATO? The Atlantic Alliance's New Strategic Concept* (DIIS, 2009), and author of *NATO Renewed: The Power and Purpose of Transatlantic Cooperation* (Palgrave, 2005). The Danish Social Science Research Council funds his 2008–10 research project *Whither the West? An Assessment of the Vitality of the Atlantic Alliance.*

Ursula C. Schroeder (PhD European University Institute, Florence) is a lecturer in International Relations at the Free University, Berlin. She was postdoctoral fellow in the European Foreign and Security Policy Studies Programme of the Volkswagen Foundation. She studies the convergence of internal and external security in Europe by looking at processes of organizational adaptation and change in EU crisis management and counter-terrorism policies. Her current research focuses on the consequences of international security assistance and security sector reform policies. She directs the project, Exporting the State Monopoly on Violence: Security Governance Transfers to Areas of Limited Statehood, in Berlin. Located at the interface of public administration and international relations research, the project investigates international transfers of security norms and institutions to areas of limited statehood.

Pascal Vennesson is Professor of Political Science, Joint Chair 'Security in Europe' at the European University Institute, Robert Schuman Center for Advanced Studies in Florence. He served in the French Ministry of Defense from 1999 to 2003 as Director of the Center for social science studies of defence. He is the author of *Les chevaliers de l'air: Aviation et conflits au XXème siècle* (Paris: Presses de Science Po, 1997), *Sociologie militaire: Armées, guerre et paix* (Paris: Armand Colin-Sociologie, 2000) (with Theodore Caplow), and editor of *Politiques de défense: Institutions, innovations, européanisation* (Paris: L'Harmattan-Logiques politiques, 2000). His articles have appeared in *Armed Forces and Society, Cultures et Conflits, European Foreign Affairs Review, Journal of Strategic Studies, New Global Studies, Politix,* and *Revue française de science politique*. He is currently working on the changing utility of military power in international politics and on the European Union's power and influence worldwide.

Index